Pastoral Inventions

AMERICAN CIVILIZATION   *A series edited by Allen F. Davis*

Pastoral Inventions

RURAL LIFE IN NINETEENTH-CENTURY AMERICAN ART AND CULTURE

Sarah Burns

TEMPLE
UNIVERSITY
PRESS
Philadelphia

*This publication has been supported
by the National Endowment for the Humanities,
a federal agency that supports
the study of such fields as history, philosophy,
literature, and languages.*

Temple University Press, Philadelphia 19122
Copyright © 1989 by Temple University. All rights reserved
Published 1989
Printed in the United States of America

The paper used in this publication meets the minimum requirements
of American National Standard for Information Sciences
—Permanence of Paper for Printed Library Materials,
ANSI Z39.48-1984

Library of Congress Cataloging-in-Publication Data

Burns, Sarah.
Pastoral inventions : rural life in nineteenth-century
American art and culture / Sarah Burns.
p.   cm.—(American civilization)
Bibliography: p.
Includes index.
ISBN 0-87722-580-X (alk. paper)
1. Country life in art.
2. Arts, American.
3. Arts, Modern—19th century—United States.
4. United States—Civilization—19th century.
I. Title.   II. Series.
NX650.C69B87   1989
973'.09'734—dc19   88-12303
CIP

Contents

Illustrations   *vii*
Acknowledgments   *xi*

Introduction   *1*

PART I
FARMSCAPES IDEAL AND REAL

1. The Iconography of the Agrarian World, c. 1825–1875   *11*
2. The Poetry of Labor   *32*
3. "Unlovable Things": Farmscapes Real   *50*
4. Beneath the Idyll   *77*

PART II
THE CHANGING IMAGE OF THE YANKEE FARMER

5. The Noble Yeoman   *99*
6. Hicks   *122*
7. Jonathans   *149*
8. Bumpkins by Contrast   *168*
9. Grandfathers and Geezers   *190*
10. Peasants   *214*

PART III
THE ANXIETIES OF NOSTALGIA

11. Rural Heavens and Urban Hells 237

12. The Homestead 258

13. Barefoot Boys and Other Country Children 297

Conclusion 335

Notes 341

Index 369

Illustrations

1. Jasper Cropsey, *American Harvesting,* 1851   20
2. *Spring in the Country,* 1858   21
3. Frances Palmer, *American Farm Scene: Spring,* 1853   22
4. Frances Palmer, *New England Scenery,* 1866   23
5. Thomas Cole, *The Pastoral State,* from *The Course of Empire,* 1833–36   24
6. Asher B. Durand, *The Hudson River Looking toward the Catskills,* 1847   25
7. *November,* 1854   26
8. George Henry Durrie, *Winter in the Country: A Cold Morning,* 1863   27
9. William Sidney Mount, *Long Island Farmhouse,* after 1854   28
10. Joseph Johns, *Farmyard at Sunset,* 1874   29
11. Granville Perkins, *An American Farm Yard—A Frosty Morning,* 1877   30
12. *Tumbledown Mansion—The House of Farmer Slack,* 1852   31
13. Jerome Thompson, *The Haymakers, Mount Mansfield, Vermont,* 1859   40
14. Alvan Fisher, *Corn Husking Frolic,* 1828–29   41

15. Winslow Homer, *The Husking Party Finding the Red Ears,* 1857   42
16. Eastman Johnson, *Corn Husking,* 1860   43
17. Eastman Johnson, *Husking Bee, Island of Nantucket,* 1876   44
18. Tomkins Matteson, *Sugaring Off,* 1845   45
19. Arthur Fitzwilliam Tait, *American Forest Scene: Maple Sugaring,* 1856   46
20. Jerome Thompson, *Apple Gathering,* 1856   47
21. John Whetten Ehninger, *Gathering Pumpkins—An October Scene in New England,* 1867   48
22. Henry Herrick, *Life on the Farm,* 1867   49
23. *The Pioneer Settler upon the Holland Purchase, and His Progress: Fourth Sketch of the Pioneer,* 1849   63
24. Ferdinand Meyer, *The Farm of Volney Lester, Esq.,* 1875   64
25. Henry R. Robinson, *The Inhuman Anti-Rent Murder,* 1845   65
26. McCormick Reaper, 1847   66
27. James Shearman, *Improved Buckeye Reaper with Table Rake,* 1860s   67
28. *Reaping in the Olden Time,* 1857   68

29. *Reaping in Our Time,* 1857   69
30. Theodore Davis, *Farming in the Great West—The "Burr Oak" Farm, Illinois, Comprising Sixty-Five Square Miles,* 1871   70
31. *Dakota Territory—The Great Wheat Fields in the Valley of the Red River of the North—Threshing by Steam on the Dalrymple Farm, Formerly a Barren Prairie,* 1878   71
32. William Allen Rogers, *Harvesting on a Bonanza Farm,* 1891   72
33. C. M. Coolidge and Edwin Austin Abbey, *"Hard Times"—Mortgaging the Old Homestead,* 1873   73
34. *Cobblestone Farm, Grover Hill, Bethel, Maine,* c. 1900   74
35. Winslow Homer, *The Straw Ride,* 1869   75
36. James Merritt Ives after Frances Palmer and J. Cameron, *Haying Time: The First Load,* 1868   76
37. Asher B. Durand, *Haying,* 1838   90
38. British School, *Dixton Harvesters,* c. 1730   91
39. Jules Breton, *The Gleaners,* 1854   92
40. George Inness, *Peace and Plenty,* 1865   93
41. W. L. Sheppard, *Harvest on Historic Fields—A Scene at the South,* 1867   94
42. *Peace and Plenty,* 1871   95
43. William Sidney Mount, *Farmer Whetting His Scythe,* 1848   110
44. *June,* 1854   111
45. *The Mower in Ohio,* 1864   112
46. Eastman Johnson, *The Evening Newspaper,* 1863   113
47. *The Farmer Pays for All,* 1869   114
48. *Gift for the Grangers,* 1873   115
49. Thomas Nast, *The Transportation Problem,* 1873   116
50. Thomas Waterman Wood, *Cogitation,* 1871   117
51. Claude Regnier after Junius Brutus Stearns, *Life of George Washington: The Farmer,* 1853   118
52. John Francis, *Joseph Ritner, Governor of Pennsylvania,* 1836   119
53. *Farmer Garfield Cutting a Swath to the White House,* 1880   120
54. *Apostle of Prosperity,* 1903   *121*
55. Richard Earlom after Francis Wheatley, *Preparing for Market,* 1799   136
56. Louis Maurer, *Preparing for Market,* 1856   137
57. T. Geremia after Francis Wheatley, *Rural Repose,* 1804   138
58. William Sidney Mount, *Farmers Nooning,* 1836   139
59. E. Scott after George Morland, *Boys Robbing an Orchard,* 1802   140
60. William Sidney Mount, *The Truant Gamblers,* 1835   141
61. William Sidney Mount, *Walking the Line,* 1835   142
62. William Sidney Mount, *Rustic Dance after a Sleigh Ride,* 1830   143
63. *The Dance,* c. 1845   144
64. William Sidney Mount, *Dancing on the Barn Floor,* 1831   145
65. William Sidney Mount, *Dance of the Haymakers,* 1845   146
66. Léopold Robert, *Return from the Pilgrimage to the Madonna dell'Arco near Naples at Whitsuntide,* 1827   147
67. Winslow Homer, *The Dance after the Husking,* 1858   148
68. William Sidney Mount, *Long Island Farmer Husking Corn,* 1833–34   162
69. William Sidney Mount, *The Long Story,* 1837   163
70. William Sidney Mount, *Bargaining for a Horse,* 1835   164
71. *George Handel Hill in Yankee Character,* c. 1835–45   165
72. William Sidney Mount, *Winding Up,* 1836   166
73. C. Knight after Francis Wheatley, *The Rustic Lover,* 1787   167
74. William Sidney Mount, *The Sportsman's Last Visit,* 1835   177

75. *Charles Mathews as "Jonathan W. Doubikins,"* c. 1824   *178*
76. Francis William Edmonds, *The City and the Country Beaux,* 1840   *179*
77. William Sidney Mount, *Raffling for the Goose,* 1837   *180*
78. William Sidney Mount, *The Painter's Triumph,* 1838   *181*
79. William Sidney Mount, *The Herald in the Country,* 1853   *182*
80. Johannes Oertel, *The Country Connoisseurs,* 1855   *183*
81. Francis William Edmonds, *Taking the Census,* 1854   *184*
82. *Country Sketches: Farmer Cronk and Farmer Bonk,* 1858   *185*
83. *Practical Experience of the Gift Book Enterprises,* 1858   *186*
84. *How the New York Merchants Received Their Country Customers Last Year: How They Receive Them This Year,* 1858   *187*
85. *How to Spend the Fourth,* 1857   *188*
86. Augustus Hoppin, *"You Want To See My Pa, I 'Spose?" "Wa'al, No; I Come Designin'—,"* 1858   *189*
87. Eastman Johnson, *The Nantucket School of Philosophy,* 1887   *203*
88. Thomas Hovenden, *The Old Version,* 1881   *204*
89. Thomas Waterman Wood, *A Pinch of Snuff,* 1891   *205*
90. After Alfred C. Howland, *Bargaining for a Calf,* 1882   *206*
91. Edward Lamson Henry, *Forty Winks,* (undated)   *207*
92. Thomas Nast, *Cincinnatus: H. G. the Farmer Receiving the Nomination from H. G. the Editor,* 1873   *208*
93. Theodore Davis, *The Centennial—State Exhibits in Agricultural Hall,* 1876   *209*
94. Alfred Gillam, *The Wily Farmer at His Old Tricks,* 1883   *210*
95. J. S. Pughe, *"Blowing" Himself around the Country,* 1896   *211*
96. Arthur Burdett Frost, *The Sick Cow,* 1904   *212*
97. Arthur Burdett Frost, *The Game between the Squire and the Postmaster,* 1904   *213*
98. Winslow Homer, *Girl with a Pitchfork,* 1867   *227*
99. Jean-François Millet, *Going to Work,* c. 1850–55   *228*
100. Winslow Homer, *The Last Load,* 1869   *229*
101. Winslow Homer, *Answering the Horn,* 1876   *230*
102. John Whetten Ehninger, *Bringing in the Hay,* 1868   *231*
103. Winslow Homer, *Gloucester Farm,* 1874   *232*
104. George Fuller, *Turkey Pasture in Kentucky,* 1878–82   *233*
105. Daniel Ridgway Knight, *Hailing the Ferry,* 1888   *234*
106. *City Sketches,* 1855   *246*
107. Stanley Fox, *Evading the Excise Law—Laying in Rum for Sunday,* 1868   *247*
108. Paul Frenzeny, *The Rag-Pickers Disposing of Their Gatherings,* 1868   *248*
109. A. Gault, *Shelter for the Homeless: Night Scene in a New York Station-House,* 1873   *249*
110. *"The Wickedest Man in New York"—Scene at John Allen's Dance House, 304 Water Street, New York City,* 1868   *250*
111. Thomas Nast, *A Warning Light,* 1881   *251*
112. *Town and Country,* 1858   *252*
113. Jules Tavernier, *Town and Country,* 1873   *253*
114. Frances Palmer, *American Country Life: May Morning,* 1855   *254*
115. Frances Palmer, *American Country Life: Summers Evening,* 1855   *255*
116. *Summer in the Highlands,* 1867   *256*
117. E. B. Bensell [?], title vignette, *"About Piazzas,"* 1866   *257*

118. Worthington Whittredge, *Home by the Sea*, 1872   276

119. Jasper Cropsey, *The Old Home*, 1884   277

120. *American Homestead: Winter*, 1868   278

121. *My Boyhood's Home*, 1872   279

122. *Home, Sweet Home*, 1869   280

123. *Johnes House* (and other old homesteads, Southampton, Long Island), 1878   281

124. Harry Fenn, *Home of John Howard Payne*, 1872   282

125. Harry Fenn, *Interior of Payne's "Home Sweet Home,"* 1872   283

126. *The Bryant Homestead*, 1873   284

127. Alfred A. Ordway, *Birthplace in Winter* (Whittier homestead), 1904   285

128. Alfred A. Ordway, *Snow-Bound Kitchen, Eastern End* (Whittier homestead), 1904   286

129. Eastman Johnson, *Nantucket Interior—Man with a Pipe* (1865)   287

130. George Cochran Lambdin, *Winter Quarters in Virginia—Army of the Potomac*, 1864, 1866   288

131. Alfred Fredericks, *And Ashes Lie upon the Hearth*, 1888   289

132. Thomas Hicks, *No Place like Home*, 1877   290

133. Edward Lamson Henry, *Figures in an Interior*, 1878   291

134. Enoch Wood Perry, *Woman Sewing by Firelight*, 1892   292

135. A. Coolidge Warren, *A New England Fireside*, 1855   293

136. Jno. Schutler after George Henry Durrie, *Home to Thanksgiving*, 1867   294

137. Frederick A. Chapman, *Thanksgiving at a New England Farmhouse*, 1871   295

138. Matthew Morgan, *Unrestricted Immigration and Its Results—A Possible Curiosity of the Twentieth Century: The Last Yankee*, 1888   296

139. James Merritt Ives after Frances Palmer and J. Cameron, *The Four Seasons of Life: Childhood, "The Season of Joy,"* 1868   314

140. Thomas Cole, *Childhood*, from *The Voyage of Life*, 1839   315

141. Eastman Johnson, *The Barefoot Boy*, 1860   316

142. John George Brown, *The Berry Boy*, c. 1875   317

143. Enoch Wood Perry, *Country Boy*, 1872   318

144. Winslow Homer, *Boys in a Pasture*, 1874   319

145. Clifton Johnson, *The New England Boy*, 1897   320

146. Winslow Homer, *Snap the Whip*, 1872   321

147. Winslow Homer, *Chestnutting*, 1870   322

148. Winslow Homer, *Gathering Berries*, 1874   323

149. W. L. Sheppard, *The Last Apple*, 1874   324

150. Eastman Johnson, *In the Hayloft*, c. 1877–78   325

151. Granville Perkins after Eva Muller, *A Visit to Grandfather's Home*, 1876   326

152. Sol Eytinge, *The Hearth-Stone of the Poor*, 1876   327

153. W. L. Sheppard after M. Woolf, *The Story of a Waif*, 1872   328

154. *Please, Sir, May I Have a Bed?*, 1880   329

155. *The Street Boy on a Farm (A Year Later)*, 1880   330

156. William Allen Rogers, *The Tribune Fresh Air Fund—Children's Excursion to Lake Champlain*, 1882   331

157. William Allen Rogers, *Let the Cloth Be White*, 1885   332

Acknowledgments

I owe thanks to Diane Chalmers Johnson, Floyd W. Martin, and Barbara Groseclose for providing opportunities for me to air some of my developing ideas during the early stages of my research. For their help in solving assorted stubborn and difficult picture-searching problems, I am especially grateful to David Alexander, Nancy R. Davison, Lee M. Edwards, Celina Fox, Jayne Kuchna, and Wendy Shadwell.

The staff of the Prints and Photographs Division, Library of Congress, have been most helpful in providing many bits of vital information. A year's sabbatical leave granted by Indiana University provided much-needed unencumbered time for the actual writing.

I also want to express my appreciation to the National Endowment for the Humanities for helping to subsidize the publication of this book.

Versions of some of this material have been published previously: "Yankee Romance: The Comic Courtship Scene in Nineteenth-Century American Art," *American Art Journal* 18, no. 4 (1986); and "Barefoot Boys and Other Country Children: Sentiment and Ideology in Nineteenth-Century American Art," *The American Art Journal* 20, no. 1 (1988).

INTRODUCTION

INCE the eighteenth century the image of the farm in American culture has been a powerful and evocative one, comprising many layers of ideas about natural goodness, republican simplicity, family continuity, and Arcadian harmony. Even today, some of us—perhaps many—when idly musing on the concept "farm," are likely to envision an idyllic place of rolling pastures and hayfields, tranquil herds of grazing cows, and a comfortable farmhouse in a bower of venerable trees. When we think of an ideal "farm," we usually do not summon up the terrain of agribusiness as it exists, for instance, in California's Central Valley, where fields of tomatoes, rice, and grapes have a gridded, standardized vastness that expresses only the utilitarian, profit-minded spirit of capitalism.

Perhaps too we subscribe to the idea of the farmer, bound to the good earth, as morally and spiritually superior to those who must live by their wits and guile in the high-tech labyrinths of the modern metropolis. Or some of us may cherish an archetypal image of the American farmer as an amiable, slightly laughable, yet grandfatherly sort with billy-goat chin whiskers, Ben Franklin glasses, straw hat, and overalls. Intellectually, we know that such notions are fictional. The media of the late twentieth century have done much, indeed everything, to bring the modern farmer into focus, yet old ideas persist.

Shoring up those images of the good farm and the good farmer is an intricate and still quite solid substructure of inherited cultural belief about the significance and otherness of American agriculture and rural life. As we know it today, this construct of ideology and values is largely the product of the nineteenth century, when art and literature—popular and academic both—played a critical role in creating enduring and iconically powerful images of country life. These images gave vivid and compelling substance to the agrarian rhetoric woven into early American political philosophy. Until the Civil War at least, they were identified with the best ideals of a society that celebrated both individualism and the breaching of fixed class barriers as the fruits of progress beyond the social order of the Old World.

The image of the good farm in the nineteenth century was the offspring of the marriage of European pastoral traditions with Thomas Jefferson's agrarian politics. The concept of the pastoral dates back to the bucolic poems of Theocritus and the *Eclogues* and *Georgics* of Virgil. These classical poets, dreaming of a perfect, unchanging Arcadia populated by primitive shepherds and simple farmers, fathered a literary and ideological tradition that persisted across centuries of European culture. At times, as in Elizabethan England, the pastoral became a dominant poetic form. In the eighteenth century the stresses of rising industrialism and social change provoked a powerful resurgence of pastoral sentiment, which was given new life by the incipient romanticism of such philosophers as Jean-Jacques Rousseau, who sought in nature, humble folk, and simple living the goodness and authenticity that modern civilization denied the individual.

It has been pointed out, rightly, that these were for the most part literary and aristocratic ideas. In England, while poets such as James Thomson and William Cowper enriched the pastoral tradition by vividly observing nature, English gentlemen invested in improvements and experimental farming on a vast scale. For every aristocrat who raised prodigious experimental sheep on his country estate, however, there were thousands of peasants, tenant farmers, and wage laborers who experienced the country not as a happy sanctuary from the city but as a hard and taxing place where survival depended in large part upon nature's (and landlords') caprices. For every play dairy, the most egregious of which was incontestably Marie-Antoinette's *Hameau* at Versailles, there were hundreds of working dairies that offered little more than the circumstantial luxury of immunity from smallpox. Few peasants, certainly, had either education or leisure sufficient to read pastoral poets, ancient or modern. Being close to nature was not romantic; it was only destiny.[1]

In America, there were to be no peasants, and no rural miseries. The idea of farm life came to be identified with the establishment of an enlightened new society where rigid hierarchies would give way to a brotherhood composed of virtuous, hardworking yeomen farmers, lords of their own soil, oppressed by no one. Often quoted but still worth repeating are passages from *Letters from an American Farmer* (1782) by Hector St. John de Crèvecoeur, the French army

cartographer who settled down for a time on a farm in Orange County, New York. Crèvecoeur painted a picture of American farm life as existence without flaw:

We are a people of cultivators scattered over an immense territory . . . united by the silken bands of mild government, all respecting the laws without dreading their power, because they are equitable. . . . If [the "enlightened Englishman"] travels through our rural districts, he views not the hostile castle and the haughty mansion, contrasted with the clay-built hut and miserable cabin, where cattle and men help to keep each other warm and dwell in meanness, smoke, and indigence. . . . We have no princes for whom we toil, starve, and bleed; we are the most perfect society now existing in the world.

Crèvecoeur's vision pictured a new American pastoral. He was not blind to the dark spots that disfigured his pristine image of rural bliss; a strain of ambivalence occasionally surfaces. He described in gruesome detail the condition of slavery in the South and deplored the luxurious indolence of the plantation masters. He was repelled by the brutal, solitary hunters and trappers of the frontier. Yet in the broad view his picture of abundance, joy, feasts, peace, cooperation, and contentment was flooded with the bright light of optimism. "It is here . . . that the idle may be employed, and the poor become rich, but by riches I do not mean gold and silver— we have but little of those metals; I mean a better sort of wealth—cleared lands, cattle, good houses, good clothes, and an increase of people to enjoy them."[2]

It remained for Thomas Jefferson to translate this picture of agrarian bliss into a more precisely political ideal: a far-flung constellation of small, self-sufficient family farms making up a nation governed by "natural" aristocrats of learning and unimpeachable character. One would hardly guess that the following lines from *Notes on the State of Virginia* (1785) were written by the master of a plantation where the actual cultivators were slaves:

Those who labor in the earth are the chosen people of God . . . whose breasts he has made his peculiar deposit for substantial and genuine virtue. . . . Corruption of morals in the mass of cultivators is a phenomenon of which no age or nation has furnished an example. . . . While we have land to labor . . . never let us wish to see our citizens occupied at a workbench, or twirling a distaff. . . . The mobs of great cities add just so much to the support of pure government, as sores do to the strength of the human body. It is the manners, and spirit of a people which preserve a republic in vigor. A degeneracy in these is a canker which soon eats to the heart of its laws and constitution.[3]

This vision of the American agrarian—incorruptible because self-reliant—was rooted in one fundamental concept: the ownership of property. Jefferson implicitly equated individual freedom and dignity with the possession of one's own acres. Like a horn of plenty, this essential right to hold and till the land spilled out all the other blessings of the agricultural life.

Jefferson's measured, glowing edifice of praise for agrarian, republican America rested on tottering foundations of contradiction, since it confronted neither the institution of the slave system nor the commercial impulses and imperatives that had begun to drive the economy. Although the bulk of the population remained on farms until the great demographic shifts beginning in the 1870s charted a momentous movement into cities and their suburbs, the earlier America might better be defined as a temporarily agricultural rather than an agrarian nation. This is not to say that agriculture did not play a critically important role in the American economy; it remained a prime resource well beyond the antebellum years. Still, long before the Civil War, industry and capitalism were on the rise, engulfing agriculture as they engulfed all else.

It is now generally recognized that the Civil War can no longer be regarded as the Great Divide between an innocent pastoral society and the disillusioned, rampantly industrializing one that sprang up in the 1870s. Regret for simpler, more bucolic days sounded as early as the 1830s, a decade

of increasing entrepreneurship and speculation. Yet despite real circumstances of every description (detailed later), it was Jefferson's vision in his *Notes on the State of Virginia* that would echo through countless future paeans to the moral nobility and political rightness of America's yeomen farmers and their way of life, as if they were invariably Jefferson's staunchly simple republicans, constituting not just the bulk but the cream of American society.

We have inherited this framework of pastoral dream and agrarian ideal. It continues to influence not only our vision of what an ideal farm ought to be but also our interpretations of country life as seen in nineteenth-century American art and literature. Yet our understanding of how it functioned in its time is still not complete. This is especially true in the study of the visual arts of the period, even though substantial revision is now taking place in American art scholarship.

Central to the ideal agrarian vision is the harmonious pastoral landscape, tirelessly celebrated during the nineteenth century in Hudson River School paintings, book and magazine illustrations, popular prints, and great torrents of poetry and prose. This outflow generated the tradition that still weighs heavily in determining our desires and expectations regarding the American farm. Only recently has the significance of the pastoral in American landscape painting and popular art begun to receive serious scholarly attention.

As Roger Stein observed, studies of American attitudes toward the native landscape used to emphasize artists' and writers' fascination with the savage and the primeval, and their deep ambivalence about the rapacious encroachment of culture. Confirmation of these arguments came readily to hand in the works of major early nineteenth-century figures: the painter Thomas Cole and his contemporaries, poet William Cullen Bryant, novelist James Fenimore Cooper. These artists exalted the wilderness as site and symbol of divine, primal creation. At the same time, they knew that this wilderness would have to die in order that cultivation and, subsequently, civilization might arise. This conflict of values was the root of their ambivalence toward both settlement and technology, and the destruction they entailed.[4]

The cultivated middle landscape or landscape of equilibrium, however, was equally important. It represented a positive good, an emblem of welcome progress, largely uncomplicated by gnawing doubts and regrets. To some extent the sanctification of the wilderness was a romantic literary and artistic idea that served as vehicle for potent spiritual metaphors. It is hardly in dispute that for those who actually tilled the earth, there was little to inspire in the forest primeval; it was something in the way. The most beautiful land was cleared, tilled, and productive. For many artists and writers too (including, in some cases, those who simultaneously venerated the ideal of a sublime wilderness), this kind of landscape was as richly stocked with ideas as with nature's bounty, and as fertile a ground for metaphor as mountain sublimity or forest fastness. In this book, accordingly, the unclouded pastoral landscape, background to the agrarian ideal past and present, will occupy the foreground of discussion.[5]

Genre paintings also have played an important role in shaping our perceptions, and although their study and interpretation have become more sophisticated, the tendency prevails to regard them as benign and optimistic, as we think rural life itself should be. Earlier scholarship accepted genre paintings and prints of rural America as truthful documents of bygone days. More recently, students of American art have recognized genre images of all types as highly synthetic, selectively composed fictions, made to reflect and promulgate cultural values rather than represent "real" life. In pursuit of meaning, accordingly, scholars have donned the spectacles of Crèvecoeur and Jefferson, the better to discern attitudes embodied in nineteenth-century pictures of farms and farmers.

Patricia Hills, for example, construes the American rural image in a largely positive light. She has argued that pictures of farmers from about 1830 to 1870 became vehicles for the transmission of values: American individualism and democracy, and hard work, thrift, and education. Concurrently, the idea of the farm represented the best of an older ideal of community, and its image served to distract attention from increasing conflicts between labor and industrialists.[6] There is a good deal of truth in this view, and I play some variations on it in the first part of this book. However, I believe that the spectacles of Crèvecoeur and Jefferson can limit as well as enlarge our vision. If we gaze through these lenses alone, we overlook other signals and clues that prompt other interpretations of country life imagery.

It is tempting, certainly, to detect in this imagery little but the upbeat and optimistic. In fact, however, the ideological messages of country landscape and life were often complex and paradoxical, and they reflected or denied real circumstances in complicated ways. At no time in the nineteenth century did art come to terms with the fact that agriculture itself had taken on all the trappings of capitalist enterprise. This denial of actuality had aesthetic and ideological causes, which illuminate the role played by art in bearing cultural messages. Beneath many of the most idyllic pastoral scenes lay subtexts bearing upon the crudest and most elemental political, economic, and cultural imperatives, all aimed at proclaiming the ascendancy of one system—northern capitalism—over another, the quasi-feudal system of the South. During the later decades of the nineteenth century, political ideology seemingly vanished from the images of country life, to be replaced by sentiment in a wide range of tones. That sentiment, however, proved to be only the guise for another set of imperatives equally crude at their deepest level.

Certainly there were images that extolled the sturdy virtues of the American yeoman, model for all society. Others, however, derived from modes of denigration and condescension widely prevalent in contemporary culture. Even while ostensibly celebrating rural life and country people, many paintings and illustrations broadcast contradictory signals, contributing generously to the establishment of a whole gallery of negative stereotypes—the hick, the bumpkin, the geezer, and the peasant—which indirectly reflect the shift-ings of power and its aggrandizement in the urban sphere of capitalism, industry, and commerce. Ultimately, these negative images shed light upon passages in the political exploitation or social expendability of farmers in the nineteenth century. Their legacy persists today in ambivalent attitudes toward rural Americans and their place in society.

In the following pages the focus is on American art first and on literature in a supporting role—or, often, the two media in a kind of reciprocating exchange—as agents in shaping and coloring a vision of rural existence that lingers yet in contemporary culture. Following a course of rigorous selectivity, art and literature created stereotypes that masked and blunted social realities even as they exalted cultural values and ideals. It is not my claim that this occurred in any conscious, deliberate manner, or that artists and writers were often overt, self-styled propagandists for specific points of view. The American art world, based very largely on an open, competitive market, had naturally to bend in the direction of what was likely to succeed there, and country scenes enjoyed decades of popularity. Their cultural messages are most often implied, submerged, taken for granted, too familiar to require pointing out, and yet—in and because of such unassuming ubiquity—they quietly reinforce over and over again, sets of beliefs, preconceptions, and assumptions about the symbolism and meaning of country life in America. This is not to say that the images necessarily reflected what the majority really believed any more than that they can be seen as self-conscious philosophical statements. What they did offer were simplified versions of reality that were easy to embrace and to accept with the lip service that can often stand in for true conviction.

It is perhaps on this level of the unobtrusive and the utterly customary that the fabrication of common beliefs is most efficiently carried out. For this reason the so-called popular arts receive a full measure of attention here, since they were and are agents for the broadest diffusion of ideas and images. In nineteenth-century America the line between "popular" and "academic" was fluid and undefined. The same subjects appear in paintings, popular prints, and magazine illustrations, and similar concerns were voiced alike by Henry David Thoreau and best-selling author Donald Grant Mitchell. In that period of American culture the academic and the popular should be seen, at least as far as the present subject is concerned, as points on a continuum rather than distinct and separate spheres. Viewed thus in panorama they resolve themselves into a paradigm of the interactions among art, society, culture, and ideology that shaped enduring types and stereotypes.

I have exercised a degree of selectivity both in my use of primary materials and in the subjects considered here. Most of the wood-engraved illustrations originally appeared in several widely circulated periodicals—in particular, *Harper's Weekly Magazine;* a lesser number come from *Ballou's Pictorial Magazine and Drawing-Room Companion, Frank Leslie's Illustrated Newspaper,* and *Harper's New Monthly Magazine.* All of these were published in Boston or New York and catered to the literate middle class. In 1860 a *Harper's Weekly* editorial made a nice distinction between "the public," and "the cultivated classes who read our *Weekly.*" The audience for the synthetic views of country life published there would be, roughly, a hundred thousand subscribers or purchasers (as of 1860) among the business and professional classes, concentrated in eastern cities and suburbs. These were still very much the power elite of the industrialized United States, the culture consumers who maintained, or struggled to maintain, cultural dominance in a changing society. This is the assumed audience for much of the material discussed here, literary as well as pictorial.[7]

Most of the popular prints I consider were issued by the firm of Currier & Ives. Nathaniel Currier established the company in 1835 and went into partnership with his brother-in-law James Merritt Ives in 1852. Although the company continued to publish until 1907, its peak period coincided with the middle decades of the century, when it dominated the market with many hundreds of images topical, sentimental, and ideal, aggressively distributed and designed to appeal to a wide audience. As Bernard Reilly has pointed out, the firm's towering reputation rested not on the superior aesthetic or technical quality of its prints but on Currier's "eccentric genius" for marketing "an eclectic collection" of imagery that adeptly pinpointed the interests of its audience. The nearly three hundred rural scenes published by Currier & Ives, then, provide a suggestive index of how rural life appealed and appeared to a broad range of image consumers.[8]

This book is less a historical survey of country life in nineteenth-century American art than an interpretation of certain themes and images within the genre. Therefore, I have deliberately bypassed such subjects as Yankee peddlers, sporting scenes, shooting contests, most overtly political narratives, and scenes of life on the frontier. Also absent is the theme of the railroad in the pastoral landscape (in Leo Marx's trope, the machine in the garden). Agricultural mechanization is important to this study, and I investigate it in detail; the railroad, however, has been the subject of extensive examination elsewhere.[9] My focus is on the imagery of rural labor, the farmer, the homestead, and the country child. More than others, these subjects evoke pastoral and agrarian ideas. My geographical focus is predominantly northeastern (New England, New York, Pennsylvania), because this region more than any other gave form and meaning to the ideas and stereotypes under review. This regional emphasis is not exclusive, however. Northern ideas formed the basis of midwestern and western agrarianism, and these western ramifications are important in considering the changing depictions of the farmer and rural life later in the century. Scenes of black labor in the South occupy only an incidental place, precisely because, as outgrowth and symbol of another social and economic system, they bear a freight of associations tangential to those inscribed in the northern imagery at the center of this study.

The sense given here to the concept of the pastoral is a general one, denoting the celebration of or nostalgia for simple country life rather than the strictly defined literary form with its conventionalized imagery of happy, sportive shepherds, shepherdesses, and flocks. Indeed, the more precise term in this context would be "Georgic," with its explicit connotations of a working, agricultural mode of existence, but I prefer "pastoral" because it has greater resonance of association. Also broad is my sense of the idea of agrarianism. It should be understood here not as a narrowly political notion but rather as a compound of general ideas associating agriculture with good life and good government.

The theme of pastoral goodness and happiness is an ancient one. I press no claim for pristine American uniqueness. American culture in its development repeated Old World patterns; American artists used the forms borrowed from British and other European sources. English society, undergoing earlier than America the stresses of industrializing a largely agricultural nation, indulged in a great vogue for idealized pastoral prints and paintings beginning in the last quarter of the eighteenth century. Many among these works have themes that reappear in early nineteenth-century American art, and for similar reasons.

Yet it was hardly a stale reworking of Old World formulas that occurred in the best American rural genre and landscape. Those formulas were merely a starting point for such artists as William Sidney Mount and Winslow Homer, who, in grafting elements of the native and local upon received conventions, created works with a memorably American accent. That accent and its meaning engage the greater share of attention in this book, in plastic, legible forms that remain as records of the thoughts and voices of other days.

FARMSCAPES IDEAL AND REAL

1 ■ *The Iconography of the Agrarian World, c. 1825–1875*

N THE 1850s a conventionalized pictorial rhetoric of the ideal American farm permeated academic and popular culture alike, and strong formal and expressive similarities tied together paintings, popular prints, and illustrations of the farm landscape. Hudson River School painter Jasper Cropsey's 1851 *American Harvesting* (Illus. 1); the wood engraving *Spring in the Country* (Illus. 2), a *Harper's Weekly* illustration in 1858; and Frances Palmer's design for the 1853 Currier & Ives lithograph *American Farm Scene* (Illus. 3) exemplify such correspondences and suggest that a fairly widespread consensus on the perfect farmscape had been reached. After analyzing these three paradigmatic images, this chapter investigates their formal and conceptual origins and surveys literary and pictorial parallels in the use and meaning of Arcadian landscape iconography during the middle decades of the century.

Visually, Cropsey's painting foretells lines in Katharine Lee Bates's hymn "America the Beautiful," not to be written for another forty-odd years. Spacious is the sky and amber are the waves of grain in the middle ground. Looming over this fruited plain, craggy purple mountains rise majestically. *American Harvesting* is a pictorial paean to the beauty of the harmonious, inhabited landscape. Its nucleus, the farm, is the center of a world of natural splendors that embellish but do not intrude upon man's domesticated acres. The dark green, shadowy foreground with its tall trees represents a vestige of the forested wilderness that once stood where the golden crops now preside. The field, whose rich yellow evokes the richness of the land, is occupied by a laden harvest wagon and several small, toiling figures. At the far end the angular flank of a farmhouse cuts a pale silhouette against a grove of trees; to its left is a large brown barn. In the distance on the right a church steeple rises above a town on the banks of the river that winds its way from a narrow notch in the mountains. The composition is nicely balanced to achieve equilibrium among its parts. Heavy, dark masses weigh against the smaller but far more vivid area of the harvest field; the ratio of sky to earth is very nearly even. Stability and resolution among the pictorial elements signify the ideal state of equilibrium associated with an Arcadian order, when neither wilderness nor civilization tips the balance.

In the wood engraving and the lithograph, content and sentiment parallel Cropsey's. The *Harper's Weekly* illustration depicts a plowed field and a pasture full of sheep, which are counterbalanced by a forested crag and a spacious vista of fertile river valley. Beyond, a mountain beneath rainy clouds terminates the view. The compositional organization is not unlike that of *American Harvesting*. The near left side, visually heavy, plays against the open distances of the right, and transitions from one plane to the next are accomplished by long, meandering diagonals. Nothing in the picture, not even the coming shower, ruffles the tranquil mood. The flock is still; their shepherdess rests against the pasture fence. Below them the man behind the plow steadily drives a long furrow in the slope. The land undulates gently down into the valley and then rises in a series of smooth rolls to the far-off foothills.

The lithograph represents the most stereotyped version of the peaceful farmscape. Palmer, an emigrant Englishwoman who executed a substantial number of such scenes for Currier & Ives, borrowed the formulas made famous by Cropsey and other Hudson River School painters.[1] These design conventions became in Palmer's hands a set of simple signals keyed to express the benign mood of American rural bliss. Her *American Farm Scene* is a self-contained pastoral microcosm. In the foreground a farmer and his boy are plowing. Half a dozen cows, invariable emblems of bucolic peace, graze in a pasture beyond the stand of lofty trees bordering the plowed field. Above the herd is the neat, clean complex of farmhouse and barn: plain, solid structures framed by graceful trees. Nothing dramatic is happening: a couple converses outside the barn door, chickens scratch in the yard, a saddle horse waits by the gate, and a wagon rolls up the lane. As in *American Harvesting*, all the elements are in perfect equipoise. Darkness and light, mass and space, foreground and background are delicately adjusted to one another and linked by smoothly curving surfaces and lines. The equations between composition and sentiment are precise (though more schematic than in Cropsey's painting); the lovely undulations and the symmetrical contrasts express pastoral tranquillity in the world of inhabited, domesticated nature.

These three midcentury images are full-blown pictorial versions of that American agrarian and pastoral rhetoric which came to fruition and assumed the status of "mass creed" in the early to middle decades of the nineteenth century.[2] More likely than not, the viewer of that day would draw a direct association between the visual harmonies of such compositions and the ubiquitous contemporary rhetoric that proclaimed the special status and blessings of agriculture in American society. Novels, stories, poems, political oratory, sermons, and plays tirelessly celebrated the agricultural life and upheld it as moral exemplar.

According to the basic rhetoric (which sounded on long after it became hollow), it was only in the country that life could be pure, simple, and good. True republican values, benefiting the entire nation, were nurtured and cherished in the American farmer's field and homestead. Self-reliant and happy in their isolation, cultivators of the soil provided the necessary antidote to the dangerous urban forces so feared by Jefferson.

What began as a political and social ideal fell under the influence of emotional associations embracing ideas of family and the character of the land itself. Edward Everett, one of the century's foremost orators, neatly tied together those political and sentimental strains in a passage that reflects many a contemporary paean to the unequaled virtue of farm life:

The man who stands upon his own soil, who feels, by the laws of the land in which he lives—by the laws of civilized nations—he is the rightful and exclusive owner of the land he tills, is, by the constitution of our nature, under a wholesome influence, not easily imbibed from any other source. . . . Perhaps his farm has come down to him from his fathers. . . . The favorite tree was planted by his father's hand. He sported in boyhood beside the brook which still winds through the meadows, . . . and near at hand is the spot where his parents are laid down to rest, and where, when his time has come, he shall be laid by his children. These are the feelings of the owner of the soil. Words cannot buy them; they flow out of the deepest fountains of the heart, they are the life springs of a fresh, healthy, and generous national character.[3]

A sense of place sounds strongly in Everett's words. Certain elements—the protective roof, the venerable favorite tree, the meadows, the brook—function (as they would in pictures) as concrete symbols betokening a universe of goodness, contentment, and deeply satisfying reward.

As the rhetoric of agrarianism evolved, so too did the rhetoric and the aesthetic of its pastoral setting. The pastoral landscape was the essential component in the formula of the good life; it was the agrarian place. It was the field of all experience and struggle. Once a wilderness ominously unfamiliar, this realm of beauties had been created by destruction, labor, and artifice. The terrain that was eventually domesticated represented a universe to which both ideology and emotion could attach themselves in an endless chain of associations centering on the pastoral configuration of beauty, harmony, peace, and plenty.

Adulation of the American land in its pastoral raiment had had a long history. Almost as early as discovery of the continent, explorers' and settlers' reports had painted sensuous pictures of an unspoiled landscape so abundant that one could exist there in blissful ease. By the late eighteenth century an American translation of the classical European pastoral ideal had emerged, as language evolved from conventional Edenic or Arcadian imagery to accommodate a more direct perception of the North American climate, geography, flora, and fauna. Even then, however, writers tended to organize observed facts into recognizably pastoral designs.[4]

The poetry of Calvinist minister Timothy Dwight, grandson of Jonathan Edwards and visionary of the New England village, illustrates that tendency. His long poem *Greenfield Hill* (1794) was inspired by the real Connecticut village of that name, where Dwight served as pastor from 1783 until 1795. Mingling the actual and the concrete with the ideal (though displaying an inclination to exalt the latter), Dwight's topographical descriptions formulated pastoral vistas with a distinctive regional accent. The opening lines of the first section, "The Prospect," depict the village at the return of spring:

> Far inland, blended groves, and azure hills,
> Skirting the broad horizon, lift their pride.

Beyond, a little chasm to view unfolds
Cerulean mountains, verging high on Heaven,
In misty grandeur. Stretch'd in nearer view,
Unnumber'd farms salute the cheerful eye;
Contracted there to little gardens; here outspread
Spacious, with pastures, fields, and meadows rich;
Where the young wheat its glowing green displays,
Or the dark soil bespeaks the recent plough,
Or flocks and herds along the lawn disport.

The Arcadian components are in place: abundant land, sportive flocks, a sense of peace and harmony. Some of Dwight's descriptions, indeed, evoked the English aesthetic of the beautiful, as when he spoke of "sweetly winding vales, / Of forests, groves, and lawns, and meadows green." Such a vista might have been painted in the eighteenth century by Richard Wilson, England's master of the classical pastoral scene. But Greenfield Hill is no abstraction. The blue hills rising to blue mountains, the populous agricultural valley, the green of the young wheat are components of a recognizable New England prospect—a place, moreover, where every "swain" is "his own lord."[5]

The image of the lovely, localized prospect, its rolling plains and winding rivers combined with the grandeur of American mountain scenery, was to become the standard for American rural beauty. William Cullen Bryant's "The Tempest" (1824), for example, depicted those beauties in a panoramic sprawl:

> I stood upon the upland slope, and cast
> Mine eye upon a broad and beauteous scene,
> Where the vast plain lay girt by mountains vast,
> And hills o'er hills lifted their heads of green,
> With pleasant vales scooped out and villages between.[6]

This was also the vision of popular New York journalist Nathaniel Parker Willis. In Willis's many letters and familiar essays, the concept and conventions of the pastoral fused, in a newly literal way, with the realities of American scenery to produce definitive and characteristic versions of the

Americanized Arcadia. His description of the valley of Owego Creek, half a mile above its junction with the Susquehanna, constructs this real and ideal realm completely:

There are more romantic, wilder places than this in the world, but none on earth more habitably beautiful. In these broad valleys, where the grain-fields, and the meadows, and the sunny farms, are walled in by glorious mountain sides, not obtrusively near, yet by their noble and wondrous outlines, giving a perpetual refreshment and an hourly-changing feast to the eye; in these valleys a man's household gods yearn for an altar. Here are . . . a river at whose grandeur to marvel; and a hundred streamlets to lace about the heart. Here are fertile fields nodding with grain, "a thousand cattle grazing on the hills." Here is assembled a specimen of every most loved lineament of nature. Here would I have a home!

Willis's rhapsodic scene-painting offers a well-stocked inventory of what had by the 1840s become standard items in the ideal American pastoral vista: the mountains, the curving streams, the golden grainfields, the grazing cows. Although he admired America's sublime, "romantic" mountain and wilderness scenery, Willis was attracted more positively to places like Owego, where "bold scenery and habitable plain" composed a balanced whole. The more cultivated, the better: he approved of landscapes with an "old country look, free from the *rawness* of most of our rural scenery."[7]

The same conventions appeared in ephemeral popular literature, where by the 1850s descriptions of the American pastoral scene had reached an equilibrium of consensus much as visual conventions had. Even as the old formulas of Eden and Arcadia faded, new ones instantly appeared, and types became stereotypes in the language of the day. The popular pastoral vista had a particular assortment of components that could be arranged in a variety of ways. The magazines of the period are especially rich repositories of pastoral stereotype. Virtually every story about farm life in the illustrated weekly *Gleason's Pictorial Magazine and Drawing-Room Companion*, for example, sang the same song of rural charm. This hymn to the joys of New England is typical:

Bright and happy and peaceful was my village home, situated in a lovely New England valley, and surrounded by a circle of lofty blue hills that rose one above the other until they were lost in the blue distance of the horizon. Thrifty fields of golden grain nodded in the breeze, and cheerful farmhouses, and fat cattle, and fragrant clover, and trellised honeysuckle, clinging fondly to overhanging eaves, and an old gray school-house, and a neat white village church, all combined to delight the senses.

A passage from another tale describes a country morning: "A flood of golden light was spreading upward in the eastern sky, and the mists were rolling off from the green hills. . . . Far as the eye could reach, were rich pastures and cultivated fields, and orchards laden with the ripening fruit—wooded forests, silver brooks . . . and then, over and beyond all, this glory of the sunlight gilding and beautifying all things."[8]

Nearly all the vistas in such fiction portray the Northeast: New England, or perhaps New York. But the same configuration served as template for a farm on the frontier. In one story a ruined New York businessman must move out to his wife's five hundred acres of "wild land" in Michigan. The scene in Michigan opens years after the businessman's urban failures and long after the land has been tamed. We are invited to imagine a glorious autumn landscape of hills, brilliant woods, a "small silver lakelet," smooth, luxuriant pastureland with picturesque groups of cattle, fields of corn, wheat, and buckwheat, and "thousands" of sheep. Odds are slim that the author of this flimsy tale based that description on any real farm in Michigan. Although by coincidence certain regions of Michigan do have a New England look, this farm is undoubtedly the quintessential, generic northeastern American farm, translated intact to the Midwest.[9]

In the literature and art of the East, this generic type continued to dominate farm imagery even after the centers of profitable farming and much of the farm population had shifted to the vast, rich fields of the Midwest and West. In purporting to represent the typical or the best American farm, however, such description was neither false nor misleading, because the concept was of greater significance than the unadorned fact, and it was to particular familiar forms that agrarian ideology most readily attached itself. Since northeastern cultural patterns migrated westward with the farming pioneers to create what Richard Bartlett called a "New England extended," ultimately stretching "all the way across the northern states to Oregon," the concept certainly held true, even if farm landscape and organization farther west became less and less like those of the East. Finally, the paintings, prints, illustrations, and writings I discuss here were for the most part either produced in east coast cultural centers or oriented toward culture consumers of those regions. It is not surprising, then, that an eastern bias should persist in defining and shaping the American agrarian pastoral.[10]

The painting by Cropsey, the *Harper's Weekly* illustration, and the Currier & Ives lithograph described at the outset of this chapter exemplify the diffusion of American pastoral conventions throughout the realm of visual culture, from the elaborate painted exhibition piece to the stereotyped but appealing popular print. The same conventions, in words rather than images, appeared in the literature of the period and took very much the same shape. Writing tended toward pictorialism much as pictures lent themselves to literary description and narrative.

Artists and writers took a similar approach toward editing nature. In each case the basic elements might be real enough; it was in the selecting and composing that the aesthetic, expressive, and symbolic aspects assumed definite form. Just as the reader of Willis's description can envision something like Cropsey's harmoniously composed *American Harvesting* or a Currier & Ives print such as *New England Scenery* by Frances Palmer (Illus. 4), so too, in viewing the pastoral compositions of American paintings or prints in the decades around midcentury, can the observer imagine them descriptively captioned by Willis, or by the forgotten spinners of

rural tales in the popular magazines. Although the whole issue of parallels between art and literature has taken on problematic dimensions in twentieth-century scholarship, such parallels were accepted easily enough in the mid-nineteenth century; indeed, they occupied a significant place in period aesthetics. Discussing Asher B. Durand's *The Beeches* (1845; Metropolitan Museum of Art, New York), for example, art critic Henry Tuckerman as a matter of course cited lines of poetry by William Cullen Bryant which conveyed in words "a remarkably just impression of the scene thus depicted." This coincidence of feeling in poet and painter indicated "how truly native is the composition of each."[11]

In early nineteenth-century painting, Thomas Cole, a key figure in the establishment of an American landscape school, played an important role in establishing the basic visual rhetoric of the pastoral, even though such landscapes occupied a subordinate place in the work of an ambitious artist fascinated by the sublime excitements and awesome meanings of untamed nature.[12] Cole's *The Pastoral State* (Illus. 5), second in the artist's moralizing five-part series *The Course of Empire* (1833–36; New-York Historical Society), is an allegory, but in form and message it is a powerful statement of the case for a just mediation between wilderness and civilization. In Cole's composition, human society has progressed from hunting and gathering (as shown in *The Savage State*) to agriculture. Where cavemen once hunted deer, flocks of sheep now graze, quietly watched by their shepherd. In the middle distance, simple huts cluster below a hill crowned by a majestic Stonehenge of a temple. The pastoral mood is reinforced by the organization of evenly balanced masses and values, the rhythms of rounded surfaces, curving lines, and smooth transitions from plane to plane. The pastoral state is one in which human culture has not passed beyond the happy stage of simplicity and intimacy with nature. No matter what triumphs of culture might succeed it, nothing could equal the beauty and goodness of this golden age—as Cole demonstrated in the last three canvases, which narrate the consummation and destruction of the mighty empire that replaced the pastoral state with the magnificent pomp of high civilization.

Similarities between *The Pastoral State* and paintings such as Cropsey's *American Harvesting* are not coincidental. Both had common sources in the classical pastoral landscapes of seventeenth-century French master Claude Lorraine, much admired and emulated by American landscape painters. Both Cole and Cropsey sought to fix a point of equilibrium between nature and artifice, and both employed the formal conventions that most clearly symbolized that ideal. In contrast to Cole's traditional Arcadian figures and archaic buildings, however, Cropsey rendered his theme in terms of a grand, synthetic, but believable American landscape with haymakers, homestead, and steeple-punctuated village. Other artists of the pastoral scene, like Cropsey, would utilize real rather than mythic elements, but one needs only to look beneath specific, localizing detail, and investigate structure and formal relationships, to determine that the implied moral is the same as Cole's: the pastoral state is the happiest.

Both Jasper Cropsey and Asher B. Durand played important roles in developing the rhetoric of pastoral harmony in contemporary American terms. Along with Cole these two were major figures in the development of the so-called Hudson River School, a true native school of landscape painters, dedicated to the celebration of American nature.[13] Durand, who had started out as a professional engraver, turned to painting in 1835 and, after an 1837 sketching trip in the Adirondacks with his friend Cole, dedicated himself to painting—and praising—the American landscape.[14]

Many of Durand's landscapes are pastoral scenes, based on the Claudian compositional devices already used by Cole. *The Hudson River Looking toward the Catskills* (Illus. 6) is characteristically serene, with its looping lines of recession, satiny river, contented cows and sheep, and grove of venerable trees welcoming some modern Arcadians on a picnic. While Durand was criticized because his work lacked the verve and sublimity so marked in many of Cole's paintings, the bucolic poetry of his rural scenes has its own beguiling charm. Essayist Charles Lanman wrote:

His best pictures are truly American. . . . he has a passion for the poetry and more beautiful sentiment of the external world; he cannot, like Salvator Rosa, dash off a bold wild picture at one heat and people it with robbers; but with Claude he would wander amid the more charming scenes of the country, like a timid but affectionate lover, portraying only those features in the sky, and upon the earth, which fill the heart with peace. He is a poet, but one who loves the sunny fields and shady woodlands of a cultivated country, more than the beetling crag and deep caverns of a mountain land.

It is difficult indeed to imagine this lover of placid scenes turning to depictions of bandits among "beetling crags." Durand himself, irresistibly drawn to the cultivated countryside, admitted that the sublime was not for him.[15]

Durand's ideal topography was also real and specific to several favored beauty spots, much visited and painted by contemporaries: the valleys of the Hudson, Susquehanna, and Connecticut rivers and the White Mountains of New Hampshire. Such places, saturated with the sentiment of rural peace and fecundity, became the haunts of Jasper Cropsey, who even more completely than Durand (whom he greatly admired) devoted himself to the the American pastoral panorama. Cropsey abandoned architecture for painting in the mid-1840s. After returning in 1849 from two years in Italy, he began to make annual sketching pilgrimages into the most beautiful countryside of New York and New England, but his sketches served only as notes for carefully planned and elaborately composed finished works. That some of these were created during his seven years' residence in England (1856–63) strongly indicates just how conceptual, as opposed to reportorial, American pastoral imagery was meant to be.[16]

Cropsey shared Nathaniel Parker Willis's taste for that pairing of "bold scenery and habitable plain" which is virtually the common denominator of landscapes in the American pastoral mode.[17] Whatever the specified site, Cropsey's compositions are gracefully structured syntheses of various rural elements: winding streams, meadows with grazing sheep or cattle, fields ripe for harvest, groves of trees, calm lakes, embosoming hills or majestic mountains, and bright, lofty skies. As Roger Stein has pointed out, there is little tension in these paintings between the sublime above and the beautiful below. The conventional, Claudian formal devices used to achieve this equilibrium constitute a strategy for bringing under control the conflicting ideas of wilderness and culture. The one is distanced and checked by the other; the ominous dangers of wilderness become mere background for settled prosperity.[18]

Not every image of American rural landscape relied on Claudian structural devices to signal the beauty and harmony of the terrain, but such conventions were quite common; they were readily accessible through imported prints after works by landscape masters past (Claude) and present (J. M. W. Turner), paintings by Durand and his colleagues and prints after those paintings, drawing manuals, and illustrated books—in particular Willis's *American Scenery* (London, 1840), illustrated by the English artist William Henry Bartlett and reprinted many times in America. The persistence of the Claudian formula suggests also the continuing significance, in landscape as well as in literary taste, of what Willis relished as an "old country look." Even those painted or printed images that did not owe their design to Claude Lorraine used the same elements—broad, fertile valleys backed by hills—to achieve effects similar to those using more conventional academic schemata. Whatever their formal devices, midcentury images portrayed over and over again the serene, expansive, rolling spaces of an American Arcadia, ideal setting for an ideal agrarian republic.

The nucleus of the pastoral panorama was the farm itself, site of virtue and poetry on a homelier, more intimate scale. Just as a virtually standardized collection of landscape elements came to be identified with the ideal farmscape, so too

did specific building styles become nearly universal in depicting the home of the farmer and his family, whether in word or in picture.

More than any other artifact, the farmhouse was central to the iconography of the paradigmatic American farm. The basic American farmhouse in paintings, prints, and illustrations was a severely plain seventeenth-century saltbox or an equally plain colonial Georgian dwelling. Regional variations occurred: in her many designs Frances Palmer portrayed an equivalent colonial Dutch type with gambrel roof and wide front veranda (see Illus. 3). The structures in the backgrounds of Cropsey's *American Harvesting* and the illustration *November* (Illus. 7) exemplify the unpretentious, archaic nature of the venerable New England saltbox, nothing more than a two-storied, gabled, rectangular solid with the steep roof sloping down over a lean-to at the back and a facade asymmetrically organized. The saltbox and the more regular Georgian type are fixtures in the paintings and prints of George Henry Durrie, whose specialty was the Connecticut farmstead. His *Winter in the Country: A Cold Morning,* published by Currier & Ives in 1863 (Illus. 8) is typical.[19] The farmhouse appears in the guise of a country inn, but its steep gable, plain trimmings, and solid boxiness proclaim its original and basic character as the archetypal farmer's home. Of whatever century, the farmhouse in art was seldom if ever a high-style building. Simple and square, it transcended fashion to become an emblem of plain virtues and changelessness in rural America.

As rendered by painters and illustrators, American farmhouses seemed as venerable as the trees that surrounded them. Even the radically simplified classical revival styles built by New England farmers in the mid-nineteenth century seldom appeared in pictures of the imagined or conceptual farm. Those stripped-down temple forms, though resembling their colonial predecessors in general outline, usually had some minimalist classical details, such as cornice returns on the gable ends. But ideal farmhouse of art lacked even those stark touches of style. Such bare simplicity was precisely consonant, of course, with the agrarian exaltation of the American farm as haven for republican values. Sturdy, sober, self-reliant yeomen lived proudly under the roofs built by their forefathers; no need had they for conspicuous display of classical porticoes or Gothic lace.

Most of the farmhouses in American paintings, prints, and illustrations did have some counterpart in reality; one can find parallels of every pictured farmhouse among existing eighteenth- and nineteenth-century structures. Some artists made sketches of farmhouses to use in composite designs, as did Palmer, whose designs for Currier & Ives were based on studies of Long Island farms, embellished and idealized. Others derived their versions from types seen in prints and paintings. Celebrated genre painter William Sidney Mount modeled the farm structures in his paintings on those of his own family and neighbors; his *Long Island Farmhouse* (Illus. 9) conveys the blunt results of direct observation in the image of a gaunt, dun-colored saltbox with an ell protruding from the rear and no ornament of any kind.[20] Durrie, who provided Currier & Ives with designs for ten large folio prints in the 1860s, based those well-known winter scenes on the farmsteads of the countryside around New Haven, Connecticut. Yet whatever the model, and whether chosen freely or used for convenience, there is so striking a family resemblance among the farmhouses in a wide range of pictures that there would be some justification for claiming the existence of a generic type, standing for all that the American farmhouse was supposed to be. In other words, although the real in this case was demonstrably there in the rural landscape, it became, by selection and consequent privileged status, the manifestation of an ideal—or at least a standard—in pictorial form.

The farmhouse was the focal point of an ensemble that almost always included a barn and perhaps other outbuildings, boundary fences, and sometimes a heterogeneous conglomeration of animals. This farm compound symbolized the agrarian world, the self-contained microcosm where the yeoman's family could produce all that their simple needs required. In paintings and prints most barns correspond roughly to structural types existent in the Northeast. Some follow the arrangement of the English barn, with the main door centered in the broad side, as in the Durrie farmyard scene. In others the main door occupies the gable end; depending on region, these were known as New England barns or Dutch barns. Palmer favored this form, especially with a picturesque roost for barn swallows in the gable, and her barns (to judge by close visual correspondences) may have served as models for Philadelphia genre painter Joseph Johns, designer of the 1874 lithograph *Farmyard at Sunset* (Illus. 10), a rustic confection one degree further removed from actuality than Palmer's own work. Other structures such as corncribs or butteries might appear as well, but the focus of meaning lay in the farmhouse, the barn, and the farmyard.[21]

Farmyard pictures are formal, itemized portraits of a typical agricultural population: the ideal farm in cross section. The second and third of Palmer's *American Farm Scenes*, companions to the plowing scene discussed earlier, undertake a kind of census, displaying a variety of cattle, swine, fowls, horses, and dogs mingling peaceably. Joseph Johns's *Farmyard at Sunset* and illustrator Granville Perkins's *An American Farm Yard—A Frosty Morning* (Illus. 11) are very much the same; assorted species mill about with serene indifference to one another. In addition to cataloguing the complete farm, both pictures layer a glaze of sentimental poetry over barnyard imagery. In Johns's design three generations work contentedly together: mother milks the cows; father grooms one horse, while grandfather holds up a small child to pet the other. A young man pitches hay into the loft inside the barn; a boy gets ready to sling a stone at the cat stalking a bird; and a little girl with a big dog attends the chicks in the center of this busy scene. Doves fly about, and backlighted clouds beautify the sunset sky. It is winter morning rather than summer sunset in Granville Perkins's illustration, but the same spirit of contented communal activity and bucolic peace prevails.

Although customs of husbandry varied from farm to farm and region to region, on most farms such promiscuous mixing of beasts would have been regarded as a slovenly practice. Crèvecoeur claimed that American farmers carefully subdivided their barnyards because "all classes of our cattle, our sheep, and our calves must be placed by themselves." Crèvecoeur, of course, had an agrarian ideal to uphold. Livestock management in early New England in fact could be a haphazard affair, and many a farmer allowed his cows and pigs to roam and shift for themselves. By the mid-nineteenth century, however, nearly every well-kept farm in this new age of improvement provided for an orderly containment of the stock. In New England, farmers designed complex systems of pens and yards to separate not only different kinds of animals but also different breeds, sexes, and ages of cattle, sheep, and swine.[22] Slipshod management was criticized. A writer in Illinois castigated the farmer who, "owning perhaps a whole section of land, lives in a miserable hut, with pigs, geese, ducks, and other filthy animals, in confused superabundance, within the very door yard."[23] The *Plow,* an agricultural magazine, published a didactic illustration captioned *Tumbledown Mansion—The House of Farmer Slack* (Illus. 12), depicting the area between house and barn overrun by the same "filthy animals" and a cow, to boot.

If American farmyard scenes did not conform to principles of sound husbandry, they could only be symbolic portraits of agrarian and sentimental ideals. There are two ways to interpret this symbolism. The pictures may be regarded as ceremonial representations of the complete conceptual farm in all its harmony, comparable to the kinds of pictures found in yearbooks: the high school glee club or the National Honor Society arranged in ordered rows, furnishing visual and captioned inventory of membership. Or they may be considered backward glances to the farms of olden days, which were seen as perennially better than those in the present, whenever that present happened to be.

Both views, or more commonly an indivisible blend of the two, may be discovered in contemporary writing. One ephemeral magazine tale carefully itemized the humble life that occupied the foreground of a resplendent pastoral panorama: here in the farmyard were fine red cows, sturdy cart horses, a flock of doves, a kitten at a milk saucer, rabbits,

and bees, all shaded by immense chestnut trees—the complete farm. In the more nostalgic vein, Samuel Goodrich—publisher and author of the popular Peter Parley books for juveniles—recalled in his autobiography the rich simplicity of old-fashioned country life. Goodrich had grown up in the early nineteenth century in the village of Ridgefield, Connecticut, where nearly all the local inhabitants were farmers. In his detailed word portrait of a neighbor's farm on the road to Salem, he described a low farmhouse with two stories in front and a lean-to in the rear; it was constructed entirely of wood, the exterior having an unpainted "dun complexion." The barn matched the house: it was "a low, brown structure, having an abundance of sheds built on to it, without the least regard for symmetry. . . . Six cows, one or two horses, three dozen sheep, and an ample supply of poultry, including two or three broods of turkeys, constituted its living tenants." Goodrich presented the entire farm world in meticulous, organized detail, which for him amounted to a strategy of possessing through re-creation a vanished yet still meaningful segment of the past.[24]

Goodrich's farm of memory, like the various idyllic barnyard scenes illustrated in this chapter, was a homely paradise where mood and sentiment, rather than practicality, were the keynotes. In midcentury culture both the pastoral panorama and the closeup farmscape were realms of idea and emotion. Whatever their counterparts in reality, they transformed and transcended those models to become symbols of basic and dearly held concepts about what America should be.

To what degree they distorted or ignored facts, whether they really meant what they said, and whether the ideal meant what it seemed to are the subjects of Chapters 3 and 4. Before turning to those issues, however, we must look more closely at the nature of farm work as seen through the lenses of art and literature.

1. Jasper Cropsey, *American Harvesting,* 1851. Oil on canvas,
$35\frac{1}{2}'' \times 52\frac{3}{4}''$. (Indiana University Art Museum, Bloomington, gift of
Mrs. Nicholas H. Noyes)

SPRING IN THE COUNTRY.

2. *Spring in the Country.* Wood engraving. *Harper's Weekly Magazine* 2 (April 17, 1858).

3. Frances Palmer, *American Farm Scene: Spring,* 1853. Lithograph, $16\frac{15}{16}'' \times 24\frac{1}{8}''$. Published by Currier & Ives, New York. (Prints and Photographs Division, Library of Congress)

22 ■ *Farmscapes Ideal and Real*

NEW ENGLAND SCENERY.

4. Frances Palmer, *New England Scenery*, 1866. Lithograph, $16\frac{3}{8}'' \times 23\frac{7}{16}''$. Published by Currier & Ives, New York. (Prints and Photographs Division, Library of Congress)

5.   Thomas Cole, *The Pastoral State*, from *The Course of Empire*, 1833–36. Oil on canvas, 39¼″ × 63¼″. (Courtesy of the New-York Historical Society, New York City)

6.   Asher B. Durand, *The Hudson River Looking toward the Catskills,* 1847. Oil on canvas, 46″×62″. (New York State Historical Association, Cooperstown)

7. *November*. Wood engraving. *Gleason's Pictorial* 7 (November 4, 1854).

WINTER IN THE COUNTRY.

8. George Henry Durrie, *Winter in the Country: A Cold Morning*, 1863. Lithograph, $18\frac{5}{16}'' \times 27''$. Published by Currier & Ives, New York. (Prints and Photographs Division, Library of Congress)

9.   William Sidney Mount, *Long Island Farmhouse*, after 1854.
Oil on canvas, $21\frac{7}{8}'' \times 29\frac{7}{8}''$. (The Metropolitan Museum of Art,
New York: gift of Louise F. Wickham in memory of her father,
William H. Wickham, 1928 [28.104])

10. Joseph Johns, *Farmyard at Sunset*, 1874. Lithograph, 13⅞″ × 18⅞″. Published by R. H. Curran, Boston. (Prints and Photographs Division, Library of Congress)

11. Granville Perkins, *An American Farm Yard—A Frosty Morning.* Wood engraving. *Harper's Weekly Magazine* 21 (January 6, 1877). (Prints and Photographs Division, Library of Congress)

TUMBLEDOWN MANSION—THE HOUSE OF FARMER SLACK.—FIG. 42.

12. *Tumbledown Mansion—The House of Farmer Slack.* Wood engraving. *The Plow,* April 1852. (Prints and Photographs Division, Library of Congress)

2 ■ *The Poetry of Labor*

ITHIN the magic circle of the farm microcosm, agricultural work, like the old-style farmhouse and the peaceable barnyard kingdom, embodied a simple but beguiling poetry—at least as artists and writers saw it. In general, they selected the most picturesque and evocative episodes of rural labor—haymaking, cornhusking, maple sugaring, apple or pumpkin gathering—in which farmers literally reaped the rewards of their virtuous and noble vocation. The language of such images constitutes an iconography of abundance and natural wealth. Barns are always crammed with hay; orchards groan with fruit; sugar maples overflow with sap. On the most obvious level, harvesting scenes proclaimed America a rich land and therefore a strong and happy nation. To urban onlookers, however, they did more: they represented the quintessential earthly idyll.

Haying scenes, which formed a perfect match with the pastoral vistas of cultivated, mountain-fringed northeastern terrain, enabled artists to combine the grand and beautiful aspects of the American landscape with the spectacle of timeless agrarian rituals. More often than not, the mode of presentation fulfilled the consumer's expectation that farm life should be "exquisitely delightful," a pastoral dream.[1] Moods of beauty, peace, and plenty pervade the haying and harvest scenes of the 1850s and 1860s, in which lush fields, noble trees, snug farmstead clusters, and sublime mountains serve to beautify and validate the spectacle of happy rural labor, the gathering-in of the bountiful rewards of agriculture.

John Burroughs, one of the most widely read nature writers of the late nineteenth century, celebrated the aesthetic appeal of the subject. "Hay-gathering," he exclaimed, "is clean, manly work. . . . How full of pictures too!—The smooth slopes dotted with cocks with lengthening shadows; the great, broad-backed, soft-cheeked loads, moving along the lanes and brushing under the trees; the unfinished stack with forkfuls of hay being handed up its sides to the builder, and when finished the shape of a great pear, with a pole in the top for a stem."[2] This represents the view of the culture creator and the pleasures of the culture consumer. Even though Burroughs himself was no stranger to farm work, he smoothly idealized his description, creating a "picture" to charm his readers.

The Reverend Henry Ward Beecher's arch report on the pleasures of haying assumed the same stance from afar, making the point that these pleasures could arise only from distance and detachment:

It is brave work to see men pitching and loading hay. We lie down under the apple-trees and exhort them all to diligence. We are surprised at any pauses to wipe the perspiration from their brows. We are very cool. We think haying a beautiful sport. We admire to see it going on from our window! We resist all overtures of the scythe and fork, for we think one engaged in the midst of it less favorably situated to make calm and accurate observations.[3]

This was the urban, and urbane, onlooker's perspective on farm labor. The same perspective was explicit or implied in art. In Cropsey's *American Harvesting* (see Illus. 1), a woman leans upon the rail fence bordering the field and watches the harvesting activity while two children play behind her. To this figure, as to the viewer outside the painting, the harvest is an edifying and aesthetically appealing spectacle. It is a picture, as Burroughs would have it, that represents concepts about farming as much as it describes the work itself.

Jerome Thompson's painting of *The Haymakers, Mount Mansfield, Vermont* (Illus. 13), exhibited at the National Academy of Design in 1859, epitomizes the idea of the harvest as the complete rural idyll, a cheerful, idealized pageant made to objectify every urban onlooker's dream of agricultural life. In the 1850s Thompson established himself as a specialist in American harvest and picnic scenes. Typically, his compositions combine the expansive structure of midcentury landscapes with the full-scale figures of genre painting. The absence of framing elements in *The Haymakers*, its structure of parallel planes stepping back into space, and the hyperclarity of foreground detail display a diligent realism inspired at least in part by Thompson's contact with Pre-Raphaelite painting during his studies in England from 1852 until 1854. Direct and without artifice as his vision may

seem, though, Thompson, like most of his contemporaries, composed his paintings in the studio with the aid of sketches taken on the spot. While *The Haymakers* appears quite different from Cropsey's *American Harvesting*, it too is a selective and artfully arranged synthesis.[4]

Its effect is nonetheless vivid and immediate. Here is a New England hill farm where the hay grows in an upland field. We look far down the amber slopes before locating the cluster of farmhouse and barn, perched above a valley of undulating, wooded terrain. The four figures grouped in the center foreground are carefully realized. A smiling young woman wearing a straw hat holds a rake; next to her stands a younger girl—a sister, perhaps—with a basket. Facing them, a young man holds his scythe tucked under his arm, while an older, bearded farmer cleans his blade with a swatch of grass. A few feet away a boy rakes cut hay into a row; and off to the left across the field three men tend a heavily laden wagon, set off by a stand of deep green trees. Behind the field, green and ochre foothills gradually rise to the massive slopes and craggy, hulking profile of Mount Mansfield, blue and mist swathed in the distance. The sky, innocent of clouds, sheds bright, glittering light upon the hayfield and its occupants. The harvesters have pleasant faces; they enjoy a moment's idleness in the sunny mountain air. The degree of concrete fact here is high: a particular kind of farm, a distinctive mountain. Yet even though this is no euphonious Claudian construction, the means tend toward the same end of exalting an agrarian ideal of cheerful labor in the Arcadian tranquillity of bounteous fields.

One critic praised *The Haymakers* as "a genuine summer idyll, which all can feel and enjoy who have had a childhood or experience in country life."[5] Again, such a response, emanating from one whose vantage point permits a vision of the farm as "exquisitely delightful," a wonderful dream, can be taken as an index (albeit approximate) to the contemporary audience's reaction to paintings of the same kind. This "genuine summer idyll" confirmed the urban view of agriculture as something set apart, a diversion both worthy and poetic to behold. That outlook is implicit within the philosophy of nineteenth-century American agrarianism, with its insistent stress on the insulation of the country from the city.[6]

Equally idyllic on a more intimate scale are scenes of husking, apple gathering, and maple sugaring, which present the agricultural family or community as cooperative, contented, and productive units. Work often seems closer to play, as in Alvan Fisher's *Corn Husking Frolic* of 1829 (Illus. 14), the initial formulation of a subject to appear later in Winslow Homer's illustrations and Eastman Johnson's paintings. Fisher, an early and very successful specialist in American landscape subjects, set his nocturnal husking frolic in the spacious interior of a barn, its loft stuffed with hay to the rafters, its floor carpeted in straw. A lantern theatrically spotlights the group of huskers, mostly young women and men. The figures are arranged in an artful crescent, which gathers momentum from the light source on the right to the rowdy climax on the left, where a youth, having uncovered a red ear, is claiming the customary prize: the right to kiss whichever one of the blooming farm girls he fancies. Just beyond the gaping entranceway are the silhouettes of several other men; one of them, head flung back, raises a bottle—whiskey or hard cider, perhaps—to his lips. Despite the allusion to drunkenness, decorum reigns here, both in composition and behavior. Even the kissing struggle is restrained. Most of the young people diligently pursue their task, yet clearly this labor is less drudgery than festivity.[7]

In literature, early national poet Joel Barlow had previously established the conventions of the jolly, convivial husking party in "The Hasty-Pudding" (1793):

> For now, the corn-house fill'd, the harvest home,
> Th' invited neighbors to the *Husking* come;
> A frolic scene, where work, mirth, and play,
> Unite their charms, to chace the hours away.
>   Where the huge heap lies center'd in the hall,
> The lamp suspended from the cheerful wall,
> Brown corn-fed nymphs, and strong hard-handed beaux,

> Alternate rang'd, extend in circling rows,
> Assume their seats, the solid mass attack;
> The dry husks rustle, and the corn-cobs crack;
> The song, the laugh, alternate notes resound,
> And the sweet cider trips in silence round.
>   The laws of Husking ev'ry wight can tell;
> And sure no laws he ever keeps so well:
> For each red ear a general kiss he gains,
> With each smut ear she smuts the luckless swains;
>
> . . . .
>
> Various the sport, as are the wits and brains
> Of well-pleas'd lasses and contending swains:
> Till the vast mound of corn is swept away,
> And he that gets the last ear, wins the day.[8]

Although Barlow's poem may or may not have been a direct source for *The Corn Husking Frolic,* the two works are very close in spirit. Barlow took a folk custom and dressed it up in phrases of politest artifice; Fisher likewise imposed the conventions of art and sentiment upon rustic revelry.

The concept of cornhusking as communal fun prevailed in Winslow Homer's lively husking imagery. Before turning exclusively to painting about 1875, Homer was a prolific illustrator of the American scene for the popular weekly magazines. At the outset of this career he created two variations on the cornhusking frolic, both so boisterous that they step into the realm of parody. In *The Husking Party Finding the Red Ears,* a *Ballou's Pictorial* illustration (Illus. 15), mayhem replaces the decorum of Fisher's painting; nearly all the youths at once have found red ears, and they lunge in unison after protesting damsels. In *Husking the Corn in New England* (published in *Harper's Weekly,* November 13, 1858), the frolicking huskers in the same manner kiss, struggle, fall off their stools, and flirt (under the eyes of their elders) in a lofty barn interior piled with hay and hung with lanterns.[9]

Homer's robust rowdiness softened into romantic folksiness in the poems of John Greenleaf Whittier and the paintings of Eastman Johnson. These two artists make a good midcentury match in that both, with their characteristic rural subjects and selective, idealizing treatment, appealed democratically to a wide audience. Both also devoted themselves to memorializing the spare beauties of New England country life.

Eastman Johnson, one of the foremost genre painters of the 1860s and 1870s, presented the theme in a characteristically quiet, gentle mood. His *Corn Husking* (Illus. 16) is set just within the shadowy spaces of the typical barn—with yawning portal and abundant hay—seen over and over again in midcentury pictures. Reflecting Johnson's extended residence in Europe (1849–55), where he acquired a high polish at the Düsseldorf Academy and subsequently in the Netherlands and Paris, this painting is expertly designed. Just off center on the left is a sturdy young farmer hoisting a loaded basket of corn on his shoulder; his weight is counterbalanced on the right by the vertical slab of barn door, a hunting rifle propped against it and a big dog curled up below. Behind the farmer, one on each side, two pyramids of husks frame two very different couples. Near the rifle and dog the huntsman, a brace of dead ducks at his feet, dallies in conversation with a young woman pausing in her work. Opposite, an old bearded man in coat, vest, and plug hat braids ears of corn together, while a little girl leans against his knee, watching. In the shadows behind are other figures, working quietly. This is no high-spirited romp but rather a romantic poem of rural labor, at once specific to the American farm with its close-knit family and universal in its allusions to the stages of life. The appeal of the subject may be measured by the fact that in 1861, *Corn Husking* was published as a lithograph by Currier & Ives, those entrepreneurs of the popular and the topical.

Sixteen years later, in his *Husking Bee, Island of Nantucket* (Illus. 17), Johnson expanded his vision of farm society to encompass what must be an entire village community. Some fifty people, old and young, have positioned themselves in two orderly rows in the middle of a field; behind them, women set up a long trestle table for the harvest feast. On the left, fields stretch to the horizon, but on the right the view is closed off by the familiar stark gables of farmhouse and barn. Johnson remained faithful to the convention of the red ear, but the tussle enacted in front of the nearest haystack is merely a ripple of horseplay in a scene of such quiet harmony as to suggest not just Arcadia but Utopia as well. [10]

When Whittier published *Songs of Labor* in 1850, he was a corresponding editor for the abolitionist weekly *The National Era*. Although he was then only at the threshold of popularity, his fame soared during the next two decades, during which his poems were collected in many editions and (after 1857) he became a member of the circle around the prestigious *Atlantic Monthly* magazine. Whittier was a democratic poet par excellence, described by modern biographer Lewis Leary as "the kind of poet, descended from simple ballad singers of all time, who made the kinds of verse which his listeners wanted to hear." [11]

Whittier said he had written the poems in *Songs of Labor* for "working, *acting,* rather than *thinking* people. I wish to invest labor with some degree of beauty." [12] These verses celebrate the toil of New Englanders in town, on dock and ocean, and in the country. "The Huskers" exemplifies the warmhearted, reminiscent tone characteristic of Whittier's treatment of rural subjects:

From many a brown old farm-house, and hamlet without name,
Their milling and their home-tasks done, the merry huskers came.

Swung o'er the heaped-up harvest, from pitchforks in the mow,
Shone dimly down the lanterns on the pleasant scene below;
The glowing pile of husks behind, the golden ears before,
And laughing eyes and busy hands and brown cheeks glimmering o'er. [13]

During this cooperative effort old men reminisce, children play hide-and-seek, and the village schoolmaster sings a husking ballad. As in Johnson's 1876 *Husking Bee,* an entire farm community joins in happy, festive labors in Arcadian harmony.

The husking pictures, in common with pastoral vistas and farmyard themes, combined the real with the ideal or fictional. Certainly there were such cooperative, neighborly activities, although it is uncertain just how often they occurred or whether they were much like their pictorial translations. Travelers earlier in the century reported similar patterns of work among the rural population. John Woods, who spent two years in frontier farm territory, wrote that "the Americans seldom do any thing without having [a frolic]. Thus they have husking, reaping, rolling frolics, etc., etc. . . . Reaping frolics are parties to reap the whole growth of wheat, etc., in one day. . . . Whiskey is here too in request, and they generally conclude with a dance." Woods's description seems objective enough; he merely reported his observations and neither embellished nor sentimentalized them. In imaginative or ideal literature, however, writers concocted visions of the husking hazed over with the glamour of legend or the charm of folkway, and—increasingly after midcentury—misted by nostalgia. As one writer observed in the late 1870s, "the husking-bees, in which girls took a part, when a red ear was a coveted treasure, are remembered only by the old."[14]

The productive, social rituals of maple sugaring seemed, if anything, even more romantic to imagemakers. New York genre painter Tomkins Matteson painted the subject in his 1845 *Sugaring Off* (Illus. 18), which was engraved as an illustration for the *Columbian Magazine*. *American Forest Scene: Maple Sugaring* (Illus. 19) by Arthur Fitzwilliam Tait—popular creator of sporting and forest scenes—was published by Currier & Ives in 1856, and the firm issued *Maple Sugaring: Early Spring in the Northern Woods* in 1872. Because it had such precise connotations of agrarian cooperative effort and such vivid local color, the theme fascinated Eastman Johnson, who made the maple sugar camp the motif for a substantial number of studies between 1861 and 1866. All these scenes share a mood of quiet pleasure. The Matteson and Tait versions combine the picturesque forest workshop with episodes of flirtation (and allusions to class differences, com-

municated by fashionable versus rustic costume). While most of Johnson's studies feature boys and codgers, his large *Sugaring Off* sketch (Virginia Steele Scott Foundation, Pasadena, Ca.) contains sparking couples among the varied, generation-spanning group.[15]

Of all rustic work festivals, maple sugaring seemed to urban onlookers the most conducive to politely amorous sentiments, as opposed to the raucous play of the huskings bees. The report of a *Gleason's Pictorial* correspondent from Burlington, Vermont, makes clear the associations between sweet syrup and sweet nothings:

At this season of the year sugar orchards become places of much resort, especially for those who love the sweet things of life. In this village parties are frequently formed, who take a trip to some sugar orchard in some adjacent town, and there regale their palates with maple molasses. These maple sugar manufactories are generally located in romantic spots—in some beautiful valley or on some delightful hill-side, where the air is pure and invigorating, and the landscape enchanting and picturesque. Vermont contains thousands of such delightful retreats; and at this season of the year . . . it is pleasant to visit these sugar orchards, drink sap, lap maple molasses, and make love. Make love! Ah! Thereby hangs a tale. Let the Vermont ladies beware; for in such places they may fall in love, while they would not dream of such a thing in their quiet homes. The delicious saccharine qualities of maple molasses, presented to the swelling lips of a beautiful lass by the hand of a smiling swain, has a wonderfully softening effect upon the head, and creates a pleasant dreamy sensation through all the nervous system, especially when it is powerfully aided by romantic wild scenes, and the music of a thousand cascades.[16]

Although maple molasses was very likely not quite the aphrodisiac rhapsodized (perhaps only half-seriously) by this writer, the passage operates on the same assumptions that animate the pictures by Matteson, Tait, and Johnson, connecting romance and the picturesque with agrarian wholesomeness and scenery both pastoral and sublime. Indeed, the thinly veiled eroticism of the text finds a parallel in

Matteson's painting, in which the young dandy on the log feeds a spoonful of syrup to his sweetheart of the hour. The sheer aesthetic attraction of such a spectacle should not be discounted either. As novelist Charles Dudley Warner said, "If Rembrandt could have seen a sugar party in a New England wood, he would have made out of its strong contrasts of light and shade one of the finest pictures in the world."[17]

Paintings and prints of other harvest themes are very similar in mood to the depictions of huskings and sugaring camps. They may be idyllic, frolicsome, or occasionally elegiac, but invariably they celebrate the pleasures, beauties, and poetry of rural toil. Jerome Thompson's *Apple Gathering* (Illus. 20) is set on a sunny hilltop above a weathered farmhouse. The old trees have brought forth a miraculous abundance of glossy, crimson fruit. Red apples lie on the ground; scarlet flowers decorate a boulder; and the two girls, holding up skirts and basket to receive the apples falling from above, wear rosy gowns. Three handsome young men, admiring visitors rather than fellow workers, lounge at their feet. The artist equates youth, love, health, and joy with the picturesque labors of the apple harvest.

John Whetten Ehninger (Eastman Johnson's contemporary and, like him, Düsseldorf trained) celebrated the farm family in his 1867 painting *October* (National Museum of American Art, Washington, D.C.) and the related illustration *Gathering Pumpkins—An October Scene in New England* (Illus. 21). Ehninger's images communicate a poetry more somber in its associations with symbols of the waning year: the dried, bound corn shocks and the gathering of the last autumn crop. The figures themselves, however, express quiet joy in working and being together. Even the horses nuzzle each other in the spirit of friendly harmony that permeates the scene.

It is significant that the title of Ehninger's illustration specifies a New England setting. All the farmscapes and harvesting scenes included here are in the same way pointedly regional in focus, not less in their references to crops than in their celebration of characteristic northeastern topography. While large-scale grain farming began to move west as early as the 1830s, the farms of New England and New York turned to mixed farming, which served the metropolitan areas of the east coast. They allotted considerable acreage to hay, vital for feeding the sheep and cattle that made up a significant part of the farm's marketable products. Fruit (apples in particular), corn, and maple sugar were important crops as well. Readers of illustrated magazines, buyers of popular prints, and viewers of art exhibitions in eastern cities were offered images that both reflected and exalted the familiar, characteristic northeastern farm, where—amid the splendors of the landscape or in the dim caverns of barns—wholesome rustics enjoyed a simple, dignified, self-sufficient existence, nurturing and harvesting the bounteous fruits of regional soil.[18]

What is absent from such pictures is of equal significance to what is in fact there. While farmers, their families, and friends are frequently seen harvesting crops, seldom did artists depict them selling the apples, maple syrup, pumpkins, or other products raised and processed on the northeastern farm. There are only a few exceptions: some gristmill scenes, George Henry Durrie's *Farmyard in Winter, Selling Corn* (1857; Shelburne Museum, Shelburne, Vermont), and painter-lithographer Louis Maurer's design for the Currier & Ives print *Preparing for Market* (Illus. 56), in which a farmer and his wife load their wagon with cabbages, carrots, fruits, eggs, chickens, and butter. The focus on harvests rather than markets accorded perfectly with agrarian ideals of the farmer's proud self-sufficiency, which separated him from the materialistic world of commerce.[19]

The fields of pictorial farms, and most literary ones as well, are also innocent of agricultural machinery, which was becoming more common by midcentury. Labor is depicted as strictly and literally manual: men scythe their grain, rake and pitch their hay without mechanical aid. This too was at least in part a matter of artistic choice, although the pattern of mechanization in the East was sufficiently erratic and selective to allow for the coexistence of archaic and modern methods, even past the turn of the twentieth century.[20]

Because the machine refused to lend itself to picturesqueness, for many artists and writers it could only tarnish the agrarian idyll. To sustain an idyllic state demands a braking of forward motion, a halcyon changelessness. Romantic perspectives on the American farm clung to traditional and therefore timeless agricultural rituals, even in the face of the knowledge that such labor could be drudgery. Looking back half-ruefully at New England farming in the early nineteenth century, a writer in 1891 commented:

Inventive ingenuity had then accomplished much in contriving machines to lessen the toil of men who worked in shops and factories; but it had done next to nothing toward relieving the labor, or lightening the burdens, of the men who labored in the field. Wheat was gathered as in the time of Ruth and Boaz, and the grain was beaten out and winnowed as by Roman slaves in the days of Nero. Most of the pastoral scenes described by the writers of the Old Testament, and by Virgil and Agricola, were presented anew every year in New England during the period under consideration.[21]

This passage and the essay as a whole exhibit a high degree of ambivalence. The author felt that in return for the benefits of material progress accrued over the last century, the farmer had sacrificed everything that had once made him special, separate, and superior. Old ways were associated with old virtues, and it is little wonder, this being the case, that artists and writers continued to present the archaisms rather than the modernizations of agricultural life.

An 1867 illustration (Illus. 22) by Henry Herrick (wood engraver, illustrator, and painter) epitomizes the persistence of that artistic, agrarian vision which shaped and dominated the image of the American farm from the beginning to the end (and after) of the nineteenth century. *Life on the Farm* is particularly interesting because two of the four central scenes in this composite design do include agricultural machinery—but in a most discreet way. "Reaping," the roundel at top left, juxtaposes old and new. In the foreground a man wields the cradle, a scythe blade paralleled by long wooden teeth, designed to cut and catch up the stalks of grain in orderly bunches, ready for tying. In the middle distance, easy to overlook at first glance, another man drives a horse-drawn reaper. More prominent in the right-hand roundel is a mowing machine, the efficient successor to the ancient scythe. While the machine cuts the hay, however, a man and a woman complete the process with traditional rakes. On the bottom right another team of horses pulls a spike-toothed harrow, not a machine but an improved traditional implement for pulverizing clods of earth after plowing. In the wake of the harrow walks the timelessly familiar sower, broadcasting the seed by hand. The large scene on the left depicts three plowmen pausing at their work. These four views summarize the farmer's productive seasons. The two machines are such minor elements in the visual complexity of the design that they scarcely even threaten to revise the agrarian pastorale; rather, they are submerged within it. Regardless of their presence, the design spells the well-known charms of farm life. Trees are venerable, and meadows undulate gently. Decorative borders of corn, wheat, apples, pears, melons, and ivy entwine among the various elements, uniting and framing them as perfect pictures of the American pastoral. Up and down the margins several small vignettes depict children's country chores, half duty and half delight: tending baby animals, trout fishing, nut gathering. Clearly, this is once more the archetypal Arcadian farmstead, unchanged in any fundamental sense.

"Unchanged" is the key word: it reveals that inherent and fatal flaw in the pastoral vision. Call it Arcadia, middle landscape, or landscape of equilibrium, such a condition entails the maintenance of absolute balance. Stasis of this nature is impossible to sustain in human and historical time, however, especially considering the accelerated temporal matrix of western European cultural advances since the Renaissance. The longing to preserve had continually to struggle against and give way to new factors (not to mention old human frailties) that could only alter and diminish what had once been whole. Probably the elusiveness of the pastoral has always been part of its charm; like the cities of gold that had earlier lured the conquerers from Spain, it was a will-o'-the-wisp vision, lovely and seductive but easier to grasp in fantasy than in fact.[22]

The agrarian and pastoral visions of the nineteenth century existed on the levels of ideology and dream which sometimes, to be sure, meshed with real circumstance but which fell short of defining and describing the sum total of experience on the American farm and in the American countryside. This is not to say that the reader or viewer does not occasionally encounter something ruder, blunter, and earthier, but before the later decades of the century such dissenting voices and views, conspicuously rare, were toads in the garden. In conformity with the pastoral ideal, visual and literary imagery for the most part presented a static world that lingered in an increasingly distant and irrelevant past while real agriculture was being transformed by expansion, technology, and capitalism.

13.   Jerome Thompson, *The Haymakers, Mount Mansfield, Vermont*, 1859. Oil on canvas, 30″ × 50″. (Private collection; photograph courtesy of Hirschl & Adler Galleries, New York)

14. Alvan Fisher, *Corn Husking Frolic*, 1828–29. Oil on panel, $27\frac{3}{4}'' \times 24\frac{1}{4}''$. (Courtesy of Museum of Fine Arts, Boston; gift of Maxim Karolik to the M. & M. Karolik Collection of American Paintings, 1815–65

15. Winslow Homer, *The Husking Party Finding the Red Ears*.
Wood engraving. *Ballou's Pictorial* 13 (November 28, 1857).
(Prints and Photographs Division, Library of Congress)

16. Eastman Johnson, *Corn Husking,* 1860. Oil on canvas,
26″ × 30″. (Everson Museum of Art, Syracuse, New York; gift of
the Hon. Andrew D. White, 1919)

17. Eastman Johnson, *Husking Bee, Island of Nantucket,* 1876.
Oil on canvas, $27\frac{1}{4}'' \times 54\frac{1}{4}''$. (Potter Palmer Collection, 1922.444;
© 1988 The Art Institute of Chicago. All Rights Reserved)

18.   Tomkins Matteson, *Sugaring Off*, 1845. Oil on canvas, 31″×42″. (The Carnegie Museum of Art, Pittsburgh; bequest of Miss Rosalie Spang, 1932)

AMERICAN FOREST SCENE.

MAPLE SUGARING.

19. Arthur Fitzwilliam Tait, *American Forest Scene: Maple Sugaring,* 1856. Lithograph, 18$\frac{11}{16}$″ × 27″. Published by Currier & Ives, New York. (Harry T. Peters Collection, Museum of the City of New York)

20.   Jerome Thompson, *Apple Gathering*, 1856. Oil on canvas, $39\frac{13}{16}'' \times 49\frac{3}{4}''$. (The Brooklyn Museum, 67.61; Dick S. Ramsay Fund and Funds from Laura L. Barnes Bequest)

GATHERING PUMPKINS—AN OCTOBER SCENE IN NEW ENGLAND.—Drawn by J. W. Ehninger.—[See First Page.]

21. John Whetten Ehninger, *Gathering Pumpkins—An October Scene in New England*. Wood engraving. *Harper's Weekly Magazine* 11 (October 26, 1867). (Prints and Photographs Division, Library of Congress)

22. Henry Herrick, *Life on the Farm*. Wood engraving. *Harper's Weekly Magazine* 11 (August 10, 1867).

3 ■ *"Unlovable Things": Farmscapes Real*

HE true historical circumstances of American agriculture contradict at nearly every point the pastoral visions of painters, illustrators, poets, and prose writers whose fictional projections of agrarian theory and pastoral dream belonged to the happy world of Crèvecoeur and Jefferson. The world they depicted had indeed existed. In the late eighteenth and early nineteenth centuries, farming was not yet much different from the way it always had been. Tools and methods were based on traditional models and ancient lore. The young United States was an agricultural nation, its highest concentration of farms (barring plantations) still in the northeastern and mid-Atlantic states for the simple reason that western expansion was yet in its exploratory and frontier phases, and the best established agriculture remained in the regions longest settled. It was also in this period that the American village, seat of rural virtue and prosperity, most nearly realized the ideal of stability and harmony that would color visions of it in later decades.[1] After that halcyon day, however, the world of American agriculture began to undergo those critical changes which, well before the century's end, would give it the character of a modern business, utterly remote from the dreams of art and literature.

The extent of divergence between real and ideal agriculture may be gauged by even the briefest historical survey.[2] Generally speaking, the attitudes of real farmers toward land, money, and work were strikingly different from those of their literary and pictorial counterparts. Even when western New York state was the fringe of the frontier, farmers regarded land as a commodity for exploitation and speculation. Often, the land hunger that drove so many to the frontier expressed not the desire to establish permanent freehold but the drive to buy cheap acreage, to be cleared, improved, and eventually sold when land values began to rise in a developing community. During his tour in America in 1831–32 the ever-observant Alexis de Tocqueville noted that given the choice, most Americans would enter into a faster way of making money than farming:

Almost all of the farmers of the United States combine some trade with agriculture; most of them make agriculture itself a trade. It seldom happens that an American farmer settles for good upon the land he occupies; especially in the districts of the Far West he brings land into tillage in order to sell it again, and not to farm it; he builds a farmhouse on the speculation that, as the state of the country will soon be changed by the increase of population, a good price will be gotten for it. . . . Thus the Americans carry their business-like qualities into agriculture; and their trading passions are displayed in that as in their other pursuits.[3]

Even at midcentury, when the rural Northeast might seem well and permanently settled, English visitor James Johnston noted, "There is as yet in New England and New York scarcely any such thing as local attachment—the love of a place, because it is a man's own—because he has hewed it out of the wilderness, and made it what it is; or because his father did so, and he and his family have been born and brought up, and spent their happy youthful days upon it. Speaking generally, every farm from Eastport in Maine to Buffalo on Lake Erie, is for sale." More scathing and particular was Henry David Thoreau's characterization of the typical Concord farmer as a small-minded, greedy skinflint "who would carry the landscape, who would carry his God, to market, if he could get anything for him; who goes to market for his god as it is; on whose farm nothing grows free, whose fields bear no crops, whose meadows no flowers, whose trees no fruits, but dollars; who loves not the beauty of his fruits, whose fruits are not ripe for him till they are turned to dollars."[4]

Many farmers also augmented the hunger for wealth with an ambition to achieve and display higher status. To wring the maximum profit from their land, they worked it intensively, planting marketable crops such as wheat year after year until the soil was exhausted. In the late 1850s agricultural writer John Johnston criticized just this greedy abuse of resources when he accused farmers in western New York state of drawing on their capital by overcropping and depleting the land in their desire to "make money faster, or build fine houses, make fine lawns, drive fine horses, and ride in fine carriages."[5]

The farmer's upward mobility was never questioned in promotional literature. Illustrations in Orasmus Turner's *Pioneer History of the Holland Purchase of Western New York* (Buffalo: Jewett, Thomas, 1849) chart the progress of settlement, from a log cabin in the first rough clearing to the final stage (Illus. 23), in which the farmer announces his much loftier rank by building a sizable mansion with a classical pediment and flanking wings. Nineteenth-century county histories also illustrate farmers' strivings toward middle-class status and its attendant symbols. Since these volumes were usually vanity-press productions, they were naturally disposed to shed the most flattering light on their subjects, who by subscribing bought—at stiff prices that generally eliminated the middling farmers—the privilege of having their farms publicized.[6] Such pictures amply illuminate John Johnston's scornful criticisms of money-mad modern farmers. New York lithographer Ferdinand Meyer's print portraying *The Farm of Volney Lester, Esq.* (Illus. 24), one of several fine estates featured in the *County Atlas of Cayuga, New York* (1875), has everything that Johnston condemned. A glossy horse pulls an elegant surrey up the drive toward the stable. The house has a fine lawn bordered by a neat white picket fence and planted with ornamental trees and shrubs. The farmhouse is a far cry from the plain, humble homes seen in paintings and popular prints. It is so resolutely stylish that it combines a modillioned Italianate cornice and window moldings with a lacy Gothic porch. Clearly, Volney Lester had made money and wanted it to show.

Until the era of big business, land remained the favorite medium for speculation. The tendency to look upon land as profitable investment rather than sacred ancestral trust had been reinforced by the federal government: in the eighteenth century the government undertook the systematic survey and subdivision of its domain and by the Act of 1796 established federal land offices charged with auctioning off townships, a few at a time. Theoretically, this practice, which replaced the seventeenth-century European system of granting enormous tracts to individuals and land companies, allowed direct public access to the domain. Instead of ensuring equitable distribution of public lands, however, the system only encouraged speculators, who, until land reform much later (and, for the most part, even thereafter), could buy up land parcels in bulk from the government and resell them for gain. The nineteenth-century campaign for internal improvements also afforded a wide arena for speculative play, since these improvements involved land rights at first for roads and canals and then for the railroads that would ultimately crisscross the entire continent.

Among the most avid speculators were the farmers themselves. During the decades when the pictorial and literary rhetoric of the agrarian pastoral ripened, there were three episodes of intense speculation, in 1815–19, 1834–37, and 1855–56. Swollen by inflation, liberal credit, a healthy balance of trade, western expansion, and heavy outlays for internal improvements, these bubbles lured great numbers of farmers into gambling with stocks; in each case, after the bubble burst, financial collapse and depression ensued. The Panic of 1837, caused in part by the eruption of wildcat banking after Andrew Jackson dissolved the Second Bank of the United States, ruined many farmers who, enticed by the prospect of dazzling fortunes, had abandoned their fields to propel themselves "into the abyss of speculation," as the *New England Farmer* put it.[7] An interval of retraction and conservatism set in following the panic, but the growth of industry and of the money economy was not to be halted. In the face of the inevitable, journalists and preachers nonetheless sounded dire warnings—in which the farmer, ironically, often shone as an *exemplum virtutis.*

A decade and a half later, traveling English theatrical manager Alfred Bunn observed that the American farmer still dreamed of wealth in its quickest, most gratifying form: "A railway scheme, a mining speculation, a Stock Exchange bargain . . . may bring about in a day what agriculture could not do for him in a year, and thus he imagines himself toiling for nothing."[8] Bunn wrote these words in the early 1850s when American prosperity flourished anew, with booms in wheat and railroad building along with overall commercial growth and expansion, especially in the prairie states. There was an unprecedented rush for the public domain, and the Illinois Central Railroad, using aggressive advertising, gave impetus to settlement in the Midwest, where nearly 200,000 new farms appeared within the decade. When the Panic of 1857 sent the economy into a tailspin, however, farmers once more found themselves burdened with enormous debts, depressed prices, and the threat of foreclosure. Although western farmers suffered the brunt of the depression, eastern farmers too lost money on the devalued stocks in which they had been investing heavily and were criticized for throwing money away on railroad, bank, and industrial stock, when they would have done better to plow it back into farm improvements.[9]

In some parts of the Northeast and Midwest a high degree of tenancy bore out the contemporary emphasis on land as commodity. Until midcentury certain regions of New York, including the Hudson River Valley around Albany and the Genesee country farther west, were organized along virtually feudal lines by great landlords who lived in aristocratic opulence by leasing millions of acres to many thousands of tenants. In 1821, freeholders barely outnumbered tenants in the state: the census showed more than 100,000 of the former to some 80,000 of the latter.

Before most of these enormous holdings were finally liquidated (by the end of the 1850s), the festering issue of tenancy provoked a long and often violent war, lasting throughout the 1840s, between the landlords of the Van Rensselaer and Robert Livingston estates and their disaffected tenants, the Anti-Renters.[10] Political caricaturist Henry R. Robinson's lithograph *The Inhuman Anti-Rent Murder* (Illus. 25) depicts one of many bloody confrontations between the enforcers of land monopoly and the agitators for freehold tenure: at the Moses Earle farm, in the summer of 1845, sheriff's deputy Osman Steele was murdered during a dispute over the sale of the farm for nonpayment of rent. This violent scene could not possibly be less like the idyllic agrarian dreams of Jasper Cropsey, Jerome Thompson, and the Currier & Ives lithographs. It indicates the existence of serious political tensions never so much as insinuated by the familiar, happier images.

The Anti-Rent conflicts were but the most gory and sensational phases of the long struggle for reform to adjust the abuses and inequities of land distribution and to make homesteads available without strings to those who desired them. The equal redistribution of all land was the goal of the National Reform Association, organized in 1844 by George Henry Evans, John Windt, and Irish Chartist agitator Thomas Devyr. This association, aiming to work in conjunction with the Anti-Renters, published propaganda and sought, with some success, to gain influence through the ballot box. To the conservatives of the day, including novelist James Fenimore Cooper, reformists like Evans represented a dangerous radicalism, a thrust toward dreaded mob democracy—which, strangely enough, in this case came not exclusively from urban stews but from the pure countryside as well.

These events forcefully contradict the agrarian pastoral. They suggest that to a farmer's eye the glorious vistas of such artists as Jasper Cropsey and Jerome Thompson symbolized dollars, temporarily in the form of landscape. This is probably putting too crass an interpretation on historical data; not every farmer could possibly have been so meanly materialistic as to see nothing but lucre in place of loveliness. The point is, though, that as the nineteenth century proceeded, most agriculturists ceased to bear any resemblance to the self-sufficient yeomen of Crèvecoeur and Jefferson. Instead, they became businessmen, as they had to do in order to compete and survive in a capitalistic economy. The historical record also belies the blissful serenity of the insulated agricultural microcosm in art and literature. Highly charged political issues could puncture that serenity, and paying rent or toiling to fill the coffers of a bank could leach away the dignity of occupying and cultivating land.

At midcentury most American farms were well entangled in an ever spreading network of commerce. By the 1850s the East depended on the Midwest for wheat, pork, and beef, transported by rail. The linking of far-flung sections by rail was a most powerful factor in the transformation of agriculture. Rapid, mechanized transport enabled western farmers to mass-produce important cash crops and ship them in bulk to distant urban markets. Between farm and consumer stretched a chain of middlemen, merchants, and business services of all kinds. Farmers, once they entered national and (following the onset of the Civil War) international commerce, inevitably became consumers themselves, buying manufactured goods that came to them via the same sprawling networks that conveyed agricultural products from countryside to cities.

The new transportation technology that speeded western products to eastern markets was more than matched in force of impact upon farming by mechanical inventions. In the process of mechanization the fabrication of agricultural tools passed out of the village blacksmith's shop and into the realm of industrial capitalism, thus forging another unbreakable link between agriculture and large-scale commerce. Machines invented in the 1830s were produced in steam-powered factories by the 1840s; they were commonly in use, particularly on midwestern and western farms, by the 1850s.[11] In 1837 blacksmith John Deere demonstrated an effective self-scouring plow that made it possible for the first time to break the obdurate sod of the prairies; by 1852 Deere's factory in Moline, Illinois, was producing 10,000 steel plows a year. Cyrus H. McCormick patented his first reaper in 1832 and moved his plant to Chicago, center of the midwestern markets, in 1848. McCormick, one of several vigorously competing manufacturers of the reaper, practiced aggressive sales techniques, featuring roving agents and attractive installment plans.

The story was the same for other new devices. By 1848 Jerome Case was producing horse-operated threshers at his steam-powered factory in Racine, Wisconsin; the hay mower, in several competing versions, came into use in the 1840s and was generally in operation on progressive farms by the 1850s. As early as the mid-1830s, horse-powered hay-presses, forerunners of the baler, were available. Scores of other implements, from horse-drawn hay rakes to steam tractors and corn shellers, appeared on the market before the end of the century. Farmers in the East adopted machinery somewhat more slowly and selectively than did their western counterparts, but the census of 1860 indicates that some had already introduced mechanized devices in their fields.

Artists and writers focused on the archaic phases of farming, which for decades did linger on coexistent with modern methods. Their reluctance to accommodate their vision to agricultural machinery was caused in part by the fact that the agrarian pictorial rhetoric simply had no place for such things. They clung to the picturesque old ways, too, as a defensive response to the threat of disruption by the new and the strange.

Any of hundreds of contemporary illustrations of machines readily reveal how foreign they must have appeared to creators of rural idylls. A wood engraving of the 1847 model of McCormick's reaper (Illus. 26) shows a complicated, factory-made contraption designed for efficient work, for the production of something that would return a profit. Even the pastoral setting contrived by New York lithographer James Shearman for an illustration of the *Improved Buckeye Reaper with Table Rake* (Illus. 27) does little to assimilate machine to landscape. The two simply do not mesh. There is no continuity between the conventional vista of cows, venerable trees, and pleasantly rolling terrain and the reaper, which with its complex components and revolving blades seems very nearly something out of science fiction (a genre then in its infancy). There is, however, one significant departure from the stereotypical bucolic background: the house on the hill above the grainfield is a high-style mansion with iron-spiked turret and porte cochère, flanked by fancy stables, rather than the virtuously plain farmhouse of the agrarian idyll. Indeed, the man driving the reaper is probably nothing more than a hired hand. Just visible on the curving drive to the mansion are the figures of upwardly mobile country people: a fashionably dressed couple and a boy rolling a hoop. Again, this reminds us that the world of the Buckeye Reaper is that of modern agricultural capitalism, commerce, and consumption.

The fateful confrontation between nature and machine in nineteenth-century America and its foregone conclusion have fascinated scholars in American studies and art history.[12] Depending on the evidence selected for support, one can argue that some or most Americans welcomed the machine, that some or most felt threatened by it, or that some or most were ambivalent. Creators of the agrarian idyll generally proceeded as if agricultural machines—threatening and disruptive—did not exist. In the larger community, however, and especially among the farm population and its spokesmen, there was a strong swell of enthusiasm for these labor-saving, profitmaking devices.

In 1842 Robert Thomas, publisher of the *Farmer's Almanac,* wrote of the technological wonders born since his young manhood only a half-century before. He marveled that the United States had gone from little sapling to mighty tree in those years and exulted over population growth in New York and other cities, but he stood most in awe of those miraculous instruments of progress, the machines:

Fifty years ago, and we had nothing of the gigantic wonders of steam; we had no boiling cauldrons traversing the land and water . . . and pulling and pushing enormous masses with fury along. . . . Fifty years ago, the worthy fathers and mothers of the present generation were willing to dress in their own homespun; the busy wheel was whirring by the kitchen fireside; the knitting needles were plied, and the wool woven in the house. . . . The water-fall and steam-engine, the improved spindles and other machines, manufacture now millions of yards, where fifty years since only hundreds were made. . . . Within the past fifty years science has done wonders for the human race. . . . The farmer, among others, is indebted to her for his well constructed ploughs, his improved breeds of cattle and swine . . . and his improved implements of every kind, from the simple apple-peeler to the steam threshing-machine.

Only four years after Thomas published his paean, the *Prairie Farmer* offered practical evidence of interest in the machines: "About thirty of these machines [McCormick reapers] were landed at our wharves early last month. They were snatched as soon as landed; while numbers of farmers who failed to get one for themselves stood looking a little like Oliver Twist when he wanted 'some more.' "[13] Later issues published farmers' testimonials to the laborsaving efficiency of the reapers.

Exultation over the agricultural machine as emblem of progress rose higher in the following decade. In 1855 eminent clergyman Henry Ward Beecher wrote his tribute to the influence of mowing machines and steam plows: the creator of such devices was a true benefactor of humanity, "an emancipator and a civilizer"; the better the machines, the better the farmer. In Beecher's view—which neatly avoided the commercial aspects of mechanization—the agriculturist, freed from the drudgery of manual labor, would enjoy "leisure for culture."[14]

The popular journals were equally enthusiastic about the progress of farming. In 1857 a reporter for *Harper's Weekly* attended the reaper trials in Syracuse, New York. Such competitions, often held during the decades of experimentation and development, attracted considerable interest and generated free publicity for participating manufacturers. The text commented, prophetically:

The days of the sickle are over. Lay it up . . . in a museum . . . label it, number it, and put the date on the label; for the time will come when the sickle will be as rare as the headsman's axe or the Spanish blunderbuss. We are too fast for so slow an instrument. We must have a machine like a steam-engine, with two horses to draw it, which shall tear devastatingly through a field of oats or wheat, cut ten feet wide of grain at a stroke, and lay it all ready for sheaving.[15]

Two illustrations accompanied the article: *Reaping in the Olden Time* and *Reaping in Our Time* (Illus. 28, 29). Although the house in the background of *Reaping in the Olden Time* is more quaint and self-consciously rustic, other features of the scene are little different from those depicted in paintings,

prints, and illustrations of the American agrarian idyll. Men swing their sickles and gather the sheaves; a majestic tree shades the man drinking from a jug brought by a farm woman. By contrast, there is nothing quaint about *Reaping in Our Time*. Ten horse-drawn reapers have methodically cut ten broad parallel swaths across the grainfield, suggesting in these precise divisions the efficiency and economy of work done by machines. The monotonous regularity of the shorn strips alternating with identical strips of standing grain evokes the uniformities of industrial production, a rigid design imposed upon nature. In such a setting the lone venerable tree occupying this field seems anomalous. Better suited to the idea of the rationalized harvest is the stark geometry of several large farm buildings in the left background.

It was in the prairie and plains states that such rationalized, mechanized farm operations most radically redefined agriculture and pushed it into the sphere of modern capitalism. Here, more nakedly than in the East, with its older traditions, the land and its bounty existed as quantifiable commodities, and machine farming seemed expressly designed for those expanses of flat terrain stretching almost endlessly toward the horizon. Even the land itself had been rationalized. The Land Ordinance of 1785 had put into motion the survey that undertook systematic subdivision of enormous inland tracts into the grid now familiar to every cross-country airline passenger: townships six miles square and divided into thirty-six parcels of 640 acres each (later to be further fragmented but always in regular divisions, 320 acres, 160, 80, 40). In the prairie lands the cost of initiating cultivation was high because of the thick-skinned sod with its almost impenetrable mat of tall, tangled grasses. The plow that broke the plains was just as likely to be the property of an entrepreneur who could buy expensive machines and hire gangs of laborers as it was to be the conquering tool of the lone pioneer. Grid, machine, and capital together determined what the future of American farming would be. As an agricultural writer noted in the 1860s, the modern farm was a kind of factory, needing vast spaces in order to realize mass production. He observed that there was now a manifest tendency toward larger farms . . . the small farmers could spare but little produce for the support of the rapidly increasing population of our cities and villages. . . . strictly speaking, this is not farming. A farmer is a manufacturer. . . . It is a great establishment, and it cannot profitably be conducted on a small scale. To talk of ten acres being enough for a *farm* is simply an absurdity.[16]

It was almost exclusively in the realm of what might be called utilitarian art and writing—in other words, straight journalistic reporting—that the real western farm, the food factory of nineteenth-century agribusiness, appeared. Early in the 1870s an illustrated article in *Harper's Weekly* summed up the character of such operations in describing the Burr Oak farm in central Illinois. What struck the reporter most forcibly was its vast size: on an estate totaling sixty-five square miles, 11,000 acres were planted in corn and 5,000 in other crops, "vast green oceans of growing grain under the bright prairie skies." Much of the article consisted of an awestruck inventory of the numbers of men and machines employed to run this "perfectly systematized" megafarm. The owner, a Mr. Sullivant, had 250 "hands," mostly German and Swedish men, divided in quasi-military fashion into gangs. Much of the work was done by machinery; in one field the writer had seen "no less than one hundred and twenty-three cultivators, each worked by one man and two mules or horses." In addition, there were 150 steel plows, 75 breaking plows, 45 corn planters, and 25 gang-harrows; the farm even had power corn shellers. As if that were not enough, the Burr Oak was also a temperance farm, and as a means of social control the patriarchal Mr. Sullivant regularly allowed his men to have dance evenings, at which he and his family were "frequent and thoroughly welcome spectators."[17]

A composite illustration (Illus. 30) based on Theodore Davis's sketches corresponds precisely to the tone of the report. Since this was a straightforward assignment intended to record information accurately, the artist was not at all hampered by fealty to the conventions of pastoral composition and sentiment. It is significant that there are none of the frills and embellishments that made such a pretty, bucolic confection of Herrick's *Life on the Farm* (see Illus. 22). There are no roundels, no twining vines or bunches of fruit, no farm pets or nut gathering. Instead, there are nine rectilinear scenes in plain borders, each one displaying a different aspect of this colossal enterprise. On the top left, men walk behind mules in an endless plowed field; opposite, they drive several of the 123 cultivators through an endless field of corn. Next down on the left is a "farm gang"; on the right, a "hedge gang." The centerpiece offers the spectacle of prairie breaking: heavy, specialized plows, each drawn by four spans of oxen, cross the empty prairie spaces. Only one scene, on the bottom right, is a close-up: here Mr. Sullivant, seated on a rustic bench with a little girl at his knee, enacts his role as farmer-general of this agricultural army and gives orders to his respectfully standing "captains." There was nothing cooperative or communal about labor performed by gangs; probably they did not have husking bees. They might just as well have been working in a mill under a similar chain of command from industrialist through foremen to workers. Also significant in these views is the absence of the village-and-church-spire configuration sometimes incorporated into the pastoral views of the Northeast. In this western land, platted upon a vast grid and occupied by far-flung farm complexes, the village evolved less as a religious and community center than as a crossroads main street built to serve commercial needs. Together, these nine pictures, views of a business in operation, utterly controvert the agrarian idyll.

The patterns established by farms like the Burr Oak became ever more standardized on yet bigger estates as agriculture moved into new territories such as the Dakotas, where so-called "bonanza farms" exploited the grain boom made possible by new seeds and planting techniques designed to withstand the aridity of the high plains. The 1878 wood engraving *Dakota Territory* (Illus. 31) portrays the Dalrymple farm, a stupendous landscape where thousands of grain sheaves in gridlike array await a turn at the threshers, mammoth machines powered by big, black steam engines that raise sooty plumes of smoke at intervals as far back as the eye can see. This is a factory in every respect save that it lacks walls and roof. In this terrain, completely rationalized and mechanized, technology has devoured nature.

William Allen Rogers' dramatic illustration of 1891, *Harvesting on a Bonanza Farm* (Illus. 32), only confirms the earlier scene. Although it shows no steam engines, the seemingly infinite column of binders (advanced reapers equipped with a self-binding mechanism) evokes the uniformity of industrial production. The writer of the accompanying text (possibly Rogers himself) appreciated this programmed regularity: "The self-binder is somewhat complicated, but it seems simple when we consider what it does. It is the most intelligent machine used on the farm. . . . All it asks is that the hired man shall keep his fingers out of it and furnish it plenty of grain to bind up. . . . It works with the precision of a steam engine." The binders are pulled by three mules each and driven by nearly identical men with slouch hats and whips. The only figure out of line is that of the overseer, riding his own mule up and down the ranks. The background vista is flat and featureless. This land and this labor are not pleasant or picturesque. There are no rolling meadows and tranquil cows. Yet in truth such scenes of agriculture have a blunt power seldom encountered in images of the agrarian pastoral. Their power and bigness were, like the machine itself, outside the range of the pastoral, and in nineteenth-century imagery the two realms remained separate: the pastoral in the sphere of art, the capitalistic farm in the arena of journalism.[18]

At their extreme point of development in the late nineteenth century, labor saving agricultural machines like the binders in Rogers's illustration relegated the farmer (or his hired man) to the status of machine tender, as factory operatives had been for much of the century. That farm workers themselves considered this degrading is unlikely, however. As nineteenth-century documents show, few farm tasks were pleasant or easy; most were physically very demanding, if not onerous—aspects of agricultural labor seldom communicated by images of the agrarian idyll.

The diary kept by New Hampshire farmer Thomas Coffin from 1825 to 1835 tells a simple and even laconic story of daily life.[19] Well established and successful at mixed farming, Coffin put some of the profits from cheese and cider, his major cash crops, into Concord Bank stocks. Not unlike the good republican yeoman of agrarian theory, he participated in state militia training and was even elected to a term in the state legislature. By necessity resourceful and versatile, he was his own wheelwright, cooper, and carpenter. With his little sons, hired hands, and an occasional neighbor, he worked almost incessantly in the barn and in his fields. The diary records no vacations or holiday festivities. The entries recite the hard facts of existence, which Coffin accepted without much complaint. Most striking in this record are the tyrannies of nature and of the agricultural cycles themselves. During the decade Coffin weathered two droughts, several seasons of torrential rains, and many winters of paralyzing snows. In summer the haying that looks so picturesque in art was an ordeal that dragged on for weeks. In 1833 Coffin began haying on July 8 and did not finish until August 14. Another year, during a July heat wave, he wrote: "Uncommon warm for three days we mowed raked got in three small jags [loads] we are almost sick." So inexorable were the demands of the hay that when Coffin's wife died during haying season, the work proceeded in the midst of funeral preparations. Such things do not happen in idylls.

Although it might seem that life was severe, even cruel, to Thomas Coffin, his general experience only repeats what was true for most ordinary farmers, as is corroborated by other records. The eminent naturalist John Muir grew up on a pioneer farm in Wisconsin, where he somehow endured an existence he later recollected as consisting of little but exhausting drudgery:

The summer work . . . was deadly heavy, especially harvesting and corn-hoeing. . . . In summer the chores were grinding scythes, feeding the animals, chopping stove-wood, and carrying water up the hill from the spring. . . . Then breakfast, and to the harvest or hayfield. . . . We stayed in the field until dark, then supper, and still more chores, family worship, and to bed; making altogether a hard, sweaty day of about sixteen or seventeen hours. . . . I was put to the plough at the age of twelve, when my head reached but little above the handles. . . . We were all made slaves through the vice of over-industry. . . . We were called in the morning at four o'clock and seldom got to bed before nine.[20]

In addition to the demands of nature, pressures to convey a solid cash crop to market played a significant part in spawning that "vice of over-industry."

Optimistic agrarian rhetoricians often pointed out that those whose wealth came from the land had the only true wealth, an absolute never subject to fluctuation. In fact, the more farmers became snared in the webs of capitalism, the more directly did external circumstances affect their prices. Erstwhile farm boy Isaac Phillips Roberts described the condition of prairie farmers during the Civil War, when prices for corn were depressed. "In the midst of plenty," he wrote, "they were really very poor."

You might suppose that I would glory in those ample granaries filled to overflowing with golden harvest, the result of making a thousand bushels of corn grow where only one buffalo grew before; but did you ever realize what it means to a farmer to sell a bushel—70 to 75 pounds—of corn in the ear for ten cents? Imagine him . . . in a climate windy and cold for six months of the year; having always more corn in the field than he can husk and no money . . . to employ help to gather in the fall harvest! Imagine . . . such a farmer, out in the field by sunrise some frosty morning, with a span of horses and wagon, husking a load of corn . . . which would keep him at work all of the short autumn day.

Roberts went on to describe the rest of the farmer's labors, which culminated in his consigning the grain to one of the long fence-board corncribs by the railroad tracks and receiv-ing for his lonely toil "only three paper dollars!" Those dollars almost instantly consumed by purchases at the general store, the farmer returned to his isolated "poorly-built pre-emption shanty" far out on the prairie, "spitefully threw a liberal supply of corn on the fire, and said: 'Damn you, burn. You ain't worth anything at the station or anywhere else, so I'll keep warm until I enlist and then I suppose the Johnnies will make it warm enough for me without burning corn!'"[21]

Eastman Johnson's paintings of cozy husking bees are roughly contemporary with the hard years when this farmer cursed the corn that he had husked alone in his field for three paper dollars. After the war, in the 1870s, the grain-growing states of Kansas, Nebraska, Minnesota, and the Dakotas were devastated by drought, and yet another financial collapse—the Panic of 1873—sent prices all over the country tumbling down once more. With only a few exceptions in the popular pictorial media, such troubles had little or no impact on depictions of country life. It had been the same during earlier boom-and-bust periods, acknowledged by only a handful of images such as Francis William Edmonds's *Speculator* (1852; National Museum of American Art, Washington, D.C.), showing a sharp trader fleecing naive country people.

The illustration *"Hard Times"—Mortgaging the Old Homestead* (Illus. 33), published in 1873, affords a rare glimpse of circumstances that were anything but rare.[22] This image refutes the many popular vistas of the sunny, secure American farmscape. The setting is a simple, homely room furnished with the plainest of country chairs and an equally plain table. Here sit a young farm couple in postures of despair, the man gripping his head as if it were about to fly off his shoulders, the woman weeping into a handkerchief. On the table rest her abandoned knitting, an oil lamp, a pair of spectacles, a sheet of paper, and a pen and inkwell: evidence of the fatal contract recently signed. Just departing through the door on the right is the reason for their distress: a man wearing a shiny top hat, attribute of the banker or the capitalist. So ingrained was the habit of seeing the American farm in an optimistic light that the text written to accompany the illustration gave the story a happy ending:

It is evidently not the fault of the young husband and wife . . . that the dear old homestead has to be mortgaged. The times have been hard, crops have failed, the live stock has been diminished by disease, and now, in order to save the home of his childhood, the young farmer is obliged to lay upon it the burden of a heavy mortgage, which he may never be able to lift. But though he seems to be overwhelmed for the present with grief and disappointment, he will undoubtedly pluck up courage, and set vigorously to work to redeem his fortunes. It is not the nature of a genuine American to surrender to misfortune without a hard struggle. . . . he takes courage from adversity, and makes failures the stepping-stones to success.[23]

Not for another few years would literature and journalism begin in earnest to debunk the cherished ideal of the agrarian pastoral. In the 1870s that ideal still held sway.

The high degree of selectivity in the agrarian idylls of Durand, Cropsey, Thompson, Johnson, Ehninger, Currier & Ives, and the popular illustrators becomes all the more obvious when viewed against the background of historical and social circumstances of American agriculture in the middle decades of the nineteenth century. Knowledge of this background makes it possible to take a more precise measurement of that selectivity and to discover that it was even narrower and more discriminating than it may at first appear to have been.

It can be argued that the narrow view of the idyllmakers did represent at least a thin slice of reality. If they remained oblivious to the western farmscape, were there not happy, well-established mixed farms of the familiar, often pictured kind in New England, New York, and the old Midwest? Does not the landscape, even today, resemble in certain places its gorgeous pictorial counterparts? Did not the physical circumstances and conservatism of northeastern agriculture, so unlike those in the developing west, weigh against the rapid adoption of farm machinery? The answer to all these queries is only a very qualified yes. The situation of eastern agriculture itself was seldom so simple or so blissful as painted and poeticized, and there are too many recorded exceptions or disagreements about its essential nature to allow us to accept the idyll as an undistorted reflection even of a highly contracted sphere.[24]

Evidence indicates that eastern farmers did adopt certain types of machinery almost as early as they became available. New Hampshire diarist Thomas Coffin was much interested in new technology. One winter he journeyed to Bethlehem and Franconia "to see the Iron Factory." Another time, in Boscawen, he went to "Mr. Benjamin Kimball's to try a machine for thrashing," and he thought of having a "horse power" built "to saw wood and thrash." Contemporaries seem to have discounted such mechanization as there was; they constantly criticized eastern farmers for their backwardness. The editors of *Homestead* declared that no other class of Yankees was "so obstinately perverse" in its reluctance to take advantage of new machines, tools, and cropping methods.[25]

Recent scholarship has corrected such probably nearsighted views. Thomas Hubka has argued that New England farmers from midcentury on responded to the demands of an increasingly market-directed economy by continually experimenting, readapting, and retooling. Oriented toward success and determined to bring about improvement, they reorganized and beautified their farms. The same was true elsewhere in the Northeast: according to Richard Wines, who conducted a study of Northville, a small community on eastern Long Island, farmers very early began using advanced techniques, and there is little evidence for the "supposedly retardant effects of cultural conservatism." By 1835 one farmer had a threshing machine; by 1844, a horse-rake. The most accelerated period of change was from 1845 to 1875. The first reapers were brought in before 1855, and they were widely used within a few years. The various changes were made in response to increased market opportunities. Although eastern farmers lagged somewhat behind their western counterparts in the early years, this gap narrowed to almost nothing later on.[26]

Photographs offer valuable evidence of the actual appearance of particular farms, which ranged from the most stark and squalid to the tidiest and most improved. A photograph of Cobblestone Farm, Grover Hill, Bethel, Maine (Illus. 34), reveals the kind of common nineteenth-century farmscape never celebrated in landscape art. The only features Cobblestone shares with the idealized farm scene are its rolling terrain and its distant background of impresssive hills. Otherwise, to those conditioned by Currier & Ives prints or Hudson River School landscapes, this bleak place is unrecognizable as an American farm. The fields are thickly strewn with granite boulders. The fences, solid enough perhaps, are rough structures, neither neat nor symmetrical. In the middle ground the house, barn, and various outbuildings form a straggling group atop a bare knoll. The few trees are not particularly venerable, and they stand a good distance from the buildings. There are no contented cows, no gently winding rivulets. This rugged farmscape recalls the observation of English traveler Isaac Weld regarding the Americans' "unconquerable aversion to trees . . . whenever a settlement is made, they cut away all before them without mercy; not one is spared; all share the same fate. . . . they are looked upon as a nuisance, and the man that can cut down the largest number to have the field about his house most clear of them is looked upon as the most industrious citizen who is making the greatest improvement in the country." It is true that the situation Weld described in 1799 was beginning to change by midcentury as farmers, urged by agricultural magazines and crusaders for beauty, began to consider the value of trees for shelter and ornament around the house. The Cobblestone Farm photograph, however, suggests that there may have been a good many homesteads not yet aesthetically improved.[27]

Only a few contemporary observers recorded unprettified views of the eastern farm. Popular author Donald Grant Mitchell, a prolific writer on farming for escapist urbanites,

described an eastern Connecticut farm on which he had lived in the 1840s. This place, he said, was "wild, unkempt, slatternly." The street of the nearest village was "dreary," consisting only of a tavern, a cooper's, a carriage-repair shop, and, strange to say, a manufactory of musical instruments. The farm was largely unimproved and far from achieving its optimal production. The only really fertile patch was the barn lot, which received leakage from animal waste; its richness, accordingly, was "due rather to lack of care than to skill." Everywhere were crazy fences and leaning walls. Like most New England farms, this one was "scrubby," with "meagre stock and wide acres." "I doubt greatly," Mitchell concluded, "if there be any people on the face of the earth, who farm so poorly as the men of New England."[28]

The most negative critique of New England farming at midcentury appeared in 1858, just at the time when such paintings as Thompson's *Haymakers* and Johnson's *Corn Husking* so warmly celebrated the harmonious goodness of eastern farming. The purpose of the article "Farming Life in New England" was to denounce such views vigorously as flagrant fictions, nothing more than the dreams of sentimental city dwellers. The writer admitted that thoughts of such heavenly places were so universal, so basic, that it was probably part of the divine plan that man should be a farmer, yet nowhere did the actual even remotely correspond to the ideal. Life as the New England farmer lived it was "mean and contemptible"; worse, it was "a pestilent perversion . . . the sale of the soul to the body . . . turning the back upon life, upon growth, upon God, and descending into animalism." The reason was that the Yankee farmer's obsessive devotion to work and moneymaking caused a deterioration both physical and mental. The writer's descriptive portrait of the typical New England farm tellingly recalls the photograph of Cobblestone:

A square, brown house; a chimney coming out of the middle of a roof; not a tree nearer than the orchard, and not a flower at the door. At one end projects a kitchen; from the kitchen projects a wood-shed and wagon-cover, occupied at night by hens; beyond the wood-shed, a hog-pen, fragrant and musical. . . . we look directly across the road, to where the barn stands, like the hull of a great black ship-of-the-line. . . . An old ox-sled is turned up against the wall close by, where it will have the privilege of rotting. This whole establishment was contrived with a single eye to utility. The barn was built in such a manner that its deposits might be convenient to the road which divides the farm, while the sty was made an attachment of the house for convenience in feeding its occupants.

The root of this deterioration lay in the fact that the farmer's life and home were "unloved and unlovable things." The farmer's children could not wait to get off the land and seek better employment in the cities, or out west. A distressing new element was the influx of kitchen girls and hired hands from Ireland, bound to "depress the tone of farming society." Only if the farmer learned to set aside time for refined "intellectual and social activity," and engaged his mind in scientific farming, might he transcend the "animal life" and "gross material utilities" that so reduced his noble calling. The tone of this article throughout is disillusioned. The writer's vitriol flows so scathingly not entirely because New England farming was in such a sorry state—although doubtless it could have been better in places—but because it seemed so mean, poor, and narrow in contrast to the agrarian ideal. Still, even granting that the writer paints an exaggeratedly dark picture, it is obvious that the literary and pictorial idylls had to be rigorously selective. For every cozy, tidy homestead in the East another was cheek by jowl with a pigsty; for every verdant pasture, there was a rocky field. [29]

The belief in or the habit of the idyll fostered ways of imaging which, however lovely, masked and distorted true circumstances. Even the cornhusking was not necessarily the innocuous fun dreamed of by urban fantasizers. Robert Thomas—who, in addition to publishing the *Farmer's Almanac,* was a practical New England farmer himself—repudiated such views. In addition to useful information about weather, animal husbandry, and crops, the *Almanac* printed maxims and moralizing tales (written by Thomas) warning farmers against wasteful practices and lax behavior. The husking bee, in Thomas's judgment, promoted both; through the years he repeatedly admonished his readers to avoid sponsoring such events. "If you make a husking, keep an old man between every two boys, or your husking will turn out a losing" (October 1805). "In a husking there is some fun and frolick, but on the whole, it hardly pays the way; for they will not husk clean, since many go more for the sport than to do any real good" (October 1808). The same message appeared in October 1816. In October 1828, Thomas embellished the warning with a long, moralizing tale that featured a youth riding off on a colt to buy four gallons of whiskey. Most damning of all was the comment of October 1833: "Get a few gallons of new rum and go at it; sing dirty songs for the entertainment of the boys; throw pumpkins, drink grog; squabble and jaw, and that's a husking." To Thomas there could be nothing less idyllic, less innocent, and less productive. His warnings coincided with rising agitation against drunkenness in New England, but even given this context, it is clear that a farmer saw rural festivals stripped of the romantic haze cast over them by urban mythmakers. [30]

Distortions could be at once gross and trivializing. Most haymaking scenes, for example—like Thompson's—insistently selected and spotlighted archaisms, presenting haying as a delightfully picturesque occupation while they glossed over the near-unanimous agreement among farmers that hay was one of the most difficult crops to translate from field to barn. While heavily mechanized harvests proceeded in the West, popular prints and illustrations in the East depicted the harvest wagon as little more than a rustic pleasure vehicle for children and vacationing urbanites. *The Straw Ride* by Winslow Homer (Illus. 35) perfectly illustrates this notion. The rough, straw-carpeted farm cart lumbering across a field of corn shocks carries a load of fashionable young men and women, most prominent among them a dandy sporting straw boater, pince-nez, and a bushy mustache, and a belle with parasol, pancake hat, and an intricately puffed and frilled dress. In such a landscape their incongruity is extreme, even ridiculous. Having as they do the status of city consumers to whom everything comes as commodity, they concern themselves with the idea of farming as recreation alone. Other images create an association betwen haying and children's play. In the Currier & Ives lithograph *Haying-Time: The First Load* (Illus. 36), the children in the oxcart, like Homer's stylish riders, are much too well dressed for work. Like gentry in their bowties and feathered bonnets, they enjoy a rustic ride while beyond them field workers rake and toss hay into rows.

Clearly, there came to be several worlds of agriculture as the nineteenth century unfurled. In one, farming was child's play, Arcadian, pretty, picturesque: amusement for tourists and spectators. In another, farming meant business and technology: a serious enterprise undertaken for profit. In a third, varying degrees of squalor and ugliness made mockery of the ideal. In the gap between real and ideal, however, lie the clues to deeper interpretation of this imagery.

23. *The Pioneer Settler upon the Holland Purchase, and His Progress: Fourth Sketch of the Pioneer.* Wood engraving. Published in Orasmus Turner, *Pioneer History of the Holland Purchase of Western New York* (Buffalo, N.Y.: Jewett, Thomas, 1849)

FARM & RESIDENCE OF **VOLNEY LESTER, ESQ.**, **EAST VENICE, CAYUGA CO.,N.Y.**

24. Ferdinand Meyer, *The Farm of Volney Lester, Esq.* Lithograph. Published in *County Atlas of Cayuga, New York*, 1875. (Prints and Photographs Division, Library of Congress)

THE INHUMAN ANTI RENT MURDER,

Of Deputy Sheriff Steele, at Andes, Delaware County New York._ Taken from a Drawing made on the Spot._ A. Sheriff Moore. B. Cattle, C. Line of Indians forming hollow Square,
D. Edgerton's Horse kill'd. E. Steele & his Horse, both brutally kill'd, F. P.P. Wright Esq. G. Spectators, H. Moses Earles House.

LITH. & PUB. BY H.R. ROBINSON, 142 NASSAU STREET   N. Y.

25.   Henry R. Robinson, *The Inhuman Anti-Rent Murder*, 1845. Lithograph, 8″ × 12½″. Published by Henry R. Robinson, New York. (Print Collection, Miriam & Ira D. Wallach Division of Art, Prints and Photographs, The New York Public Library, Astor, Lenox and Tilden Foundations)

26.   McCormick Reaper, 1847. Wood engraving. *Ohio Cultivator*,
3 (1847).

27. James Shearman, *Improved Buckeye Reaper with Table Rake*, 1860s. Lithograph, 17″×24″. (Prints and Photographs Division, Library of Congress)

28. *Reaping in the Olden Time*. Wood engraving. *Harper's Weekly Magazine* 1 (August 1, 1857).

29.   *Reaping in Our Time*. Wood engraving. *Harper's Weekly Magazine* 1 (August 1, 1857).

30. Theodore Davis, *Farming in the Great West—The "Burr Oak" Farm, Illinois, Comprising Sixty-Five Square Miles.* Wood engraving. *Harper's Weekly Magazine* 15 (September 23, 1871). (Prints and Photographs Division, Library of Congress)

31.   *Dakota Territory—The Great Wheat Fields in the Valley of the*
Red River of the North—Threshing by Steam on the Dalrymple Farm,
Formerly a Barren Prairie. Wood engraving. *Frank Leslie's Illus-*
trated Newspaper, October 19, 1878.

HARVESTING ON A BONANZA FARM.—Drawn by W. A. Rogers.—[See Page 663.]

32.   William Allen Rogers, *Harvesting on a Bonanza Farm*. Half-tone engraving. *Harper's Weekly Magazine* 35 (August 29, 1891). (Prints and Photographs Division, Library of Congress)

33. C. M. Coolidge and Edwin Austin Abbey, *"Hard Times"—
Mortgaging the Old Homestead*. Wood engraving. *Harper's Weekly
Magazine* 17 (June 21, 1873).

34. *Cobblestone Farm, Grover Hill, Bethel, Maine*, c. 1900. Photograph, $3\frac{1}{2}'' \times 5\frac{1}{2}''$. (Courtesy of The Bethel Historical Society)

THE STRAW RIDE.—[See Page 619.]

35. Winslow Homer, *The Straw Ride*. Wood engraving. *Harper's Bazar*, September 25, 1869. (Prints and Photographs Division, Library of Congress)

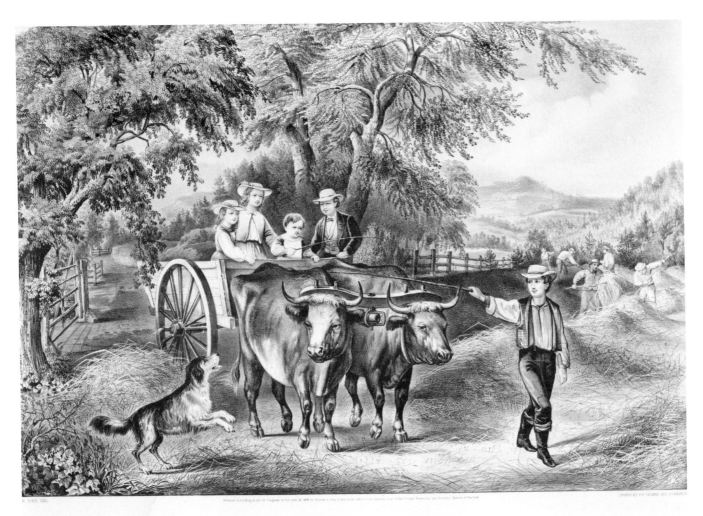

HAYING-TIME. THE FIRST LOAD.

36. James Merritt Ives after Frances Palmer and J. Cameron, *Haying-Time: The First Load*, 1868. Lithograph, $15\frac{7}{8}'' \times 23\frac{7}{8}''$. Published by Currier & Ives, New York. (Prints and Photographs Division, Library of Congress)

4 ■ *Beneath the Idyll*

HY did such a yawning disparity exist between American farms as they were and the ideal farms of art and literature? Why did the latter remain petrified in pastoral amber while agriculture in the real world developed into a capitalistic enterprise driven by new technology? How could painters, illustrators, and writers of all kinds so obdurately ignore the actuality of American farming as to suppress much of the genuine in their agrarian dream? The answer has to do with the function of those pictorial and literary images as message bearers. Their purpose was not and never had been documentary. Their purpose was to communicate and validate the articles of belief that had coalesced about the idea of the farm in America.

These images expressed and defined certain social, cultural, and political values professed by the literate middle class, the capitalists, the politicians, and the culturemakers of midcentury America.[1] In some cases, they did not so much ignore as mask the reality of what was really happening, or they rendered that reality in a visually palatable disguise. The content borne by these images was fundamentally political in the sense that they embodied ideas about the structure of society and its concepts of property. Rarely was such political content stated outright. It existed as a subtext, enscripted behind the webs of sentimental associations that so often constituted the primary appeal of rural imagery. Given that essentially political, rhetorical function, it no more mattered whether they gave a true accounting of the American farm than it mattered in Christian art whether a scene of the Nativity was historically accurate.

One of the basic, overt, and unvarying components of country-life imagery was its appeal to escapist yearnings. This was equally the case both early and late in the nineteenth century. The antebellum decades encompassed a great wave of social, economic, and technological transformations that exerted enormous pressures on the culture. Those pressures could be eased by escapist fantasies, which provided at least a temporary release. Harvest landscapes and happy homestead scenes clearly served such a purpose, as did images of wilder nature. The New York-based American Art-Union, whose activities contributed strongly to the support of American painting in the 1840s, outlined that purpose in its promotional literature:

To the inhabitants of cities, as nearly all of the subscribers to the Art-Union are, a painted landscape is almost essential to preserve a healthy tone to the spirits, lest they forget in the wilderness of bricks which surrounds them the pure delights of nature and a country life. Those who cannot afford a seat in the country to refresh their wearied spirits, may at least have a country seat in their parlors; a bit of landscape with a green tree, a distant hill, or low-roofed cottage—some of these simple objects, which all men find so refreshing to their spirits after being long pent up in dismal streets and in the haunts of business.[2]

In his *Letters on Landscape Painting,* published in the art magazine *The Crayon* in 1855, Asher B. Durand reiterated these ideas, describing nature as an oasis of refuge from tumultuous city streets. For those who could not afford a painted landscape, there were the engravings distributed by the Art-Union itself, or picturebooks of American scenery, illustrated magazines, and popular prints.[3]

In assigning such a function to country scenes, American imagemakers directly followed English precedent and echoed English sentiment. Developing industrialism and capitalism in England had made their first inroads into the edifice of tradition and the structure of society early in the eighteenth century. New manufacturing towns burgeoned, as did a new lower class of wage earners—many of them refugees from the countryside, where the enclosure of common lands had ruined thousands. Oliver Goldsmith's elegiac poem "The Deserted Village," published in 1769, looked back with bittersweet nostalgia at traditional rural life and values, then all but extinguished by the forces of change. Foremost among the latter were the Parliamentary Enclosure Acts, which, by the early decades of the nineteenth century, had authorized the enclosure of some six million acres of land, thereby furthering the concentration of ownership among a wealthy minority.

Enclosure was only one of the innovative farming techniques that revolutionized English agriculture in the last half of the eighteenth century, but the benefits of that revolution were not shed upon all. In the country as in the city, relentless poverty afflicted the laboring class. The longing for

a simple, rustic life was chiefly an escapist fancy cultivated by the middle and upper strata of the urban hierarchy; to the extent that this fantasy of idealized and moneyed rural bliss was real, it was possessed only by aristocratic and bourgeois landlords whose country houses crowned the pyramid of the rural hierarchy. This class cultivated a taste for pictorial images intended not so much for escape as to justify the status quo and to gloss over the misery of the rural poor by depicting them as both contented and industrious.[4]

Although certain changes in America followed the pattern already mapped by England and generated the same escapist impulse, others were specific to the history of this country alone. American images of the ideal farm and the agrarian dream did not merely pander to idle escapist fantasies, nor did they uphold the social order in quite the same way. Their messages and symbolism represented a deep engagement with two key circumstances: the ever accelerating rate of social and economic change in the antebellum decades, which to some extent duplicated the process long since underway in England; and, during the same period, the intense sectional conflicts that led finally to the Civil War. The first, which opened wide the issue of what American society was to become, provided the context for didactic images of the farm as the embodiment of moral values and social order that Americans would do well to heed. The second, intertwined with the first, inscribed within the image of the farm its basic political subtext: the rightness of the northern capitalist system of freehold property and free labor.

Rapid social change was not a phenomenon that erupted suddenly just before or after the Civil War. Since the establishment of the republic there had always been a frontier, and it was always expanding. Although change proceeded from east to west, the older, more settled region enjoyed the briefest phase of equilibrium. The shift from a relatively stable agricultural economy to a dynamic market economy began before 1800. By then the traditional ties of kinship, community, and religion had already begun to unravel in the basic social unit, the small agricultural village. As early as

1815 this self-contained world had been dismantled by the forces of trade, war, geographic migration, and political participation.[5]

The rampant speculation that careened into the Panic of 1837 was possible only in a society swerving more and more toward individualistic enterprise and industry in a market-oriented economy that discouraged self-sufficiency while it fostered specialization, division of labor, and an interconnected system of money and credit. Fed by huge profits from the American carrying trade during the Napoleonic Wars, manufacturing mushroomed during the 1830s. By 1850 the value of manufactured products exceeded that of agricultural products. The period 1820–60 marked a great surge in urban growth: by its end the population living in towns of 2,500 or more had swelled from 2 percent to nearly 20 percent. The consolidation of the new industrial working class, the rise in immigration, and the growth of the commercial middle class all contributed to the formation of an American society where class barriers were fluid and mobility high (although in truth the social pyramid retained its shape). In broad outline, these were the transformations that buffeted American culture as early as the 1820s, giving rise to the anxieties and fears that seldom fail to accompany the process of moving from the familiar to the unknown.

With urbanization and a commercialized money economy came the materialism and love of conspicuous consumption which, together with speculation, many saw as grave threats to republican simplicity, integrity, and self-reliance.[6] Cultural critics of the period deplored the love of luxury that would ultimately only enslave. In 1833 the *New England Magazine* editorialized: "Is any sturdy republican inclined to demand of me, in a tone half indignant, 'What! Cannot free-born Americans, who are lords of themselves in every thing around them, escape from the toils and bondage of fashion?' Alas! he, who would propose such a question, knows but little of human nature. Free-born Americans are as ardent and inflexible votaries of fashion as the world contains. There is reason to believe they are the most so." A newspaper in 1838 complained that young American men returned from their European tours "rogues and fops, with extravagant, anti-American notions," condemning frugality as "an old-fashioned and dirty foible." As the economy grew, so did display. In the 1850s a commentator noted disapprovingly that "the rich man of today expends more upon the architecture of his residence, to say nothing of its furnishings, than the whole capital of the so-called rich man of forty years ago. . . . the sum total required for the annual expenses of a fashionable family is colossal, appalling."[7]

Rehearsing a Jeffersonian optimism, writers turned to the American farmer's way of life as the hope for salvation of a society threatened by the disease of materialism. At the height of speculation fever in the mid-1830s, one critic castigated contemporary society for its utter abandonment of higher values, cast off in the rush to bow "at the crowded shrine of Mammon." Everyone wanted money and would stop at nothing to get it; as a result, America was becoming fundamentally unsound: "The canker of gain hath eaten deeply into the very heart's core of society." If such tendencies continued unchecked, Americans would ultimately dwindle down to "a puny and degenerate race." The only hope of reform and restoration resided in the "noble stock" of the physically and morally healthy farmer. The incorruptible farmer was above materialism and had no need for the petty status symbols of the small-souled:

With what consciousness of superiority must the farmer look down upon those who are childishly triumphing in the possession of fine house, fine furniture, and splendid equipages; and with what pity must he regard those who are wearing out their lives and energies, to gain those gilded playthings and gew-gaws of mature age. As for him, he treads the imperial carpet with as much indifference as he does the dusty pathway; and the grassy bank affords a more inviting seat than the most luxurious ottoman or fauteuil.[8]

This is all quite familiar; it is the basic stuff of agrarian philosophy. Jefferson himself had used the metaphor of the canker eating into the heart of a society that deviated from agrarian virtue, and the imagery of sickness would be repeated in countless future complaints associating cities and commerce with the feverish, the unwholesome, and the depraved.

Viewed against the maelstrom of ominous change and the onus of materialism, scenes of American farm life were clearly more than idylls. If the farmer embodied all that was naturally good and noble, and if farming—alone among vocations—preserved republican values, then paintings, prints, and illustrations of the farm bore a full load of moralizing matter. They were pictorial lessons in the simple, saving virtues of life in the country, where all that is beautiful and rich comes from nature.

The elevated moral worth conferred upon the plain rural cottage or farmer's house supports this symbolic reading. A writer for the *New England Magazine* condemned the excessive "slavery to fashion and custom" that drove men to build large, showy houses. Such expensive piles would visit disaster on the younger generation, heaping insupportable debt upon their heads and forcing them at last to "yield their paternal acres to some stranger." In place of the grandiose, the writer recommended to the reader's attention the "little cottage" that combined "neatness, comfort, and taste." If only Americans would spurn their unworthy greed for luxurious show, there might come a future time when "neat, snug cottages and farmhouses . . . where nature, art, and economy shall all combine—shall be scattered through the land and mark the abodes of comfort, and true Republican independence."[9]

In the 1840s Andrew Jackson Downing, landscape architect and tastemaker, enlarged the association between moral values and architecture into a coherent philosophy embracing the entire spectrum of American society, proposing to house everyone from cultivated gentleman to humble mechanic in a style that best expressed the character of the dwelling's occupant. The farmhouse, he thought, should be entirely without pretension, since the farmer was more sincere than anyone else and less sophisticated in "manners or heart." "His dwelling," wrote Downing, "ought to suggest simplicity, honesty of purpose, frankness, a hearty, genuine spirit of goodwill, and a homely and modest though manly and independent bearing in his outward deportment." Such a man's house, accordingly, should present "a certain rustic plainness" commensurate with a "substantial and solid construction," which together symbolized "a class more occupied with the practical and useful than the elegant arts of life."[10] Such "rustic plainness" is exactly what characterizes the American homesteads of art and literature.

The fact that Downing thought more in symbolic than in practical terms was duly noted and criticized by farmers. But it was precisely those symbolic terms that carried the message and the moral. Lewis F. Allen, who wrote his volumes on country architecture with the practical farmer in mind, refuted Downing's ideas yet shared his conviction that the farmhouse—a plain abode for plain people—stood for a moral well-being vital to the health of American society. It was literally the cradle of democracy: "the chief nursery on which our broad country must rely for that healthy infusion of stamina and spirit into those men who, under our institutions, guide its destiny and direct its councils. They, in the great majority of their numbers, are natives of the retired homestead."[11] Whether glimpsed across golden fields, as in Cropsey's compositions, or seen close up, as in Francis Palmer's designs for Currier & Ives, the farmhouse—and by extension the farmscape and everything it contained—amounted to sermons in paint, teaching true, solid republican values.

In this light, idyllic paintings like Asher B. Durand's *Haying* (Illus. 37) take on denser meaning. Shown simply as *Landscape* at the National Academy of Design in 1838, this painting exhibits the blandness characteristic of Durand's early style, yet the familiar conventions are already in place. On the left is a stand of majestic old trees; on the right, an open vista; in the foreground, grassy slopes and curving path; in the background, the complete American village, with a plain white church and a one-room schoolhouse from which lively children stream. Under the trees a man with a pitchfork hails the milkmaid walking down the path. Opposite, a loaded hay wagon draws up to the hayrick next to a pair of open barn doors. There are cows and chickens in the barnyard and ducks in the pond. A more tranquil scene of rural felicity is not to be imagined. This beauty, however, cloaks a serious admonitory message, reminding Americans that this, rather than the temple of Mammon, should be their ideal.

In fabricating his didactic landscape, Durand may well have been thinking of his friend and mentor Thomas Cole's serial work *The Course of Empire*, which had recently been exhibited in the rooms of the National Academy of Design. Its five paintings—*The Savage State, The Pastoral State, Consummation, Destruction*, and *Desolation*—embraced several overlapping themes concerning the balance of nature and civilzation, of wilderness and progress. In dramatic and elaborately symbolic visual language, Cole preached a warning against disturbing the precisely modulated balance represented by the ideal pastoral state. To these dominant meanings he appended a sermon against the evils of materialism, graphically depicted in the large centerpiece of the quintet, *Consummation*, and its sequel, *Destruction*. Intended to display the fateful connections between (in Cole's words) "luxury" and "the vicious state, or state of destruction," this pair coincided precisely with the rampant speculation and status display that preceded the Panic of 1837. Cole was simply expressing in paint what anxious commentators had been expressing profusely in print during that period.[12]

Less transparently allegorical than *Consummation, Haying* is just as much a sermon. Durand's determination to invest landscape with moral and spiritual significance was as powerful as Cole's, but although he occasionally invented an explicitly programmatic landscape such as *Thanatopsis* (1850; Metropolitan Museum of Art, New York), after William Cullen Bryant's poem of the same title, for the most part he preferred to divest his compositions of obvious symbolic baggage and deliver his sermons in terms of nature itself. *Haying*, then, while it does not address the issue of materialism and luxury head on as do *Consummation* and *Destruction*, incorporates within the idyll an implied homily on the beauty and value of simple, traditional country living. The fact that *Haying* appeared hard on the heels of the Panic of 1837 is of particular consequence. In the wake of exploded bubbles and crumbled banks it offered a sensible, safe alternative to which Americans must return—spiritually if not physically. Encapsulated in this painting is the essence of the agrarian ideal; these, surely, are Jefferson's "chosen people," self-sufficient and indifferent to the shallow pleasures and playthings of the urban world.

So entrenched in the antebellum decades was the notion of the improving, elevating mission of art that such content doubtless existed on some level in most illustrations of ideal farm life. It need not have been overt or even entirely deliberate; it may have been as much a matter of rote and reflex as a great deal of the agrarian rhetoric of that time seems to be. But the idea of the moral value of farm life was so tightly bound up with agrarian theory itself that American farm scenes, whatever their creators' other intentions, had to be on some level the pictorial embodiments of that lesson. Certainly by contrast with real events, if in no other way, farm scenes shone all the more with goodness and virtue. Jerome Thompson's *Haymakers, Mount Mansfield, Vermont* (see Illus. 13), standing in the same relation to the Panic of 1857 as Durand's *Haying* did to the earlier panic, may have functioned in the same way as a timely reminder of the enduring values of country life.

Rural images did more than preach agrarian, republican ideals; they proclaimed and validated the concepts of property underlying the entire structure of American society or, more precisely, of the northern sections that emerged in opposition to the South when the controversy over slavery began to intensify in the 1830s. Here again we are dealing with subliminal or subtextual messages, ever present beneath surface meanings and representing a set of assumptions so basic that they needed little exposition beyond the simple fact of their unspoken presence. We are concerned once more with the realm of symbol—existing apart from the imperfect conditions prevailing in reality—in which nearly all fictional or idealized images of the harvest, the homestead, or the barnyard read as depictions of the property of the northern freeholder. There is no question of tenancy or mortgages. As embodiments of an agrarian dream, American pictorial farmscapes routinely associated the freedom of the individual with the right to own land.

Land ownership, one of humankind's "natural rights" as postulated by Enlightenment thought, was a central element in Jefferson's agrarianism, in turn derived partly from John Locke, who argued that every man had a right to land which, by occupancy and use, he could claim as his own. This potentially radical idea was to become the basis of the Homestead Act campaign in the 1840s and 1850s. But the equation of property with liberty, of natural rights with the freedom to own, had been common currency in the evolving definition of American citizenship ever since the Revolutionary War. Indeed, one of the slogans of the revolutionary movement had been "Liberty and Property," referring to basic rights that British colonial policies had violated. Although by the early 1830s (in most states) enfranchisement ceased to be contingent on owning property, such ownership still promised to confer worth, dignity, status, and independence. In theory, the prime duty for which the government had been constituted was to protect and defend those rights. Whereas in England and Europe traditional class hierarchies had made landowning the basis of sovereignty, the American freeholder was neither ruler nor ruled. If the farmer was the backbone of healthy, virtuous republican society, it was his right to the land he tilled that shored up everything else.

The idea of the independent yeoman and his farm, which contrasted so vividly with the situation of rural classes in England or on the Continent, naturally became a source of nationalistic pride. As one orator said, American farmers were not, like those of the "old continent," fixed by birth into class rank: "We know no such distinctions among us. We recognize neither the hereditary distinctions conferred by birth nor wealth." An agricultural reporter who wrote an account of his travels in England noted that the lower ranks of rural society there were a miserable, groveling lot:

The condition and character of the [rural] laboring population in England, is widely different from that of the same class of persons in this country. The laborers there have no more association with the nobility, gentry, and larger tenant farmers, than have the slaves at the South with their masters. The line of demarcation is as decided and as stringent in the one case as in the other. Never have I seen a laborer approach the farmer without doffing his hat, and in various other ways manifesting the utmost servility.

He went on to describe those laborers' lack of education, their bestial ignorance, and their starvation wages. The implication was that in America no such gross inequities existed; there might be richer and poorer farmers, but they were politically equal.[13]

The political edge of such comparisons sharpened in the late 1840s when Europe became the scene of mass unrest among the working and peasant classes and, in 1848, of revolutionary action in several countries. One commentator in that year exhorted American farmers to rise to the challenge of meeting their responsibilities as American citizens. "Especially at this crisis, when the old world is rocking to its center, would we preserve the integrity of [the republic's] institutions. We would hold out for those who struggle for freedom, the example of a virtuous and noble republicanism."[14] Against the tottering hierarchies of Europe, the American farm became emblem of an enlightened, stable social order based on natural rights. The recent Anti-Rent wars might never have happened; the symbolic importance of sustaining the illusion of a classless, agrarian, landowning society—infinitely superior to that of the Old World—outweighed any discrepancies between fact and fiction.

The concepts of American freedom to own property and of European society as a rigid, oppressive social pyramid complemented each other and wrote a few phrases, at least, of the political subtext within images of the American farm. European versions of the harvest theme help sharpen the focus on the presence of such ideas in scenes of American farming. An eighteenth-century panorama of haying on the Dixton Manor in Gloucestershire, England (Illus. 38) offers a clear picture of the rural hierarchy so ferociously scorned by agrarian apologists in America. Here are sprawling hay-fields surrounded by other enclosed plots, which continue out of sight into the distance. This huge tract of land is occupied by some 150 figures, men and women, engaged in the activities still seen in American haying scenes of the nineteenth century: swinging scythes, raking grass into long swaths, and pitching it up into hay wagons. These are not happy, independent farmers working their own land, however: all of it is the property of the resident lord of Dixton Manor, and the platoon of figures toils for him. Explicit in this harvest scene are the social divisions and inequities that the American concept of independent land ownership was meant to rectify. Ironically, illustrations such as those of Burr Oak Farm (Illus. 30) seem like little more than capitalized, mechanized versions of that archaic English scene.

Contemporary with the American pictures under review is *The Gleaners* (Illus. 39), a monumental early work of Jules Breton, one of the most successful and popular painters of French peasants. Like the Dixton Manor painting, *The Gleaners* diagrams the structure of authority and subordination. Here, the harvest is over, and the rural poor of the French countryside have by custom been permitted into the field to pick the meager leavings from the stubble. An overseer with a badge, a sword, and a dog watches the women and children as they stoop to their painstaking search. Their very postures express their lowliness in the rural hierarchy. In the background a loaded wagon and several fat hayricks testify to the harvest abundance reserved for the more privileged. Both the English and the French painting—random selections from many—illustrate aspects of the stratified social order in traditional rural communities. Both show rural workers whose importance as individuals is trivial; rather, they play preordained roles in a tightly organized system. Against such a background American farm scenes, with all they imply of freedom and individuality, seem almost manifestos proclaiming the self-evident superiority of a new social order in the New World. What these images declare is that in the American countryside no man has a master.

The political meanings underlying images of the freeholder's domain, however, go beyond affirmation of an equitable, enlightened social order, symbolized by the individual's right to possess and till his own acres. In subtle but unmistakable ways the American farm as represented in such images validated the northern system and the northern causes that ultimately contributed to disunion and the Civil War. Paradoxically, these tranquil images seemed on the surface to deny the storms seething around them during the three decades before the war, when waves of political and social problems beset the North. Levels of anxiety rose and remained high at the ever more likely prospect of sectional separation, which might be triggered not by the issue of slavery alone but by the sheer expansive force (of which the Mexican War was a symptom) that propelled masses of Americans into increasingly distant western lands. Of course, not everyone was anxious; it would be a gross oversimplification to press such a claim. The process of expansion was in the main an exhilarating adventure that promised aggrandizement in every conceivable form. At the same time, the prospect of change and the threat of shifting balances of power, along with the ever present and ever worsening controversy over slavery, tempered exhilaration with apprehension. In this context American farm scenes—idyllic, peaceful, harmonious—stood as configurations of cohesion, unity, and order in a world that seemed to be inexorably crumbling into danger and chaos.

Such configurations amount to a symbolism of denial, yet there was also a more positive symbolism operating on the subtextual level. The American farm scenes reviewed here were produced by northern artists for northern consumption, and they depicted identifiably northern scenery, much of it specific to New England and New York state. By their scale and organization these farms were obviously small freeholds, each owned by an independent yeoman and worked by a single family. All these elements concurred with the ubiquitous agrarian rhetoric of the period. At bottom, however, they did more: they posed as emblems of the northern vision of agriculture—and labor—in refutation of the southern plantation/slavery system.

In abolitionist literature the southern landscape mirrored what was thought to be the fundamental corruption of a society whose prosperity rested on the bondage of an entire race. John Greenleaf Whittier, who from 1833 until the end of the Civil War devoted himself almost exclusively to the cause of abolition, devised an iconography of southern decay for his early attack on slavery, the 1835 prose pamphlet *Justice and Expediency*. Whittier claimed that the slaveholding states were neither free nor prosperous:

We are told of grass-grown streets, of crumbling mansions, of beggared planters and barren plantations, of fear from without, of terror within. The once fertile fields are wasted and tenantless, for the curse of slavery, the improvidence of that labor whose hire has been kept back by fraud, has been there, poisoning the very earth beyond the reviving influence of the early and the latter rain. A moral mildew mingles with and blasts the economy of nature. It is as if the finger of the everlasting God had written upon the soil of the slave-holder the language of His displeasure.[15]

Of course, Whittier had never beheld the South with his own eyes, but it mattered little whether this was a factual picture as long as it was morally and emotionally true. Later, in the long political poem "The Panorama" (1856), Whittier described a plantation in similar terms:

> Look once again! The moving canvas shows
> A slave plantation's slovenly repose,

> Where, in rude cabins rotting midst their weeds,
> The human chattel eats, and sleeps, and breathes;

. . . .

> Of ampler size the master's dwelling stands,
> In shabby keeping with his half-tilled lands,—
> The gates unhinged, the yard with weeds unclean,
> The cracked veranda with a tipsy lean.
> Without, loose-scattered like a wreck adrift,
> Signs of misrule and tokens of unthrift;
> Within, profusion to discomfort joined,
> The listless body and the vacant mind.[16]

It was for the most part New England abolitionists who created the plantation-centered image of a diseased and rotting South. Like Whittier, abolitionists and their sympathizers such as Wendell Phillips, William Lloyd Garrison, Henry Wadsworth Longfellow, and James Russell Lowell had limited experience or none of the real South in all its complexity. Their high-pitched rhetoric of decayed plantations, blacks groaning under the whip, and weeping families torn asunder presented a vivid but vastly oversimplified and melodramatic picture. Nor can their views be taken as broadly representative of American sentiments in the 1840s and 1850s; some New York-based writers and journalists—such as William Cullen Bryant, Frederick Law Olmsted, and Walt Whitman—considered abolitionism an extreme position and took great pains to present the South with fairness, objectivity, and even sympathy. Rather than do away with slavery—which these writers viewed as protected by the Constitution—they sought to prevent its extension into the territories. But the new Republican party, in its campaign for power during the 1850s, contributed tirelessly to a critique of the South as a land and society both decadent and threatening.[17]

To what degree northerners in general held extreme or moderate views is difficult to say; it is impossible to guess how many carried about in their minds Whittier's image of barren, infected southern acres. If the galloping popularity of Harriet Beecher Stowe's *Uncle Tom's Cabin* (1852) is any index, however, the northern reader of the 1850s must have been powerfully impressed by Stowe's scenes of the South, portraying gracious estates and kindly patriarchs but offsetting these with the noxious atmosphere and merciless tyrannies of villainous Simon Legree's plantation. As the conflict came closer, perhaps more subscribed to the metaphor of a tainted South. Such was Henry Ward Beecher's vision in a speech made shortly after John Brown's raid on the federal arsenal at Harper's Ferry, Virginia: "There was a time when I thought the body of death would be too much for life and that the North was in danger of taking disease from the South, rather than they our health. That time has gone past." The North alone, he announced, had the healing power that represented the only hope for mending and regenerating the Union.[18]

Whatever their status as counterpoints to abolitionist visions of the South in decline, the northern farms of art and literature invariably presented a picture of thriving, blooming health. Symbolizing the virtue of the northern way, they were clean, sound, and neat. Their homesteads never had so much as a cracked shingle; their fat fields were green and gold, their inhabitants confident and justifiably proud. If God's finger had smeared a moral mildew over southern lands, it had gilded the farmsteads of the North with the sunshine of approval. Even the northern climate was morally and spiritually superior: whereas the South, as Larzer Ziff has argued, represented everything that was hot, teeming, earthy, and passionate, the severe landscape and purifying winters of the North had fostered moral rectitude and the worthy, godly life of the mind.[19] Even characteristic northern crops were morally better. Maple sugar, wrote Robert Thomas in his *Farmer's Almanac,* "is a most wholesome and pleasant sweetening, and every true American will prefer it to that which is seasoned with the tears, sweat, and blood of the miserable slave."[20] If such sentiments were shared by northern viewers of the 1840s and 1850s, then even those romantic, picturesque paintings and prints of sugaring-off parties may have carried an implied political spark.

The idea of the northern homestead and the yeoman's freehold had even more explicit political and ideological connotations. The concept of the independently owned farm—free soil—operated by free labor became the leading edge of debate over the question of slavery and its expansion into the territories. It was more than a leading edge: it was a weapon against slavery. The idea was tied in with the effort to reform federal land policy in order to ensure that government lands be made available to settlers rather than speculators. During the mid-1840s several factors coalesced to give birth to the campaign for the passage of a Homestead Act, a campaign later appropriated by the Republican Party. Although it was not directly caused by the Anti-Rent war, that struggle gave impetus to the program of George Henry Evans's National Reform Association. Evans followed the Lockean natural-rights principle of land ownership and dedicated himself to propagandizing for federal land reform measures that would provide a free homestead to anyone willing to settle on and cultivate it. Central to Evans's philosophy was a vision of homesteads in the West inhabited by impoverished refugees from the overpopulated cities of the East. The poor workingman, rightfully endowed with land, would shed his degradation and rise to become a self-respecting agrarian yeoman. Broadcasting the slogan "Vote Yourself a Farm," Evans sought to apply pressure on legislators through the ballot box, and the issue gained considerable public support.

While there was some doubt about the wisdom of opening up the West to questionable classes, there was no doubt among reformist agitators that the homestead measure would act as a natural deterrent to slavery. This rationale was proffered by Anti-Rent congressman John Slingerland, who, in introducing the first federal Homestead Act, argued: "An effectual bar against the progress of slavery will be found in the creation of small homesteads sufficient for the maintenance of single families and requiring not a host of slaves or laborers to cultivate. Slave labor is profitable only when it is extensively employed." Even New York landlord Gerrit Smith was moved to declare that free farms were the mightiest of all antislavery measures. Western agrarian George W. Julian argued along the same lines in 1851: the ideal society, he said, would be based upon a single principle, "the distribution of landed property, and its cultivation by freemen." Walt Whitman, in an editorial for the *Brooklyn Daily Eagle*, characteristically focused on the human element and voiced his concern that the territories should be reserved for free labor: the western lands must be open to the "millions of mechanics, farmers, and operatives, of our country"; the welfare of America depended on these workingmen and not upon "the few thousand rich, 'polished', and aristocratic owners of slaves at the South." The interconnected issues involving slavery, land, and work, distilled down to the slogan "Free Soil; Free Labor," became the core of the northern—more specifically, the Republican—cause in the 1850s.[21]

The homestead issue heated up as controversy about the status of slavery in the territories grew more and more bitter. The Republican Party was organized in the north in 1854 in response to the threat posed by the passage of the Kansas-Nebraska Act, which repealed the Missouri Compromise of 1820 and left to popular sovereignty the issue of free labor versus slavery in those territories. The Republicans, committed to halting the least further extension of slavery, took fruitful advantage of the homestead debate after the Panic of 1857. Democratic President James Buchanan's veto of the latest effort to pass the homestead measure, along with his order to sell the land out from under settlers who had claims but could not afford to pay, drove multitudes of farmers out of the Democratic Party and into the embrace of the Republicans, who wooed them with the promise that a Homestead Act under the Republican aegis would finally be passed.

The intended impact of the Homestead Act, which did become law in 1862, was obviously on the western states and territories where the government still held millions of acres. The act acknowledged and sought to extend into the West the northern ideology of land ownership and free labor. In the sense that pictures of the American farm coherently embodied those assumptions, they functioned as a form of low-keyed yet persuasive validation of the northern system—and its right (and Manifest Destiny) to dominate the expanding nation—during the turbulent years preceding the Civil War. This is not to say that they were ever meant to be overtly propagandistic or that the artists who created them were necessarily Republicans. Nonetheless, simply by appearing when and where they did, images of the northern farm served tacitly to support the unquestionable rightness of the northern cause. Their subtext read as a justification of the fight against slavery by depicting lovely landscapes, blessed landscapes, occupied by free people upon their own soil. Slaves, by contrast, could not own property because they were property themselves; the southern system, with its aristocrats and vassals, seemed little more than a thinly disguised revival of medieval feudalism.

The religious justification for the North's assumption of such hegemony came out of a long tradition of millennial interpretations of northern society, especially that of New England. In the millennial vision (inspired by Isaiah in the Old Testament, and the Revelation of Saint John in the New) the rural villages and pastoral life of the North foreshadowed the imminent spiritual rule of Christ on earth, a time of peace and prosperity in a new, perfected Eden. Henry Ward Beecher's image of the healing, regenerative power of the North grew out of millennialism, as did the Peaceable Kingdom paintings of Quaker artist Edward Hicks. In the 1850s Jasper Cropsey, one of the most zealous celebrants of the American pastoral, painted two variants on the theme: *The Spirit of Peace* (1852; Woodmere Art Gallery, Germantown, Pennsylvania) and *The Millennial Age,* or *The Golden Age* (1854; Mrs. John C. Newington). The latter, an elaborate allegory in the spirit of Thomas Cole, depicted a Temple of Peace embellished with the symbols of Isaiah's prophecies: the lion, the lamb, and the child; the setting, a landscape with shepherd and flock, suggested the Arcadian peace of the new age to come. It is conceivable that Cropsey's agricultural landscapes embody this millennial content in secularized form.[22]

Underlying the ideological and moral controversies between North and South, however, were the bare facts of economic reality; at the most primitive level the claims of Manifest Destiny or a foreordained northern millennium were merely very effective rationalizations of an unswerving drive for power. The North and the South were competing for domination of the enormous western territories, and the economic stakes were high. To the southern vision of expanding a paternalistic empire of cotton and slavery, the North opposed its own expanding free-soil empire. Even more basic, the North and the South stood for competing forms of agricultural capitalism. The southern planter grew his crops for the commercial market; his slave labor force unwillingly contributed the muscle that produced surplus, profits, and accumulated capital. The northern farmer had become an entrenched part of the developing northern capitalist economy, an economy thriving on the mechanical revolution and a free market system which, while it did not permit enforced human labor, did tolerate exploitation in the commercial sense: prices, and profits, rose and fell depending upon (among other things) terms of credit and the dealings of middlemen. The farmers of the North sided with the antislavery, pro-homestead Republicans to improve the chances that their culture, their system, and their fortunes—not the South's—would dominate America's capitalistic agricultural economy. Ultimately, of course, no one could deny that slavery was a moral issue of supreme importance, but the zeal to restrict and then abolish it could hardly be detached from the fact that it was the essential driving force of the rival southern economic system.[23]

What the American farm scenes were about thus had to do with their affirmation and support of the status quo, of the entire creed of northern beliefs that exalted liberty, individualism, and middle-class values: the basis of the capitalistic, free enterprise system. In agrarian guise, or disguise, they proclaimed the ideology of personal freedom and the right to private property, which the government had been constituted to protect. Lest it be objected that such a burden of symbolism is too weighty for those uncomplicated pastoral idylls, it should be emphasized that the seemingly innocuous, when linked with political or moral matter of sufficient interest or controversiality, can become potent. A case in point is the famous presidential election of 1840, in which Whig candidate William Henry Harrison soundly trounced Democratic incumbent Martin Van Buren. Harrison's victory was immeasurably assisted by his cleverly orchestrated advertising campaign, which co-opted the images of the log cabin, the cider barrel, and the plain farmer to stir up public sentiment against the supposedly aristocratic Van Buren, said to live regally in the White House, sipping imported champagne from silver goblets. In the Log Cabin Campaign, Harrison's allegedly popular political stance was completely identified with and expressed by those humble rural objects which, in a highly charged political context, became powerful and effective symbols.

Although American farm scenes were a part of the northern free-soil and free-labor campaign by association rather than intention, as cultural products of the northern system they accepted and reflected its values. Certainly they were idylls and escapist dream pictures before they were topical political statements. But in putting upon canvas, or paper, designs that symbolized dominant beliefs (dominant in the sense that politicians, religious organizations, and sympathetic public media sanctioned and exploited them), artists tacitly said "yea" to the status quo. It is unlikely that the contemporary viewer made these connections at the conscious level. Virtually every farm scene, however, embodied the message "This is the way things are and the way they should be; this social and economic order, and no other, must prevail in North America." Who could doubt that such a painting as Jerome Thompson's *Haymakers, Mount Mansfield, Vermont,* produced on the very eve of the Civil War, was more than a detached, innocent depiction of happy country life? And did not the images of northern rural work, such as Thompson's *Apple Gathering* and Eastman Johnson's 1860 *Corn Husking,* resonate with emotional affirmations of free labor?

The Civil War itself was a vast watershed in American history, even though its aftermath, rather than marking a sudden new beginning, only brought into sharp and sometimes painful focus the economic, technological, social and cultural transformations that had been well under way long before the war. Writers and preachers of the North defended the righteousness of the war by applying to it the veneer of divine sanction. The war was a sacred cause, dedicated to preserving the Union; it was a divinely ordained purging, like the biblical Deluge, that would bring about a spiritually reborn, greater, unified America in the end. During the war, poets, illustrators, and preachers used metaphors drawn from an ancient tradition equating battlefields with harvest fields, sacrificial bleeding with the sowing of seed in the earth, and death in battle with reaping. One of the most famous and grisly images of the war, Timothy O'Sullivan's 1863 photograph *The Harvest of Death* (published in Alexander Gardner, *Photographic Sketch Book of the War* [Washington, D.C., 1866]), showed soldiers' corpses on the battlefield of Gettysburg.[24] Again, such religious rhetoric essentially served the economic and territorial needs of the North. It served as well to help cement the case for the northern hegemony that so deeply imprinted American politics, society, and culture for many decades thereafter.

Postwar rhetoric followed the same lines. Commentators looked back and discovered in the bloody detritus of the conflict a design full of spiritual meaning. In 1865 the influential Congregational minister Horace Bushnell delivered at Yale University a commemorative oration on the end of the war. A new and greater unity and national identity would rise from the war as seeds from the soil, he said. It was like the time after the Deluge when, the waters having receded, "the oaks and palms and all great trees sprung into life, under the dead old trunks of the forest, and the green world reappeared even greener than before." More explicitly agricultural were the metaphors used by Henry Ward Beecher in his novel *Norwood* : "War ploughed the fields of Gettysburg and planted its furrows with men. But though the seed was

blood, the harvest shall be peace, concord, and universal intelligence."[25]

The redemptive imagery of such rhetoric was also reflected in paintings, prints, and illustrations during the first few years after the war. In 1865 George Inness—one of the greatest landscape painters of the late nineteenth century—painted the radiant *Peace and Plenty* (Illus. 40), which depicts a serene world of abundance and beauty. The wheat harvest taking place in the broad Arcadian spaces of this landscape is to be read as more than a gathering-in of grain; it represents the hope of social and spiritual rebirth. The harvest metaphor is most transparent in William L. Sheppard's illustration *Harvest on Historic Fields—A Scene at the South* (Illus. 41), in which black and white workers together are cradling and binding grain on the very site where battle once raged. The poem accompanying the illustration spells the meaning out:

> To-day another harvest stands
>   Where once Death trod the bleeding plain,
> Ripe for the reapers' ready hands
>   That bind in sheaves the golden grain.[26]

The last two lines portray a benediction: "In mellow radiance flooding all,/ The golden light of peace is shed." Though the words are hackneyed and the picture prosaic, the meaning here parallels that of Inness's transcendent *Peace and Plenty*. The same title was bestowed on a Currier & Ives lithograph of 1871 (Illus. 42), in which all the familiar elements of the agrarian idyll appear once more: the plain, boxy house, the tall, sheltering trees, the barn crammed with hay, the contented animals in the pasture, the loaded wagon rolling down the lane. Although the war was by then six years in the past, the symbolism clearly speaks to a postwar era still conscious of its scars.

Even in these hopeful images apotheosizing peace and celebrating the nation's renewal, the rock-bottom meaning still pertains to the balance of power. In the war the South had been crushed; it had been beaten, not led, back into union with the North. Religious rhetoric and harvest symbolism painted pictures of a sanctified war, a divinely ordained victory, and a blessed reunion full of hope; but the real subject was conquest and domination. Northern business and agricultural interests had prevailed, and the competition had been vanquished. From then on the expansion and aggrandizement of American lands would be tailored to the pattern for which the North had fought and won. Tranquil and beatified on the surface, postwar harvest imagery was at bottom as much victory celebration as thankful prayer for the reestablishment of peace and unity.

From the 1830s through the 1860s the image of the agrarian pastoral derived its strength from the rock of social, political, and economic conviction out of which it grew, and promulgated a metaphorical picture of the culture that achieved decisive hegemony by 1865. With the postwar era, however, the portrayal of country life in American art and literature shifted into different modes of meaning. There was no clean line of demarcation between old and new imagery; elements of earlier agrarian and pastoral ideology, moralism, and sentiment joined almost seamlessly with the new strains of nostalgia that were to become dominant in the last third of the nineteenth century. With increasing poignancy through the close of the century, the image of the farm came to symbolize what had been lost—not so much the old methods of agriculture as the cultural values and (relatively, in retrospect) the peaceful stability of a predominantly rural society in earlier years. What had begun as an idealization of the real would metamorphose into the stuff of dreams, expressed through an iconography of reminiscence.

37.   Asher B. Durand, *Haying,* 1838. Oil on canvas, 36″×54″.
(The Vose Galleries of Boston, courtesy of James Bradshaw)

38. British School, *Dixton Harvesters*, c. 1730. Oil on canvas, 42″×113⅜″. (Cheltenham Art Gallery and Museum, Cheltenham, England)

39.   Jules Breton, *The Gleaners,* 1854. Oil on canvas, $36\frac{5}{8}'' \times 54\frac{3}{8}''$.
(National Gallery of Ireland, Dublin)

40. George Inness, *Peace and Plenty*, 1865. Oil on canvas,
$77\frac{5}{8}'' \times 112\frac{3}{8}''$. (The Metropolitan Museum of Art, New York; gift
of George A. Hearn, 1894 [94.27])

HARVEST ON HISTORIC FIELDS—A SCENE AT THE SOUTH.—DRAWN BY W. L. SHEPPARD.—[SEE POEM, PAGE 452.]

41. W. L. Sheppard, *Harvest on Historic Fields—A Scene at the South*. Wood engraving. *Harper's Weekly Magazine* 11 (July 20, 1867).

PEACE AND PLENTY.

PUBLISHED BY CURRIER & IVES.   ENTERED ACCORDING TO ACT OF CONGRESS IN THE YEAR 1870 BY CURRIER & IVES IN THE OFFICE OF THE LIBRARIAN OF CONGRESS AT WASHINGTON   152 NASSAU ST. NEW YORK.

42. *Peace and Plenty*, 1871. Lithograph, $9\frac{15}{16}'' \times 16\frac{13}{16}''$. Published by Currier & Ives, New York. (Prints and Photographs Division, Library of Congress)

THE CHANGING IMAGE OF THE YANKEE FARMER

5 ■ *The Noble Yeoman*

N AGRARIAN theory the American farmer was the ideal American citizen, the ultimate and fundamental republican. Such was the breed that was meant to inhabit the rural houses envisioned by Andrew Jackson Downing and Lewis Allen: plain, sturdy homes for plain, sturdy people. The idea that the American farmer was uniquely blessed in this plainness and in manliness, honesty, and common sense developed in the selectively factual accounts and fictional idealizations that did so much in the antebellum decades to shape the enduring stereotype of the noble yeoman.

English traveler James Silk Buckingham admired the wholesome simplicity of a rural church congregation near Schenectady, New York:

The men . . . were all decently dressed, in plain and coarse cloth garments, without the least attempt at fashion or finery. They had the large hands of laboring men; and the bronzed complexions of those who work much in the open air. . . . The young men were good looking and athletic; the old men healthy and cheerful, and, with their low-crowned and broad-brimmed hats, and gray locks often flowing over their shoulders, looked grave and venerable.

Such farmers needed no frills or garnishes to refine their behavior; they were natural gentlemen. As popular genteel novelist Catherine Maria Sedgwick wrote, "I have never seen better models of manners . . . than in the home of a New England farmer." Others saw the very stance of the yeoman as symbol of the manly independence that elevated him above the urban worker:

From my heart, I honor the countryman, in whatever situation he may be found. Look at the wagoner beside his team; the manliness of his gait, the flourish of his whip, the very wearing of his hat, show that he is a freeman—that he feels no superior. Contrast him with the journeyman mechanic of the city. The latter is either a copyist of others, in a different station of life, or he is embittered by jealousy and envy of that class whom he styles the aristocracy, and whom he imagines to be leagued in an unholy alliance against the rights and privileges of his fellow-workmen.

Proud yet not haughty, the farmer remained unaffected by the burdensome pressures of conformity and social aspiration. He was a whole man, sufficient unto himself, the complete American.[1]

In the realm of fiction and art, two key midcentury images epitomized the character of the noble yeoman, master of the antebellum northern farm. Donald Grant Mitchell's evocation of a venerable New England farmer in his ever-popular *Dream-Life: A Fable of the Seasons* (1851) fleshed out abstract notions, and William Sidney Mount's 1848 painting *Farmer Whetting His Scythe* (Illus. 43), gave forceful visual life to the concept.

Self-sufficiency is the salient trait of Mitchell's "New-England Squire," a "good specimen" of the old-fashioned New-England farmer:

Frank's grandfather has silver hair, but is still hale, erect, and strong. His dress is homely but neat. Being a thorough-going Protectionist, he has no fancy for the gewgaws of foreign importation, and makes it a point to appear always in the village church, and on all great occasions, in a sober suit of homespun. He has no pride of appearance, and he needs none.

The town's board of selectmen defers to the Squire, and as justice of the peace he arbitrates local disputes. His country domain conforms precisely to the pastoral stereotype, and even his "peculiarities" are evidence of his unshakable yeoman's spirit:

He has a great contempt . . . for all paper money, and imagines banks to be corporate societies skillfully contrived for the legal plunder of the community. He keeps a supply of silver and gold by him in the foot of an old stocking, and seems to have great confidence in the value of Spanish milled dollars. He has no kind of patience with the new doctrines of farming. . . . Scientific farming, and gentleman farming, may do very well, he says, "to keep idle young fellows from the city out of mischief; but as for real, effective management, there's nothing like the old stock of men, who ran barefoot until they were ten, and who count the hard winters by their frozen toes."[2]

The Squire, having achieved the silvered wisdom of age, represents the evolution of those barefoot boys into village elders, hardy as the ancient oaks sheltering their homesteads, and vital principals in the social and civic affairs of their New England towns.

Mount's farmer, in the prime of manly strength, might be read as one of those erstwhile barefoot boys, now vigorously fulfilling his promise. The monumental simplicity of the composition belies its small size. The design is characteristic of Mount's rigorous formalism combined with naturalistic observation. Although it was, as he recorded in his notebook, "painted on the spot," there is little that seems spontaneous in this carefully mapped and delineated image.[3] The farmer's stance coincides with the vertical axis of the canvas, which is horizontally divided into nearly equal portions of earth and sky. His legs are silhouetted against the background of hayfield, groves, and pastures; his upper half rises above the horizon to merge with the serene, silvery heavens. Bending just enough to the left to relax the rigidity of the compositional grid, the farmer strokes the blade of his scythe with a whetstone. He wears the plain working garb which, with certain variations, appears so frequently in pictures of the nineteenth-century American farmer that it amounts to an agrarian uniform: low-crowned hat with broad brim, white shirt, baggy trousers held up by suspenders, and thick boots. Young, solidly built, brightened by clear sunshine, Mount's farmer expresses strength, vigor, and competence in every line of pose and gesture. The precisely plotted design places him quite literally at the center of his rural universe. This configuration functions metaphorically to express the fabled self-sufficiency of the archetypal American yeoman.

Many midcentury images bore the same connotations of strength, vigor, and proud American yeomanry. The 1854 wood-engraved illustration *June* (Illus. 44) depicts a haying scene, with men raking swaths and loading a wagon on the right; in the left distance another high-piled cart lumbers toward an ample barn with wide-open portal. The two men in the left foreground dominate the design. They wear variants of the functional agrarian uniform: low hats, rolled shirtsleeves, loose open vests, baggy trousers. The older, bearded man holds a whetstone and wipes his blade clean with a whisk made of field grasses; the younger man to the right assumes a simple yet self-possessed pose, one hand on hip, the other lightly steadying his upright scythe. These men, with their quasi-classical poise and their air of quiet physical confidence, exemplify the ideal conception of the northern farmer. The same is true of the two men with scythes in the foreground of Thompson's *Haymakers, Mount Mansfield, Vermont* (see Illus. 13): elder and younger; one grooming his blade, the other casually, even elegantly posed; both attired without pretension; both tough and strong. Likewise, the rugged young farmer hoisting a bushel basket of corn in Eastman Johnson's *Corn Husking* (see Illus. 16) conveys the same sense of competence and self-sufficiency. *The Mower in Ohio* (Illus. 45), published in *Harper's Weekly* in 1864, is a New England squire translated to the Midwest; like Mount's farmer he whets his scythe against a background of fields, orchard, and homestead. Once more, this illustration is primarily an emblem of the hardy, independent yeoman, though in this case with additional dimensions of tragic patriotism; as the accompanying verses tell, two of the farmer's sons have fallen in battle, and the third and last marches with General Grant's army, advancing on Richmond.[4]

Like the serene farmscapes of midcentury art and literature, such images had distinct nationalistic connotations. The American farm was the symbol of an egalitarian social order based on natural rights rather than inherited and rigidly fixed class hierarchies. The upright figure of Mount's yeoman and the erect, hale posture of Mitchell's Squire represent the happy state of the free man, unbent by oppressive systems. Although opinions varied quite widely as to the real condition, for example, of the rural population of England in comparison with that of America, writers seemed to agree that the opportunities enjoyed by the American farmer had produced a better man. This was Buckingham's conclusion, although the Englishman may have based his remarks too heavily on his acquaintance with the more well-to-do farmers of upstate New York:

All those idle disputes and distinctions about old families and new ones, people of high birth and people of low . . . are here happily unthought of. . . . In England no one . . . will deny the fact of the farmers and farm-labourers being among the least intelligent and most uneducated portion of the population. Here, on the contrary, they are among the most intelligent and best informed . . . the farm-labourers and their families are well fed, well dressed, well educated in all the ordinary elements of knowledge, intelligent in conversation, agreeable in manners, and as superior to the corresponding class of farm-labourers in England as all these advantages can indicate. There are no beer-shops . . . no haunts of vice and debauchery, at which they concoct the plans of the poacher, the smuggler, or the robber, to make up by illicit gains the deficiencies of honest industry.

As an American tourist noted, the degraded peasants of England wore "frocks, corduroy breeches, gray stockings, and thick, solid hob-nailed boots." No such costume deflated the status of the American farmer, whose garb, if rough and simple, was not the archaic symbol of a place near the bottom of the social pyramid.[5]

A particular point of pride in contrasting American and European farm systems was the fact that women were seldom to be seen working in American fields. Francis Pulszky, a Hungarian politician who visited the United States in 1852, reported a conversation with a gentleman in New York, who told him that, "in Europe, women even work in the fields and they must assist the husbands to earn a subsistence; with us, even in the factories, the girls work until they marry, but once married, the maintenance of the family is the care of the husband, and an American farmer would feel degraded if his wife or daughter should hoe the corn or break the flax."[6] In American art few antebellum harvest scenes do depict women participants, although there are exceptions, as in some of Jerome Thompson's paintings. Even in his *Haymakers, Mount Mansfield, Vermont*, however, the young woman is posed so prettily that it would take only the substitution of shepherd's crook for hay rake to transform her into the perfect Arcadian shepherdess. By contrast, any cursory glance through images of peasants in nineteenth-century European painting reveals a strikingly high incidence of lowly women in the fields, working often with other women, sometimes with men.[7] Like nothing else, the presence of women engaged in strenuous field work betokened a peasant class. American farmers, with their middle-class aspirations, subscribed to the middle-class division of labor, which consigned domestic (if arduous) tasks to women and breadwinning labors to men; this ethos found reflection in the preponderance of American farm scenes of midcentury, although the emphasis shifted somewhat in the later decades.

Possibly the greatest point of pride in contrasting the rural populations of Old World and New was a belief in the American farmer as a literate, politically responsible citizen. The allegedly typical English farmer described by Donald Grant Mitchell, who had many reservations about his own actual rural countrymen (not to be confused with the mythical "Squire"), was clearly inferior in intellect, whatever his worth as a tiller of the soil; he was "less of a man, by far" even if "more of a farmer" than his New England counterparts. This farmer, according to Mitchell, was a "staunch, rosy-faced man" who lived "within easy distance of the taproom of the inn," in addition to keeping his own excellent home brew. He was only "vaguely informed on politics, reading the Sunday Times, perhaps." The high point of his life was market day, when he would drive to the market square in a "jaunty dog-cart," get drunk, and drive home on roads that were, fortunately for him, good enough to permit a safe return. The general impression is of a genial but muddleheaded rustic, greedy for his creature comforts and existing on a fairly low plane of intellectual development.[8]

The American farmer was considered altogether keener. Noah Webster declared that "the American yeomanry . . .

are not to be compared to the illiterate peasantry of England. . . . [The former] not only learn to read, write, and keep accounts; but a vast proportion read the Bible, sermons, treatises, and newspapers every week." Traveling British barrister Alexander MacKay elaborated on the American farmer's political acuity:

Enter, for instance, in the evening, an unpretending farm-house, and it is a chance if, after the labor of the day, you do not see the occupant in his homespun grey, reading his newspaper by the fireside; for both he and his family can invariably read, and he thinks that the least he can do for his party is to sustain the local party newspaper; many receiving, in addition to this, their daily metropolitan paper. In conversing with him, you will generally find . . . that, as a duck takes to water, so does he very soon take to politics. The market and a few other topics may receive a passing attention, but the grand theme is politics; and you will be surprised by the ease and readiness with which he speaks upon the most intricate national questions.

As with any traveler's account—native or foreign—a great deal of allowance must be made for distortion and bias. The tourists were not methodical pollsters, and what they learned was limited to whatever segments of American life they actually experienced, augmented by hearsay, anecdote, and various sorts of published information. MacKay's description of the politically zealous agrarian immersed in his newspaper (after a typical fourteen-hour day in the fields, no doubt) finds contradiction in the pages of agricultural journals, which exhorted farmers to rouse themselves from their near-vegetable mental state and improve their minds to become worthy of their special status as free citizens in a great republic. As is often the case, there was a vast middle ground between those extremes, encompassing many degrees of literacy and political enthusiasm. In light of the approval shed upon the exemplary, politically keen American yeoman, however, pictures of farmers in that character take on a significance equal to that of the men with their scythes.[9]

Eastman Johnson's painting *The Evening Newspaper* (Illus. 46) portrays a strapping young farmer out of the same mold as Mount's scythe-whetter but here in the role of an alert reader of the news. The setting is a rustic interior: plank floor, plain woodwork making up the fireplace surround, the baseboard, and the door, with only a whiskbroom hung up under the mantelpiece for ornament. In the narrow space between hearth and door the countryman sits, tilting his chair back against the wall and propping his large, booted feet on the rungs. In addition to the sturdy boots, his costume displays the usual components of the agrarian uniform: low slouch hat, white shirt and loose vest, a casually knotted cravat of sorts, and roomy trousers. Newspaper on lap and clay pipe jutting from the corner of his mouth, the man looks up as if momentarily distracted, a solemn cast dignifying his well-cut features. The date of Johnson's picture, 1863, lends historical particularity to what would otherwise seem a more general celebration of the American yeoman as reader and thinker. It is most likely that the newspaper reports on the progress of the war between North and South. A decade and a half earlier, ordinary Americans of various types had appeared reading newspapers in paintings contemporary with the American war against Mexico. The theme of war news is also implied by Arthur Fitzwilliam Tait in *The Latest News* (1862; New York Public Library), showing a barn interior in which a farmer with a pitchfork considers the information read to him from the newspaper by a visiting friend. Farmers such as Johnson's and Tait's could hardly be less like the florid, boozy, fuzzy-thinking English farmer described by Mitchell. American agriculturists were depicted as laudably literate. Far from the front lines and secure in their kitchens and barns, they maintained nonetheless a vital connection with the great events of the day, as democratically diffused through the agency of print.[10]

The most transparently and aggressively political image of the proud American yeoman came out of the Midwest in the decade following the Civil War, when the National Grange Order for the Patrons of Husbandry—better known simply as the Grange—emerged as a formidable alternative to free enterprise capitalism.[11] In the early 1870s the Grange and its mushrooming membership (from 10,000 in the late 1860s to more than a million in 1875) represented an agrarian radicalism disturbing enough to prompt magnates like Jay Gould on the east coast and Collis Huntington on the west to label them a "pack of communists." The order had its origins in (but was not under the aegis of) the United States Department of Agriculture, where in 1867 clerks Oliver H. Kelley, William Saunders, and several colleagues conceived the idea, drew up the constitution and bylaws, and strenuously propagandized for the establishment of chapters in rural districts throughout the country. The greatest activity and political power of the Grange eventually localized in the Midwest, where the farmers, dependent on a string of middlemen for getting their crops to metropolitan marketplaces, felt most keenly the grip of railroad monopolies, which kept storage and freight costs artificially and intolerably high.

The railroad issue was the focal point of a complex of problems that had long since begun to sour farmers' relations with cities, capitalists, and government. The speculators and middlemen who stood between the farmer and maximum profit; low wholesale prices that failed to compensate for the high retail costs the farmer was obliged to pay as consumer; protectionist trade legislation aiding industry but not agriculture; tight federal restriction of the money supply, and disproportionate tax laws—these were some of the financial inequities besetting farmers. Kelley's plan was to organize farmers for their economic, social, and cultural improvement and thus to create a dynamic group capable of fending off predators far more effectively than the farmer acting alone could do. At first the Grange remained a sleepy organization, more social than political, elaborately dressed up in the paraphernalia of a secret society. In 1869, however, steeply falling wheat prices, coupled with the refusal of banks and railroads to respond sympathetically to the farmers' dilemma, exerted a galvanic impact that launched the Grange upon several not unproductive years of political lobbying and economic experimentation.

The economic aims of the Grange were patterned on those of Rochdale, a radical English cottage weavers' cooperative that shared resources, production, and profits and sold its goods directly to London outlets. Once radicalized, Grange chapters in the midwestern states began quite daringly to try out Rochdale concepts. They opened cooperative stores, maintained cooperative grain elevators, even established Granger factories to make agricultural machinery and formed Granger life insurance companies—none of which, except the grain elevators, were notably successful. Of greater value were their lobbying activities and court cases to press for laws giving states the power to regulate railroad freight charges and impose uniformity on the rates paid by farmers. Although such regulatory legislation bore the name of "Granger laws," the Grange constitution in fact prohibited political action; however, Grangers could and did engage in political activity as members of independent farmers' clubs. So politicized were the farmers in eleven midwestern states that by 1874 the Independent, Reform, Anti-Monopoly, and Farmers' parties were all aggressively present in the political field. Many of the Granger laws were subsequently repealed, most in the wake of the Panic of 1873, when widespread railroad bankruptcies and skillfully orchestrated lobbying provoked reaction against the radical, would-be communistic agrarians, hell-bent on destroying free enterprise.

The progress of the Grange in the Midwest was accompanied by pictorial propaganda. Prints published for or about the organization reformulated the classical agrarian ideal and presented an emblematic image of the farmer restored to a dominant and central position in society. The lithograph *The Farmer Pays for All* (Illus. 47) exemplifies the expressive configuration of such designs. Like a sun, or a god of sorts, the farmer occupies the center of the composition and achieves commanding stature through hierarchical scale. Ranged around him, as if in orbit, are seven figures, each less than half the size of the colossal farmer. They represent the spectrum (skewed and male, to be sure) of American society: soldier, railroad capitalist, doctor, legislator, lawyer, merchant, and preacher. Each man has his own motto: "I fight for all," "I prescribe for all," and so forth, culminating finally in the farmer's declaration, "and I PAY FOR ALL." Above the farmer's motto a dove with an olive branch and an eagle flank an airborne liberty cap, which, surrounded by its own aureole of light, hovers over the farmer's head like the Holy Ghost. The seven vignettes and the dominating farmer are framed and laced together by borders of oak trees and their spreading branches, grapevines, wheat and corn stalks, and laurel leaves.

The ruggedness of the farmer's physique suggests his dauntless individualism. The broad shoulders, thick torso, and muscular thighs; the pose with one booted leg flexed, about to bear down on the shovel with which he will break the soil; the simplicity of his agrarian costume; and his heroic composure, suggestive of a David triumphant over a Goliath or a hunter victorious over his prey; all proclaim the American farmer as first among men and lord of the pastoral acres in the background. That the pose had specific associations with heroic, independent manliness is suggested by Eastman Johnson's painting *Woodcutter* (c. 1868; Smith College Museum of Art, Northampton, Massachusetts), in which the axeman's pose, mirror image of the farmer's, symbolizes his hard-won conquest of the forest giant he has just felled.

In contrast to the brawny yeoman in the lithograph, the satellite men in their sleek suits or uniforms, with their tapering feet and elegant posturings, seem trivial. At the farmer's right and left hand are the merchant trader and the railroad capitalist, villainous middlemen. Each one—the merchant with his ship and the capitalist with his locomotive engine and map of the United States—reaches toward the pile of coins spilling from the mouth of an upended cornucopia of money. Here the essential point of the design becomes clear: such outpourings of gold, gathered by others, originate with the commodities produced in the farmer's fields and by his labors.

Other Granger prints followed the identical format. In the lithograph *Gift for the Grangers* (Illus. 48) virtually the same farmer appears, stern-faced, sleeves rolled up, elbows and knee cocked, shovel at the ready. In this design, however, the satellite scenes in their roundels and rectangles epitomize and preach the ideal of agrarian life. This is the vision of Crèvecoeur and Jefferson, revised and perfected by the Grange. The landscape behind the farmer represents the farm world in microcosm, with plowing, digging, and chopping going on; animals frisking in their pasture, a fine upwardly mobile farmhouse on a hill, boasting a gazebo and a fountain; and a church spire in the distance. The "Farmer's Fireside" in the upper left roundel displays the fabled cultural richness of country life in a cozy, well-appointed parlor where every member of a large country family is reading, making music, or playing wholesome games. Some of the remaining scenes depict typical pastoral activities, while others portray Grange life: a formal meeting in the upper right, and, to the right of the farmer's shovel, a Granger cooperative store. The ancient and godly tradition of agriculture is the subject of the bottom right roundel, "Ruth and Boaz." An oval below the farmer's feet contains symbols of what the Grange was intended to counteract: a decrepit, sway-backed log cabin standing in a yard occupied by trash and wallowing pigs, signposted with boards reading "Ignorance" and "Sloth." Over this entire scheme the figure of the farmer—"I Pay for All"—presides as focus, hero, and even guardian: staunch emblem of agrarian idealism, economic muscle, and political clout.

The superyeomen of the Grange were, like many symbols, as much ideal and wishful thinking as reality, and probably more so. Actual political and economic circumstances were not so clear-cut as the Granger images tried to show, although no one would deny the fundamental importance of the farmer's role as foodmaker. Thomas Nast's shrewdly perceptive cartoon *The Transportation Problem* (Illus. 49), published at the time of the Panic of 1873, offers a concise graphic paradigm—or parody—of the two sides at loggerheads. On the right stands the "Railroad 'Monopolist'" in the capitalist's top hat and frock coat. Back turned to the

spectator and hands in pockets, he beholds the train wreck that symbolizes the ruin of his business. On the left a lantern-jawed farmer, hands likewise in pockets, scowls over his shoulder at the railroad monopolist. He wears the familiar farmer's garb and carries a large drover's whip. Behind him is the railroad station, liberally inscribed with mottoes and warnings: "Down with Railroad Monopoly"; "Look Out for Wicked Trains." Hogsheads and baskets of produce, now destined for nowhere, wait on the platform. The Granger addresses his foe: "I say, Mr. Wildcat Speculator, what am I to do now?" The capitalist retorts, "Solve your own problem, Mr. Farmer Despot." The figure of this slouching, chopfallen farmer implicitly contradicts the Granger image of the defiant, commanding yeoman looming grandly over American society. The cartoon suggests, moreover, that the farmer was well and truly engaged with capitalism and dependent on its institutions. The Grange and other farmers' clubs faced a formidable adversary in an age when big business was enjoying lusty and virtually unchecked growth and power. While their efforts were creditable, they were insufficient to effect fundamental changes in the economic balance of power. Although rural political agitation continued through the end of the century with the formation of Farmers' Alliances in the mid-1880s and their affiliation with Populism in the 1890s, other forces were overwhelmingly dominant, and the stature of the heroic yeoman dwindled with the the farmers' political hopes.

The image of the noble yeoman did endure for a time in the art of Thomas Waterman Wood, a native of Montpelier, Vermont, and so successful a self-taught painter of meticulously realistic anecdote that he ultimately became president of the National Academy of Design. In the 1860s and 1870s Wood turned many times to the theme of politics in the lives of rural Americans, although his later works leaned more and more toward nostalgia and sentiment.[12] Wood's 1871 *Cogitation* (Illus. 50), comparable to Mount's *Farmer Whetting His Scythe* in its spare monumentality and formal strength, shows a dim barn interior where a farmer leans on the handle of his pitchfork while he ponders out some problem. This man is very similar in type to Mount's farmer and the heroic Granger; he is in the prime of manhood, well built, clothed with rustic republican simplicity. The title offers a clue to this farmer's mental worth: "cogitation" connotes not daydreaming or woolgathering but intent, serious thought. This farmer's face, like few others among pictorial farmers, is a visage expressing deep reflection: brows drawn together, forehead furrowed, mouth stern.

There is no precise clue to the subject of the farmer's meditations. Could he be thinking about the price of corn, or building a new pigpen? Given Wood's predilections during this phase of his career, these are possible but not likely. The viewer is meant to understand that this man ruminates on something weightier: religion, perhaps, or philosophy, or—most probably—politics. In 1871 the issue of the impending 1872 presidential campaign was heating rapidly, with Liberal Republicans opposed to President Ulysses S. Grant splitting off from the established Republican Party, and Democrats scheming desperately to topple Grant out of the White House. In such a political climate one would expect the ideal yeoman to take seriously his duty to be an informed and intelligent voter. It is difficult to say how much of this should be read into Wood's *Cogitation*. In the following year, though, a wood engraving after Wood's picture was published in *Harper's Weekly*, with a far more explicit title: *The Farmer's Question—"Is Horace Greeley a Fool or a Knave?"*

Horace Greeley, the farm boy who became editor of the crusading *New York Tribune,* had been nominated in May 1872 as presidential candidate on the third-party ticket of the Liberal Republicans. Soon thereafter the Democrats followed suit and nominated him as their candidate as well. Almost at once, Greeley resigned from the *Tribune* and threw himself passionately into the campaign. Perhaps the farmer in Wood's illustration asks his question because Greeley had, throughout a lifetime of espousing controversial causes, declared himself a friend of the farmer. In the 1850s he had even taken up experiments in scientific farming at his coun-

try house in Chappaqua, New York, and enthusiastically preached his ideas about farming (which he maintained should be scientific and cooperative) in two books, scores of newspaper columns, and dozens of speeches delivered at state and county fairs throughout the nation. In the 1840s he had supported George Henry Evans's National Reform movement, and in 1860 he was one of the chief authors of the Homestead Act plank in the Republican platform. After the Civil War he had become more and more disillusioned with the Grant administration and its ruinous policies of Reconstruction in the South. Gradually, he divested himself of ties with the Republican Party, and when the Liberal Republicans organized themselves to seek universal amnesty for the South and civil service reform, Greeley promoted the new party in his *Tribune*. His presidential candidacy proved highly controversial; his critics accused him of everything from political hucksterism to unholy alliances with Tammany Hall and the Ku Klux Klan. Although he preached a "New Departure" toward a "New Dawn" of clean, efficient government, full political rights for all, and the preservation of public lands for cultivators rather than railroads, he was crushingly beaten by Grant, who had the business vote behind him.[13]

Wood's farmer, then—at least in his *Harper's Weekly* incarnation—reflects on the issues of a highly charged campaign. The caption may at second glance give the reader pause: the choice is between foolhardiness and knavery, rather than worth and its obverse. The farmer, we are meant to understand, is not trying to decide whether or not to vote for Greeley, but merely—at this juncture—whether he is a political *naif* led unwittingly into corruption (and therefore to be leniently judged) or a money-corrupted trickster from the beginning (and therefore deserving of damnation). One wonders whether it was the magazine editors, rather than the artist, who rechristened the painting—quite likely, given the fact that Thomas Nast's vicious anti-Greeley cartoons also appeared in the pages of *Harper's Weekly*, which despite nonpartisan avowals had consistently sided with the Republicans since the early 1860s. Although the possibility certainly tints the illustration with shades of bias, it does not alter the basic expressive and symbolic impact of the imagery. Unquestionably, this is the yeoman in the exemplary role of thinking, judging citizen.

The idea of the exemplary yeoman naturally lent itself to symbolic and didactic representations of leaders and would-be leaders in the nineteenth century. A number of politicians (or their caricaturists) used the yeoman's guise to symbolize their own fitness for office, or their worthiness to keep it. The yeoman of the agrarian ideal provided an unimpeachable model, but other well-known associations reinforced such symbolism: the patriotic minuteman of the American Revolution, and George Washington in his role as a modern Cincinnatus.[14] The story of Israel Putnam, who left his plow to join the fight against the Redcoats, was a popular tale well represented in prints and illustrations. The image of Putnam shed its virtues on the idea of the typical revolutionary farmer-warrior as well, and by midcentury a strong link between selfless patriotism and agriculture had been forged. A whole constellation of agrarian ideas clustered about the ever more mythic figure of George Washington. Resigning his miltary commission and returning to his farm in 1783, Washington seemed a reincarnation of the Roman general Cincinnatus. He did not stay down on the farm for long, but the image endured, and Washington was glorified as the first farmer of his country. His early mythologizer Mason Locke Weems, whose idealized Washington so powerfully shaped the nineteenth-century image of the Father of His Country, eloquently drew the hero in this mode:

He abhors war; but, if war be necessary, to this end he bravely encounters it. His ruling passion must be obeyed. He beats his ploughshare into a sword, and exchanges the peace and pleasure of his fame for the din and dangers of the camp. Having won the great prize for which he contended, he returns to the plough. . . . Happy among his domestics, he does not regret the shining ranks, that, with ported arms used to pay him homage. The *useful citizen*

is the high character he wishes to act—his sword turned into a ploughshare is his favorite instrument, and his beloved farm his stage.[15]

An iconography of Washington with his plow was established by the late eighteenth century, and his role as gentleman farmer, both patriarchal and paternalistic, became the subject of several midcentury pictorial works. The fountainhead of these, according to Mark Thistlethwaite's study, was the 1851 painting *Washington as a Farmer, at Mount Vernon* (Museum of Fine Arts, Richmond, Virginia) by Junius Brutus Stearns, a Vermont-born genre and history painter best known for a series of works depicting events in the life of Washington. In 1853 M. Knoedler published Claude Regnier's lithograph after this painting, with the title *Life of George Washington: The Farmer* (Illus. 51). Other prints included Nathaniel Currier's *Washington at Mount Vernon 1787* (1852), and *Washington at Mount Vernon* (1859), an engraving by John Rogers after John McNevin.

All three prints portray Washington benevolently overlooking harvest rituals in the fields of Mount Vernon. In none does he turn a hand to physical labor, but given his patriarchal role—both on his plantation and in American history—it is fitting that he should appear as a kind of elder statesman of agriculture. In the Regnier lithograph the harvest spectacle conforms to agrarian stereotypes in some respects. The workers are vigorous, handsome, and sturdy; their picturesque labor suggests pastoral pleasure rather than arduous toil. They are graceful and happy whether they load a wagon, bend to cut the stalks of grain, or pause for drink proffered by an amiable young farm girl. The glaring difference, of course, is that all of these workers are black, and slaves. They mime actions that bear no meaning for them with reference to the concepts ennobled in agrarian thought. Yet there is no irony intended; if anything, the Stearns picture and its successors seek to affirm an ideal of pastoral harmony that somehow binds together aristocrat and slave in a reciprocal relation of willing subservience and paternal protection. The structure of authority here is clearly but unobtrusively spelled out in the figures on the right. Turning from the observation of his workers, Washington confers with a white overseer, and behind them grazes Washington's horse, traditional attribute of kings and warriors. The other prints vary somewhat in design, but the basic situation is the same. Considering the climate of controversy in the 1850s, such images might be read as rather feeble palliatives, showing the nation's great hero as the good master of contented subjects. This is somewhat beside the main point, however, which is that the image of Washington himself in these pictures reaches the summit of agrarian virtues rolled into one with patriotism, wisdom, and right-minded leadership.

Given the power of these associations, it is not surprising that nineteenth-century politicians should occasionally be portrayed as patriotic agrarians themselves, even when such imagery could have fooled nobody. Pennsylvania portrait painter John F. Francis's 1836 lithograph (after the painting, at Lafayette College, Easton, Pennsylvania) of Joseph Ritner, governor of the state (Illus. 52), is transparently intended as symbol only, a ceremonial affirmation that yeomanlike virtues and republican simplicity—appearances to the contrary—still dwell within. The governor stands under an old tree in a half-plowed field, with a rail fence and hilly, pastoral landscape behind him. One hand on a wooden plow, he turns to favor the viewer with a straightforward look of command and resolution. That all this is a sham is attested, however, by the governor himself: he is a tall, fat man obviously addicted to soft living. Like a real yeoman, he is in his shirtsleeves, but he also wears a buttoned satin vest. Reposing next to a stump nearby is his dark beaver top hat, the headgear of the city gentleman, not the practical agriculturist. Despite contradictory signals sent by costume, the rustic accoutrements and environment deliberately evoke the minuteman abandoning his plow and the virtues of Washington as soldier-citizen-farmer. They manage to suggest in a more general way the incorruptibility and sterling worth

of the American yeoman. The effectiveness of such contrived simple-agrarian imagery was proved only four years later when Whig candidate William Henry Harrison, styled by his supporters as a rough, honest farmer in a log cabin (though he in fact dwelt in a substantial mansion), won decisively over the Democratic incumbent Martin Van Buren. One campaign print, entitled *William Henry Harrison, the Farmer of North Bend* (1840; Historical and Philosophical Society of Ohio, Cincinnati) depicts yeoman Harrison posing with a plow much in the manner of Governor Ritner, though more ruggedly attired.[16]

Later in the century, agricultural metaphors continued to serve presidential aspirants. Although Horace Greeley's candidacy drew fierce criticism both in prose and pictures, his campaign supporters heavily stressed his country simplicity and honesty. A cartoon in *Frank Leslie's Illustrated Newspaper* (which was anti-Grant) depicted Greeley as a farmer with birds and squirrels around him as he chopped down the tree in which the raccoon Grant was attempting to hide. Another showed him as a farmer-blacksmith, doing in fact what Washington had done symbolically: beating swords into plowshares. There was even a songbook entitled *The Farmer of Chappaqua*.[17] In the campaign of 1880, Currier & Ives published the lithograph *Farmer Garfield Cutting a Swath to the White House* (Illus. 53), which used the harvest metaphor to symbolize James Garfield's probity in a field of weeds and hissing snakes that bar his progress toward a strange hybrid of the United States Capitol and the presidential mansion. Stripped down to his shirtsleeves (rolled up to display brawny arms), wearing a neckerchief and big farmer's boots, Garfield swings a scythe bearing on its blade the motto "Honesty, Ability, and Patriotism." Under his feet he crushes the large snakes Calumny and Falsehood, and with his next swing he will demolish the serpents of Venom, Fraud, Hatred, Defamation, and Malice. Given the scandals of government corruption uncovered after the end of Grant's second term, this reaper imagery, recalling again the idea of the yeoman as the soul of integrity, the purest of citizens, remains consistent with the tradition of the agrarian ideal while shrewdly exploiting it.

In 1904 the honest yeoman image appeared yet again in a poster for the campaign of Theodore Roosevelt (Illus. 54), depicting the former Rough Rider as a sort of updated Cincinnatus; in the elaborately programmed design all components are carefully labeled to ensure correct understanding of the message. Yeoman Roosevelt, who in dress very much resembles the proud farmers of Granger lithographs, is the "Apostle of Prosperity." Like sowers of old he broadcasts by hand the seeds of this prosperity from a shoulder pouch. Next to him are piled bulging sacks full of the other things he will sow and cultivate if elected: agriculture, forestry, and mining; industry, commerce, and navigation; arbitration, justice, and law; and even literature, science, and art. An old-fashioned plow, hoe, and shovel rest at the edge of the neatly tilled field awaiting Roosevelt's seed. In the background is a homestead with a modern windmill, a lake, and some rolling hills, behind which sinks a celestial orb labeled "strife": the day of contention is ending. To all this are added uplifting quotations: "He who sows wind will reap storm— / But from good seed springs prosperity!", and, from Goethe's *Faust,* "Take spade and hoe thyself; dig on— / Great shalt thou be through peasant toil."

This is all a clever masque, of course, but the use of such symbolism, worked out in such expository detail, demonstrates the persistence and hardihood of an ancient ideal, translated into persuasive political metaphor. Long after the image of the farmer himself had subsided into good- or ill-natured caricature, the potency of the idea continued to serve politicians and their imagemakers, who could still rely on the plow, the sower, or the reaper to conjure up associations with a tradition of American rural rectitude.

43. William Sidney Mount, *Farmer Whetting His Scythe,* 1848. Oil on canvas, $23\frac{7}{8}'' \times 19\frac{7}{8}''$. (The Museums at Stony Brook, New York; gift of Mr. and Mrs. Ward Melville, 1958)

44. *June*. Wood engraving. *Ballou's Pictorial* 6 (June 17, 1854).

45. *The Mower in Ohio*. Wood engraving. *Harper's Weekly Magazine* 8 (August 6, 1864). (Prints and Photographs Division, Library of Congress)

46. Eastman Johnson, *The Evening Newspaper*, 1863. Oil on academy board, $17'' \times 14\frac{1}{2}''$. (Mead Art Museum, Amherst College; gift of Herbert W. Plimpton, The Hollis W. Plimpton, '15 Memorial Collection, 1977.62)

47. *The Farmer Pays for All,*
1869. Lithograph, $19\frac{7}{8}'' \times 15\frac{7}{8}''$.
Printed by Chicago Lithographing.
(Prints and Photographs Division,
Library of Congress)

48. *Gift for the Grangers*, 1873.
Lithograph, 21½″ × 17⅛″. Published
by J. Hale Powers, Cincinnati.
(Prints and Photographs Division,
Library of Congress)

49. Thomas Nast, *The Transportation Problem*. Wood engraving.
Harper's Weekly Magazine 17 (November 22, 1873).

50. Thomas Waterman Wood, *Cogitation*, 1871. Oil on canvas, 30″ × 27″. (By permission of The Fine Arts Museums of San Francisco, Mildred Anna Williams Collection)

51. Claude Regnier after Junius Brutus Stearns, *Life of George Washington: The Farmer*, 1853. Lithograph, $21'' \times 25\frac{15}{16}''$. Published by M. Knoedler, New York. (Prints and Photographs Division, Library of Congress)

52. John Francis, *Joseph Ritner, Governor of Pennsylvania*, 1836. Lithograph, 14″ × 11½″. Published by John Francis, Philadelphia. (The Harry T. Peters "America on Stone" Lithography Collection, Smithsonian Institution)

FARMER GARFIELD
Cutting a Swath to the White House.

53. *Farmer Garfield Cutting a Swath to the White House*, 1880. Lithograph, 13″ × 10⅝″ (plate and text). Published by Currier & Ives, New York. (Prints and Photographs Division, Library of Congress)

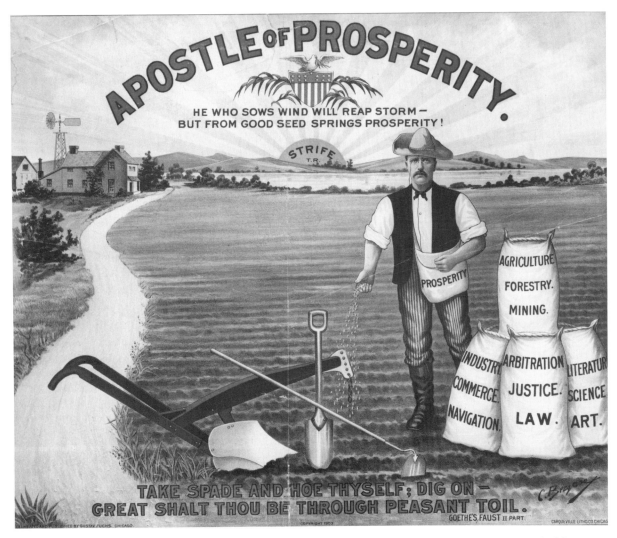

54. *Apostle of Prosperity*, 1903. Lithograph. Published by Gustav Fuchs, Chicago. (Courtesy of The New-York Historical Society, New York City, Landauer Collection)

6 ▪ *Hicks*

N AGRARIAN philosophy the American yeoman was the backbone of the republic and chief source of its virtue and strength. The sturdy scythe-wielder, the serious farmer-citizen with his newspaper, the patriot dropping his plow to fight for liberty—all these images affirmed the farmer's natural nobility and his high moral status in American society. Other conventions of representation, however, tempered and contradicted these celebratory images. In a tradition that had begun to take root even before the opening of the nineteenth century, the Yankee countryman was a comic figure, shrewd of wit but more often than not a laughable bumpkin. Nineteenth-century prose, poetry, plays, and pictures firmly established this type of the countryman as rustic oddity or clown.

A long history of European antecedents played a major role in shaping the comic American rustic. For decades after independence, American artists remained heavily dependent on European and perhaps especially British cultural authority and pictorial models. This was of necessity: no matter the rising nationalism of the new age, American art traditions were inescapably wedded to those of the Old World. In a republic initially so ill equipped with institutions for

teaching, exhibiting, and underwriting the pictorial arts, where there was little to teach that did not reflect a cultural debt to the mother country and her cousins, American artists inevitably depended on received conventions and regarded European models as foundations or templates for American pictures.

American depictions of the farmer as bumpkin ultimately derived from the art of the Netherlands in the seventeenth century, when the painting of daily life emerged as an important genre in a competitive, secular market catering to the tastes of the rising bourgeoisie. Specialists in peasant themes—David Teniers, Adriaen Brouwer, Adriaen van Ostade, and dozens of others—followed a path well paved by such predecessors as Pieter Breughel, whose peasants behaved with an earthy heartiness entirely appropriate to their status: a notch above the beasts whose shelter they customarily shared. Often incorporating a moralizing message—cautioning against excessive sensuality or alluding to man's bestial nature—seventeenth-century Dutch paintings of country people portrayed them as boors: dancing, guzzling, smoking, and playing cards in rural taverns, occasionally brawling, seldom less than coarse and lusty. Not every image showed the peasant as a rowdy, however. Van Ostade's country people, for example, tended to be genial and well behaved, as the urban bourgeoisie even then liked to see them. Other paintings and prints depicted seasonal activities—plowing, sowing, reaping—in which humble farm people uncomplainingly performed the ageless rituals of agriculture.[1]

Although even homebound American artists had ample opportunity to study Dutch pictures (a few paintings, many prints, and illustrations in painting and drawing manuals), much of the Dutch spirit came to Americans filtered (and given better manners) through English art, along with a newer strain of sentiment about the bliss of bucolic existence. In the last quarter of the eighteenth century in England, the pressures of change in both the agricultural countryside and the newly industrializing towns fostered the cultivation of sentiment and rosy, escapist dreams of a serene, pastoral existence. The visions of rural felicity proffered by Thomas Gainsborough in his "fancy pictures" were only the most famous among an outpouring of such images; the works of George Morland, Francis Wheatley, for example, widely circulated as engravings or book illustrations, were well known to many American artists. Ultimately exceeding them in popularity was the Scottish painter Sir David Wilkie, whose often humorous "narratives" of rural and village life (also much indebted to Dutch prototypes) continued to satisfy the desires of urban patrons and audience for warmhearted scenes of folk life.

The range of subjects treated by Morland, Wheatley, and Wilkie was very nearly duplicated by American artists (William Sidney Mount in particular) a generation later. Wheatley, a highly successful painter whose vision hovered somewhere between rococo make-believe and genuine observation, won a large, admiring public with his pretty, sentimental country imagery. His subjects included haymaking scenes, harvest home festivities, peaceful farmyards, children hunting birds' nests, peddlers, and rustic courtships in humble cottage interiors. Morland, prolific but always bedeviled by drink and debt, created perhaps 4,000 rural scenes: stable interiors, farmyards, field laborers, rustics drinking in country inns, country children playing or misbehaving. His work of the 1790s had subversive undertones sometimes expunged by the engravers who reproduced hundreds of his paintings for publication. These images, akin to some Dutch forerunners, showed the rural poor as shiftless, slovenly, and drunk. A larger number of Morland's other works, however, were more neutral—or positive—and embodied the country charm for which he achieved enormous popularity well into the nineteenth century.[2] Wilkie, whose themes ranged from rude cottages to intricately stage-managed spectacles of village society, retained the Dutch spirit of reverence for the ordinary while purifying his designs of any suggestion of Dutch ribaldry.

Looking at some representative British and American paintings or prints side by side, an observer unfamiliar with the art of the period might be hard pressed to distinguish one from the other. In the engraving after Wheatley's *Preparing for Market* (Illus. 55), and in Louis Maurer's Currier & Ives lithograph *Preparing for Market* (Illus. 56) for example, the rituals depicted scarcely vary from one picture to the other. In Wheatley's design a sturdy cart with two dray horses stands before a picturesque thatched shed. A young man arranges the farm produce on the wagon bed while two comely young women hand up baskets of vegetables. Below, heaps of cabbages, turnips, and carrots spill onto the ground from large wicker hampers. The left-hand corner contains an interesting assortment of rural artifacts: a keg with a knothole, a twig broom, and a lantern. While there is even more detail in the Maurer print, the activity is virtually identical: farm cart, dray horses, man loading, woman handing up baskets, and an abundance of produce spread out on the ground. The house and barn are clapboarded and gabled rather than plastered and thatched, and the rendering lacks Wheatley's contrived prettiness. Despite a half-century's difference in style and costume, though, the two images hum the same tune of pastoral tranquillity. Both suggest that rural life is rich in its simplicity and homely charm, and its populace contented with humble but picturesque labors.

Rural Repose, another engraving after Wheatley (Illus. 57), bears a similar relation to William Sidney Mount's *Farmers Nooning* (Illus. 58). Again, there are obvious differences in style. Wheatley's forms are conventionalized and his scenery artificial; Mount's are sharply individualized, and his landscape scintillates with the immediacy of direct observation. Once more, however, situation and mood correspond. Both depict groups of harvesters relishing moments of ease during their noon dinnertime, and in each the major focus is a haycock where a slumbering figure lolls in luxurious indolence. In *Rural Repose* a spaniel ransacks the lunch basket of the sleeping maid and her inattentive companion. In *Farmers Nooning* a roguish boy with a straw tickles the ear of the sprawling black man. Behind Wheatley's haycock a youth and a girl, both pretty enough to be painted on porcelain, steal a few moments' dalliance while their cohorts dream or daydream. The male emphasis in Mount's picture precludes any such tender byplay, but the workers enjoy desultory pastimes: one stretches prone on the grass, and one watches the tickling scene. Only the last, who hones his scythe sharpener, makes productive use of his time at leisure. A minor but interesting instance of formal parallelism occurs in the placement of a foreshortened rake on the right slope of the haycock in both compositions. This is not solid enough evidence to support an argument for direct influence, although it is conceivable that Mount, avidly interested in prints, was familiar with *Rural Repose.* In any event, there need not have been direct influence for this consanguinity of mood to arise; shared attitudes toward country life and people dictated the creation of imagery emphasizing not diligence and productivity but vegetation both mental and physical. In Mount's painting there is a sly injection of moralism in the contrast between the diligent sharpener and his slothful comrades. Even so, the general effect is of the country as a sleepy place.[3]

Moralizing intentions ally pictures such as George Morland's *Boys Robbing an Orchard* (Illus. 59) and Mount's *The Truant Gamblers* (Illus. 60), which humorously treat the subject of bad boys and their imminent punishment. The boys in Morland's design scramble out of a tree to flee in frantic but comical haste as an angry farmer bears down on them with his dog. Mount's gamblers are four barefoot, gleeful urchins pitching pennies in a barn; on the left a farmer stalks them, ire in his eye and in one hand a long switch to arrest their waywardness. The boys' game only appears innocent; it is really a foreshadowing of the more serious adult vices (speculation in every form) to which this seemingly harmless activity will inevitably lead. Another allusion to temptation is embodied in the shiny, corked earthenware jug on the ground just below. In Morland and Mount, as in many antecedent Dutch pictures, the comic surface cloaks and renders palatable a more serious message.[4]

In depicting country life as bucolic bliss, vegetative torpor, or slapstick comedy, British and American images betray the presence of underlying attitudes resembling each other more than might at first be suspected, given the oft-proclaimed American pride in contrasting independent New World farmers so advantageously with the servile peasants of the Old World. The more sentimental or romantic aspects arose as a response to similar conditions in both countries: industrialism, urban growth, and social change, while permanently altering traditional rural cultures, at the same time made them more desirable. Other images, however, suggest the kind of seemingly good-natured condescension that prevails when one social group looks, from some point of advantage, at another comfortably lower in the social hierarchy. In England, where sharp class divisions had been fundamental to the social order for many hundreds of years, to find peasants portrayed as inferiors is not surprising. America, however, had in place a seemingly more fluid social system—not classless, to be sure (economic differences automatically imposed a stratification of groups) but allowing for mobility and encouraging all citizens to regard themselves as equal to any others. Nonetheless, a discernible ambivalence shadowed attitudes toward the farmer, at least as we find them expressed by the culture producers of the time. Paintings like Mount's *Farmers Nooning,* much as they seem to extol the agrarian ideal, at the same time subtly denigrate it, make it an object of fun, portray country folk not as simple but as simpletons and layabouts. Natural and unrefined, these types could be used to point a moral yet be unacceptable to cultured society.

The evidence suggested by Mount's works (discussed below) also finds support in a variety of contemporary literary sources. In some writings the author's overt intention was to criticize by satire not country people but the urban fashionables who scorned their simplicity as offensively common. This was the strategy of Knickerbocker author James Kirke Paulding, who took didactic aim at elegant urban snobs in a chapter of his novel *Koningsmarke:*

> With a considerable portion of romance readers, everything, not fashionable, is of course vulgar. A worthy farmer, or mechanic, in a clean white frock and thick-soled shoes, is vulgar, and therefore ought not to be introduced into a genteel novel. The picture of a village group dancing, is of necessity vulgar, because they are not fashionably dressed, dance with the most unseemly zeal, vigor, and activity, as if they actually enjoyed themselves, and above all are egregiously ignorant of the waltz, the gallopade, and the mazurka. In short, with this class of readers and critics, every trait of nature, and every exhibition of character, or manners, or dress, which does not come up to the standard of fashionable elegance, is necessarily low and vulgar.[5]

Here Paulding was sending out a set of very mixed signals. On the one hand, his defense of unaffected country manners was but another manifestation of that romantic sentiment which had animated the thoughts of Jean-Jacques Rousseau and had more recently given rise in England to the early poetry of William Wordsworth, seeker after revelations of truth in the simple and the natural. The same sentiment had prompted the upsurge of pastoral longing in late eighteenth-century England and would spur identical impulses in America. On the other hand, Paulding, himself a cultivated New Yorker, was writing for an audience of those whom he was gently chiding. He rebuked his readers for an excessive gentility that would banish farmers and country dancers even from the pages of their novels, yet if he did not share their feelings that farmers were vulgar, it is easy to see that he thought them lowly, as the description of the "worthy" farmer's costume reveals. The farmer's frock is clean and therefore an emblem of his decency, yet no polite drawing room would countenance such dress. Likewise, thick-soled shoes were for the country clod, not the urban gentleman.

Paulding's farmers and country dancers should be welcomed into the new literature because they were picturesque and colorful types, truthful touches of nature that would enliven the stilted forms of romance. More than anything else, perhaps, they were entertaining, just as the spectacle of haying was entertaining to the writer who beheld it from a comfortable distance. As entertainers, they inhabited a different world, somewhat akin to that of actors or circus clowns. It was a world that spectators could enjoy, that might even offer edification of some kind; however, beyond the limits of the enjoyment and edification it provided, it was low and déclassé. A farmer or village dancer would be as surely and sorely out of place at a fashionable soirée as a clown.

It was implicitly an urban perspective, whether or not exaggerated by satire, that viewed the farmer in this role, just as it beheld him in the role of noble agrarian. This is made clear in a bit of dialogue from *The Politicians,* a satirical play by Cornelius Mathews, another prolific and versatile Knickerbocker author. In this excerpt, the character Kate and her suitor Blanding argue about the merits of country life and country people:

> *Kate:* Well, Blanding, you are the better pleader, and all I can say is, that your cause requires your ingenuity, but the country still has charms, honest hearts, cheerful faces, simple manners.
> *Blanding:* Faces uniform as sheep, and one everlasting pair of lin-

sey-woolsey pantaloons. The manners are simple enough, for there the three acts of a man's life are, to cut hay in summer, fodder his cattle in winter, and attend a town-meeting in spring, to elect overseers of the poor. The poor!—they are all poor in spirit, if not in pocket, and deserve nothing better to look out upon than one huge, green page, with half a dozen dreary-looking trees, by way of interjection![6]

Blanding, rehearsing the urban view, in effect declared farmers dirty and dull. This kind of interchange was repeated, with many variations, over and over in the plays of the time.

Donald Grant Mitchell later echoed Blanding's assessment of the American yeoman:

If a man perspires largely in a cornfield on a dusty day, and washes hastily in the horsetrough, and eats in shirt-sleeves that date their cleanliness three days back, and loves fat pork and cabbage "neat," he will not prove the Arcadian companion at dinner. . . . A long day of close fieldwork leaves one in a very unfit mood for appreciative study of either poetry or the natural sciences.[7]

Mitchell's attitude toward farmers, riddled with unresolved contradictions, fairly represents the ambivalence detectable over the wide range of American cultural expression—uttered, for the most part, by urban voices. Despite his interest in and actual experience with farm life, Mitchell retained at bottom an urban orientation. On one hand, the author of *Dream-Life* could apotheosize that agrarian pillar of a bygone New England community, the Squire, keen and upright in body and mind, who surely did not sit down in unclean linen to feast dumbly on greasy pork. On the other hand, he could dismiss the farmer, as described above, with a few decisive strokes, portraying the same type envisioned by the Blanding character: a lowly creature, dirty and dull.

This same ever changeable Mitchell also adopted tactics similar to Paulding's, using the eccentric, entertaining simplicity of country manners as a goad to prod the ultrarefined sensibilities of the fashionable world. In *The Lorgnette,* a

collection of commentaries on urban life, Mitchell poked fun at the empty-headed, superficial lady of fashion while offering tongue-in-cheek advice on how to avoid the social embarrassments that might be visited upon her by rural acquaintances:

She should be cautious . . . of meeting any shabby country friends . . . and to this end, should carry on an active correspondence for a week or two in advance, with her country cousins—engaging to meet them *late in the season.* A thin old lady in calico, who says "our folks," or a young man who dresses in a flimsy, black dress coat of a morning, who carries a baggy cotton umbrella, and blows his nose on the "stoop" with a "silk handkercher," might do her serious damage.[8]

The tone here is light and spirited, the fun benign. Yet again, as in Paulding, there is just a note—no more—of condescension, as if Mitchell were saying that there really was something inherently absurd about the dress and manners of country people with their scraggly bodies, runny noses, rustic outfitting, and unrefined speech.

During the antebellum years there was plenty of such fun to be had at the expense of rural society. The couple described in a sketch entitled "Mr. and Mrs. Cowpen" are cut from the same cloth as Mitchell's "shabby country friends." In this *Gleason's Pictorial* piece the Cowpens are presented as "an eminently homespun couple" from that most homespun of regions, the state of Maine. Their lives and consciousness extend not much beyond the limits of their potato patch, and they believe that at least three-quarters of the stories they read in the newspaper are lies. Informed that trains travel at the speed of twenty miles per hour between Boston and Portland, they refuse to take such "gammon" (nonsense) seriously.[9]

When one recalls that in *Gleason's* and other contemporary magazines a reader could sometimes go from the Cowpens to the noble yeoman in a matter of pages, the inconsistencies in the farmer's social and cultural status become all the more apparent. This was a fundamental paradox, not to be resolved in the nineteenth century or indeed in the twentieth. For all the exaltation of the yeoman and the goodness of his life, a countercurrent of humorous commentary worked to undermine, trivialize, and ridicule the image of American country people. Little of such writing was bad-spirited, and its negative undercurrents may have stolen in without a writer's conscious collaboration; some of it, indeed, displayed a certain chauvinistic pride in American peculiarities. But the fact remains that there lay before the literate public a great deal of printed matter which, by presenting the American rustic as a figure of fun, probably helped to shape readers' perceptions along the same lines.

Nowhere did all the ambivalences coalesce so thickly as in the work of William Sidney Mount, foremost among American genre painters from the 1830s until the early 1850s. His own background and life experiences were paradigmatic of the contrasts and conflicts between rural and urban values in the first half of the nineteenth century. Born on rural Long Island, he nourished throughout his career a deep attachment to the people and places of his youth. The world of creative stimulus, acclaim, and success, however, lay within the New York metropolis: there, at the National Academy of Design and the American Art-Union, his work could be seen; there too were the patrons, the camaraderie of fellow artists and writers, the entertainments, the critics, the audience. For all that, Mount's time in the city was relatively brief: the years 1824–26, initially as apprentice to his brother Henry and then as student at the National Academy of Design, and—following an interval back in his native Stony Brook—the years 1829–1836, after which he returned to Stony Brook for good.

Aside from some portraits and a few early attempts at history painting, his entire output consisted of scenes from country life, using in many cases local models and setting them in and around the old family house, barn, and fields. A devoted student of nature, Mount diligently sketched and painted outdoors, capturing in certain pictures—notably in

Farmers Nooning— effects of astonishingly precise and brilliant naturalism. Yet he produced very few works that were other than elaborately synthetic constructions. Seen on a continuum, Mount's paintings depict an American rural scene populated by amusing rustics, clowns, and clodhoppers of various types, complemented occasionally by the noble yeoman, as in *Farmer Whetting His Scythe.* Some paintings offer a political metaphor: *Cider Making* (1841; Metropolitan Museum of Art, New York) probably alludes to the log-cabin-and-hard-cider motif of the 1840 Whig bid for the presidency. Others, notably the famous *Eel Spearing at Setauket* (1845; New York State Historical Association, Cooperstown), are freighted with luminous, nostalgic poetry, and some of Mount's country boys are grave and thoughtful rather than rambunctious and devious urchins.[10]

But many of his other characters present a low spectacle of rustic manners: they loaf, they drink, they gamble; they outfox each other in wily trading; they perform crude dances in taverns and barns; they court farmers' daughters in ludicrous parodies of romance. In certain works such behavior is meant to point a moral against the evils of intemperance, cardplaying, and games of chance—as is obvious, for example, in *The Truant Gamblers,* and in *Loss and Gain* (1847; The Museums at Stony Brook, New York), which depicts the comic despair and impending salvation of an old bumpkin who cannot clamber quickly enough over a wall to rescue his toppled whiskey jug before its contents (happily) drain away into the ground instead of down his gullet.[11] Whether or not moral messages are the ultimate point, it is still true that Mount's works include a considerable number of comical boors whose antics and peccadilloes afforded abundant entertainment to their largely urban audiences. The fact that so many of Mount's comical pictures were engraved and made widely available (in gift books, through distribution to American Art-Union subscribers, and by the agency of art merchants Goupil, Vibert and Company) ensured an even wider public for these amiable but ever so subtly denigrating portrayals of life in America's rustic outposts.[12]

Denigration is somewhat too strong a term to describe what happens in these paintings. It might be more precise to say that Mount's work deftly balances on a cusp between admiration (his family and old friends were country people, after all) and condescension. In his own jottings, which belie the often merry, celebratory spirit of his country pictures, his complaint about existence in the country became something of a litany. If he had to stay in the country his art would stagnate: "I am not in the way of improving myself in painting in the country as quickly as if I lived in the City. More pictures and characters to be seen there. My feeling for painting would burn with a brighter flame by living in New York." He felt sometimes as if he were living in exile, as he wrote more than once to a friend and correspondent, the essayist and artistic dabbler Charles Lanman: "I shall not be able to reside in the City for some time, owing to some commissions I have lately received requiring close observation in the country, which I regret on some accounts, as the City is the place for the artist. [Sir Joshua] Reynolds considered . . . the three years he spent in the country as so much time lost." Later, Mount returned to the subject in even more emphatic terms: "I often ask myself this question, am I to stay in old Suffolk County as long as the Children of Isreal [sic] did in the wilderness." There is obviously a component here of intense personal frustration, symbolically vented by disparaging the country as a desert wilderness that contained no food for Mount's hungry spirit, but there is also a kernel of truth derived from his own experience. He had surprisingly little to say about the people who lounged, drank, frolicked, and danced in his paintings, but one comment about his farmer neighbors on Long Island is revealing:

Long Island appears to be very atractive [sic]. Some of the farmers have not been to the City of New York in thirty years—I know a farmer he is now about forty years old, he never was in the city. Notwithstanding all the modern improvements in traveling. . . . This feeling, bound to one place for life, I do not believe in. It is all habit. It may do for farmers—but it will not do for artists.

Mount regarded himself as substantially separate from and in some respects superior to the rustics of his native place. This attitude is consistent with the perspective of the urban sophisticate: amused, tolerant, distanced; ready to be entertained, edified, or mystified by the customs of the rustic species.[13]

Contemporary critics made a habit of comparing Mount with his English and Dutch predecessors; they coupled his name very frequently with those of David Teniers, Wilkie, and Morland. Mount's art, they found, was akin both in subject and in spirit to that of his exemplars. Like theirs, it dealt with the common, the rustic, the low, and the unrefined. The only attribute Mount lacked (which no one missed) was the vulgarity so often to be deplored in the Dutch. Although the most forthright criticism was reserved for his tavern scenes, such as *Walking the Line* (Illus. 61), one can infer that the attitudes expressed there probably extended to a wider range of Mount's themes.

Walking the Line portrays a sparse tavern interior where five male figures observe a man seen from the back, who is performing a vigorous shuffle along a crack in the barroom floor. This figure obviously embodies the crux of the moral tale: his clothes are in tatters; the upended mug he brandishes, along with the corked jug on the floor beside an axe and a plug hat, explicitly indicate the association of strong drink with dereliction. The other figures represent a cross section of the rural male population: a wonderstruck boy, an old man with a long clay pipe, two young men (one of them something of a blade), and on the right, physically very much isolated from the group, a smiling black man.

Critics who saw *Walking the Line* exhibited at the National Academy in 1835 were reminded of Wilkie and Teniers, and they appreciated Mount's comic spirit, tipped with its moral point. One expressed his satisfaction that although Mount's rustic scenes had "all the nature and humor of the Dutchman," they were "entirely free from [Teniers's] occasional grossness." Another, however, was perturbed by the debased subject:

We might be disposed to wish that such superior talents and skill as here displayed had been exercised on a subject of a higher grade in the social scale; but when we stand before this admirable picture and contemplate the expression of the several characters who are attracted from their poisonous potations by the clownish agility and conceited skill of the dancer, who balances his shuffle by the extended arms and empty mug from which his inspiration and his rags are derived, we cannot regret the time or exertion which this extraordinary young artist has bestowed on the scene. . . . With all our admiration of this picture (and it has its moral in the rags of the pot-house Vestris) we hope that the American Wilkie will select such subjects as will, at the same time, give scope to his talent for expression both of face and attitude, (in both of which he excels) and tell such stories as shall improve the hearts and instruct the minds of his admirers.

Reviewing the engravings published as illustrations in the 1842 crop of gift books, Edgar Allan Poe voiced a similar reaction to J. J. Pease's engraving *The Tough Story* (in *The Gift* for 1842), after Mount's painting *The Long Story* (see Illus. 69). Also a barroom scene, this work depicts a ragged old cardplaying toper regaling the landlord and a bird of passage with an interminable tale. "Mr. Mount's merits," Poe wrote, "are those of acute observation and fidelity. These merits, although not of the highest order, have the advantage of being universally appreciable. This is an advantage which he secures—*clinches*—by dealing only in homely subjects." It is not particularly surprising that such a subject would call forth these responses, half praise, half demurral. In England the same had been said of an engraving (published in 1801) after Morland's *Alehouse Politicians*, which John Hassell, one of the artist's earliest biographers, criticized as "too low a subject" to merit much attention; taverns, after all, were not places where one would expect to encounter polite society.[14]

The subject did not need to be an overtly degraded one, however, to provoke those comments. By its very nature, Mount's art was without elevation, without ideality of content, despite the rigorous purity and precision of his design.

His expected function was to provide comic relief along with occasional gentle reminders of morality and righteousness. Looking back on Mount's contributions to American art, Charles Lanman wrote:

He was unquestionably one of the most original artists of his day, and exerted a happy influence on the public taste. He was the pioneer, and continued the unequalled master in his special department; and he accomplished, to some extent, for American country life what David Wilkie did for the country life of Great Britain, or David Teniers of his fatherland. . . . In a few instances, the mere execution of his pictures was quite equal to that of the famous Scotchman; but he contented himself with a single humorous thought, instead of touching the heart with the elevating sentiments born of rustic life. Unlike the Flemish painter, he was never vulgar, and we can only regret that he did not pay more respect to the higher and better feelings of our nature.

Contemporary with Lanman's was art critic Henry Tuckerman's assessment, which indicates clearly how outlandish Mount's characters might appear to urban sophisticates (even taking into account the fact that to Tuckerman, who preferred the suave polish of European training as manifested in the art of Eastman Johnson, Mount's style seemed awkward, crude, and homemade): "Very expressive and clever are Mount's happy delineations of the arch, quaint, gay, and rustic humors seen among the primitive people of his native place; they are truly American."[15] More than anything, it is the use of the word "primitive" that reveals Tuckerman's bias.

Frequently coupled with observations on Mount's comic power and low subjects was enthusiastic approbation of his fidelity to natural facts. Even his earlier efforts, created before his skills had quite matured, won admiration on that score. Regarding his *Dancing on the Barn Floor* (see Illus. 64), shown at the National Academy in 1832, a commentator made note of Mount's "natural bias," joined to a singular "comic power." Soon his work was being taken as the next best thing to life itself, to judge by critics' remarks. A spectator looking at *The Truant Gamblers*, for example, "is at once convinced that he sees nature before him, and feels as if he had seen that man entering with the whip a hundred times." Likewise, *Bargaining for a Horse* (see Illus. 70) was "true to nature; and the oldest farmer is an old acquaintance of every beholder of the picture." Even better, *Farmers Nooning* was "nature itself, a perfect transcript from life."[16]

Mount's designs were anything but perfect transcripts from life, though most observers of the exquisitely wrought detail, animated expressions, and naturalistic surfaces of his best would be persuaded to comply with the intended illusion. What is significant is that images of country people as entertainers, clowns, and bumpkins were accepted, apparently, as convincing facsimiles of the genuine article. An important aspect of Mount's contribution, then, was to vivify and confirm what were already becoming deep-seated stereotypes.

Through such imagery the idea of rural Americans received the stamp of triviality, and their separation from the urban spheres of power became more complete. Like stereotyped nineteenth-century blacks, and not too far above them on the social scale, the farmer was jolly, placid, content with his lot, and happy to sing and dance the time away. John Barrell has proposed a similar reading of certain British paintings of rural life. Of Wilkie's *Village Politicians* (1806; Collection, the Earl of Mansfield) he observes that while the alehouse customers are "grotesquely and condescendingly portrayed," the painting was much admired for the truth of its representation. In explaining what it was that admirers thereby wished to believe about the rural poor, Barrell argued that in pictures like Wilkie's the "politicians" are made to appear obviously too stupid "to initiate any action which their opinions, however radical, might prompt them to," the message being one of reassurance to the classes above them, willfully oblivious to the true state of affairs in English rural life. While the signals in Mount are more muted, there is evidence that his comic works communicated the same kind of message.[17]

Mount scored his first success with *Rustic Dance after a Sleigh-Ride* (Illus. 62), a lively depiction of rural revelry, and he returned to even more rustic treatments of the subject in later works (see *Dancing on the Barn Floor*, Illus. 64; and *Dance of the Haymakers*, Illus. 65). In these paintings, dancers act out the role imposed upon them of country people as entertainers, performers of ungainly, impolite figures for the amusement of a more genteel audience. *Rustic Dance*, like so many of Mount's pictures, treads a narrow line between the painter's actual experience and knowledge of country life and the world of artifice.

Rustic Dance after a Sleigh Ride was exhibited in October 1830 and won first prize at the third annual trade fair of the American Institute of the City of New York. So great was its success that it made Mount's reputation, virtually overnight. Still crude by comparison with the works he would produce by the mid-1830s, *Rustic Dance* is nonetheless exuberant. The simple, boxlike room holds twenty-nine figures; two more peer around the partially open door in the rear wall. In the center is a pair of dancers, the young woman pinching up a fold of her gown and tripping on the toe of her tiny black slipper, the young man energetically prancing with one hand outstretched and the other in his pocket. On the right another couple seems to be on the verge of joining the dancers, and all around the walls on that side of the room are more dressed-up girls and attendant youths. A tall clock in the right rear corner shows the time to be sixteen minutes past midnight. The left side of the room is considerably more rowdy. A grinning black musician saws away on his fiddle; behind him is a man who—with his gaping mouth (shouting or singing, perhaps), wilted collar, and pitcher on the floor between his feet—is evidently intoxicated, as are others among the all-male crowd clustered between the door and the mantelpiece, where a goblet of rosy liquor keeps company with the three candles that illuminate the scene. A man at the rear brandishes aloft another such goblet in a toast. In front of the fireplace is a jolly-faced black boy holding a bellows. Although certain effects may be only the result of Mount's stiff, unpracticed rendering, some of the faces in the crowd barely escape grotesquerie, and even among the well-dressed couples on the right there are hints of awkwardness or clownishness—especially in the prancing youth, whose hand in pocket could hardly be considered good form.

Did we not know better, it would be easy to take this as a carefully composed but otherwise truthful account of rustic customs on Long Island, so near and yet so far from its metropolitan neighbor. Mount had grown up in a rural community where music and dance were a vital part of cultural life. He was himself a skilled amateur violinist who performed at country dances, collected dance tunes, and wrote a piece or two of dance music. Dancing schools had begun to open in Long Island villages early in the nineteenth century, and Mount's brother Robert Nelson Mount was a dancing master—itinerant as were many during that period. Dancing took place at social gatherings of every description. There were even actual prototypes for the black fiddler in *Rustic Dance*: in his childhood, Mount had been powerfully impressed by Anthony Hannibal Clapp, a rustic virtuoso of jig and hornpipe. There can be little doubt that Mount's painting commemorated—in essence—aspects of a familiar world.[18]

Reservations and contradictions, however, demand to be registered. It would be more accurate, in the first place, to say that Mount's experiences may have coincided with the subject of *Rustic Dance* but that the painting itself is entirely a fabrication, related as much to pictorial and literary sources as to real life on Long Island. As a number of scholars have established, the direct source for the composition was Philadelphia genre specialist John Lewis Krimmel's *Country Frolic and Dance* (c. 1820), a painting now lost and known only by the Childs and Lehman lithograph after it, called *Dance in a Country Tavern*. Krimmel's painting, in turn, was indebted to Wilkie's *The Blind Fiddler* (1806; Tate Gallery, London), one of the several Wilkie compositions that Krimmel copied. Although the manner of Mount's actual contact with Krim-

mel's *Country Frolic* is still problematical, the striking visual parallels confirm that somehow the influence was transmitted. Many details vary, but the basic design of the two works is the same, with a boxlike interior space, a couple (considerably more suave in Krimmel) dancing in the middle, and a fireplace on the left. Most interesting in the Krimmel is the presence of a black man—in the same place, with the same grin—playing the violin. It is just as likely that Mount's black musician came from Krimmel's example as from Anthony Clapp or any other local figure Mount may have known.[19]

Previous literary stylings of the rustic dance theme may also have played a part in shaping Mount's conception. Before the turn of the century a number of well-educated urban writers had indulged in what amounted to a fad of writing poems in New England rustic (or Yankee) dialect verse. The country poems probably originated in the circle of author and playwright Royall Tyler. Their creators included poet and journalist Thomas Green Fessenden, Isaac Story, and Tyler himself, along with a number of anonymous hands. The verse spread rapidly, appearing in New England newspapers such as the *Federal Orrery* (Boston), *Dartmouth Eagle*, *Columbian Centinel*, and Joseph Dennie's widely read *Farmer's Weekly Museum*. After the turn of the century they were reprinted in such magazines as *The Port Folio* of Philadelphia and in early anthologies of American verse. In virtually every case, the rustic poems are self-consciously vernacular pieces written by literate sophisticates. Part parody and part celebration of rural American peculiarities, they dwell on the subject of rustic courtship (considered further below), and other aspects of rural social and political life.[20]

Tyler and Fessenden both devised romping anecdotes of the country dance. Humorous, energetic, and satirical, their poems foreshadow the spirit and content of Mount's painting. Tyler's "Ode Composed for the Fourth of July, Calculated for the Meridian of Some Country Town" portrays a scene of rambunctious, rustic merrymaking: a house party where the drink is plentiful, the dance more vigorous than graceful, and the participants emphatically folksy:

Squeak the fife and beat the drum,
INDEPENDENCE DAY is come!
Let the roasting pig be bled,
Quick, twist off the cockerel's head,
. . . .
Send the keg to shop for brandy
Maple sugar we have handy,
. . . .
Sal, put on your russet skirt,
Jotham, get your boughten shirt,
Today we dance to diddle diddle.
—Here comes Sambo with his fiddle.
Sambo, take a dram of whisky
And play up Yankee Doodle frisky.

The black fiddler ("Sambo" had come into use as an all-purpose black nickname very early in the eighteenth century) is urged to "saw" as fast as he can, to rosin his bow so that the merry company can "have another go." When the squire, a local man of substance, arrives, he is heartily invited to "drink until you're blind." The poem rounds off triumphantly: "Thus we drink and dance away / This glorious INDEPENDENCE DAY!"[21]

Only two months later Fessenden published in the *Farmer's Weekly Museum* his response to Tyler, "The Country Junket, or Rustic Revel," very similar to the earlier piece but even more a lampoon of rustic ways. The first part of the poem describes preparations for the "village kickup": engaging the ballroom at the local inn, the arrangements made by those invited to ride and drive there, and the like. They send for "Sambo with his fiddle, / Tiddle diddle, tiddle diddle," and the fun begins. In Fessenden's poem more attention is directed to the dancers: they cut droll capers and blunder through their figures, ending up "all higgle piggle." Among the various individuals described are: Miss Airy, who "dances topping, / Lighter than a cricket hopping," and the true clodhopper Sammy Snyder, who "trots like thunder, / Sure he'll split the floor asunder." After the dancing concludes, serious flirtation begins: arming himself with lem-

onade, wine, and porter, each young blade must "sit by lass, and strive to court her." Another poem by Fessenden, "Horace Surpassed; or, A Beautiful Description of a New-England Country-Dance," pictures a similar scene, combining finery and awkwardness:

How funny 'tis, when pretty lads and lasses
Meet altogether, just to have a caper,
And the black fiddler plays you such a tune as
Sets you a frisking.

Again, the fiddler is black. The country gallants are sleek and spruce and the ladies arrayed in silk and muslin, but their deportment—especially the men's—reveals their basic bumpkin nature: "Clumsy Ralph Lumberlegs treads on Tabby's gown, and / Tears all the tail off!"[22]

It is difficult to determine the chances of Mount's having been acquainted with these poems. Given their wide diffusion, however, it is possible that he knew them, or variants of them, perhaps even as transmitted by the lively oral traditions of the region. It is conceivable, in fact, that the same sources also contributed to the local color of Krimmel's *Country Frolic and Dance,* in which many elements correspond to those in the poems.

Vernacular prose tales on the same themes were also in circulation during the early decades of the nineteenth century. They appeared, like the poems, in newspapers and even in almanacs. One in particular, "A Sleigh Ride," corresponds so closely to Mount's *Rustic Dance* that it is difficult to discount it as a direct source. It was first published early in 1829—more than a year before the painting made its debut—and proved so popular that it was widely and frequently reprinted. This tale, which has been attributed to John Neal (in whose *Yankee and Boston Literary Gazette* it first appeared), recounts a gleeful evening sleighing party, planned by a boisterous group of young fellows who shout with joy at the prospect of "gals—fiddles and frolic." They find some willing "gals," and, with the fiddler in the lead, set off in their sleighs to Peter Shaw's inn:

And when we arrived the floor was swept, the best Japan candlesticks paraded, the fireplace filled with green wood, and little Ben was anchored close under the jam [mantel-tree] to tug at the broken winded bellusses [bellows]. . . . As soon as we had taken a swig of hot stuff all round, we sat the fiddler down by the other jam [the other side of the fireplace]—took the floor, and went to work might and main, the fiddler keeping time with the bellusses. Not to be lengthy, we kept it up frolickin' and drinkin' hot stuff til midnight.[23]

Details in this description—the boy with the bellows, the placement of the fiddler near the fireplace, the candlesticks parading on the mantelpiece—strongly suggest a connection between story and painting. Given the immediate fame of "A Sleigh Ride," it could even have been the primary literary stimulus for Mount's conception of *Rustic Dance*. If this was the case, it reinforces the argument for viewing Mount's picture as containing more artifice than nature, and relating more closely to an urban or sophisticated tradition of laughing at country people than to the simple facts of rural society alone.

Mount's *Rustic Dance* shares the rollicking energy of the dances described by Tyler, Fessenden, and the author of "A Sleigh Ride." Like the poets, Mount mixes refinement (the ladies arrayed in their best muslins and hung about with chains, lockets, and lace; the beaux in their starched collars and dancing pumps) and rowdiness (the cavorting bumpkin who appears quite capable of treading on his partner's feet, if not ripping off a piece of her gown; the crowd of celebrating tipplers on the left). While Mount's dancers may not appear to our eyes so very rude and risible, a comparison with the popular print *The Dance* (Illus. 63), published some ten years later, shows how broad was the gulf—conceptually, at least—between elegant and inelegant diversions. *The Dance* portrays the urban ideal of a genteel mingling of the sexes, where decorum reigns and the dancers glide rather than bounce or frisk. Instead of a black fiddler, there is a lady at a piano. Neither whiskey jugs nor glasses of wine are to be seen. When it is recalled that even the dancing schools of Long Island stressed manners as much as steps in the training they offered, it becomes all the more apparent that Mount's *Rustic Dance,* like the country poems, includes a measure of parody in its conception. It is meant to depict country amusements as buoyant yet rough-edged and faintly ridiculous affairs.[24]

As Mount matured and became more and more his own artist, he was less inclined to rest his compositions so obviously on literary or pictorial models. I would argue, however, that in important ways *Rustic Dance* set a pattern that continued to shape his works and their meaning. Many of his subsequent paintings corresponded in mood, situation, and character to the matter in contemporary prose, poetry, and plays; they continued to present country people as entertainers—musicians, dancers, clowns, unwitting moralizers; they purported to relate the natural truth yet remained, on the whole, fabrications, though increasingly sophisticated and polished as Mount grew into his finest powers.

Dancing on the Barn Floor (Illus. 64) again casts rustic characters as entertainers, this time in the much more recognizably rustic setting of a barn interior, with the fiddler (white this time) sitting on the threshold and a girl and youth dancing within. In the rear of the barn is another partially opened door, from which a woman with a hayrake looks out and beckons. This painting displays an impressive advance in technical refinement; the figures are less puppetlike and the surfaces more naturalistic. Beyond that, however, the work is once more rigorously contrived, using the stagelike geometry of the barn as a frame for the precisely counterbalanced figures, who appear carefree and jolly but self-consciously so, as if they were actors. Self-consciousness is especially marked in the young male dancer, whose mannered pose, professional smile, and, especially, red sash slung like a bandolier across his chest recall conventional academic poses and costumes used to signify peasants, banditti, and other picturesque types in European art. These features also indicate possible connections with contemporary theater, which, in tune with the rising nationalism of the 1820s, had witnessed the growing popularity of plays featuring Yankee characters and life in pastoral American villages.

One of the most successful and durable of these plays, *The Forest Rose: or American Farmers* by Samuel Woodworth, was produced at the Chatham Theatre in New York in October 1825 and May 1826, when Mount, still in his first tenure as city resident, could have seen it. Although this play combined plentiful comedy with its pastoral sentiment, it communicated a serious agrarian moral: that the farm and village were havens of peace and prosperity, and the city the haunt of wickedness and materialism. The iconography of the agrarian message included, at the end of the first act, a spontaneous, joyous country dance by harvesters on their way to dinner after the morning labors. The grand finale also featured harvest celebrations: dancing, singing, feasting, and praising the worthiness of the American farmer. What was meant to appear spontaneous, natural, and simple here would have been the result of choreography devised to create a theatrical set piece, both idealized and stylized and far more aesthetically coherent than any actual barn dance was likely to be. Mount's precisely placed and artfully poised figures may very well have owed some inspiration to *The Forest Rose* or other pastoral plays in which musical set pieces were standard offerings. Compounded more of art than of nature, *Dancing on the Barn Floor* is a work of pictorial stage-craft and choreography, presenting rustics as performers who with their lively steps and ingratiating looks seek to win the spectator's applause.

Dance of the Haymakers (Illus. 65), the third and last of Mount's country dance scenes, is more complex than *Dancing on the Barn Floor* and seems less inclined to woo the observer with obvious ploys. It is still a performance, however, the considerably more polished production of a painter in his prime. From the barn—stage framing device to the interesting array of watchers (including two girls, one black and one white, in the hayloft, segregated like Jewish women in an orthodox synagogue), the ragged black boy outside beating time on the door with a pair of sticks, the violinist with his grin, and especially two dancing men hopping and skipping one around the other, the composition is the kind of coherent, smoothly coordinated ensemble that might be seen in a still from some Hollywood musical of the 1950s. Paradoxically, individual elements of *Haymakers* are intensely real. Not only are details and textures recorded with masterly skill, but several of the models have been identified as inhabitants of Stony Brook, including the violinist; those still unidentified were very likely locals as well.[25] The conception, however, is just as intensely theatrical, and although the men's steps are thought to represent a jig, very similar stylized academic attitudes were used, for example, by the French neoclassical peasant painter Léopold Robert in his salon productions, such as *Return from the Pilgrimage to the Madonna dell'Arco* (Illus. 66). Like Mount's nearest dancer, Robert's peasants even wore their shirts unfastened, exposing their chests, as if to proclaim their freedom from the suffocating restrictions of polite society.

Despite their pedigreed poses, Mount's haymakers are unmistakably meant to be seen as capering yokels. Compare the decorum required by Long Island dancing classes, as spelled out in a list of rules by Nelson Mathews, a local teacher. Rule 10 stated: "No gentleman will be permitted to dance in boots, or an overcoat, or any fantastic dress whatever, on penalty of being expelled from the School."[26] Mount's haymakers would not have lasted five minutes in such a class; their big boots, flying shirttails, unfettered necks, and strange headgear (one wears a red and black striped stocking cap) brand them as country clowns, amusingly occupied in a rude frolic. As in the other pictures, the dancers and their companions are putting on a show, filled with theatrical merriment and deliberate uncouthness, for the diversion of urban onlookers.

Mount's dancing pictures do admit of other readings. They

could be seen as celebrations of natural, happy manners in the country, where nothing more is needed for pleasure than a fiddle, a drink, and a floor to dance upon. They could be seen as idealizations of actual circumstances familiar to Mount from his rural upbringing. A work like *Dance of the Haymakers* could even be perceived in a moralizing light. The presence of the slightly tattered, somewhat disreputable man in a tailcoat, with a corked earthenware jug (identical to the old drunkard's in *Loss and Gain*) nearby, at least hints at a subtext about the devil's finding work for idle hands—and feet. It is also true that there is little overt condescension in the painting. Mount depicted these celebrants—people he knew—as individuals, without obtrusive caricature.[27]

For all that, there remains the image of the barn as a stage where rustic louts cavort to the tunes sawed out by a country fiddler. An urban viewer would not fail to recognize the differentness of the players in Mount's scene, players who were, in Henry Tuckerman's words, the "primitive people of his native place." Like modern Hawaiians going through the motions of the hula for off-islanders, Mount's high-steppers were putting on their act for the art-gallery promenaders or for armchair tourists who purchased the lithograph issued by Goupil, Vibert & Co. (as *Music Is Contagious*) in 1849.

Although the country dance was not a major theme in rustic genre after Mount, such scenes as there were did exhibit the same apparatus of contrivance and spectacle. The performance aspects emerged clearly in Asher B. Durand's 1851 *Dance of the Haymakers* (private collection), a much more mellifluous pastoral than Mount's vigorous "kickups." Here, several harvesters engage in a round dance, while others—one clothed like a peasant in smock and leggings—watch the dance as they rest and picnic in graceful groups. But from afar, on the left, the entire cast of harvesters is observed by a country gentleman and his lady—well dressed, well mounted, obviously leisured. Discounting its marked sentimentality, Durand's painting reveals the likely structure of the relation between viewers and imagery in the case of Mount's dancing pictures: viewers well distanced and detached; performers suitably rustic in dress and action, miming simple rustic happiness.

In the popular visual media, the case was the same. Winslow Homer's wood-engraved illustration *The Dance after the Husking* (Illus. 67) closely recalls Mount's *Rustic Dance after a Sleigh Ride*. Again, in a sparsely appointed New England inn, blooming country girls pair off with energetically capering country bucks. Refreshment comes from a cider keg; and a fiddler and a trumpet player provide the tunes. The Currier & Ives 1868 lithograph *The Old Barn Floor* repeats Mount's barn-dance formula in blackface. In this idyllic scene a black banjo player accompanies a dancing black boy for an audience (whose ever-smiling condescension is implicit, given the climate of the times) comprising the white farmer, his wife, and their baby.

While the legacy of Mount's country dances was relatively insignificant, his own designs, popular and widely reproduced, surely made a strong impression on the picture-consuming audience, helping to strengthen unconscious prejudice and reinforce stereotypes. His works represented the quintessence of that class of country genre that invited amused condescension. The audience that saw those dance scenes beheld a charming, convincing, but subtly distorted and trivialized image of American country life as musical comedy. At bottom, such images were paradigms of what was even then well under way: the subordination of the country and agriculture to the expanding and powerful world of the city and capitalism.

PREPARING FOR MARKET.

55.   Richard Earlom after Francis Wheatley, *Preparing for Market*, 1799. Mezzotint, 18″ × 23¾″. Published by B. B. Evans, London. (Reproduced by courtesy of the Trustees of the British Museum, London)

136 ▪ *The Changing Image of the Yankee Farmer*

PREPARING FOR MARKET.

56.   Louis Maurer, *Preparing for Market*, 1856. Lithograph,
18″ × 27¼″. Published by Currier & Ives, New York. (The Harry
T. Peters Collection, Museum of the City of New York)

Rural repose

57. T. Geremia after Francis Wheatley, *Rural Repose*, 1804.
Stipple engraving, $13\frac{1}{4}'' \times 16\frac{3}{4}''$. (Reproduced by courtesy of the
Trustees of the British Museum, London)

58. William Sidney Mount, *Farmers Nooning*, 1836. Oil on canvas, $20\frac{1}{4}'' \times 24\frac{1}{4}''$. (The Museums at Stony Brook, New York; gift of Mr. Frederick Sturges, Jr., 1954)

59. E. Scott after George Morland, *Boys Robbing an Orchard*,
1802. Stipple engraving, 11½″×15″. Published by Peter Brown,
London. (Reproduced by courtesy of the Trustees of the British
Museum, London)

60. William Sidney Mount, *The Truant Gamblers*, 1835. Oil on canvas, 24″ × 30″. (Courtesy of The New-York Historical Society, New York City)

61. William Sidney Mount, *Walking the Line,* 1835. Oil on canvas, 22¼″ × 27½″. (Mr. and Mrs. William Owen Goodman Collection, 1939.392; © 1988 The Art Institute of Chicago. All Rights Reserved)

62. William Sidney Mount, *Rustic Dance after a Sleigh Ride*, 1830. Oil on canvas, 22″ × 27¼″. (Courtesy of Museum of Fine Arts, Boston; bequest of Martha C. Karolik for the M. & M. Karolik Collection of American Paintings, 1815–65)

THE DANCE.

63. *The Dance*, c. 1845. Lithograph, $8\frac{1}{2}'' \times 12\frac{3}{4}''$. Published by
E. B. and F. O. Kellogg, Hartford, Connecticut. (The Harry T.
Peters "America on Stone" Lithography Collection, Smithsonian
Institution)

64.   William Sidney Mount, *Dancing on the Barn Floor,* 1831. Oil
on canvas, $24\frac{5}{8}'' \times 29\frac{5}{8}''$. (The Museums at Stony Brook, New York;
gift of Mr. and Mrs. Ward Melville, 1955)

65. William Sidney Mount, *Dance of the Haymakers,* 1845. Oil
on canvas, 24½″ × 29⅞″. (The Museums at Stony Brook, New York;
gift of Mr. and Mrs. Ward Melville, 1950)

66.   Léopold Robert, *Return from the Pilgrimage to the Madonna dell'Arco near Naples at Whitsuntide*, 1827. Oil on canvas, $55\frac{7}{8}'' \times 83\frac{3}{4}''$. (Musée du Louvre; Cliché des Musées Nationaux, Paris)

THE DANCE AFTER THE HUSKING.

67.   Winslow Homer, *The Dance after the Husking*. Wood engraving. *Harper's Weekly Magazine* 2 (November 13, 1858). (Bowdoin College Museum of Art, Brunswick, Maine)

7 ▪ *Jonathans*

HATEVER the degree of clownishness displayed by Mount's characters, ranging from none at all (the deadpan nobility of the farmer with his scythe; see Illus. 43) to outright foolishness (the dancing drunkard in *Walking the Line;* see Illus. 61), in their roles as either edifiers or entertainers they displayed a strong national and regional identity. However laughable or outlandish these rustic figures, their peculiarities were authentically American and therefore a cause for exultation. The good-humored condescension with which commentators regarded them was often tempered by a note of nationalistic pride—which the artist himself no doubt shared—that diverted attention from the less positive attitudes embodied in many of Mount's paintings.

This patriotic spirit, however, was an important component in the symbolic content of Mount's imagery, since it reflected the demand being sounded on nearly all cultural fronts—especially from the 1820s through the 1840s—for native arts based on American life and American manners. Mount's nationalism found expression in the figure of the Yankee, or "Jonathan," as typical American. His conceptions corresponded closely with the idea of the Yankee as it developed on the stage and in print during the same period.[1]

The origin of the term "Yankee" is obscure. It is thought to have been used by British soldiers during the Revolutionary War as an insult to the American rebels, but the colonists embraced it as a defiantly patriotic label declaring their separateness from the British enemy. After the war the name took on a more regional indentification with the Northeast and especially New England, but it continued to be understood more generally to designate an American. Explaining his decision to resist the temptations of Europe and remain at home, Mount told Charles Lanman, "I have always had a desire to do something before I went abroad. Originality is not confined to one place or country, which is very consoling to us Yankees." From whatever region, however, and whether clown, trader, peddler, or farmer, the Yankee was invariably a rustic. George Handel Hill, one of several actors who developed and popularized the role of the stage Yankee in the 1830s, defined Yankees as "country boys." Together, the image of the eccentric rustic and the connotations of strong, self-conscious national identity became the principal ingredients in the recipe for the figure of the quintessential Yankee.[2]

Writers tended to treat this character with a mixture of celebration and embarrassment. On one hand, the Yankee represented traits thought to be unique to American culture: he was unaffected, real; he was a farmer-philosopher and the trickiest trader anywhere. His language was richly colloquial. On the other hand, he symbolized a dire, clownish provincialism that could never mesh smoothly with the refinements of correct urban society. Nevertheless, the Yankee was, for a time, a triumphantly appropriate figure to represent the aggressively self-proclamatory Americanism of the antebellum decades. His ubiquity was reflected in a spate of humorous magazines: *Yankee Miscellany, Yankee Blade, Yankee Notions,* and *Yankee Doodle.* He appeared frequently in antebellum political cartoons as a symbol of America and stands as ancestor to the modern figure of Uncle Sam.[3]

The type of the Yankee had its genesis in Royall Tyler's play *The Contrast.* First performed in 1787, *The Contrast* pitted a homespun but canny American countryman (in a minor but vivid role) and his friend Colonel Manly against the foppish affectations of fashionable New York society. Tyler's salty prototype inspired imitations that gradually elaborated and refined the character. Dialect poems by Tyler, Thomas Green Fessenden, and others contributed to the formation of the archetypal Yankee, as did the popular Yankee monologue, drawn from folk sources, newspapers, and almanacs and used originally as a filler to enliven the intervals during long theatrical evenings. The term "Jonathan" gained wide currency through its repeated use as a name for Yankee characters: Jonathan Jolthead in Fessenden's poem "The Country Lovers" (1804); the representative American versus the British in James Kirke Paulding's political satire *John Bull and Brother Jonathan* (1812); and, most memorably, Jonathan Ploughboy in Samuel Woodworth's *Forest Rose* (1825).

By the mid-1830s, when Mount began to create his own memorable gallery of Yankee characters, the Yankee Jonathan had become an extraordinarily popular character in prose and on the stage. As a contemporary observer of the theater commented, "There cannot be a doubt, that among the many mirth-moving subjects which are so greedily caught up by the caricaturists of the day, none are so irresistible as those which come under the title of 'national peculiarities,' and that among all the nations of the globe none are more open to ridicule, or possess more laughable peculiarities, than a certain portion of the American continent who vegetate in that section of the universe, known and distinguished by the very definite *soubriquet* of 'Down East,' and who rejoice in the euphonious appellation of 'Yankee.' "[4] Until the 1850s, Yankee plays flourished in the theaters of New York, Philadelphia, Boston, and even western towns such as Cincinnati. Actors James Hackett, George Handel "Yankee" Hill, Danforth Marble, and Joshua Silsbee enjoyed great success impersonating Yankee characters in *The Forest Rose, The Green Mountain Boy* (1833) by Joseph Jones, and the Cornelius Logan play first called *The Wag of Maine* (1834) and later retitled *Yankee Land*—among the most typical of dozens of such plays.[5]

The first of the true Yankee plays, Woodworth's pastoral opera *The Forest Rose; or, American Farmers,* at once summarized the development of the Yankee in earlier writing and established, in the character Jonathan Ploughboy, a vivid model for subsequent stage Yankees with their backwoods monikers: Solomon Swop, Jedediah Homebred, Lot Sap Sago, Solon Shingle. It remained among the most popular of Yankee theatrics as well, enjoying regular revivals for some forty years after its first performance on October 7, 1825, at the Chatham Garden Theatre in New York. Yankee agrarian and crafty trader, Jonathan Ploughboy serves as foil for the conventional manners and predicaments of the serious characters. He describes his occupation to the smooth city gentleman Blandford as "a little in the marchant way, and a piece of a farmer besides." In his shop he sells the same collection of oddments one might find in a Yankee peddler's pack: "whiskey, molasses, calicoes, spellingbooks, and patent gridirons" (1.3). He wears homespun, plays the mouthharp, and speaks in the vernacular. He is singularly inept in the field of love, being spurned by one maiden and held up as buffoon by another. In questions of gain, well- or ill-gotten, his conscience struggles against acquisitiveness. When the corrupt English dandy Bellamy gives him a purse full of money to help carry out a nefarious scheme of seduction, the Yankee muses, "I don't calculate I feel exactly right about keeping this purse; and yet I believe I should feel still worse to give it back" (2.3). Despite his apparent simplicity, in the end Jonathan helps vanquish the scheming Bellamy, thereby affirming the superiority of rustic American sense and decency over foreign affectation and duplicity.[6]

Joining the stage Yankee in fame was the figure of the Down East political philosopher, first incarnated by Seba Smith as Major Jack Downing. Descended from Tobias Smollett's peripatetic heroes Peregrine Pickle and Humphrey Clinker and Benjamin Franklin's Poor Richard, Jack Downing was himself the ancestor of such rustic sages as Thomas Chandler Haliburton's Sam Slick, James Russell Lowell's Hosea Bigelow, and, after the Civil War, Henry Wheeler Shaw's Josh Billings. Smith, editor of the *Portland* (Maine) *Courier,* published the first Major Jack Downing letter in January 1830:

To Cousin Ephraim Downing, up in Downingville
Dear Cousin Ephraim:

I now take my pen in hand to let you know that I am well, hoping these few lines will find you enjoying the same blessing. When I come down to Portland I didn't think o' staying more than three or four days, if I could sell my load of ax handles and mother's cheese and Cousin Nabby's bundle of footings. . . . I've been here now a whole fortnight and if I could tell ye one half I've seen, I guess you'd stare worse than if you'd seen a catamount, I've been to meeting and to the museum, and to both Legislaters, the one they call the House and the one they call the Sinnet. I spose Uncle Joshua is in a great hurry to hear something about these legislaters.[7]

Major Downing soon graduated from local legislative gossip to reports on the national scene. From Washington and other places he sent his rustic relatives a long series of rambling accounts, touching on everything from congressional wrangling (members "shooting" their speeches at one another louder than guns and cannons) to the nullification crisis, Manifest Destiny, and the war with Mexico. In the early years it was Smith's conceit to make the Major the unofficial right-hand man and confidante of the "Gineral," President Andrew Jackson, from which vantage point he could deliver his homely, deceptively naive rustic's opinions on the American political scene.

The original Smith/Downing letters were published and widely read in Smith's book *The Life and Writings of Major Jack Downing of Downingville, Away Down East in the State of Maine, Written by Himself* (1833), which went through eight editions; Downing's later adventures were collected in *My Thirty Years out of the Senate* (1859). There were also numerous spurious and pirated editions, and individual letters (both the genuine and imitation) were widely circulated, especially in 1833, when at least twenty-nine newpapers (probably many more) published them. Iron merchant Charles Augustus Davis, Mount's friend and patron, wrote his own series of Downing letters, which in book form went through ten editions between 1834 and 1836.[8] The Major, his family, and various cronies even joined the stage Yankee in several plays or theatrical sketches during the mid-1830s, when, to judge by the outpouring of publications, Jack Downing's popularity was at its peak. In 1834 W. F. Gates had the Major's part in the skit *Life in New York; or, the Major's Come.* Almost at the same time the more famous Yankee comedian James Hackett starred in *Major Jack Downing; or, the Retired Politician.* In 1835 George H. Hill played Jack in *Lion of the East* (perhaps meant as a kind of complementary piece to *Lion of the West,* a play made famous by Hackett, featuring Colonel Nimrod Wildfire, backwoods frontier cousin of the Major).

Nothing could have been more folksy than the Major and

the environment from which he emerged and drew his character. His relatives had quaint names—Grandfather Zebedee, Cousins Ephraim and Nabby, Uncle Joshua, "Ant" Keziah—and they planted their gardens in "punkins" and " 'arbs." They stood in plain, countrified counterpoint to the muddled, mystifying political scene described by Jack in letter after letter, often in homely rustic metaphors: cornhuskings refer to elections, or to the passage of bills through the legislature.

Jack's innocent rustic perception, however, thinly veiled his role as a critic of Jacksonian democracy and Jacksonian policies. Ostensibly the common man, Jack was in truth the blunderbuss for a conservative view of Jackson and his sycophantic entourage as a volatile, arbitrary, potentially destabilizing force that encouraged political incompetence (the making of policy by those as untutored and naive as Jack himself) in the name of mass democracy. If this was a subtle undercurrent in Smith's Downing letters, it was overt in Davis's, which concentrated, with a Whig's dismay, on Jackson's high-handed attack on the Second Bank of the United States. It is possible, then, to view Jack in at least two ways: as a pastoral innocent somehow sly and shrewd enough to cut to the bone of truth in his observations, or as an untutored, bumbling *naif* (type of the common man), a kind of political idiot savant whose remarks—couched in rude Down East vernacular—hit home in spite of himself.[9]

The distinguishing Yankee qualities of Jonathan Ploughboy and Jack Downing were reproduced in dozens of other Yankees and Jonathans. The composite Yankee would be very much like the one described in the mid-1820s by actor James Hackett:

The *Yankees* are
> *Enterprising and hardy—cunning* in *bargains—back* out without *regard to honour—superstitious* and *bigoted—simple* in *dress* and *manners—mean* to degree in *expenditures —free of decep.—familiar* and *inquisitive,* very fond of telling *long* stories without any *point,* which just as they appear to approach is diverted by some new digres-sion—when they finish, will laugh *themselves,* and never care whether the listener does or not—the only sure way of knowing when they are done is their throwing away a chip or stick, which they invariably keep whittling while telling a story, and putting their *knife* in their waistcoat pocket, after sitting an hour on a wood-pile.[10]

Despite its standardization, the concept of the Yankee was as much folk reality as literary conceit. Jonathan Ploughby and Jack Downing were neither entirely false nor absolutely true; they represent seamless conjunctions of the real and the ideal. The case of George H. Hill demonstrates how such conjunctions were forged. In 1835 Hill and playwright Joseph Jones visited the Massachusetts villages Raynham and Taunton, where the actor had passed some years of his boyhood. Notebooks in hand, Hill and Jones wandered about the area, a rich repository of Yankee folk and legend, and sought to record the genuine raw material out of which they would later devise new Yankee plays. Still, they obviously not only selected a limited amount of the available material but also later polished it and shaped it to conform with popular stereotypes. Travel writers too were more likely to describe the colorful and eccentric sorts encountered during their peregrinations rather than the truly common and unremarkable man.

Such selective description, like selective breeding, produces a homogeneous race in the end; thus, descriptions of Yankees, whether in fiction or in documentary prose, became virtually interchangeable. In *John Bull and Brother Jonathan,* Knickerbocker writer James Kirke Paulding drew an elaborate picture of the typical Yankee country boy; he was

a rawboned, long-sided, rosy-cheeked, light-haired lad, who seemed gaping about as if he had just thrust his nose into the world. He wore a light-blue linsey-woolsey coatee, no waistcoat, and a pair of tow linen trousers, that, by reason of his having outgrown them, reached just below the calf of his leg; but what they wanted in length they made up in breadth, being of that individual sort called by sailors cannon-mouthed. But what most particularly fixed the . . . attention was a white hat, which, on account of its having been often caught in the rain, had lost its original outline, and marvellously resembled a haystack in shape and color.

This figure was leaning over a gate, with one hand scratching his head, and supporting his chin with the other, in the true style of listlessness and simplicity.

The "genuine Yankee" described by the traveler Alexander MacKay in the mid-1840s seems older brother to Paulding's imaginary character. While waiting for the departure of a steamboat from Washington, D.C., MacKay beheld this singular figure:

Apart from the rest was one whose demeanor and attitude soon attracted my attention. In leaning against a post, his tall emaciated figure fell into a number of indescribable curves. . . . His face was so sunburnt that it vied in brown with the long, loose, threadbare frock coat which, from his reclining position, hung perpendicularly from his shoulders. Deep furrows traversed his sallow cheek. . . . In his hand was a large clasp-knife, with which he was whittling to a very fine point a piece of wood he had sliced from the post. In this occupation he appeared absorbed; but on closely watching him, you could see that from under his matted eyebrows he was looking at everybody and observing everything. . . . He was a thorough type of the genuine Yankee, concealing much curiosity, cunning, and acuteness beneath a cold, impassive exterior.[11]

During his idyll on his estate Glenmary (near Owego, New York) in the late 1830s, Nathaniel Parker Willis took almost as much interest in his rustic neighbors as he did in the beautiful, pastoral valley of Owego Creek, with its Claudian delights of curvilinear, cultivated scenery. He too had a Yankee acquaintance of the same family as Paulding's and MacKay's. This man, a small farmer, would stop to exchange cordialities whenever he encountered the writer ensconced in his favorite spot under a picturesque bridge:

He is a shrewd man withal, likes to talk, and speaks Yankee with the most Boeotian fetch and purity. Imagine a disjointed-looking Enceladus, in a homespun sunflower-colored coat, and small yellow eyes, expressive of nothing but the merest curiosity, looking down on me by throwing himself over the railing like a beggar's wallet of broken meats. . . . Now, is not this a delicious world, in which, out of a museum, and neither stuffed nor muzzled, you may find such an Arcadian?

There is an ironic accent in the use of the term "Arcadian" to describe this exotic fellow, adorned by Willis's tongue-in-cheek classical erudition, with its references to a mythological Greek giant and the provincial boorishness associated with the Boeotians. Later in the same series of letters Willis sketched a similar type whom he summed up as a "genuine Jonathan."[12]

Even historical figures might coincide with stereotype, as in the case of Horace Greeley, who throughout his career retained—as a badge of distinction, perhaps—the rough-edged rusticity of his youth. Dr. Thomas Low Nichols wrote in his autobiography, "If I were asked to select a model Yankee, I should take the young Horace Greeley." This green New Hampshireman, arriving in New York, was "tall, lanky, near-sighted, awkward" and dressed in a "suit of blue cotton jeans," in addition to which he owned "two brown shirts." Later on, Greeley cut a peculiar, anachronistic figure in long coat, old white hat, and the chin-saucer beard that admirers cultivated and christened a "Greeley."[13]

Mount's pictorial conceptions should be examined in the context of this varied Yankee lore. The connections between Mount and the theater are direct. In New York in 1825 the young artist boarded with his uncle Micah Hawkins, who kept a tavern and grocery on Catherine Slip, wrote songs, and created the comic operetta *The Saw Mill; or, A Yankee Trick,* which was performed at the Chatham Garden Theatre in 1824. This piece set an important precedent for Yankee plays soon to follow. Mount's years of closest involvement with New York culture coincided precisely with the rise of Yankee theater, and there can be little doubt that he saw or heard about a number of these productions. He appears to have been a regular and enthusiastic theatergoer.

He even made a few sketches of characters in plays he had seen, although not all of these were from Yankee plays.[14] Since Mount knew Charles Augustus Davis, he must have been familiar with Davis's Jack Downing letters and probably knew Smith's as well. There can be little question that the image of the Yankee existed in Mount's mind as a representative and highly paintable American type. A culturally engaged, nationalistic artist in the 1830s could scarcely avoid being well acquainted with the archetypal Yankee in his various manifestations.

In his paintings of the mid-1830s Mount drew upon the popular fund of Yankee types for his portrayals of country folk. It is true that his farmers and barflies do not bear much physical resemblance to the lanky scarecrows described by writers. Mount used local models and was probably fairly faithful to them, as it suited his needs. One could even protest that Long Island was not a part of Yankee-land at all, but that would be to insist on an arbitrary geographical limit. Mount's farmers may have been Long Islanders, but they were substantially Yankee in spirit, action, and attributes, as contemporary criticism demonstrates.

Critics of Mount's paintings praised his American, Yankee spirit almost as often as they compared him to Wilkie or marveled at his perfect imitation of nature. *Farmers Nooning* (Illus. 58), for example, was "truly American." *Raffling for the Goose* (see Illus. 77), exhibited as *The Raffle* at the National Academy, prompted a reviewer to say: "We can never enough admire the talent for observation which this gentleman's compositions evince. They are all American. We could almost say that they are all of Long Island. And this is in our estimation a beauty." Later, Edgar Allan Poe, remarking on A. Lawson's engraving after *The Raffle,* admired the "varied expression of the Yankee faces" grouped intently around the table where the prize, a fat goose, reposed. *Coming to the Point* (1854; New York Public Library), a later variant on the theme of *Bargaining for a Horse* (see Illus. 70), impressed one journalist as "an image of pure Yankeeism and full of wholesome humor." Even *Who'll Turn the Grindstone?*

(1850; Whitney Museum of American Art, New York), a literary painting not strongly regional in accent, was described as one of Mount's "characteristic Yankee incidents."[15]

Mount produced some of his most Yankee-flavored paintings in a very short span of time during the mid-1830s: *Long Island Farmer Husking Corn,* 1833–34; *The Long Story,* 1837; *Bargaining for a Horse,* 1835; and *Winding Up,* 1836 (see Illus. 68, 69, 70, 72). Their creation coincided with the height of Jack Downing's fame and with the true flowering of Yankee theater. On at least three occasions the paintings exerted a reciprocal influence, generating Yankee stories based on their imagery.

Long Island Farmer Husking Corn (Illus. 68) was one of the latter. This little canvas, which Mount said had been painted "in the open air—the Canopy of heaven for my paint room," foreshadows *Farmer Whetting His Scythe.*[16] The farmer must have been a local, a neighbor, and his irregular profile, with long nose and double chin, suggests that Mount copied his model faithfully enough. His costume is the standard farmer's garb of white shirt, vest, and neckerchief; soft, low-crowned, broad-brimmed hat; baggy trousers and work boots. He stands in the autumnal cornfield, stripping the husk from an ear of corn, with a big wicker basket of naked ears behind him.

There is little here to associate with Yankee notions except in the general sense that the painting represents a countryman in work clothes. The image became "Yankee-fied" post facto, in 1844, when Robert Hinshelwood's engraving after the painting, retitled *Uncle Joshua,* appeared in the gift-book annual *The Wintergreen,* accompanied by a bit of Jack Downing folklore in the style of Seba Smith:

This ere pictur is as much like Uncle Joshua, when he was about forty-five years old, as two peas in a pod. And well it may be, for it was drawed from real life; and there aint no more nateral picters in the world, than them that's drawed from nater. I well remember when it was made, and the way it was done. It was a good many years ago, a little before Giniral Jackson was elected president, Uncle Joshua was in the field one day, harvesting corn. He was in his shirt sleeves, for he always worked with his coat off, unless the weather was cold enough to freeze a bear. He had on a pair of green fustian trowses, and an under-jacket of the same.[17]

Mount's image of the farmer husking corn, which was also engraved on more than twenty-five denominations of currency in ten or more states, gained a cultural pedigree by virtue of this paragraph, and Uncle Joshua acquired a pictorial counterpart.

The Long Story (Illus. 69) probably derived from the lore of the Yankee as a teller of pointless, interminable tales, an attribute noted by James Hackett in the Yankee character sketch quoted above. This characteristic was brought to the stage, first in monologue form and then incorporated into the Yankee play itself by George H. Hill, who made sure that his writers allowed ample flexibility for the insertion of a few Yankee stories and high jinks. By 1830 the notion of endlessly meandering labyrinths of speech was virtually inseparable from the idea of the Yankee—except when he attempted to court a girl: in that situation he often became tongue-tied.

The Long Story is clearly descended from Dutch and English tavern scenes, but its classical triangular composition lends an uncommon, spare geometry to the homely figures grouped around the woodstove of the tavern. Encircling the stovepipe, which precisely bisects the canvas, are the traveler, mysterious in his long, dark cloak and masking cap; the stolid landlord puffing on his clay pipe, and the storyteller, whose bandaged head, swaddled leg, crutch, whiskey glass, and overturned hat spilling out playing cards neatly summarize the temperance moral. There is a carefully arranged litter of painstakingly described props: fire tongs and shovel, a log, and the plain board base of the stove; the pipe, mug, and glass on top of it; and even a handbill, tacked to the rear wall, advertising the "Long Island Rail Road."[18]

In a letter to his patron Robert Gilmor, Jr., of Baltimore, Mount broke his usual reticence about the expressive and narrative content of his paintings to create a miniature scenario for *The Long Story:*

The man puffing out his smoke is a regular built Long Island tavern and store keeper, who amongst us is often a General or Judge, or Post master, or what you please as regards standing in society. . . .

The man standing wrapt in his cloak is a traveller . . . only waiting the arrival of the stage. . . . The principle [sic] interest to be centered in the old invalid who certainly talks with much zeal. I have placed him in a particular chair which he is always supposed to claim by right of profession, being but seldom out of it. . . . A kind of Bar room oracle, chief umpire during all seasons of warm debate whether religious, moral, or political, and first taster of every new barrel of cider rolled in the cellar, a glass of which he now holds in his hands while he is entertaining his young landlord with the longest story he is ever supposed to tell, having fairly tired out every other frequenter of the establishment.[19]

Certain references and word choices here suggest that Mount was offering Gilmor his own long story, compounded from current Yankee mythology. He noted that men like the landlord were often known as "General" or "Judge," honorifics of the same sort as Jack Downing's "Major" and indicating the same class of half-mythical folk-heroic types. He refers to the chair that the old toper is always "supposed" to claim, and the longest story he is ever "supposed" to tell, thereby offering a clue that his own tale is but hearsay, the transmittal of what are commonly understood to be Yankee traits.

It was this painting, engraved by Joseph Ives Pease and published as *The Tough Story* in another annual, *The Gift for 1842,* that gave Seba Smith his own opportunity to devise a long story. While much more fully elaborated, Smith's tale was strikingly similar to Mount's narrative, which he could not possibly have known. The similarities could only have come about because both painter and writer were so well acquainted with the same pool of lore and stereotype. In Smith's tale, called *The Tough Yarn,* the traveler is Major

Grant, who, stopping for the night at a "snug tavern" in a small Maine village, falls into talk with Dr. Snow, the local physician. Dr. Snow bets the Major that it will be impossible to get a straight answer to a plain question within half an hour from Jack Robinson, who just then hobbles on his crutch into the barroom. The Major blithely takes up the wager but soon discovers how stiff a challenge he has before him. To even the simplest query, Robinson has an interminable response. When the Major offers him a tumbler of hot flip, he says:

"I could drive twenty miles in a cold day with a good mug of hot flip easier than I could without it. And this *is* a cold day, gentlemen, a real cold day, there's no mistake about it. This norwestern cuts like a razor. But taint nothin near so cold as 'twas a year ago, the twenty-second day of this month. That day, it seemed as if your breath would freeze stiff before it got an inch from your mouth. I drove my little Canada gray in a sleigh that day twelve miles in forty-five degrees, and froze two of my toes on my lame leg stiff as maggots. Them toes chill a great deal quicker than they do on 'tother foot. In my well days I never froze the coldest day that ever blew. But that cold snap, the twenty-second day of last November, if my little gray hadn't gone like a bird, would have done the job for my poor lame foot. When I got home I found two of my sheep dead, and they were under a good shed, too. And one of my neighbors, poor fellow, went into the woods after a load of wood, and we found him the next day froze to death, leaning up against a beech tree as stiff as a stake. But his oxen was alive and well. It's very wonderful how much longer a brute critter will stan' the cold than a man will. Them oxen didn't even shiver."

Major Grant takes out his watch finally and—thinking that he has hit upon the right question—asks Robinson whether his lameness is in his foot or his leg. Robinson then launches into a kind of Yankee stream-of-consciousness monologue, touching on his innocent boyhood involvement in a theft, his narrow escape from death under a water wheel, and the time a big, black bear nearly gnawed off his feet. The half-hour elapses, and the Major loses the bet.

Though the details vary considerably in the Mount and Smith scenarios, their essence is the same. *The Tough Yarn* was collected in Smith's *'Way Down East; or, Portraitures of Yankee Life,* which was first published in 1854 and had gone through five subsequent editions by 1884. Unrelated to the Jack Downing letters, the tales in *'Way Down East* were homely, rustic sketches of ordinary and extraordinary episodes of Yankee life, most of which had been published previously in various journals: the *Knickerbocker Magazine, Godey's Ladies' Book,* and the like. What had originally been a pictorial fable had passed into prose as the definitive version of one of the most common Yankee stereotypes.[20]

Mount's *Bargaining for a Horse* (Illus. 70) is in the same way as definitive, as complete, as Smith's *Tough Yarn.* It is a perfectly staged Yankee anecdote, presenting stereotypes in a manner so fresh and lively that they seem newborn, not stereotypes at all. In this picture the artist synthesized two more Yankee hallmarks—sharp trading and whittling—into a comical picture intimately tied to established traditions of Yankee legend. Once again, a severe compositional understructure is layered over with polished detail and rustic humor. Each farmer is the other's counterpoint. One is silver-haired, the other young. The older one looks down as he cuts a fresh sliver from the twig he is whittling; the younger looks up, flourishing his knife at the end of a stroke. The elder wears a battered, broad-brimmed farmer's hat; his antagonist sports a dented top hat. They stand in a littered space of ground in front of an open shed. On the other side the horse for which they are presumably dickering (the original title was only *Farmers Bargaining*) stands silhouetted against a plank wall. On the left, at the end of the wall, space opens up into the background, giving a glimpse of a distant farmhouse and a woman squinting across the field as if to check on the progress of the deal.

Being a Yankee meant possessing the ability to drive a wily bargain, bring about a sharp trade, sell wooden nutmegs, and otherwise make an honest or dishonest profit handily. Peddlers and sly traders abounded in the Yankee stories and plays. Often, the main Yankee character in a play was a peddler with a name to match: Solomon Swap, Hiram Dodge, Zaccharia Dickerwell. Significantly, Micah Hawkins's comic opera *The Saw-Mill* was subtitled *The Yankee Trick*. Stories specifically concerned with sharp horse trading by or among Yankees included an anecdote told by Paulding in *John Bull and Brother Jonathan,* in which a Down Easter tricks an "Oatlander" (Canadian) in a horse-swapping deal:

The youth, after the fashion of Down East, first asked him [the Oatlander] what was his name, what countryman he was, where he came from, and where he was going; together with other questions equally necessary.

Having received satisfaction in these points, they fell to work, and our Oatlander never had tougher work in his life. At last, however, a bargain was struck, and he went on his way, chuckling at having taken in the clodhopper. All at once, however, his horse insisted on lying down, and his mirth came to the ground with him.[21]

Donald Grant Mitchell sketched a folksier, milder picture of farmers whittling away the time between morning and afternoon church services in a New England village:

Two or three of the more worldly-minded ones will perhaps stroll over to a neighbor's barn-yard, and take a look at his young stock, and talk of prices, and whittle a little; and very likely some two of them will make a conditional "swop" of "three likely ye'rlings" for a pair of "two-year-olds."[22]

Whittling was not only a ritual of bargaining; it was often associated with storytelling or time-killing. Captain Frederick Marryat, an Englishman who visited the United States in 1839 and reported his encounters with and thoughts about the Yankees (as did a considerable number of other foreign visitors), noted early in his travelogue that "the Down Easters, as the Yankees are termed generally, whittle when they are making a bargain, as it fills up the pauses, gives them

time for reflection, and moreover prevents any examination of the countenance." Later, he penned a passage about whittling so exaggerated that it stands as a tall tale in its own right:

Whittling . . . is a habit, arising from the natural restlessness of the American when he is not employed, of cutting a piece of stick, or anything else, with his knife. Some are so wedded to it from long custom, that if they have not a piece of stick to cut, they will whittle the backs of chairs, or anything within their reach. A Yankee shown into a room to await the arrival of another, has been known to whittle away nearly the whole of the mantel-piece.[23]

There were probably not many Yankees who whittled to the lengths—or depths—claimed by Marryat, but such exaggeration was intrinsic to the legendary aura of this all-American type. Whittling was a ubiquitous bit of stage business for Yankee character actors, too, as a contemporary print of Hill in a Yankee role (Illus. 71) suggests.

Like the *Long Island Farmer Husking Corn* and *The Long Story, Bargaining for a Horse* inspired a Jack Downing scenario, although it is not clear who wrote it. In this case it was the painting itself, not an engraving in a gift book (though *The Gift* did publish the illustration in 1840, engraved by Joseph Andrews), that stimulated the writer. In 1835 quite a few people, apparently, had seen the work at the home of Luman Reed, who had commissioned it. In October Reed sent Mount a copy of the *New York Gazette* containing a Downing story that included, as Reed told Mount, a scene based on the painting that "hits it exactly." In this sketch each of Mount's figures was given a Downingville name, and the pictorial moment was reinvented to include a role for the distant woman at the fence:

Seth suspended for a moment the whittling [of] his twig, and there seemed a crisis in the argument—*a silent pause*—when a shrill voice from the front gate adjoined [sic] the meeting instanter. It was the voice of Aunt Nabby herself, breathing authority and hospitality: *"Joshua, come to dinner, and bring the folks along with you."*

Mount responded: "I think the author studied the picture closely, please give my respects to the writer and tell him I was perfectly delighted with his conception."[24]

Of course, he had not set out to create a tableau featuring Uncle Joshua and Aunt Nabby, but the fact that the author of the sketch was able so effortlessly to translate picture into prose indicates once again the strength of agreement among forms of cultural expression during these antebellum years. Fact, fiction, folklore, and theater had generated a vivid image of the American rustic as a smooth haggler and indefatigable whittler, and this was the content that Mount's painting so clearly signaled. The two men are scarcely to be thought of as ordinary Long Island farmers at all. Rather, they are, and were meant to be seen as, quintessential Yankees—not particularly clownish figures but indeed part clown, in the sense that they enact eccentric, provincial Yankee rituals for the entertainment of the sophisticated onlooker.

Even more, the figure of the hopeful suitor in *Winding Up* (Illus. 72) embodied that aspect of the Yankee. Like some of Mount's other works, *Winding Up* was based on Dutch and English models, especially the rustic courtships devised by Francis Wheatley and Sir David Wilkie. Mount may have been familiar with prints after Wheatley's paintings, such as *The Rustic Lover* (Illus. 73), a pretty, idealized cottage scene overflowing with humble, rural charm. The tidy interior contains simple furniture and evidence of industry in the workbasket and spinning wheel. The cottage maiden, her fichu in becoming disarray, feeds a saucer of milk to a kitten on her lap, while her swain leans over the back of her chair and teasingly tugs the kitten's tail. The essential situation in both works is the same: humorously viewed love-in-a-cottage. Mount, however, preferred downright joking to the affected delicacy and sentimental treatment of the typical English rustic courtship motif.[25]

In *Winding Up*, a young woman stands near the fireplace in a rough cottage interior. Against this background, she seems incongruously fashionable in her coral dress with hugely puffed sleeves, her rope of shimmering beads, and her dainty black slippers. Her suitor, on the other hand, is clearly a farmer or perhaps another sort of bumpkin. Huddled into his shapeless, fur-collared overcoat, wearing a broad-brimmed hat and rough farmer's boots, he thrusts out his hands to hold up the hank of yarn from which his sweetheart winds her ball. Under his chair is a half-whittled stick. Although the subject is courtship (which was also the original title of the painting), there are no flowery sentiments here, no romantic sighs. Mount's presentation is light and sportive, as if the scene were a bit of business in a Yankee play.

The native roots of Mount's comedy extend back to the flurry of Yankee dialect "courtin' poems" written by the parodists in Royall Tyler's circle. Cast, like the country dance epics, in the New England vernacular and often set to the meter of "Yankee Doodle," these poems lampooned the insipid, floridly romantic Della-Cruscan love poetry recently in vogue in England and took a few swipes at the conventions of the pastoral poem as well. Deliberately deflationary, the Yankee dialect courtin' poems sang of love among country bumpkins who knew nothing of romantic conventions and rituals and who spoke in the homely figures and hilarious country metaphors of their native haunts.

Thomas Green Fessenden's "The Country Lovers; or, Mr. Jonathan Jolthead's Courtship with Miss Sally Snapper" is typical. It was published as a broadside in 1795 and collected in Fessenden's *Original Poems* in 1806. Fessenden's Jonathan, who can count to a hundred and has been to school "to spell a-bom-in-a-ble," is sent by his mother to court the deacon's daughter Sal, who is "as good a gal / As ever twisted yarn, sir." Sal is a sensible farm girl who will have a marriage portion of a hundred pounds. She has been to Boston market and "knows all about affairs"; she

> Can wash and bake and brew, sir,
> Sing "Now I lay me," say her prayers,
> And make a pudding too, sir.

Jonathan is a country innocent, ignorant and afraid of girls. His actions upon confronting Sal in her father's house are typical:

> Now Jonathan did scratch his head,
>   When first he saw his dearest;
> Got up—sat down—and nothing said,
>   But felt about the queerest.

After many uneasy minutes, Jonathan begins his declaration:

> "Miss Sal, I's going to say, as how,
>   We'll spark it here tonight,
> I kind of love you, Sal, I vow,
>   And mother said I might."

Too cowed by her bold look to "smack her," Jonathan proceeds to paint a vision of their married future, when they will live happily in "father's t'other room," which will be quite spacious for the pair once the loom is moved elsewhere. Sal, veteran of many a courtship duel, taunts Jonathan for being a green hick who went to Boston in his "streaked trowses" (striped trousers) and vowed he "could not see the town, / There were so many houses." Finally Jonathan suffers from such a fit of embarrassment that Sal has to douse him with a pail of cold water, reducing him to the status of "a drowned rat."[26]

This is the stuff of rustic romance in the Yankee courtin' poems. Deliberately uncouth and irreverent, they send up the lachrymose excesses of fashionable sentimentality. Commensurate with this spirit, Yankee Jonathans described themselves and their loves in the most stubbornly unromantic terms. The Jonathan in "Yankee Phrases" declares that his heart was "lighter than cork," and his body "fatter than pork" before he met the fatal temptress Jemima, "tall as a hay pole," with a smile "like a basket of chips." Because his passion is unrequited, Jonathan dwindles. He becomes "dull as a hoe," "weak as a rat," and expects soon to be "dead as a hammer" unless Jemima relents. Another Jonathan is in even worse straits, but Yankee common sense prevails in the end. After gazing longingly from behind a tree while his Jemima milks a cow, he creeps away in despair and decides to commit a Wertherian suicide for love:

> I took a rope and went away. . . .
>   My heart was sorer than a bile. . . .
> But when I got it round my neck,
>   I says, thinks I, it an't worth while.

Just as flowers become brambles in these verses, so do grand, tragic gestures become small and ridiculous.[27]

The Yankee courtin' poems figured as models for the Yankee plays, many of which included comic courtship scenes between either a bumpkin and a country maid or a bumpkin and a genteel young lady. Woodworth's *Forest Rose* had Jonathan Ploughboy in both situations, but by far the funnier is his browbeaten romance with Sally Forrest, the deacon's daughter. (Their names and Sally's paternity suggest a more than coincidental connection with Fessenden's "Country Lovers.") Woodworth's Sally is as mocking and teasing as Fessenden's Sal. When Jonathan pays a courting call, he reproaches her for her heartless flirtations with another bumpkin. She reminds him of her recent favors:

Sally: Now, Jonathan, didn't I sit on your knee last Sunday evening? Answer me that.
Jonathan: And, 'cause I happened to get asleep, didn't you get up softly, and put the big Tom-cat in your place? And didn't your father find me hugging it when he got up in the morning? Answer me that. I wouldn't serve a negro so.
Sally: Ha, ha, ha! Now, Jonathan, what difference can it make to a man that is fast asleep, whether he is hugging me or a Tom-cat? [1.2]

Repelled by Sally's tricks, Jonathan courts Harriet, a serious heroine who, though a farmer's daughter, is well-bred and refined, too good for him. After praising her as the smartest girl in the country, able to "milk a cow, make a cheese, and boil a pudding," Jonathan confesses his hesitation about proposing: "But . . . thinks I to myself, there can be no great harm in axing the question; and if I get the sack, says I to myself, I shan't be the first that's got it by hundreds." To this romantic declaration, Harriet retorts, "That is true, Jonathan, and you won't be the last by thousands" (1.4).

Winding Up shares the antic spirit of courtship in the Yankee poems and plays. A contemporary critic's appreciation reveals how closely painting and theater converged on the theme of the Yankee bumpkin, and how recognizable these types were to viewers of the period:

The group consists of a clown, rather beyond the median of life, who has been whittling a stick—(the employment painters have adopted for all Yankee clowns)—while admiring, and perhaps wishing to address a beautiful girl, young enough to be his daughter. . . . Jonathan's knife and half whittled stick is [sic] abandoned, and lies on the floor, while he sits, with crossed leg over knee, and wide-extended arms, awkwardly holding the damsel's yarn, stretching his clumsy fingers far apart to prevent its escape from his bony wrists.

The commentator went on to marvel at the beauty and tasteful apparel of the young woman, which "would be unnatural in the peasant-girl of Europe; but is perfectly characteristick of the yeoman's daughter of America." When the painting hung in the National Academy of Design exhibition the following year, another critic—or possibly the same writer—also remarked on the elegance of the farmer's daughter while he savored the visual puns in the composition: "Here is another Long Island scene by our American Wilkie. Can anything be more beautifully correct than the graceful figure, arch (yet modest) expression, of this American farmer's daughter? She has tasked her clownish admirer to hold the skein, while she *holds the ball in her own hands,* and is winding up a courtship not to her taste." [28]

Why did the first piece of criticism refer to the suitor as a clown and call him Jonathan? The clue of the whittled stick would immediately signal which stereotype this bumpkin represented; beyond that, surely this writer attended the theater and had seen Yankee plays with scenes that reminded him of this one. In identifying a certain type with the figure in *Winding Up* (although it remains unclear, from the pictorial evidence, why he thought "Jonathan" so much older than his companion; preconception may have played a role), he might have been thinking of Jonathan Ploughboy or other ill-fated Yankee suitors and of their bumbling attempts to "spark" their would-be sweethearts. He could have been familiar also with the Yankee courtin' poems, their inept Jonathans and confident Jemimas, never hesitant to "give the bag" to suitors who failed to please.

That Mount regarded his pictured suitor in the same way is suggested by the presentation. His "Jonathan" is very much the butt of a visual and verbal joke, centering on the winding of the yarn. To the distinctiveness of the Yankee whittler, Mount added this particularly American twist: the cleverly punned notion of "winding up." On one level there is the simple depiction of useful feminine employment: the young woman has been knitting a stocking, which lies nearby on the backless chair by the fireplace, and she has enlisted the help of her would-be lover to hold the skein while she winds up yarn into a fresh ball so that she may continue her work. But as the *New-York Mirror* commentator so readily understood, the visual presentation of the activity punned a familiar colloquialism. John Russell Bartlett's 1848 glossary of Americanisms defined it: "To Wind Up: To close up; to give a quietus to an antagonist in debate. Also intransitively, to shut up, to stop business." In Bartlett's political example of usage, a Whig senator from Tennessee effectively "wound up" a senator from Michigan, his opponent in debate. [29] The well-dressed farmer's daughter is quite clearly doing the same thing to her visitor. This winding up, as the critic perceived, signals the termination of her suitor's advances. This Yankee is as much a dupe and figure of fun as Jonathan Ploughboy in *The Forest Rose,* when Sally puts the "big Tomcat" in his lap or when Harriet gives him "the sack." The light touch here, indeed, recalls the spoofing of romance in the dialect poems. One can imagine that if this Jonathan gets the bag, he too will decide that hanging himself because of it "an't worth while."

Mount's Jonathans and Joshuas ranged from the merely provincial to the ridiculous, but they were all essentially types of the Yankee. Clearly, he found as much to celebrate as to satirize in these figures, yet it cannot be said (as older writings on Mount claimed) that they have any but the most remote relation to the real America of the 1830s and 1840s. Mount's America was the land of the theater, the Downing letters, and the vernacular poem. It is in these images, too, that his ambivalence is unquietly present. It is now barely tenable to claim that Mount's compositions are simple exaltations of the Common Man in the age of Jacksonian De-

mocracy. There are far too many negative, denigratory, or satirical nuances threading his imagery to allow for that sunny interpretation. Like Seba Smith's Jack Downing, Mount's rustics appear now witty and shrewd, now naive and thickheaded. They may even be regarded as slyly undercutting the common man while seeming to glorify him. The circumstances of Mount's patronage do little to discourage this view. The men who commissioned his genre scenes included wealthy New Yorkers Henry Brevoort and Charles Augustus Davis, solid merchants Luman Reed and Jonathan Sturges, and Philadelphia publisher Matthew Carey. While some of these had rural or small-town roots, it seems plausible, from pictorial evidence alone, that what they required of Mount was less often a nostalgia piece than the staging of a comic performance by the Yankee boors of popular fame. At the same time, however, Mount's imagery cannot be detached from the cultural nationalism of his age. His Yankees were indubitably Americans—even though they might be but risible ones.

68. William Sidney Mount, *Long Island Farmer Husking Corn*, 1833–34. Oil on canvas, 21″ × 17⅛″. (The Museums at Stony Brook, New York; gift of Mr. and Mrs. Ward Melville, 1975)

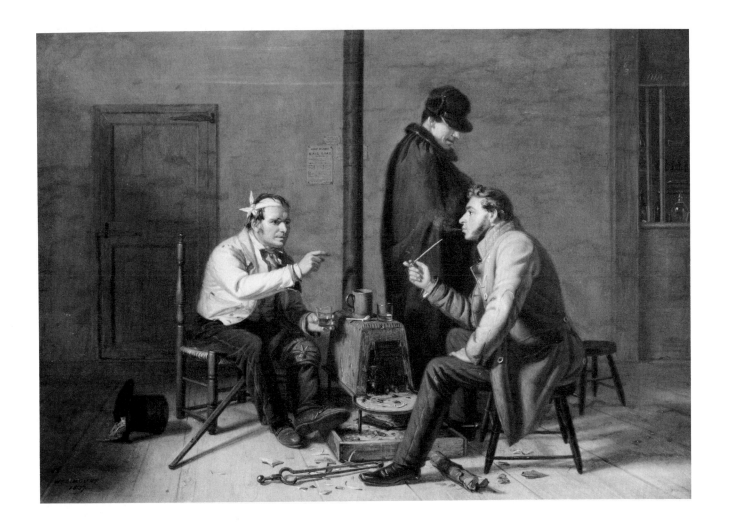

69. William Sidney Mount, *The Long Story,* 1837. Oil on panel, 17″×22″. (In the collection of the Corcoran Gallery of Art, Washington, D.C., Museum Purchase, Gallery Fund, 1874)

70. William Sidney Mount, *Bargaining for a Horse,* 1835. Oil on canvas, 24″×30″. (Courtesy of The New-York Historical Society, New York City)

71.   *George Handel Hill in Yankee Character,* c. 1835–45. Lithograph, $10\frac{13}{16}'' \times 8\frac{7}{16}''$. (Harvard Theatre Collection)

72. William Sidney
Mount, *Winding Up*,
1836. Oil on panel,
$18\frac{1}{2}'' \times 15''$. (The Nelson-
Atkins Museum of Art,
Kansas City, Missouri;
acquired through the
Enid and Crosby Kemper
Foundation)

THE RUSTIC LOVER. LE RUSTIQUE AMOUREUX.

Published 2d March 1787, by Bull & Jeffryes, Ludgate Hill.

73. C. Knight after Francis Wheatley, *The Rustic Lover*, 1787. Stipple engraving, 17″ × 14″. Published by Bull & Jeffryes, London. (Reproduced by courtesy of the Trustees of the British Museum, London)

■ *167*

8 ■ *Bumpkins by Contrast*

OR Mount's paintings of Jonathans, Yankees, and country dancers, the audience was by implication urban, as surely as if these painted figures had been brought to life to caper behind the footlights of New York's Park and Bowery Theatres. In several works by Mount and others, however, the urban view was made explicit, posing the rustic and the sophisticate side by side, most often to the detriment of the countryman. Like the images of happy rustics, these pictures had roots in England, where the encounters of urban fop and country bumpkin furnished humor for popular prints in the eighteenth century. The American contrast pictures are of value not only because they so clearly spell out the condescension visited upon the American countryman but also because their unambiguous content helps to confirm the likelihood that the images of rustics by Mount and his contemporaries are not to be taken at face value as hymns to the worth of the Common Man.

The Sportsman's Last Visit (Illus. 74) epitomizes the contrast picture. Unlike most, however, even in Mount's own *oeuvre*, it does not exploit the opposition of types to make the rustic appear an unadulterated fool or clodhopper. Although it does contain unexpected nuances, the painting merits extended consideration because of its pictorial discourse, which deliberates with a certain subtlety on issues of cultural and national identity.

In this courtship anecdote, one man's suit has been abruptly curtailed, and he stands by haplessly while his rival presses successfully on. In type, costume, and manner, each wooer is in complete contrast to the other. Stuffing one hand into the pocket of his bulky tan hunting jacket, the sportsman raises the other to scratch his head in a pantomime of bewilderment. Opposite him, the neat young man in black leans forward and gestures gracefully as he murmurs to his fair one. The sportsman is nonplussed; the suitor in black, self-assured. It is this pairing of opposites that generates the comic charge of the picture. The young woman plays a straight role. Like the farmer's daughter in *Winding Up* (see Illus. 72) she is fashionably dressed. In her high-style white gown with balloon sleeves and fancy black apron, she seems at odds with the plainness of her surroundings, but this mismatch is not part of the joke. She is the romantic interest of the trio, and there is no call for her to be funny.

Mount's strategy of pairing opposites paralleled and may

have been derived from the Yankee plays, which almost invariably advanced the plot and salted the comedy by staging intersection and conflict among various social types. The Yankee character sometimes attempted to court the genteel heroine; representatives of the rural and urban spheres routinely scoffed at, scorned, and insulted each other. In Woodworth's *Forest Rose,* for example, the heroine Harriet's only weakness is the longing to see city lights. In the first act the English fop, Bellamy, carrying a double-barreled gun for bird hunting, appears just as Harriet informs her earnest suitor William that since he is not gallant enough to take her to town, she must find someone who will.

William: Then, fare you well, for here comes a verification of the old proverb—the very thing you are speaking of—a scarecrow from the city. . . .
Harriet: A scarecrow! Why, he is a genteel, delightful looking fellow, neat as a starched tucker fresh from a bandbox. Why do you call him a scarecrow?
William: Because he frightens the birds without killing them.[1]

When he spies William through his quizzing glass (an urban affectation), Bellamy returns the compliment: "Who can the bumpkin be? By his dress, I take him to be damn'd low." He concludes that William is "a mere clodhopper" from whom Harriet may with perfect ease be detached. By such remarks, the mutual spheres of antagonism are established early in the play. Harriet sighs for the glamour of Bellamy, who is "a sportsman, and a foreigner" and, best of all, "dresses so genteelly." She is even foolish enough to consider his offer (tainted with ulterior motives) to make her the present of an expense-paid visit to New York. Events of the play, however, soon lead her to recognize the superior worth of honest yeoman William, and in the end Bellamy is unmasked as a villainous seducer.

Similar situations and banter are present in J. S. Jones's *Green Mountain Boy* (1833). In this play there is a romantic triangle consisting of a well-bred heroine; her suitor, a Navy officer; and an aristocrat, whom the heroine's father very forcefully wishes her to marry, though that wish is predictably thwarted in the end. There are also comic lovers, the servant girl Lucy and Jedediah Homebred, who introduces himself as "the smartest chap at a huskin' or log-rollin' in our parts, besides knowin' something about grammar." In one exchange of unpleasantries, the Yankee character expresses a contempt for urban and foreign refinements equal to the contempt the urban and the foreign profess toward lowly clodhoppers. Swapping insults with the lofty Lord Montague, Jedediah parses the noun "gentleman": "Gentleman is a distracted noun, ridiculous mood, past tense, and governed by the feminine gender."[2]

Another representative comedy, Cornelius Logan's *The Wag of Maine* (1833) revolves around thwarted serious lovers and the comic actions and misadventures of Mischievous Joe, a bear-hunting bumpkin who yearns for the unobtainable heroine Lavinia Marshall, daughter of an expatriate English lieutenant. After attempting in a ludicrous courting scene to steal Lavinia's affections from her gentleman lover, Mischievous Joe—like Jedediah Homebred—does his part in fending off the dangers that threaten a happy outcome.

In these plays, class and role distinctions were accentuated and symbolized by costume. The 1856 prompt book for *Yankee Land* (the 1842 version of *The Wag of Maine*) describes dress in careful detail, adhering quite closely to what had become established stereotypes derived from early performances of the plays. Lot Sap Sago (Mischievous Joe's new name) wears "Drab long tail coat, broad striped vest, eccentric striped trousers; straps and boots; yeoman crown hat; bright-colored cravat."[3] This describes the outfit of the stage Yankee, introduced in the 1820s by actors such as the Englishman Charles Mathews and the American James Hackett. For his debut at Covent Garden in 1827, Hackett wore a "genuine Yankee" costume: black hat, blue coat, flowered waistcoat, and blue striped trousers. On his second London tour in 1832, Hackett walked onto the Drury Lane stage in a long-tailed coat, bright vest, striped trousers, and red wig (see Illus. 71).[4] The stage Yankee's garb, reinforcing the message communicated by his bizarre accent and strange habits, marked him as a rustic eccentric. The serious characters wore more conventional dress. In *Yankee Land* the genteel lover Harvey is dressed in correct but not dandified fashion: "Blue coat, gilt buttons; black velvet vest; gray or black trousers; black hat." Such garb befits his role as romantic lead. As their contrasting costumes make plain, Harvey is a gentleman; Lot Sap Sago is a clown. Josephine (the erstwhile Lavinia) is described merely as wearing "white muslin," appropriate to her status as an English officer's daughter.

Costume and comic tone in Mount's *Sportsman's Last Visit* correspond on a number of points to elements in the Yankee plays. The comedy of Mount's scene recalls an episode in *The Wag of Maine* in which rustic bear-hunter Mischievous Joe, clumsy as the bumpkins in the courtin' poems, attempts to declare his devotion to Lavinia, only to be routed by her gentlemanly admirer. In *The Sportsman's Last Visit* the practiced, smooth-mannered gentleman has vanquished the unrefined country boy in the contest of love. Mount's young woman—like Ellen Tomkins of *The Green Mountain Boy* or Lavinia in *The Wag of Maine*—is genteel. She wears an ornamental apron and does fancywork instead of utilitarian sewing. The successful rival is impeccably arrayed in black. His high white stock rising to stiff points under the chin, his bow-tied cravat, tight sleeves, and long coattails squared off at the ends conform tastefully to the fashion of 1835.[5] The sportsman, though his costume falls short of caricature, has none of his rival's modishness. His plain tan coat falls loosely to his knees; his hunting gear is slung about his shoulders. His huntsman's dress recalls that of a character played by Charles Mathews: Jonathan W. Doubikins, a rifle-toting Yankee in sealskin vest and long, heavy, greenish-brown cloth coat (Illus. 75).[6] The sportsman's rust-colored vest is in style, with its double-breasted front and notched lapels, as are his bow-tied cravat and stovepipe hat—but he wears the latter indoors, committing a breach of correct manners.

In *The Sportsman's Last Visit* the suitor in black symbolizes urban manners, culture, and values. His garb would be recognized in that day as an expression of urban elegance and high status (though later this sober costume would take on more democratic connotations). Cornelius Mathews, one of the Knickerbocker writers, used the same costume symbolism in his satirical account of a New York City campaign between patrician and plebeian. The patrician candidate was "Herbert Hickock, Esq., a wholesale auctioneer and a tolerably good Latin scholar: a gentleman who sallied forth at nine o'clock from a fashionable residence in Broadway, dressed in a neat and gentlemanly suit of black, an immaculate pair of gloves, large white ruffles in his bosom, and a dapper cane in his hand." His opponent, Bill Snivel, was a shoemaker who wore layers of "unclean garments" and a "rusty, swaggering hat." Unequivocally, the gentleman was known by his correct dress, and the worker by his slovenliness.[7]

Despite its equally sharp contrast of costume, however, *The Sportsman's Last Visit* seems to equivocate. It presents the alternatives—city and country—in a relatively even-handed way. It weighs the respective merits of urban values and village culture; it measures the man of the parlor against the man of field and forest. Neither is made to appear repulsive or ridiculous, although viewer bias could easily color the perception of the imagery. Even the seemingly clear signals broadcast by costume blur a bit when one recalls that in *The Painter's Triumph* Mount depicted the figure of the artist in the dark, gentlemanly suit of a "Herbert Hickok, Esq.," but in *The Herald in the Country* he dressed his idealized self-portrait in a natty sportsman's outfit (see Illus. 78 and 79). In the Yankee plays the bear-hunting Mischievous Joe was not the only sportsman. In *The Forest Rose* both the treacherous dandy Bellamy and the pure-hearted city gentleman Blandon wore hunting costume.

Such garb, then, did not automatically signify a clodhopper. Mount's suitor in black may be the gentleman and the winner of the girl, but it is not clear that he represents an intrinsically superior human type. The sportsman is tall, trim, and handsome; although probably a country man, he is not a booby. His plain, functional dress and even the unmannerly hat on his head do not represent something intrinsically inferior to the gentleman but symbolize the exurban world where, as myth would have it, the best and most independent Americans led their lives.

To some, independence meant discarding the formalities and civilities of the aristocratic or upper-class behavior associated with American cities and European culture in general. The regular taunting, thwarting, and unmasking of dandified, villainous aristocrats in Yankee plays expressed that impulse, which had its foundation in the intense nationalism of the period. The lack of public decorum in America regularly appalled visitors from abroad. The Englishwoman Frances Trollope observed with dismay that in a Cincinnati theater "men came into the lower tier of boxes without their coats; and I have seen shirtsleeves tucked up to the shoulder; the spitting was incessant. . . . The bearing and attitudes of the men are perfectly indescribable; the heels thrown higher than the head, the entire rear of the person presented to the audience. . . ." Americans criticized their own countrymen as well. James Fenimore Cooper, no advocate of mass democracy, wrote in *The American Democrat:* "There is no doubt that, in general, America has retrograded in manners in the last thirty years. Boys, even men, wear their hats in the houses of all classes, and before persons of all ages and conditions. This is not independence but vulgarity."[8]

Defenders of American manners contended that republican citizens had no need for fancy frills of behavior, and if published commentaries are any index, Americans rather cherished their unique churlishness. The ever popular Nathaniel Parker Willis deplored the vogue for correct etiquette, which had set in, he thought, in reaction to Mrs. Trollope and other scornful critics: "Gracious heavens! Are we to have our national features rasped off by every manner-tinker who chooses to take up a file! . . . All well-bred people are monotonously alike. . . . Long live our . . . 'abom-

inations.' Long live *some* who spit and whittle, *some* who eat eggs out of wine glasses and sit on four chairs, *some* who wear long naps to their hats, *some* who eat peas with a knife, . . . and *some* who are civil to unprotected ladies in stagecoaches!"[9] In their republican independence, in short, Americans possessed a natural civility and a sense of right action that had nothing to do with how they ate their peas or sat on their chairs. In this light it is not so clear that Mount's sportsman is merely unmannerly because he has neglected to remove his hat. Rather, the omission offers a clue to his identity as the natural American, the rural American, the uncorrupted and unaffected product of farm or village, who needs neither starched collar nor suave gestures to disguise or "rasp off" his rough edges or to embellish the Republican simplicity of his deportment.

Such a meaning would reflect the emerging concept of a fundamental barrier between the two major yet antagonistic cultural regions of American life: rural and urban; an already fading vision of agrarian simplicity and the expanding urban world driven by a money economy. Considering the climate of moralistic opinion regarding the dangers of speculation and fashion display in urban America of the 1830s, it could be that Mount's sportsman is well away, now that his sweetheart has cast her lot with urban gentility and style. Given the fact that a number of observers then and later deplored the gradual surrender of village life to this same urban frivolity and materialism, there may be a spark of truth in this reading. There could be a trace of ruefully ironic folk wisdom here as well; one is reminded of a proverb in the *Farmer's Almanac:* "Flattery sits in the parlor, when plain dealing is kicked out of doors."[10]

The Francis William Edmonds painting *The City and the Country Beaux* (Illus. 76) was almost certainly inspired by *The Sportsman's Last Visit,* but in Edmonds's hands the contrast is intentionally ludicrous. Edmonds, a New Yorker who managed to juggle careers in banking and painting, admired and studied seventeenth-century Dutch genre painting, the work of Sir David Wilkie, and the art of Mount. He too chose subjects from American country and village life, presenting them as carefully crafted, miniaturized theatrical tableaux. Like *The Sportsman's Last Visit* but more strikingly, *The City and the Country Beaux* reminds us of the comic social contrasts in plays like *The Forest Rose* and *The Wag of Maine*. Edmonds's country beau is unmistakably a boor. His porcine torso and sprawling legs, his pantaloons—recalling the "eccentric, striped trousers" of Mischievous Joe—Lot Sap Sago—his cigar, spittoon, wilted collar points, and vacuous countenance overstep the border between description and caricature. Here is a true country booby of the sort satirized in a *Godey's Ladies' Book* story in which a bowlegged village dandy wore skintight pantaloons and combined a yellow vest with green coat and a purple-and-crimson plaid cravat.[11] The city beau is similar to Mount's in dress but altogether more self-conscious in action. Flourishing behind him his silk hat and cane and daintily holding his quizzing glass, or monocle, he smirks, bows, and makes a leg in the direction of his swinish foe. The pretty young woman who introduces the beaux to each other is as stylish as Mount's. Edmonds's painting bears the same relation to the Yankee plays as Mount's but is far more theatrical in the breadth and exaggeration of its stereotypes, gestures, and body language. It is this exaggeration that distinguishes Edmonds's version of the theme from Mount's, deprives it of nuance, and, for all its humor, announces a value judgment. There can be no contest between the coarse, lolling manner of the country lout and the exquisite, disciplined etiquette of the urban gentleman—unless the mincing mannerisms of the city beau are also the target of Edmonds's satirical pencil. Even so, the country beau is repellent, the city beau only slightly ridiculous.[12]

Mount used a similar strategy in *Raffling for the Goose* (Illus. 77). Here the town-bred elegance of the two men on the right serves to enhance the bumpkin coarseness of their companions. These fastidious visitors to a shabby rural dive (set in the tavern that once adjoined the Mount family house) wear visored caps, then the headgear of choice for the well-

dressed sportsman, and dashing greatcoats with frog fastenings, the height of fashion for urban dandies.[13] The other men, gathered closely around the makeshift plank table on its cider-keg base, form a motley provincial crew. All exhibit a raggle-taggle appearance, with the exception of the hatless man looking over the shoulder of one of the rafflers on the left. Given his relative spruceness, he too may be a city visitor; it is in his shiny, medium-tall top hat that the raffle tickets are being shuffled. The man looking out the door in the background, in his out-at-elbows coat and head scarf, is surely cousin to the dilapidated tale spinner of *The Long Story*. The remaining three surrounding the goose offer a spectacle of picturesque rustic variety: one wears a bulky tan jacket and low-crowned hat; another is in vest and shirt-sleeves, with the front brim of his hat rolled jauntily back from his forehead; the last displays a battered plug hat and ill-fitting vest. Their features are plain and their expressions animated.

The well-dressed pair, symbolizing a superior urban class, would by inference hold something like Nathaniel Willis's point of view in *Letters from under a Bridge*. During the time he played farmer at Glenmary in the late 1830s, Willis described the picturesque costume of his rustic hired helpers on the threshing-room floor: Jem the groom, a stout fellow wearing a rusty black broad-brimmed London hat, and a tenant who vaguely resembled a sailor in his "ripped and shredded" secondhand velvet redingote. Willis himself wore what he considered tasteful pastoral attire: cowhide boots, fustian frock, and straw sombrero. Not surprisingly, his tone in the *Letters* was that of the tourist, sending back to the metropolis reports of the outlandish locals. Like Willis's threshers, Mount's rafflers were rustic oddities whose dress, manners, and rituals would furnish a rich fund of amusement for their sophisticated tourist visitors. At the same time, *Raffling for the Goose* may embody a moral message, directed against the speculation mania of the mid-1830s.[14]

In *The Painter's Triumph* (Illus. 78) Mount makes the cultural division between sophisticate and rustic even more explicit. This painting depicts a studio interior where an excited painter shows off the canvas on his easel to a farmer, whose delighted expression reflects his comprehension and appreciation. The artist—symbolizing culture—wears a well-tailored ensemble of dark tailcoat, frilled shirt front, yellow vest, and stylishly narrow, dark brown pantaloons anchored by stirrups to shiny boots. The probably uncultured yeoman visitor—representing the popular audience—wears the familiar garb of the agricultural laborer. Instead of a cravat he has a knotted neckerchief. He is in vest and shirtsleeves, and his trousers fall baggily to rolled-over cuffs. Next to the figure of the artist, dapper as the city beau in Edmonds's painting, the farmer looks crude. His drover's whip is as much a symbol of his lowly occupation (on the level of the animals) as the painter's brandished palette and brushes are of his privileged existence on higher planes of culture, from which he can visit and beguile the popular mind. Even their postures speak eloquently of the cultural gap between them: the painter in a mock-heroic pose like a classical warrior about to hurl a javelin; the farmer, having perhaps just risen from the chair, still awkwardly bent over like a beast of burden, hands braced on wide-apart knees, smile unveiling the gaps among his teeth. Mount established the same kind of contrast later in *The Herald in the Country* (Illus. 79), in which a farmer with a pitchfork and a sportsman reading the *New York Herald* stand on either side of a rail fence with the top bar lowered. The well-dressed hunter, trim and sleek, makes the thick-bodied farmer, in his shapeless coat with its ragged holes, seem all the more a dull, stolid laborer. Possibly because of the newspaper but just as likely because of costume, one critic without hesitation identified the sportsman as a man from the city.[15]

The Painter's Triumph has often been seen as a canonical image, symbolizing the egalitarian aspirations of art during the Jacksonian era, but the very nature of the contrast between the two men contradicts this notion, as do Mount's private reflections in his journal: "Paint pictures that will take with the public, in other words, never paint for the few, but for the many—Some artists remain in the corner by not observing the above." Mount's assessment of the situation was at least as practical as it was democratic. He had his eye on the market, on what would enhance his reputation, what his patrons would buy. Whether or not he communicated with farmers was of secondary importance, if that; farmers were not his buyers. This is not to say that *The Painter's Triumph* overtly belittles the farmer, or that it does not have bearing on the contemporary issue of nativism, with its emphasis on the need to create an art of and for ordinary America. Nonetheless, the distinct though covert language spoken here subtly puts the rustic in his place.[16]

The subject of the farmer confronting Culture reappeared some seventeen years later in German-born Johannes Oertel's *Country Connoisseurs* (Illus. 80), which brings Mount's submerged meanings to the surface so that no viewer can mistake the meaning. Oertel, who had emigrated from Nuremberg in 1848, must have come across Albert Lawson's engraving *The Painter's Study* after *The Painter's Triumph*, published in *The Gift: A Christmas and New Year's Present for 1840* (Philadelphia: Carey & Hart, 1839); the resemblances are far too close to be merely coincidental. Oertel eliminated the painter, however, and marshaled a representative cross-section of rural society to posture before a canvas which, like Mount's, is turned away from the spectator beyond the picture frame. No contrast was needed in this case; by the 1850s the condescending or satirical stereotype of the rustic—diffused by Yankee comedies, Mount's paintings and the many prints after them, and works by followers such as Edmonds—had been thoroughly assimilated into midcentury culture, or at least the media that broadcast that culture. The two most prominent figures in the composition are those of the young man wearing a very tall stovepipe hat and huge red bowtie, whose thumbs-in-lapels stance suggests a certain cockiness; and, to the right, a shambling adolescent drover in baggy coat and trousers, his broad-brimmed hat and the whip under his arm confirming his lowly rusticity.

A reviewer of the painting at the 1855 National Academy of Design exhibition instantly understood that here was an opportunity to share in the artist's laughter at rustic pretensions and rustic ignorance. The painting was altogether "mirth-moving," he wrote. "A parcel of 'country chaps,' a village buck, an old farmer, etc., are in a painter's studio, and are complacently viewing and criticizing a large picture on his easel. The long, gawky figure of the mud-bespattered wagoner is absolutely distracting. It is a decided success."[17] *The Country Connoisseurs* invited just this sort of condescension from spectators; they could snigger at the complacency of the "country chaps" in pretending to judge high art. The amused contempt recorded by the critic is echoed in the composition itself by the écorché (muscular) figure at lower right, whose outstretched arm, pointed commandingly at the wagoner's slinking mongrel, banishes this entire coarse assembly from the realms of art and refinement.

The broad-brimmed hat and the drover's whip in the foreground were also clues to low status and intellect in Francis William Edmonds's *Taking the Census* (Illus. 81), nearly contemporary with Oertel's painting. The setting is a rustic interior with a Dutch accumulation of detail—including, over the mantelpiece, a portrait of George Washington, to announce this household's good citizenship. The elaborately contrived anecdote here hinges on the comic figure of the farmer, enumerating his brood by counting on his fingers, and the children's fun of hiding behind Mother's chair as if to confuse the reckoning process and fool the census taker. The latter, in his sober frock coat, exemplifies clerical respectability. The farmer once more is presented in rougher attire. Although the presence of books on mantelpiece and table indicates literacy in the family, the farmer himself sends a contradictory signal, which a contemporary reviewer detected:

Here we have represented the census-taker, with an important official air, noting down the family statistics; his assistant, a lad standing in a business-like attitude . . . ; farmer _____, rough and awkward, reckoning in brown study the number of the "boys and girls," evidently more at home in the use of the ox-goad, which lies on the floor, than in "figuring."[18]

Edmonds's farmer is not even a Yankee type, who was at least quick with numbers. Like the counterparts in works by Mount and Oertel, this finger-calculating worthy is a humble and laughable tender of animals and crops, comparable in many ways to the European peasant.

By the 1850s the stereotype of the stage Yankee had entered the world of cartoon journalism, thus ensuring the further diffusion of comic-countryman imagery. This was a great decade in the rise of popular illustration (efficiently produced by the wood-engraving technique and the steam press) in mass-marketed magazines. *Harper's Weekly*, for example, while by no means revealing an accurate or objective cross section of concerns in American culture and society, did reflect—like *Life* magazine in the 1950s—what was topical and popular. Some of the bumpkin cartoons in *Harper's Weekly*, which began publication in 1857, depicted farmers either as true grotesques—in the tradition established by Dutch art—or as Yankee Jonathan types. In some, the contrast with city refinement and power is explicit; in others, it is implied. In the Yankee images the laughable and the nostalgic were variously compounded, but they generally reinforced the notion of the farmer as a clown. This corresponded to the status of the Yankee plays (still popular) in that decade, in which the figure of the Yankee became less a symbol—however comic—of downright, uncompromising Americanness and increasingly a figure of outlandish archaism, cultural continents from the customs and manners of contemporary America.

Some *Harper's Weekly* cartoons of the later 1850s express undisguised condescension. Farmer matches animal in *Country Sketches* (Illus. 82), which records the conversation of Farmers Cronk and Bonk in Yankee vernacular. Cronk is a rustic grotesque with a proboscoid nose, scraggly whiskers, battered hat, and peasant's smock. Bonk and his enormously fat hog, which is the subject of their exchange, are so similar that no one could fail to comprehend: Bonk's snouted profile and obese bulk are matched exactly by the hog, whose forward-flopping ears even mime the forward sweep of Bonk's hat brim.

Other images show the Yankee as dupe and victim of city slickness. The cartoon *Practical Experience of the Gift Book Enterprises* (Illus. 83) discusses the fleecing of a Yankee Jonathan, here coyly dubbed the "Verdant Countryman," by an urban con man. A "City Friend" enlightens his gullible country cousin, who has just bought, for a mere dollar, a volume of noted missionary David Livingstone's African travels and a gold ring for "Sairey." He brags, "Pretty slick, I guess! Oh! We're up bright and early in our section of the country, I tell you." When the city man tells him he has been taken— "your Livingstone is not perfect and you can buy Rings like yours by the Bushel for Two Cents apiece"—the verdant one exclaims, "Je-e-e-rusalem!" The worldly and fashionable City Friend wears the urban uniform of frock coat, tight pants, and high silk hat and flourishes a slim walking stick. The Verdant Countryman, beefy and thickset, wears a badly fitting version of Yankee costume: round hat, cutaway tailcoat, and high-waisted pantaloons much too short in the hem. What is especially notable here is that the Yankee is represented as the swindlee, not the swindler—a complete reversal of the older conception. Along the same lines is a double cartoon showing the farmer's relations with city merchants before and after the Panic of 1857 (Illus. 84). In the first panel he is welcomed by ingratiating smiles and gestures; in the second he gets cold shoulders and stony backs. The countryman, with his carpetbag, shaggy locks, and long, thick coat, looks ridiculously out of place among the suave, well-coifed, well-groomed tradesmen. The reality beneath the joke is, of course, that the farmer was in just this way at the mercy of the urban market.

The stage Yankee's costume invariably branded the wearer as an outright hick. This was certainly its meaning in the cartoon *How To Spend the Fourth*, which depicts "Farmer Whilty" and his wife visiting a patriotic monument (Illus. 85). The farmer, with his sorely outdated tailcoat, nappy beaver hat, short striped trousers, and voluminous umbrella, makes an eccentric figure, true type of the Yankee clown. His outfit is, in fact, a near duplicate of the Jonathan Ploughboy costume worn by G. E. "Yankee" Locke, a popular character actor of the 1850s. The farmer's wife, in her poke bonnet, shawl, and limply draped skirts, is equally dowdy and antiquated. Both have long noses and prominent chins, and both seem to be goggling—as one would expect rustics to do—at a statue so huge that only its feet are visible at eye level; the rest soars up out of sight. Their costumes and stance recall some of the snide, semisatirical remarks cited previously about the embarrassing young men with baggy cotton umbrellas, and those ignorant provincials the Cowpens. Popular literature of this decade offers very explicit descriptions of the "Whilty" type of country cousin, such as the farm couple dressed for Christmas in their egregious best:

In a smaller room sat the farmer and his wife. The former was clad in a new suit of homespun cloth, with immense brass buttons, a checked neckcloth, high-heeled brogans, and a scarlet vest. His wife appeared in the glory of a new cap, and a smart calico gown, with figures as large as a dinner-plate on its white ground. Both sported immense bandanas, but the lady's was blue and the gentleman's red.[19]

The indoor wear sketched here is different from the Yankee traveling costumes in the cartoon, but the spirit and intent of the description are much the same. The clownishness of this rustic couple is betrayed by such details as "immense" brass buttons and "immense" bandanas, similar in effect to the immense red bowtie worn by the country buck in Oertel's *Country Connoisseurs*.

Augustus Hoppin's illustrations for James Russell Lowell's rustic poem "The Courtin'" (1857) also featured the Yankee as buffoon.[20] Lowell's poem is directly in the tradition of the older Yankee dialect poems and Yankee plays—it even preserves the "Yankee Doodle" meter—but it is more self-conscious even than the originals. The dialect is more laboriously countrified, which is not surprising considering that Lowell was, among other accomplishments as poet, diplomat, and critic, founding editor of the intellectual *Atlantic Monthly* in 1857. The simple narrative, however, echoes the stories of tongue-tied Jonathans and arch Jemimas in the old courtin' poems.

Hoppin's illustrations, published in *Harper's Weekly* in 1858 to accompany an abbreviated version of the poem, remain faithful to its archaisms and stand in relation to Mount's courtship pictures as Lowell's verse does to the old dialect poems. The later images offer a humor of mannered quaintness, whereas Mount's, contemporary with the best years of the Yankee plays, have the vital high spirits of living comedy. A picture depicting Zekle's first hesitant address to the farmer's daughter Huldy (Illus. 86) epitomizes the new treatment of the Yankee. As Huldy, her lap full of apples, turns to ask Zekle if he has come to call on her father, the suitor hovers behind her and hopefully begins to pull up a chair. Whereas Mount's country suitors were merely inelegant, Hoppin's Zekle is decidedly anachronistic. Like Farmer Whilty, he is arrayed in the fully evolved getup of the stage Yankee, badge of the obsolete bumpkin. The figure of Huldy is less startling; she plays the role of beautiful farmer's daughter much as Mount's young women did.

Hoppin's stage-Yankee Zekle represents the latest phase of rustic stereotyping, marked by the reduction of the character to a kind of pictorial one-liner and the increasingly ludicrous gulf between the rustic clown's garb and current city style. Oversimplified though it is, it is consistent with the developing tradition of the previous half-century. The patterns established by Mount, the Yankee plays, and the Downing letters had shaped a stereotype that reflected a popular taste for rustic wit and idiosyncrasy while it invited a patronizing attitude. Such an image, fabricated as it was, stood just as distant from the real countryman as had the image of the noble yeoman—and functioned just as effectively to burden the farmer with an unwelcome weight of symbolism and obfuscation. Images of countrymen in the last third of the nineteenth century would perpetuate these simplistic conceptions in the figure of the American farmer as grandfather, geezer, or peasant.

74. William Sidney Mount, *The Sportsman's Last Visit*, 1835. Oil on canvas, $21\frac{1}{2}'' \times 17\frac{1}{2}''$. (The Museums at Stony Brook, New York; gift of Mr. & Mrs. Ward Melville, 1958)

75. *Charles Mathews as "Jonathan W. Doubikins"* (second from right), in *A Trip to America,* c. 1824. Lithograph, 3″×4″. (Harvard Theatre Collection)

76. Francis William Edmonds, *The City and the Country Beaux*, 1840. Oil on canvas, $20\frac{1}{8}'' \times 24\frac{1}{4}''$. (Sterling and Francine Clark Art Institute, Williamstown, Massachusetts)

77.   William Sidney Mount, *Raffling for the Goose,* 1837. Oil on
wood, 17″×23⅛″. (The Metropolitan Museum of Art, New York;
gift of John D. Crimmins, 1897 [97.36])

78. William Sidney Mount, *The Painter's Triumph*, 1838. Oil on panel, $19\frac{1}{2}'' \times 23\frac{9}{16}''$. (Courtesy of The Pennsylvania Academy of the Fine Arts, Philadelphia; bequest of Henry C. Carey [The Carey Collection])

79. William Sidney Mount, *The Herald in the Country*, 1853. Oil on panel, $17\frac{1}{4}'' \times 12\frac{3}{4}''$. (The Museums at Stony Brook, New York; gift of Mr. and Mrs. Ward Melville, 1955)

80. Johannes Oertel, *The Country Connoisseurs*, 1855. Oil on canvas, 36″×42″. (Shelburne Museum, Shelburne, Vermont)

81.   Francis William Edmonds, *Taking the Census,* 1854. Oil on canvas, 28″ × 38″. (Courtesy of James Maroney, New York)

FARMER CRONK. "Wal now, Deacon, that's a purty nice hog o' yourn."

FARMER BONK. "Wal, I can't say much for him now, but he'll look purty smart when I get him fattened up a bit."

82. *Country Sketches: Farmer Cronk and Farmer Bonk.* Wood engraving. *Harper's Weekly Magazine* 2 (October 16, 1858).

CITY FRIEND. "Why, Nathan, what have you been doing?"

VERDANT COUNTRYMAN. "You see, Mr. Brown, we know a thing or two up our way, so I've just bin and subscribed to that there Gift Enterprise, and see here: Livingstone's Travels and this splendid Gold Ring for Sairey—both for a Dollar. Pretty slick, I guess! Oh! we're up bright and early in our section of country, I tell you."

"CITY FRIEND. "The only misfortune is, Nathan, that your Livingstone is not perfect, and you can buy Rings like yours by the Bushel for Two Cents apiece."

VERDANT COUNTRYMAN. "Je—e—e—rusalem!"

83. *Practical Experience of the Gift Book Enterprises*. Wood engraving. *Harper's Weekly Magazine* 2 (April 17, 1858).

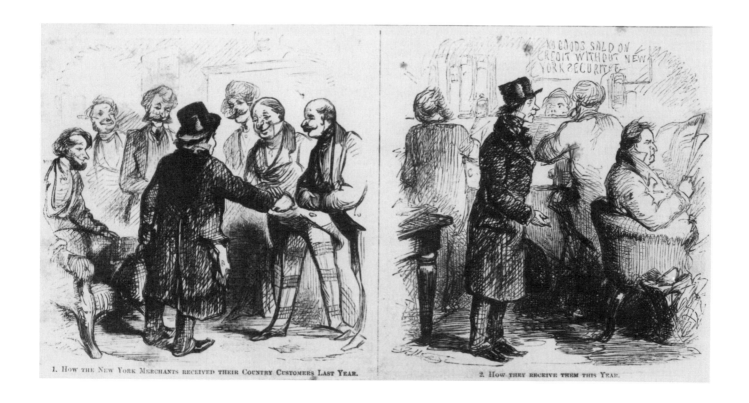

1. How the New York Merchants received their Country Customers Last Year.

2. How they receive them This Year.

84. *How the New York Merchants Received Their Country Customers Last Year; How They Receive Them This Year*. Wood engraving. *Harper's Weekly Magazine* 2 (April 3, 1858).

85. *How To Spend the Fourth.*
Wood engraving. *Harper's Weekly
Magazine* 1 (July 4, 1857).

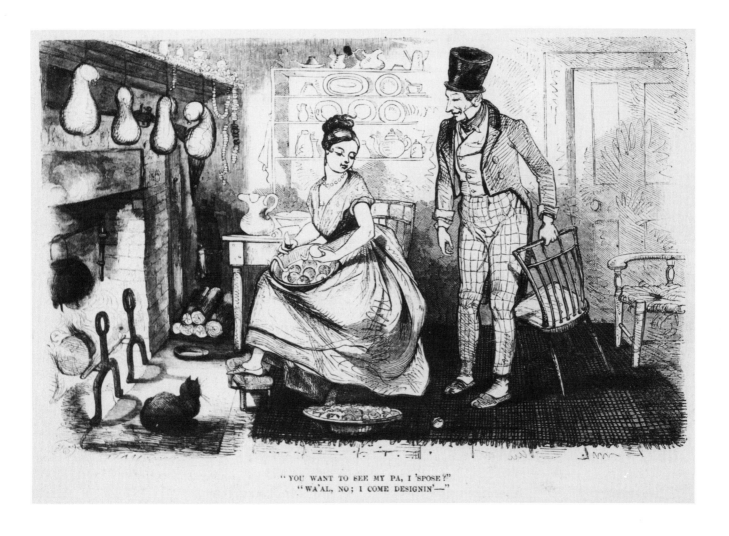

"YOU WANT TO SEE MY PA, I 'SPOSE?"
"WA'AL, NO; I COME DESIGNIN'—"

86. Augustus Hoppin, *"You Want To See My Pa, I 'Spose?"*
"Wa'al, No; I Come Designin'—." Wood engraving. *Harper's
Weekly Magazine* 2 (October 23, 1858).

9 ■ *Grandfathers and Geezers*

HE last third of the nineteenth century, epoch of accelerating progress and transformation, encompassed demographic shifts that profiled a society in the process of being regrouped, reshaped, and restructured. During this time the population more than doubled, surpassing seventy-five million by 1900. More than ten million immigrants arrived, many of them settling in the already crowded eastern cities, and an even greater number of the farm population left the countryside to seek a different way of life in the urban world. By the mid-1880s, industrial production had outstripped that of agriculture. This was an advantage which, once gained, never ceased to grow. Correspondingly, the number of factory workers increased tenfold. Communities large and small, once relatively self-contained, underwent reconfiguration to become increasingly interdependent components in the far-flung networks of transportation, consumption, and communication. Within towns the same kind of interdependence was gradually imposed by new corporate structures (both political and economic) that built and controlled the networks for delivering energy and commodities. The new urban environment became more and more the realm not only of laborers, factory operatives, merchants, and financiers but also of a burgeoning middle class of bureaucrats and professionals of various kinds. Their number jumped from about 750,000 in 1870 to 5.5 million by 1910. These transformations had been in the making, of course, decades before the Civil War, but in the 1870s they seemed to leap ahead with a propulsive force that could not be retarded.

It was a period of tangled cultural complexity as well. As the United States became an industrial power and began to play a role in international politics, culture creators fashioned new styles in a grander image expressing both might and sophistication. Cosmopolitanism became the common denominator of mainstream architecture and painting during this time, and older modes—represented by the Hudson River School and genre painting in the spirit of William Sidney Mount—were attacked and dismissed by new critics as dismally provincial and painfully homespun. Simultaneously, popular or mass culture became an industry unto itself, while various ethnic subcultures attempted to resist the weight of an Anglo-Saxon cultural hegemony attempting to expunge the expression of alien (and therefore threatening) racial or national identities.[1]

It should be understood that any discussion of society and culture in the late nineteenth century must perforce either generalize broadly or define its terms narrowly. The terms here are for the most part consistent with those applied to the discussion of earlier decades: we are speaking of the predominantly urban culture producers and cultural critics who addressed or represented any of the several levels composing the white, urban and suburban, middle to upper-middle classes. It is mainly through their eyes, and their art, that we read the changing image of the American farmer in the last decades of the century.

The antebellum era nourished the dream of an agrarian America even while the patterns of industrialization and urbanization charted the real future course of development; the social changes that seemed so remarkable in the later nineteenth century were only repeating, on a bigger and more complicated scale, what had already occurred. The mass migration of rustics into cities, for example, had been a phenomenon of the 1840s; at about the same time, immigration had been an equal cause for dismay—only the ethnic groups were different. And certainly the furor over speculation and materialism in the 1830s was symptomatic of the spasms of cultural conflict. Then, however, the rhetoric of agrarian pastoralism had prevailed over the emergent energies of social and technological change. There remained space to fantasize an agrarian social order that might contain all. Rural values, preached explicitly or implicitly in the media, were still the standard by which to judge the health of society. The virtuous yeoman existed as a noble concept, even though his alter ego, the Yankee bumpkin, showed how easily hero could metamorphose into hayseed.

The later decades of the century witnessed the rise of urban values that seriously challenged older assumptions. It is possible to find antebellum precedents for these attitudes as well; what is significant, though, is a new tone. It was no longer *de rigueur* even to feign deference to the superiority of country standards, country goodness. More and more, the city came to represent something positive, dynamic, and self-creating, a place that did not draw its nourishment from the same sources that fed the countryside. Champions of urban life and values spoke with increased confidence, and debunkers of the agrarian ideal allowed a much harder edge of cynicism to shred the beauties of the pastoral dream. Before the 1870s the debunkers of country life had been light-spirited satirists, sour cranks, or occasionally the farmers themselves; thorough and devastating critiques though not unheard of, were uncommon. But what had been a mere contradictory trickle became in the closing decades of the nineteenth century a flood of words, disparaging the country, country people, and the entire construct of the agrarian ideal.

The very title of urban reformer Frederic C. Howe's treatise *The City, the Hope of Democracy* (1905) proclaimed the shift in attitude. It was not much more than a century before that Thomas Jefferson had written those influential passages on the country as the hope if not of democracy (in the modern sense), then at least of rational republicanism; the city was a necessary evil, a disease best kept quarantined. By contrast, Howe saw the modern city as marking "an epoch in our civilization," creating a new society, and bringing "a revolution in industry, politics, society, and life itself. Its coming has destroyed a rural society, whose making has occupied mankind since the fall of Rome. It has erased many of our most laborious achievements and turned to scrap many of our established ideas. Man has entered an urban age." Howe saw the city as a positive force for a genuine democracy, a mass leveling that would in time demolish the hierarchies of industrial capitalism:

For the first time in history we have a really democratic city, safeguarded in its democracy by law. Through this fact the city has become a tremendous agency for human advancement. . . . It is an organism capable of conscious and concerted action, responsive, ready, and intelligent. . . . The city is to be the arena where the social and political forces that are coming to the fore will play.[2]

Howe's position, of course, represented a radical extreme of affirmation and optimism. The urban problems of the day remained profound, complex, and even nightmarish; the specters of crime, poverty, and alien races seemed as terrifying to urbanites then as they do to many today. Even so, the terms of reform were largely urban, although nature—still a panacea for social ills—might be pressed into service when needed.

A more flippant but equally revealing celebration of the modern city was R. K. Munkittrick's story "Farming," (1891), which ended with the meditations of a city dweller who, having found farm life not at all to his liking, gloried in the comforts he rediscovered back in his natural habitat:

> But in truth I cared nothing for farming since being initiated into its mysteries. I cared not if all the crops failed, because, no matter how signally they fail, the city markets are always overstocked. I did not care if the whirlwinds tore the topknot foliage off the turnips of Russia or the beans from the gaunt and scrawny poles, I could sit in my air-tight, snow-proof flat, and puff the room full of delicate wreaths of smoke from a tobacco so spicy that it would be difficult for me to believe that it ever grew in the country, for the reason that in the rural districts I had never found any fit for use. . . . I would be perfectly willing to do my farming in the future at the corner grocery, where the finest specimens of everything desirable and green could always be had. . . . My luxurious lounge, covered with a flowered Persian rug, would be the flower bank into which I could sink with a sweeter forgetfulness than I ever knew on nature's sward. And there I could dream and dream . . . and wander in fancy by the margins of leaping runnels befringed with dewy flowers and gently sloping meadows sweet with the song of birds. . . . I could dream of even the unmortgaged farm being the home of the free—because the farmer is independent—and the home of the slave—because the farmer is not independent, except in the imagination of the poet.[3]

Munkittrick made no pretense of delighting in the picturesqueness of rural toil. His observations, forcefully proclaiming the superior quality of urban life, confronted and exposed the essentially romantic, imaginary character of the pastoral vision. One could live or, rather, dream it just as well—and probably better—by never leaving his urban couch at all.

For some writers, the state of the American farmer seemed all the sorrier in comparison with his situation in the past, nostalgically viewed as a time when the agrarian ideal had meshed with reality. Rodney Welch, for example, had grown up on a New England hillside farm, which in retrospect symbolized the quintessence of upright self-sufficiency and hard but decent and fundamentally satisfying rural life. In the 1890s, however, he realized with dismay that little of that life remained; indeed, the very locus of American farming had shifted to the "great prairies of the West."

But the new farmer Welch described with such disapproval had existed for many decades. Actuality was finally catching up with and dispelling illusion. Modern farmers, he complained, bought as many "things" as did town dwellers. They had large grocery bills because they no longer maintained kitchen gardens. They no longer bartered; they no longer manufactured their cloth, clothing, and other necessities at home. They were in debt; they used machines. In the old days, on the other hand,

> several of our . . . presidents were farmers, as were the governors of most of the States. More than one congressional directory shows that the majority of the senators and representatives were farmers; even Daniel Webster and Henry Clay took pride in being classed among them. At that time the legislation for States, counties, and towns was the work of farmers. . . . In short, farmers constituted a class from which men could be selected who were, by virtue of their intellect and learning, competent to fill almost any public position.

We have heard all this before, in antebellum agrarian rhetoric, and found it true only in a limited sense. To Welch, however, this was the way things had really been—or so he claimed—whereas modern farmers had plummeted in status and were still falling. They had lost "their place and influence in the councils of the State and the nation." New England farmers had deserted their farms to work in towns, and most western farms were owned by absentee landlords who had subdivided large tracts into many smaller ones, which were then rented to "persons of foreign birth" while the landlords moved into cities in order to take advantage of urban social, educational, and religious institutions. They left behind a landscape where English was seldom spoken, where the intellectual condition of tenant farmers was "not above that of the lowest class of laborers in our large cities." What had once been a noble breed of American had degenerated to "an ignorant rural peasantry."[4]

A number of determined debunkers, coming forth at this time, only reiterated in more virulent terms what Welch had sorrowfully detailed. Schoolteacher John M. Welding set out systematically to dismantle—ideological brick by brick—the entire edifice of agrarian idealism and the many myths and assumptions that shored it up. Rebutting with statistical data the notion that most great figures in American culture and politics had come from the country, Welding cited a whole page of eminent Americans (Franklin, Emerson, and Poe, among others) who had been formed by the city. To build a city, he contended, "is the first step of a people that commences a career of civilization and greatness." Tartars and Bedouins built no towns, and their very names were synonymous with "brutality, cruelty, and barbarism." Like Welch, Welding pointed out that the American countryside harbored many a miserable tenant, living in wretchedness equal to that of the urban proletariat. Farmers who owned their land were not much better off, because like John Muir's family forty years before, they suppressed family life and cultural pursuits in order to satisfy a terrible hunger that drove them to work relentlessly in order to buy more land. "The farmer is a slave, and his wife (alas for the farmer's wife!) is the slave of a slave. . . . Now, harp all you will about the pure air and free sunshine of the country life, but account, if you can, for the generally stunted physical and mental growth of country children." Rural education was minimal and the horizon constricted. Children clustered around the door of the country school appeared "joyless and tired." Farm food, which the urban fantasist expected to be fresh, bounteous, and delectable, was in fact monotonous slop: "Greasy biscuit, fat pork swimming in gravy, and the everlasting pie are the main items of the farmer's bill of fare." The urban mechanic, Welding declared, had a diet of greater variety and far better quality. Paradoxically, the only constructive tendencies in modern country life were fueled by urban energies, which furnished the "bulk of the brains and skill of the nation." The Dakota bonanza farms, for example, were "owned and operated by men born in the cities and educated in the public schools."[5]

Notions of decay and degeneracy accompanied the new, bleaker vision of American rural life. The old region of New England, in particular, invited such perceptions, but farm life in the Midwest was far from immune. In prose tours of the erstwhile Yankee land, such popular writers as Rebecca Harding Davis conjured up pictures of a monochromatic wasteland populated by haggard specters, the only folk remaining after mass migration by the young into eastern towns or western spaces. The visitor to rural New England in the 1890s would discover "somber atmosphere, the gray cabins and gray rocks cropping out of the mat of grass and wild roses. The grim old men and delicate, sad-eyed women are fitting figures for the melancholy background. . . . the eventless drama of their lives is . . . the symptom of the decadence of a race." Davis liberally strewed her essay with adjectives such as "stooped," "dull-eyed," "listless," "grim," "subdued," and "ashy-faced" to describe the pathetic remnants of once-vigorous Yankee stock in the lonely farms and "worn-out villages" of the region. By contrast, the urban New Englander was hearty and prosperous, and the western farmer all but bursting with health and vitality.[6]

Another writer described isolated New England hamlets as so quiet, their ugly, angular white houses so devoid of any signs of life, that they evoked a graveyard atmosphere:

Even the hens step gingerly, as if fearing to make a noise on the grass; the dog may bark a little at you if he be young; but, if he is old . . . only turns his head languidly at the noise of wheels. At sunset, you may possibly see the farmer sitting on the porch, with a newspaper. But his chair is tipped back against the side of the house; the newspaper is folded on his knee, and his eyes are shut.[7]

The same images of decrepitude and senility had also emerged in poetry and fiction. In "Among the Hills," written in 1869, the normally optimistic John Greenleaf Whittier for once put aside his rosy spectacles and portrayed the New England rural scene in a harsher light:

> old homesteads, where no flower
> Told that the spring had come, but evil weeds,
> Nightshade and rough-leaved burdock in the place
> Of the sweet doorway greeting of the rose
> And honeysuckle, where the house walls seemed
> Blistering in the sun, without tree or vine
> To cast the tremulous shadows of its leaves
> Across curtainless windows, from whose panes
> Fluttered the signal rags of shiftlessness.
> . . . .
> And, in sad keeping with all things about them,
> Shrill, querulous women, sour and sullen men,
> Untidy, loveless, old before their time,
> With scarce a human interest save their own
> Monotonous round of small economies
> Or the poor scandal of the neighborhood.

Unwilling to leave such a taste of ashes, Whittier ended with a trumpet call for the elevation of farm life into what it had been before the war, in the golden days of his own boyhood: the yeoman must again become "A man to match his mountains, not to creep / Dwarfed and abased below them."[8]

An often pained awareness of the present characterized the work of New England literary regionalists Rose Terry Cooke, Sarah Orne Jewett, and Mary E. Wilkins Freeman. These writers, who developed and matured in the 1870s and 1880s, sought to commemorate the distinctive or mythic qualities of regional life and local landscape. The same impulse fueled regionalism in every section of the United States after the Civil War, when progress and social change seemed more than ever to threaten traditional cultural patterns. The New England regionalists' stories exhibited varying proportions of nostalgia, combined with the modern realist's desire to confront and examine a present where lived the descendants of Puritan and Yankee, a dying race psychologically deformed, ingrown, and narrow. In these tales, life and landscape were more often than not sterile, desiccated, and cruel. Cooke's story "Some Account of Thomas Tucker," about the spiritual deformities of an obsessively Puritanical minister, opens with a sketch of his childhood environment. Father Amasa Tucker, stern and hard as the "granite rocks beneath the sward he tilled . . . ploughed the brown sod of the sad New England hills under the full force of the primeval curse." His wife, like many of the wives in these tales, is "meek and spiritless." To this pair are born ten children, of which two survive:

Abundant dosing, insufficient food, and a neglected sink-drain had killed all the others . . . but those two evaded the doom that had fallen on their brothers and sisters, by the fate which modern science calls survival of the fittest, and spindled up among the mullein-stalks of their stone-strewn pastures as gray, lank, dry, and forlorn as the mulleins themselves.

Freeman's stories, too, depict an often decrepit rural landscape grudgingly supporting lean women in calico; shrunken, melancholy old maids; laconic, leathery men; and lovers poor and plain. Farmhouses are often unkempt, weather-stained, landscaped with moss and weeds rather than cheerful, cultivated plants. Even though some spark of human love or sympathy now and then warms and redeems stunted lives and constricted souls, this is indeed a far cry from Donald Grant Mitchell's idealized New England village, where the hale, venerable Squire held sway.[9]

In the same spirit but far more coldhearted in its onslaught against the rural idyll was Harold Frederic's *Seth's Brother's Wife* (1886), which centered on the decadent rural Fairchild family, living in a bleak region of New York state. Their barns are rickety and paintless, their cows—shuffling about in the black mire of the barnyard—lean and dingy, their gates broken, their wellcurb mildewed. Patriarch Lemuel Fairchild is a "bowed, gray-haired, lumpish man . . . feebly rocking himself by the huge wood-stove"; his funereal sister Sabrina is a "grim old maid in a rusty bombazine gown and cap." Among seedy surroundings the Fairchilds, especially the degenerate younger branches, engage in very ignoble yeomanry indeed: duplicity, adultery, murder.[10]

The new weapon in the debunkers' attacks, whether rueful or virulent, was a realist aesthetic, still somewhat tentative, perhaps, and still too circumspect (or melodramatic) in some cases but signaling nonetheless a major new direction in late nineteenth-century literature. By its very nature, realism was incompatible with the agrarian ideal. No realist could in good conscience have penned Donald Grant Mitchell's description of that agrarian paragon the Squire or, like John Burroughs, extolled the cleanliness and manliness of haying. Objectivity and an analytical temper demanded scrutiny of all that the agrarian ideal had edited out: weakness, vice, failure, ugliness, crudity, pain, monotony. This realist imperative tempered the nostalgia of the New England regionalists and more astringently permeated the farm and village novels that began to come out of the Midwest (culturally an extension of New England in many places) after the Civil War.

The innocuous title of Edgar Watson Howe's novel *The Story of a Country Town* (1883) belied the content, which in essence denounced the agrarian ideal—here, to be more precise, the village ideal—as fraudulent and morally bankrupt. The dusty prairie town of Fairview, ironically advertised in full-throated agrarian terms as the "garden spot of the world," is the home of gloomy people oppressed by religion. Far from being exemplars of the happy republican community, the farm and village families are rotten with human weaknesses and passions, which lead to dreadful crimes. Chief among the villains is the shifty operator Lytle Biggs, whose activities in organizing farmers' political protest groups (the alliances that merged into the Populist Party of the 1890s) are but steps in his own self-aggrandizement and quest for power.[11]

In *Main-Traveled Roads* (1891), Hamlin Garland attempted to paint the American farm in the light of truth rather than of Gothic excess. Garland based these stories on his own memories of boyhood in the rural Midwest, combined with the adult bitterness experienced upon his return visits to the miseries of his father's farm in South Dakota after several years of escape, teaching and writing in the genteel ambience of Boston. In Garland's vision of the true West, the grand, empty beauty of the prairies and their skies served as background for dramas of frustration, failure, and endurance in squalid villages and elemental homesteads. Although Garland's intention was to tell his tales from the authentic perspective of one who knew those farms from prolonged, firsthand experience, several of them nevertheless hinged upon the urbanized perspective of sons who (like Garland himself) return to their old homes after long absences in distant parts, only to find all somehow diminished. In "Up the Coulee," Howard McLane—successful actor and playwright, ex–farm boy become international sophisticate—comes home after ten years away. Arriving at the dreary farm where his mother and brother now live, he sees a huddle of humble buildings and

a barnyard full of mud, in which a few cows were standing, fighting the flies. . . . the pigs were squealing from a pen nearby; a child was crying. . . . he could hear . . . the impatient jerk and jar of kitchen things, indicative of ill temper or worry. The longer he stood absorbing this farm scene, with all its sordidness, dullness, triviality, and its endless drudgeries, the lower his heart sank. All the joy of homecoming was gone.

A minute later, incongruously elegant in his tailored suit, Howard stands facing his brother Grant, who is "ragged, ankle-deep in muck, his sleeves rolled up, a shapeless old straw hat on his head." The development of the narrative rests upon Grant's sullen refusal to accept his brother, and Howard's tormenting itch of guilt at having neglected to help his wretched family while in New York he had taken pleasure in his yacht, his horse, and his paintings.

Again he saw his life, so rich, so bright, so free, set over against the routine life in the little low kitchen, the barren sitting room, and this still more horrible barn. Why should his brother sit there in wet and grimy clothing mending a broken trace, while he enjoyed all the light and civilization of the age?

To exculpate his sins of neglect and regain his brother's regard, Howard plots to buy back the old homestead, lost through foreclosure several years since. His self-serving generosity, however, runs into the blank wall of Grant's resignation: "Life ain't worth very much to me. I'm too old to take a new start. I'm a dead failure. . . . You can't help me now. It's too late." Nothing could be further from the old, optimistic world of agrarian idealism and cheerful rustic stereotypes than this scene of dead hopes and tattered failure.[12]

In the lighter branches of contemporary writing, the reduced status of the farmer found reflection in an increasing trivialization of the yeoman character. This version of the farmer was an amusing fossil, mired in temporal backwaters and impossibly distant from modern urban culture. The rustic humor of Josh Billings—one of the later descendants of Major Jack Downing—revealed the new pattern. Billings was the creation of Henry Wheeler Shaw, who abandoned his irreproachable New England background for a life of adventure in the West, then eventually settled in Poughkeepsie as an auctioneer. In 1860 he placed his comic piece "An Essa on the Muel bi Josh Billings" in a New York newspaper. Subsequently, his reputation flourished as he produced more comic Billings sketches and appeared as a speaker around the country. He published his first *Farmer's Allminak* in 1870,

and for ten years these spoofs were enormously popular, selling hundreds of thousands of copies overall.[13]

The egregious misspellings in the Josh Billings letters and aphorisms offer a not-so-subtle clue to the new status of the rustic clown. Whereas in the writings of Jack Downing, and most other antebellum "philosophers," the misspellings often corresponded to the pronunciations of vernacular speech— "jist," "Gineral," "spose," and the like—the Billings letters appear to have been produced by one who can write just sufficiently to set down on paper the ludicrous perversions of correct orthography that confirm his low status, even as they provoke chuckles. The subject matter too reveals a countrified commentator substantially different from Downing and his ilk, who sounded forth on the nation's politicians and their foibles. Billings told folksy stories, gave folksy advice, and had little to say about national affairs. His "Letter to Farmers" is characteristic:

Beloved Farmers:
   Agrikultur iz the mother ov farm produce; she iz also the stepmother ov gardin sass.
   Rize at haff past 2 o'clock in the morning, bild up a big fire in the kitchen, burn out two pounds ov kandels, and grease yur boots.
   Wait pashuntly for da brake. When da duz brake, then commense tew stir up the geese, and hogs.
   Too much sleep is ruinous tew geese and tew hogs. Remember yu kant git ritch on a farm, unless you rize at 2 o'clock. . . .
   What iz a lawyer?—What iz a merchant?—What iz a doktor? . . . I answer, nothing!
   A farmer is the nobless work ov God; he rizes at 2 o'clock in the morning . . . then goes out tew worry the geese and stir up the hogs.
Beloved farmers, adew.[14]

This letter not only exemplifies Billings's own image but also symbolizes the descent of the noble agrarian and the shrewd Yankee clown into the rank of dumb drudge, however diverting.

   The antebellum motif of comic rural-urban contrasts remained a stock item in the rural plays that enjoyed a vogue in the last decade of the century.[15] The remodeling of the stereotype in the later plays was in some cases slight but still telling: the farmer became more laughably countrified and more simpleminded in his reactions to urban marvels and peculiarities. Typical were Joshua Whitcomb and Jonas Larkin, characters in *The Old Homestead* and *Farmer Larkin's Boarders*. *The Old Homestead*, first produced in 1886, featured Down East impersonator Denman Thompson, so popular in this role that he played it exclusively until his death in 1911. The plot requires farmer Joshua—who describes himself at sixty-four as "hard as a hickory nut and spry as a kitten"—to visit New York City in search of his son, who has succumbed to urban vices and become a drunken tramp. Once there, Joshua makes the most of every opportunity to deliver opinions that loudly broadcast his rustic naiveté. In the fashionable drawing room of his successful city friends, Joshua beholds a nude alabaster Venus and is shocked: "What do you do with it when the minister comes?" he inquires of the servant with whom he is democratically conversing. "I'm glad Tilda didn't come. She'd have put for home when she saw such sights as that. If I put that figure up in my cornfield the sheriff would have me in jail before night."[16]

Farmer Larkin's Boarders creaks along on a similar run-of-the-mill plot involving comic clashes with city people and an errant country-boy son. Larkin is even more a caricature than Joshua Whitcomb. The hick-versus-sophisticate dialectic commences immmediately in the first act, when the city boarders' children have gone off on a bicycle ride. Farm wife Liza tells her husband that the cyclists had departed on "them spinnin'-wheel things," and Larkin exclaims: "Wall, I'll be danged! Spinnin' wheels! It does beat all what them city folks does git into their heads." "Dang it" is, in fact, Farmer Larkin's favorite expletive. The costume directions are also revealing. Farmer Larkin's garb lacks even the natty eccentricity of the stage Yankee's and seems intended to express his utter irrelevance to the realms of fashion and culture: "Wig of thin gray hair, gray chin whiskers, blue overalls, checked shirt, blue 'jumper' [loose overgarment], and heavy plow shoes"; his wife Eliza wears "print or checked gingham gowns."[17] Like Joshua Whitcomb, Larkin is old but not particularly venerable; he represents the geriatric diminuendo of the noble yeoman and the Yankee clown.

The unsentimental realism of the new fiction about rural life did not often appear in contemporary pictorial images of the American farmer. Realism of technique (thanks in part to the new vogue for European training) was reaching levels of sophistication seldom attained by antebellum artists, but the kind of bold realist sensibility needed to treat themes of rural poverty and despair was absent, as was the market for such work. Instead, paintings and illustrations in the last decades of the century closely followed the lighter literary patterns described above. As if reflecting the antiquation of the agrarian ideal itself, or the idea of decay in rural sections of New England, the farmer became a rustic old codger, either quaint and wise or simply torpid. But the popularity of even these homespun subjects declined as new themes (the upper-class urban world and the aestheticized landscape) ascended, though there remained a market for some old-time country-life specialists such as Thomas Hovenden, Edward Lamson Henry, Thomas Waterman Wood, Alfred C. Howland, and (until the 1880s) Eastman Johnson.

Like many of the later country genre painters, Johnson dedicated himself to one particular rural backwater: in his case, Nantucket. In the 1870s and 1880s he produced paintings and studies of ancient Nantucket Islanders. Though his old men are obsolete seafarers rather than farmers, like their agricultural counterparts they are symbols of a vanished way of life (whaling, in this instance), and they function as eloquent witnesses to the notion of regional decline so prevalent in contemporary fiction and commentary. Two of Johnson's paintings—*Nantucket Sea Captain* (1873; private collection) and *Embers* (c. 1880; private collection)—depict old men sitting by cottage firesides. The second is particularly melancholy, both in its suggestive title and in the figure, who wears the stage Yankee's top hat and tails but slumps wearily over his cane to gaze pensively at the dying fire on the hearth. Though more convivial, with its gossiping codgers around a Franklin stove, *The Nantucket School of Philosophy* (Illus. 87) has the same effect of metaphorical twilight; these old men have nothing but bygones to sustain them. Johnson's paintings have the flavor, without the grimness, of Rebecca Harding Davis's evocations of coastal places with their gray rocks and gray cabins. They also recall the somber ambience of Deephaven and Dunnet Landing, fictional towns created by Sarah Orne Jewett as paradigms of the declining, depopulated New England seaport, the home of ancient men and women living on memories of happier days. Like the regionalist writers, Johnson cherished what was distinctive to Nantucket—its tidy cabins and seafaring tradition—while revealing, at the same time, its deliquescence.[18]

Thomas Hovenden exploited the inhabitants of Plymouth Meeting, Pennsylvania, to create images of elderly country people, the surviving relics of early days. Seven years of training in the Paris studio of Alexandre Cabanel—academic painter par excellence—had equipped Hovenden to overlay his homespun subjects with that veneer of sophistication requisite for success in the increasingly competitive and cosmopolitan art market of the 1880s. *The Old Version* (Illus. 88) displays both his skill and a pair of quintessential rustics, portrayed with no obvious condescension or caricature yet meant to be understood as awkward (if endearing) anachronisms. The interior is that of a fairly prosperous farmhouse, well garnished with comfort and ornament: a padded rocking chair and footstool, a wall clock with a decorative landscape panel, a china cabinet, and a framed engraving of a figure worshipping a cross, evidence of household piety. Beneath the print sit the farmer and his wife. The woman is almost severely plain and antifashionable with her calico gown and skinned-back hair. The man, cousin of sorts to Johnson's old sea captains, has a ruff of whiskers and wears the shirt, vest, and boots of a laborer. He is reading from the Bible on his lap. These people are dignified and devout, yet in comparison with the urban styles and mores of Hovenden's intended audience, they are oddities divorced from the mainstream of American life. The title itself has a double meaning. A revised version of the Bible was published in the early 1880s, but this old pair, emblems of the old-fashioned conservatism then associated with American country people, of course prefer the "old version." The implications go beyond the Bible to embrace the man and wife themselves and the way of life they represent.[19]

A Pinch of Snuff (Illus. 89) by Thomas Waterman Wood (whose special territory was provincial Montpelier, Vermont) shows the elderly rustic in full-fledged late nineteenth-century form. Unlike Hovenden's couple, these two farmers or (farmer and peddler, possibly) offer a comic contrast in modes of rusticity. The plump man on the left, with leonine chin whiskers and loose overalls, extends a snuffbox to his companion, a shaggy scarecrow whose rumpled box coat, shapeless hat, and baggy umbrella read as the uniform of a country clown. The very act of taking snuff, an indulgence almost exclusively rural by that time, brands these men as inhabitants of some quaint but culturally moribund New England backwoods.

In the same vein, Alfred C. Howland's *Bargaining for a Calf* (present location unknown; wood-engraving after the painting, Illus. 90), which was exhibited at the National Academy of Design in 1882, amounts to a geriatric paraphrase of William Sidney Mount's *Bargaining for a Horse* (see Illus. 70). Since Howland specialized in nostalgic, sometimes poetic rustic subjects, one could quite legitimately perceive these figures as Mount's farmers, now great-great-grandfathers, doddering under the gnarled apple tree as they dicker over the price of an animal somewhat less imposing than a horse. A third old man tilts his chair back against the tree trunk and observes the negotiations of his elderly friends. Very explicitly, this painting constructs an image of the American countryside as devitalized, a kind of rural convalescent home where redundant antiques fritter away their remaining time in quaint but useless occupations. Appreciating the sentiment of Howland's farm scenes and landscapes, journalist Marguerite Tracy compared his "homely country figures" to those of New England regionalist writer

Mary E. Wilkins Freeman. Like Freeman, Howland combined decay and decline with glimmers of unexpected lyricism, giving a strange beauty to the cultural twilight of the rural East.[20]

The subject of rural torpor appeared also in the work of Edward Lamson Henry, who divided his output into the categories of carefully researched, historicizing nostalgia and treatments of modern country life that often emphasized the weary monotony of old age. *Watching for Crows* (1880; Terra Museum of American Art, Chicago), *Uninvited Guests* (1883; Warner Collection of Gulf States Paper Corporation, Tuscaloosa, Alabama), and *Forty Winks* (Illus. 91) are variations on the latter theme. The first depicts Peter Brown, a grizzly old denizen of remote Cragsmoor, New York (Henry's regionalist territory), gazing idly out the window in his gloomy cottage, rifle propped against one knee and a glass of toddy on a table within easy reach. The second shows a man who appears to be the same model, now soundly dozing at his kitchen table while hens troop in through the open door and plunder the remains of his meal. In the third an old man naps in a chair, and his cat sleeps on the warm windowsill, while a square of sunlight penetrates the dusk of the interior. Like Howland's, such images corresponded to the prevalent regionalist mood of rural decline.[21]

The old men painted by Johnson, Hovenden, Wood, Howland, and Henry exemplify the late nineteenth-century stereotype that became virtually inseparable from the idea of the antiquated provincial, whether of farm or of seaport. Like others, this stereotype had some basis in actuality; the country genre specialists almost always derived their pictorial characters from carefully studied local models. This being the case, one might argue that it was no stereotype at all but simply a matter of fact observed. Again, however, in the process of selection and crystalization certain real individuals merged in a generic concept of character that came to stand for a certain class of American: the superannuated bumpkin, often nostalgically quaint, sometimes pathetic.

For the most part, this type conformed to the description of Farmer Larkin in the play discussed above. Costume was as much a reliable indicator as it had been with the stage Yankee. Sometimes, as in Eastman Johnson's *Embers*, the top hat and tailcoat functioned as clues to the recognition of essentially the same character type, grown ever more obsolete with the progress of the century. Yankee Jonathan gear was less common than various sorts of laborer's garb, marking a persistence of earlier conventions for depicting the yeoman but with increasing exaggeration of effects. Clothing became shabbier and more ill-fitting. The more modern overalls (which evolved from outdoor workers' high-waisted pantaloons with button suspenders) functioned as the unmistakable uniform of one who worked with his hands, not his head.

One telling sign of identity was the beard: a fringe of chin whiskers, sometimes goatish, sometimes rufflike, and only rarely completed by a mustache (there were numerous exceptions: this is less a rule than a guideline). Beards of any sort had become acceptable and stylish only as recently as the 1850s; before that they had been tainted by association with various forms of radicalism and Bohemianism. Abraham Lincoln, the first president in office to grow a beard, wore the fringe later identified with farmers, as did Horace Greeley, who deliberately cultivated a rustic image. Thomas Waterman Wood's portrait of Franklin Hoyt in 1855 (Wood Art Gallery, Montpelier, Vermont) shows a village carpenter similarly bearded. Other styles—the full beard with mustache, the Imperial, the bushy Dundreary side-whiskers—coexisted with the fringe, and as early as the 1870s the style began to surrender its popularity to other fashions in facial hair. Those who failed to relinquish their chin saucers were more and more likely, therefore, to stand out as irrelevant rural buffoons.

Contemporary cartoons and illustrations provide further evidence that the chin beard was the badge of bumpkinhood. The ever sardonic Thomas Nast exploited Horace Greeley's actual appearance to depict him as a crassly scheming rustic in the cartoon *Cincinnatus: H. G. the Farmer Receiving the Nomination from H. G. the Editor* (Illus. 92), which suggests that Greeley took advantage of his editorial prominence to pump up support for his nomination as presidential candidate. Greeley's notoriously inelegant backwoods Yankee guise is displayed in the long, light coat, the sagging top boots, and the trademark chin-saucer beard. Since Greeley had only recently published his book *What I Know of Farming* (1871; parodied here by Nast in papers protruding from Greeley-the-Editor's pocket, bearing the title *What I Know about the Presidency*), his association with things agricultural and rural was particularly strong. In contrast to this uncouth figure, the bearded men (an anti-Grant cabal of Republican senators, including Carl Schurz of Missouri and Reuben Fenton of New York) behind Greeley the Editor seem all the more sleek and sophisticated in their neatly tailored business suits. Even their top hats are more perfectly cylindrical than the agrarian newspaperman's. Of the three, only one has a clean-shaven upper lip; the others have beautifully groomed, fashionable whiskers of patriarchal lushness.

Theodore Davis incorporated the same dichotomy in his illustration of the interior of the Agricultural Hall at the Centennial Exposition in Philadelphia (Illus. 93). The artist's intention here was only to furnish pictorial information, but there is no mistaking the provincialism of the man on the right who, to an audience of shabby urchins, gestures toward the Ohio state display. Like Greeley, this rustic has the accoutrements of bumpkinhood: the out-of-true top hat, the long, flapping coat, a baggy umbrella, and a tuft of chin whiskers. The woman behind him in dowdy bonnet, spectacles, and bunchy shawl is probably his wife. Beyond this pair, the young city couple promenading down the central aisle are a study in elegance. The man has a full complement of well-shaped facial hair. The illustrator had no need to engage in any overt editorializing; the contrast between well-groomed urban style and rumpled, fusty provincialism is self-evident. It is as if the cartoon figures of Farmer Whilty and his wife (Illus. 85) had become flesh and walked abroad.

While Davis's illustration did not have explicitly pejorative intentions, later cartoons, exaggerating still more the distinctive attributes of the ancient rural buffoon, deliberately denigrated the image of the rural American. Alfred Gillam's cartoon *The Wily Farmer at His Old Tricks* (Illus. 94) and J. S. Pughe's caricature *"Blowing" Himself around the Country* (Illus. 95) exemplify this mode of crude disparagement. Gillam, one of *Life*'s stable of comic artists, sketched the farmer as a gleeful spider, baiting his web with rural temptations—fresh eggs, home comforts, cool springs—to ensnare the hapless city boarders, human flies with greenback wings, fluttering above the New York skyline. The farmer—or his head, at least, since the rest of him is a clump of spider legs—is a rustic grotesque, a perversion of the innocent Farmer Larkin type, absurd with his bulging eyes, lank locks, almost toothless leer, and billy-goat whiskers. Such cruel ridicule finally brings to the surface the sentiments better submerged in earlier depictions of the rural clown.[22]

The cartoon by Pughe, who worked for Joseph Keppler's satirical weekly *Puck,* is the definitive version of the American farmer as ignoble yeoman and political nincompoop. The main figure on the platform of the railroad car is William Jennings Bryan, presidential candidate by virtue of an alliance of convenience that temporararily united the Democrats with the radical Populists on the issue of free silver versus the gold standard. This issue, the last to fuel agrarian radicalism in the nineteenth century, had been fermenting ever since the 1870s, when Congress had passed a law to halt domestic silver coinage and limit the legal-tender value of silver coins already in circulation. Egged on in part by concerned mining interests, which presented the gold standard as a conspiracy against agriculturists, debt-beset farmers of the South and West made the campaign for free silver a central interest of the Farmers' Alliances that had begun to form in the mid-1880s. Unlimited silver coinage at the ratio to gold of sixteen to one, they argued, would solve rural financial troubles by putting into circulation money sorely needed to meet the demands of creditors. The fact that those measures would depreciate the currency was of little importance in relation to problems that became sharply more urgent with the Panic of 1893 and the depression that followed.

Big business interests of the East, ardent supporters of the gold standard, viewed the Farmers' Alliances as rural rabble, their demands dyed in the deepest shades of radicalism, even anarchy. The real danger of such radicalism seemed to increase when leaders of the Alliances joined with labor leaders to constitute the Populist Party, sworn enemy of capitalist, Republican powers. Like the Grange, the Alliances had some success in stirring up zeal and placing supporters in Congress (thirteen in 1894), but their candidate Bryan lost decisively to William McKinley in 1896 and 1900. The revival of prosperity in the late 1890s had the predictable effect of dampening farmers' protests, and the century closed with the status quo intact, at least as far as agriculture was concerned.[23]

The Pughe cartoon exemplifies a group of anti-farmer, anti-Bryan caricatures of the 1890s in which the iconography of the yokel finally became a full-fledged visual language of disparagement. By its very nature, political cartooning holds little sacred, but the figure of Bryan is nearly a straightforward portrait, and the newspaper reporters—though subjected to some satirical touches—are no match for the hoard of hicks ecstatically receiving Bryan's populist wind, pumped out of a huge bellows bearing the legend "16 to 1." Nearly every one of these cheering figures wears some variation on the telltale rustic chinwhiskers. The hats they wave are broad-brimmed and high-crowned: clowns' hats. Not one wears any sort of jacket. Not one has a tie, and there is but a single neckerchief. All have round, staring eyes and grinning, frog-like mouths. This is the rural electorate. The cartoonist's distortions are signals of the American farmer's long descent from the elevated status bestowed by the agrarian idealists of the young republic. In relation to urban-industrial powers, the farmer's political clout was puny indeed.

In a more benign but no less denigratory form, such types entered the realm of popular illustration about the turn of the century in the work of A. B. Frost, one of the best known illustrators of his time, remembered today especially for his pictorial interpretations of Joel Chandler Harris's "Uncle Remus" stories. A specialist in subjects drawn from the depressed and primitive realms of the rural North and South, Frost perpetuated the archaic hayseed stereotype in his pictures of New England farm life—many of which appeared in his 1904 *Book of Drawings*—presenting rural customs as genuine and often laughable folkways preserved in New England rural society.

The Sick Cow and *The Game between the Squire and the Postmaster* (Illus. 96, 97) demonstrate his half-sentimental, half-humorous tone. *The Sick Cow* represents a tragicomic drama in the monotonous lives of American rustics. The cow stands listlessly, surrounded by a bustle of consternation. Gawky women look on while an old farmer with a white fringe beard crouches over an assortment of potions. A youth is about to gallop off bareback to get more medicine, or perhaps to fetch the veterinarian. Chickens flap and scuttle away from the horse's hooves; on the left, a curious pig gazes at the scene, trotters neatly hooked over the top plank of its pen. Such is the stuff of rural life: farmers, their families, and their animals exist virtually on the same plane. Wallace Irwin's jingle, written to accompany the picture, makes those low connections clear:

> My! She looks so thin and meek
> With 'er sort o' listless eye
> And 'er nose all hot and dry—
> Seems to mean to me, somehow,
> Somethin' more'n just a cow:
> Shows how trouble, bustin' in,
> Draws us closer to our kin.[24]

The Game depicts a congregation of codgers similar to the group in Eastman Johnson's *Nantucket School of Philosophy* (see Illus. 87). Once more, the rural scene takes on shades of torpor as ancient yeomen and villagers—nearly every one with his billy-goat whiskers—pass the sleepy hours near the general store's potbellied stove, pushing counters across the checkerboard.

Representing a devolution of Eastman Johnson's rustic nostalgia combined with the condescending caricature of the late nineteenth century, Frost's illustrations of farm life—pictorial ideas in their most popular form—only serve to confirm the blunter message of the cartoons that preceded them. As a class, farmers had become unambiguously déclassé. As if rural New England (and other provincial regions) were the Galápagos Islands, the insularity of their lives had produced a species apart, curiously distinct from and in some ways inferior to the urban race evolving in the cultural mainland of American cities.

87. Eastman Johnson, *The Nantucket School of Philosophy*, 1887. Oil on panel, $23\frac{1}{4}'' \times 31\frac{3}{4}''$. (Walters Art Gallery, Baltimore, Maryland)

88. Thomas Hovenden, *The Old Version*, 1881. Oil on canvas, 24″ × 18½″. (Private collection; photograph courtesy of Kennedy Galleries, New York)

89. Thomas Waterman Wood, *A Pinch of Snuff*, 1891. Watercolor on paper, 20″ × 30″. (In the collection of the T. W. Wood Art Gallery, Montpelier, Vermont)

90.   After Alfred C. Howland, *Bargaining for a Calf*. Wood engraving. *Harper's Weekly Magazine* 26 (April 15, 1882).

91. Edward Lamson Henry, *Forty Winks*, undated. Oil on panel, 14″ × 10¼″. (High Museum of Art, Atlanta, Georgia; gift of Susan J. and George E. Missbach, Jr.)

CINCINNATUS.
H. G. THE FARMER RECEIVING THE NOMINATION FROM H. G. THE EDITOR.

92.   Thomas Nast, *Cincinnatus: H. G. the Farmer Receiving the Nomination from H. G. the Editor.* Wood engraving. *Harper's Weekly Magazine* 17 (November 22, 1873).

93.   Theodore Davis, *The Centennial—State Exhibits in Agricultural Hall*. Wood engraving. *Harper's Weekly Magazine* 20 (December 16, 1876).

94. Alfred Gillam, *The Wily Farmer at His Old Tricks*. Wood engraving. *Life* 1 (June 21, 1883).

"BLOWING" HIMSELF AROUND THE COUNTRY.

95. J. S. Pughe, *"Blowing" Himself around the Country.* Lithograph, *Puck* (September 16, 1896). (Prints and Photographs Division, Library of Congress)

96.   Arthur Burdett Frost, *The Sick Cow*. Halftone engraving.
Published in *A Book of Drawings by A. B. Frost* (New York: P. J.
Collier & Son, 1904)

212 ■ *The Changing Image of the Yankee Farmer*

97. Arthur Burdett Frost, *The Game between the Squire and the Postmaster*. Halftone engraving. Published in *A Book of Drawings* by A. B. Frost (New York: P. J. Collier & Son, 1904).

10 ■ *Peasants*

OEXISTENT with the image of the American farmer as antiquated hayseed was the image of the farmer as peasant. The two were so closely intertwined in meaning that they should rightly be seen as points on a continuum rather than distinct categories of rustic imagery. Antebellum artistic and literary versions of the American farmer frequently embodied subtle undercurrents or overt strains of patronizing sentiment, comparable to that of European depictions of peasant societies. The emergence later in the century of the American farmer as peasant type represented only the realignment of an older and essentially similar configuration so that other aspects of the design received new and significant emphasis. What had been mitigated or submerged in earlier imagery later became unambiguous.

Regionalism and the rise of urban values contributed to a leveling of the farmer's caste, as did the influx of immigrants who, displacing the older stock, threatened to form the nucleus of what one writer called an "ignorant rural peasantry." American "peasants" were but one component of the agricultural population—found in remote northeastern byways, prairie wastelands, the settlements of Appalachia, and the hardscrabble farms of sharecroppers in the South—but they were the predominant figures to emerge in the disenchanted fiction and debunking literature of the period. As represented in contemporary media, the American farmer had many characteristics of the lowly European peasant: hidebound traditionalism, insularity, provincial crudeness, and suspicion of all things urban.[1]

Winslow Homer's images of country people most eloquently expressed the concept of the American farmer as New World peasant. Raised in Cambridge, Massachusetts, Homer learned the lithographer's trade in Boston and then worked as an illustrator for the popular journals, including *Ballou's Pictorial* and *Harper's Weekly*. He began to paint in the 1860s while he was artist-correspondent for *Harper's Weekly* during the Civil War. Homer's art of the later 1860s and the 1870s, when he produced most of his farm paintings, did not fit entirely comfortably within the context of its time. Predicated on an uncommonly blunt and monumental optical realism, it lacked the refinements admired in the art of rustic genre specialists—such as Eastman Johnson and John George Brown—who were closest to Homer in style and sensibility. Confronted with his unsoftened and seemingly crude vision, uncomfortable critics voiced repeated reservations. Although he did not lack buyers during the first two decades of his painting career, his works generally fetched rather low prices.[2]

This is not to say that Homer was alien to the period. He painted the homely rural subjects that were still in favor (as the success of the already seasoned Johnson affirms), and his realism accorded with strong American precedents. That Homer's magazine illustrations so often featured rural themes is an index of their contemporary appeal; other successful artist-illustrators—Edwin Forbes, Arthur Lumley, C. S. Reinhart—published country scenes of the same sort. Homer's reticent, forceful images, however, were the boldest new formulations of an American peasantry.[3]

Homer's early painting *Girl with a Pitchfork* (Illus. 98) already embodied the qualities essential to his version of the American rustic. In this composition the single figure of the young farm woman nearly fills the pictorial space. Solemn profile facing left, the prongs of her pitchfork stabbing the sky above her kerchiefed head, the girl possesses an archaic, sculptural stillness little ruffled by the breeze that lifts her skirt much as it might fill the sails of a majestic barque. The largeness and simplicity of the figure endow it with a monumentality that belies the small scale of the canvas. In the darkening field behind the girl the hemisphere of a haystack on the left provides counterpoint to the stabbing prongs, and there is a spire in the right background—nothing else. Beyond her existence as a type of the field worker, the girl has no individuality. Seen without sentiment, she is intensely physical, an object massively poised and as earthy as the field upon which she stands.

Homer painted *Girl with a Pitchfork* in France during his visit there in 1866–67, coinciding with the exhibition of his prizewinning war painting *Prisoners from the Front* (1866; Metropolitan Museum of Art, New York) at the Exposition Universelle in Paris. It was there that he had his first extensive confrontation with French Barbizon landscape and peasant painting, which he had previously known mainly through prints after Constant Troyon, Narcisse Diaz, and others; these had become available to Americans in the 1850s. At the Exposition itself hung a comprehensive exhibit of the work of Jean-François Millet. Homer thus had ample opportunity to study the art of this master, visionary of heroic, enduring men and women of the soil. While earlier scholarship maintained that whatever Homer's contact with French art in 1867 or at any other time, he remained an independent, more recent studies see in his work clear evidence of close attention paid to the example of Millet and other French peasant painters.[4] Though neither a worshipful imitator nor a calculating borrower, Homer evidently learned from Millet a code of style and expression appropriate to the simple, earthy beings that both chose as subjects. The "girl with a pitchfork" herself, who must be a French peasant rather than an American farmer's daughter, bears a distinct family resemblance to Millet's statuesque shepherdesses and rugged field workers. The compositional format echoes Millet's in *The Sower* (1850; Museum of Fine Arts, Boston) and *Going to Work* (Illus. 99).

Going to Work expresses Millet's reverent concept of the peasant: primitive yet heroic, and spiritual in a rude and vital way that throve somehow under conditions of unceasing hardship. The design exemplifies the spare strength of Millet's pictorial language, focusing exclusively on the severely simplified figures of the peasant and his wife, who stride across a gray-green pasture slope in the early morning light. The man's profile is in shadow and the woman's face partially obscured by the basket she wears, like a grotesque bonnet, on her head. They are not to be seen as individuals; rather, they represent the universal peasant engaged in the timeless rituals of labor on the land.

Though increasingly tempered by the artist's own developing language, the Millet family resemblance persisted in Homer's depictions of American farm people throughout the 1870s. The wood engraving *The Last Load* (Illus. 100), which appeared in *Appleton's Journal* in 1869, evokes Millet's economy and concentrated focus. The design is dominated by three large figures, a man and two young women, who cast long twilight shadows as they make their way from the hayfield down a grassy hill toward their evening's rest. Solidly formed, crisply outlined, and described with a minimum of fuss, these three—like Millet's peasants—have the most generalized and conventionalized of features. The young man's lowered head and slouching hat brim make him the Everyman of the American hayfields, and the girls' features, prettier than the coarse lineaments of Millet's typical peasant women, are conventionalized far beyond individuality. The girl on the right, with her kerchief and pitchfork, is in fact the figure from the 1867 painting, translated to the American scene. In the background a haywagon rolls down the slope, and a man and child crest the distant hilltop, but these objects scarcely distract from the monumental, poised threesome in the foreground.

Answering the Horn (Illus. 101) plays another variation on the same theme, this time with a rustic couple.[5] Their upper bodies backlit by the silvery sunset behind them, they pause to acknowledge the sound of the distant horn that calls them from the fields. The tall young man who salutes the horn with his raised arm has regular, inexpressive features; the girl behind him achieves Everywomanhood with her capacious, lappeted sunbonnet (a native article replacing the Gallic kerchief of the earlier pictures) and hand raised to cover the lower portion of her face. Again, the monumental figures display Homer's stringent elimination of all but the most elemental; they are almost primitive in their simplicity.

In both the illustration and the painting, Homer's men and women have the same kind of unadorned physicality and dumb reticence as the peasants in *Going to Work* and many of Millet's other pictures. They seem to have no contact (beyond an elemental sort of physical togetherness) with each other, nor do they acknowledge the viewer's presence. They are self-enclosed yet give no hint of an interior life. Engrossed as deeply in his study of light and atmosphere as in the depiction of human beings, Homer accorded his figures the status of objects, as interesting, perhaps, as cattle in the meadows. Unlike the figures in the fields of Jerome Thompson or Eastman Johnson, Homer's are neither buoyant nor supple; they express no joy or satisfaction in their work but only the undeniable fact of it. Their wooden stiffness further enhances the sense of a mute, animal acceptance of or immersion in their existence.

On the whole, Homer was less sentimental than Millet, who interspersed his severe labor scenes with tender spectacles of rustic maternity and the like. For all its apparent straightforwardness, Millet's imagery bore a haze of romantic, quasi-religious nostalgia for an uncomplicated life close to nature. Even though he portrayed his peasant subjects hard at work, his paintings wrought poetry from the reality of brutal, monotonous toil. Homer remained cool and distant. Although with this reticent artist it is never wise to be too certain, visual evidence suggests that his farm workers were not often vehicles for statements on heroism, nobility, or rural virtue. Fashionable middle-class men and women—surely not the repositories of any noteworthy moral qualities—are treated to the same kind of neutral observation in his croquet scenes.

Despite French ideas, Homer was still operating within a basic, established framework of traditional American rural imagery. His subjects find numerous past and contemporary parallels in painting and popular illustration. It is reasonable to inquire why one cannot read his rural scenes, as one would a work by Eastman Johnson or John W. Ehninger, as a pictorial celebration of the agrarian ideal. On the surface, Homer's is no less idyllic. Yet if we set *The Last Load* side by side with an image almost exactly contemporary, such as Ehninger's *Bringing in the Hay* (Illus. 102), the coolness of Homer's sensibility precisely asserts itself. The figures in Ehninger's painting play their expected roles, expressing happy, graceful harmony with each other and with the serene rural landscape that contains them. The group to the left of the haywagon, a young man and two girls, bears a surprising resemblance to Homer's figures, even down to the fact that one of the young women wears a kerchief and short jacket, like the "French" maiden in *The Last Load*. Ehninger's haymakers, however, form a circle of connection: they touch, they chat, they smile. The more distant couple hang back to enjoy a few moments of romance, and the boy on top of the wagon merrily waves his hat. Even the solitary man driving the oxen looks across at the happy threesome as if to share in their company. Homer's trio forms only a circle of disconnection; they are barely aware of one another's existence. No less intimately contained within their landscape than Ehninger's figures, their presence there is not so much happy and graceful as a simple and inevitable circumstance of their lives. Their monumentality endows them with heroic largeness merely in the physical, not the moral, sense.

Homer's undercutting of the agrarian ideal is subtle but unmistakable. Indeed, his vision approximates the tenor of real farm life, as recorded in laconic diaries and disillusioned recollection, more honestly than do the sweeter fictions of an Ehninger or a Johnson. This is not to say that Homer can be counted among the outright debunkers. His figures are only stolid and plain, never disfigured by brutal toil, but he discarded completely the narrative and sentiment conventionally utilized as vehicles for expressing the agrarian spirit. By refusing to comment, by treating his rustic figures as part of a visual rather than conceptual or philosophical design, he stripped away the veneer of the older ideal. What lay beneath had a formal beauty little indebted to the tradition. In place of the smoothly interlocking components of the old pastoral, Homer introduced a matter-of-factness that relished the elemental beauties of rural light and air while declining to exalt the felicity of rural life.

Gloucester Farm (Illus. 103) exemplifies the pronounced flatness of human relations so often embodied in Homer's work. Several of his paintings in oil and (as he became more interested in the medium in the 1870s) watercolor featured young rustic couples feeding animals, resting in meadows, or cautiously confronting each other. Although these situations imply courtship, the couples for the most part remain curiously detached or, more precisely, mute in each other's presence, as if silenced by tensions vibrating between them. In *Gloucester Farm* the girl hefting her milk pail looks aside and down as the big-footed farm lad with the hoe drinks from a dipper. The pasture slope upon which they stand is vivid with red and white flowers, and the sun beautifully irradiates the girl's rosy flesh and the pale fabric of her skirt. Behind them a bare plane of ground slants up to the stark angles of a red barn and a white house behind it. This is not the suave, vernal farmscape of a Jasper Cropsey or of Currier & Ives prints. The backward boy and girl have none of the witty liveliness of Mount's farmers in *Bargaining for a Horse*, nor are they depicted as amusing country clowns after the fashion of *Winding Up*. There is no spark of animation between the two, only that undercurrent of unspeaking tension. They are shapes in the light, dull caretakers of animals and tillers of the rocky, grudging New England soil.[6]

In the sense that Homer's farm people appear to be lowly, inarticulate toilers, bonded to the land and by dress and attitude widely separated from urban society, they conform strikingly to a peasant model. Even the fact that women emerge here as active and equal workers represents a shift. Americans cherished the notion that the Yankee farmer refused to let his women degrade themselves by toiling in the fields like European peasants. Significantly, Homer's treatment of his New England farm laborers differed little from that which he accorded to black field workers in paintings derived from a trip to Petersburg, Virginia, in 1875. *The Cotton Pickers* (1876; Los Angeles County Museum of Art) portrays two classically monumental black women, New World equivalents (in social as well as pictorial fact) to their French counterparts in the works of Millet or Breton. Though vestiges of the agrarian tradition clung about the conceptual edges of Homer's farm scenes in the 1860s and 1870s, their real message was different, contradicting yet not debasing the older ideals, simply offering an alternative vision, unadorned and forcefully designed.

As Lloyd Goodrich has noted, critics in the 1870s complained constantly about the lack of finish in Homer's paintings; to many they seemed crude, glaring, and sketchy. In 1876 the *Art Journal* fretted: "Mr. Homer is always perplexing. There are so much truth and vigor in his compositions that one can but admire them; and yet half-expressed thoughts, strange eccentricities of drawing, rude handling of material, seriously offset the charm." And the *Atlantic Monthly* grumbled, "The most prominent fault of his pictures has always been their baldness." In the farm scenes, Homer's lack of sentiment and conventional ideas probably baffled commentators as much as his lack of technical refinement. The subjects themselves and the artist's direct approach, were startling and unfamiliar, at least in the world of art. As one journalist wrote:

He paints the life that he sees as he sees it; he never softens a line nor modifies a feature, nor yields for a moment to any soft seduction of beauty. He is wholly in sympathy with the rude and uncouth conditions of American life; he likes the men, the women, the boys, and the girls, of the rustic by-ways of our land—and he likes them as they are, awkward in dress, spare in form, tanned and freckled by the sun, with no sensuous warmth, no dream of beauty.[7]

Clearly, this reviewer found little to admire in the angular, slab-sided denizens of the American countryside. Whereas earlier writers praised the American rustic's plain garb and ruddy health as visible evidence of a virtuous life, the critic of the 1870s struck the condescending note reserved for inferior, outlandish beings. However much these folk might belong to their provincial hamlets and pastures, they had no business inhabiting paintings, at least in their natural state.

It was the sophisticated eye of Henry James that detected, down to the minutest point, what was unacceptable about Homer's American peasant imagery. James recorded his comments as part of a broad retrospective of the 1875 exhibition season, especially at the National Academy of Design, where the three paintings Homer had showed included *The Course of True Love* (unlocated), depicting a straw-chewing country girl with her farm-boy suitor, and *Milking Time* (1875; Delaware Art Museum, Wilmington). James's words, which have appeared in many a study of Homer, remain one of the most penetrating, if negative, contemporary analyses of the artist's vision. With a great show of reluctance, he admitted that Homer's strength of design had a force that one could not help admiring. The subjects, however, he found altogether repellent.

The most striking pictures in the [National Academy] exhibition were perhaps those of Mr. Homer. . . . Before Mr. Homer's little barefoot urchins and little girls in calico sunbonnets, straddling beneath a cloudless sky upon the national rail fence, the whole effort of the critic is instinctively to contract himself . . . so that he can creep into the problem and examine it humbly and patiently, if a trifle wonderingly. Mr. Homer's pictures . . . imply no explanatory sonnets; the artist turns his back squarely and frankly upon literature. . . . Mr. Homer goes in, as the phrase is, for perfect realism. . . . He is a genuine painter; that is, to see, and to reproduce what he sees, is his only care; to think, to imagine, to select, to refine, to compose, to drop into any of the intellectual tricks with which other people try to eke out the dull pictorial vision—all this Mr. Homer triumphantly avoids. He not only has no imagination, but he contrives to elevate this rather blighting negative into a blooming and honorable positive. He is almost barbarously simple, and to our eye, he is horribly ugly; but nevertheless there is something one likes about him. What is it? For ourselves, it is not his subjects. We frankly confess that we detest his subjects—his barren plank fences, his glaring, bald, blue skies, his big, dreary, vacant lots of meadows, his freckled, straight-haired Yankee urchins, his flat-breasted maidens, suggestive of a dish of rural doughnuts and pie, his calico sun-bonnets, his flannel shirts, his cowhide boots. He has chosen the least pictorial features of the least pictorial range of scenery and civilization; he has resolutely treated them as if they *were* pictorial, as if they were every inch as good as Capri or Tangiers; and, to award his audacity, he has incontestably succeeded. . . . Mr. Homer has the great merit, moreover, that he naturally sees everything at one with its envelope of light and air. He sees not in lines but in masses. . . . If his masses were only sometimes a trifle more broken, and his brush a good deal richer—if it had a good many more secrets and mysteries and coquetries, he would be, with his vigorous way of looking and seeing, an almost distinguished painter. In its suggestion of this blankness of fancy the picture of the young farmer flirting with the pie-nurtured maiden in the wheat field is really an intellectual curiosity. The want of grace, of intellectual detail, of reflected light, could hardly go further; but the picture is the author's best contribution, and a very honest, and vivid, and manly piece of work. Our only complaint with it is that it is damnably ugly! We spoke just now of Mr. La Farge, and it occurs to us that the best definition of Mr. Homer to the initiated would be, that he is an elaborate contradiction of Mr. La Farge.[8]

Paradoxically, John La Farge and Homer were friends, and La Farge greatly respected Homer's art. James's opposition of the two painters, however, touched the core of a fundamental issue: the great new wave of cosmopolitanism nudging American art into its typical late nineteenth-century mainstreams and in the process creating a climate of rejection for the old native schools or for any traits that betrayed provincial unrefinements. While Homer was considerably more sophisticated than James allowed himself to perceive, he was neither suave, dexterous, nor erudite, as the younger Americans trained in France and Germany were learning to be. Whereas La Farge fit smoothly into the category of refined cosmopolitan, Homer had too many angles that had not been filed down and polished. In James's eyes, Homer's crude Yankee subjects, set forth in a style equally crude if powerful, were well beyond the pale of well-bred art.

In the same review, James had kinder words for Eastman Johnson, in particular for a painting of a Yankee peddler that had all the felicities of technique and expression James had missed in Homer's paintings: "The old hawker, with his battered beaver hat, his toothless jaws and stubbly chin, is charmingly painted. The painting of his small wares and of the stove near him, with the hot white bloom, as it were, upon the iron, has a Dutch humility of subject, but also an almost Dutch certainty of touch."[9] Johnson's rural subjects were analogous to Homer's during the 1870s. Like Homer,

he pursued a strong interest in the accurate depiction of form in natural light and atmosphere. Yet Johnson was altogether more ingratiating. He painted what was probably a "damnably ugly" old Yankee peddler "charmingly"; he rendered his still-life accessories in an exquisite Dutch (read: non-American) manner. Although his themes were homespun, his technique was not. It was only through such treatment that the plain Yankee rustic could become at all palatable, even though, as James pointed out, Johnson was essentially a homely painter rather than an elegant one.

James reacted as he did to Homer's paintings not only because the works themselves seemed ugly but because he considered those rustics to be equally so. He all but shuddered at the thought of so crude a dish as "rural doughnuts and pie," and the coarseness of such things as calico sunbonnets filled him with dismay. An urbanite and soon-to-be expatriate in an increasingly urban and cosmopolitan era, James voiced the emerging values of the age. Even so, he would have looked more favorably upon Homer had the artist been less impassively literal, willing to add a few grace notes of feeling to his stark designs. A painter like Johnson was ingratiating not only because of his fine handling of the brush but also because his works breathed a gentle sentiment that beautified his humble subjects and evoked feeling (warm, nostalgic) in the beholder. Such a tactic would fall into James's category of the "intellectual tricks"—imagining, thinking, composing—by which the plain might be transformed into something more nearly ideal.

In the 1880s Homer finally achieved real prominence among American painters, but his rising reputation coincided with his shift to a different range of themes: the perils of the sea and the Darwinian dramas of the wilderness. Observers of the 1870s certainly respected Homer's talents (so often wrongheaded, as they thought); a few praised his freshness, liveliness, manliness, and sincerity; but many failed to grasp his meaning or appreciate fully the content of his paintings of rural life. His vision of the New England agricultural scene—unpicturesque, unembellished with humor, sentiment, or moral message—seemed mystifyingly blank. His sunburned youths and strapping maidens, naturalized versions of Millet's monumental peasants, were the inhabitants of a new American pastoral too close to the truth to exert a strong appeal. Undistorted reflections of the American farmer's real status and the true tenor of rural existence, Homer's paintings—popular subjects painted in an unpopular way—confronted an audience that still demanded rustic fancy dress, in both the literal and the metaphorical sense. It is a telling instance of such taste that in the late 1870s Homer's Houghton Farm paintings, a number of which featured girls in rococo shepherdess costumes—white ruffles and laced bodices—enjoyed an overwhelmingly favorable reception.[10]

It was not so much that Homer painted the American farmer as peasant as that it was the wrong kind of peasant. Peasant signals, cloaked in guises of nobility or buffoonery, had been present all along in representations of American rustics. The current taste, however, dictated not only sentiment of some kind but also a smooth, foreign look, in emulation either of traditional sources or of the immensely popular French peasant painters Millet, Jules Breton, and Jules Bastien-Lepage. In view of Homer's debt to Millet, it may seem paradoxical that the French painter won an adoring American audience while Homer did not; but Homer had studied selected aspects of Millet's formal expression, ignoring the reverence and emotion whereby the French painter transfigured common clay into something higher. Favor, accordingly, fell upon those Americans who did likewise.

Critic H. T. Tuckerman, who approved of European refinements, routinely praised those whose paintings admitted such influence. His remarks on John W. Ehninger's work reveal his bias. Ehninger had studied extensively in Paris at the atelier of Thomas Couture, and he spent much time abroad, but he specialized in scenes of American rustic life. Ehninger, wrote Tuckerman, had French skills that lifted him well above the ranks of those American painters who were hampered by "careless habits and incomplete discipline." Ehninger's early painting of a Yankee peddler (1853; Newark Museum, Newark, New Jersey) was fine precisely because of those skills: "There is nothing Yankee in it but the subject; a patient handling and an expressive significance are manifest; nothing crude, hasty, or extravagant. . . . the general artistic effect is almost too good for a subject of this class; though very apt in their treatment, a higher range is more appropriate for this artist." Tuckerman's complaint about the baseness of the theme was nothing new. Critics had regretted the same tendency in Mount to dwell on planes lower than his talents merited. But none of Mount's contemporary admirers, even while calling him the Wilkie of America and the like, would have dreamed of praising his paintings because only the subject was Yankee! Ehninger had painted peasants in Europe, and to his American subjects he brought a Europeanized peasant sentiment, depicting farmers in the fields as warm family units; in the happy group of *Gathering Pumpkins* (see Illus. 21), even the horse in harness has her foal gamboling alongside. One such picture Tuckerman found especially pleasing and full of "sympathy and truth." The subject was "a farmer halting his plow in the furrow, while his gudewife sets the baby on the horse." Tuckerman's epithet "gudewife" for the woman is significant: he applied this affected archaism to individuals perceived as worthy yet lowly and archaic.[11]

It was the same with with Eastman Johnson, who also owed much of his style and technique to Europe. Tuckerman admired the truth, naturalness, and pathos of his works depicting the "American rustic." He had the "truth and tenderness" of Edouard Frère, another venerated French painter of humble life. Frère was associated with the school of "sympathetic art," so named because his portrayals of the peasant milieu, like Millet's, were suffused with expressions of sympathy for those who nobly endured lives of hard labor and frequent sorrow. Art critic S. G. W. Benjamin later ranked Johnson with another enormously popular French painter of peasant sentiment. Praising Johnson's 1876 *Husk-*

ing Bee (Illus. 17), Benjamin wrote: "In tone and color and in the acute perception of rural human nature it loses nothing by comparison with the work of Jules Breton."[12]

Such comparisons, made casually enough, perhaps, are not without deeper implications. Ehninger, Johnson, and other popular imagers of American country life in the decades after the Civil War were comparable to French peasant painters because—matters of technique aside—the Americans' subjects were alike regarded as peasants. The painters' embellishments of gentle feeling and their romantic allusions to timeless ritual veiled the harder reality expressed so much less compromisingly by Winslow Homer. Such devices, like the images of the farmer as geriatric buffoon or lovable archaism, also served the purpose of subtle belittlement or unconcealed condescension.

However strongly they reminded critics of European painters, Johnson and Ehninger were not allied with the central developments of postwar cosmopolitanism. Others, notably Bostonian William Morris Hunt, owed much more to Barbizon mentors. Hunt was a key figure in the genesis of American taste for French Barbizon painting and its offshoots. He spent two years following and studying Millet after leaving the Paris atelier of Thomas Couture. His subsequent career in Boston combined teaching and painting with such energetic promotion of Barbizon art that Boston became an early and zealous center of Barbizon collecting. A figure painting such as *The Little Gleaner* (1854; Toledo Museum, Toledo, Ohio) reveals Hunt's debt to Millet in the simple unity of the figure, the subdued, closely related tones, and the pensive mood projected by the little harvester herself, frail sibling to Millet's peasant girls. Hunt's landscapes disclosed their French ancestry in their broad generalizations and subordination of detail to soft, poetic effects.

Contemporary observers found much to admire in Hunt's Boston-French style, which represented a modern alternative to the tight realism of antebellum native schools. Still, some complained that he lacked the true regional touch. In pointing out this deficiency, one review of Hunt's figure and landscape paintings also yielded valuable insight into the new attitudes toward both pictorial style and the New England farmer. The author Edward Wheelwright (a Harvard classmate of Hunt and likewise a student of Millet) devoted a long section of his review to an autumnal twilight scene in which two men with an oxcart gathering the last corn shocks from a bleak and withered field. The mood of the painting, wrote Wheelwright, was intensely poetic, but strongest in expression was the

poetry of incident, the story proper which the artist had chiefly in his mind to tell: that sad, pathetic story of the hard, laborious, joyless life of the small farmer in New England,—a life of which, for the most part, we have had, in painting at least, only caricatures, but which contains, when rightly seen, as many of the elements of poetry as that of the French peasants whom Millet has made immortal.

"Rightly" seeing this mode of existence meant spinning poetry out of deprivation, as Millet did. No longer the wily, idiosyncratic bumpkin, the Yankee farmer as seen through Barbizon spectacles was becoming a minor but mildly tragic peasant hero. Images of his life were less celebrations of American identity than evocations of melancholy. In Hunt's painting the muted tones, the dead plants, and the celestial afterglow conjured up thoughts of the dying year. Whereas Millet's images were truly French, however, Hunt's were not precisely American:

Admirably, on the whole, as the story is told . . . Mr. Hunt has not quite succeeded in giving it in the genuine Yankee dialect, with a strong flavor of the soil about it, as Burns or Millet would have done had they been born in New England. Neither the men, nor the oxen, nor even the apple-trees, are of the pure Yankee type; and the whole picture has something of a foreign air. There is a want of that perfection of local coloring which we can never hope to see fully realized in the portraiture of the rural life of New England until some youth, "native here, and to the manner born," shall, as Millet did, quit the plow handle and the scythe for the palette and brush, and . . . qualify himself to render a tardy justice to the race from which he sprang.[13]

Winslow Homer, though he had not literally "quit the plow handle and scythe" for painting, better met those criteria, but his art lacked that suggestive Barbizon poetry which cast a haze of glamour over the commonplace.

In contemporary opinion it was George Fuller, not Homer, who succeeded where Hunt had failed to strike that regional chord. Fuller, success phenomenon of the 1870s and 1880s, was no less indebted to Barbizon examples, particularly Millet and Camille Corot. Yet perhaps because he was not the celebrity that Hunt was, and because he had returned to the art world after fifteen years of tobacco farming in Deerfield, Massachusetts, many reviewers praised his paintings as purely native creations. Prominent critic Mariana Van Rensselaer spoke for many:

We are grateful for his poetry, since poetry is not too common in our art. . . . And we are still more grateful that, being poetical, he could at the same time remain national, local—could be the interpreter of his own people. If he is rare among our painters for being poetic, he is unique as yet . . . in being both poetic and American.[14]

Some of Fuller's most Gallic paintings are scenes of agricultural life in the South, with black herders and field workers standing in for French shepherdesses and gleaners. Like his French exemplars, Fuller populated his fields predominantly with young women. *Turkey Pasture in Kentucky* (Illus. 104) depicts a muted, misty field in which some pensive black girls watch over their feathered flock. The close harmony of earthy tones symbolizes the harmony of figures with nature. The mood here, as in many French peasant paintings, is tranquil and a little melancholy. The subject of turkey herding itself, at first glance so purely American, also had Barbizon precedents, such as Millet's *Autumn Landscape with a Flock of Turkeys* (c. 1870–74; Metropolitan Museum of Art,

New York), and Constant Troyon's *La Gardeuse de dindons* (c. 1863; Louvre, Paris).

Fuller gallicized his New England farm scenes as well. *The Afterglow* (c. 1880; Phillips Collection, Washington, D.C.) shows an autumnal forest where several women are gathering faggots. The choice of this theme, which evoked the idea of hardship and diligence among the rural poor, represented the wholesale assimilation of European models. Like gleaning, such activities had once held no place in the idealized American farmscape. Now, however, the romance and poetry of the primitive rustic life had staked a claim upon American cultural territory, while the growing taste for European styles had begun to discredit older modes of American pictorial vision.

It was ultimately the younger generation that went to extremes in emulation of the French, assimilating not only French style but also French peasants themselves as subjects: cosmopolitanism could hardly go further! Some, like the immensely successful Daniel Ridgway Knight and his rival Charles Sprague Pearce, even took up permanent residence abroad (at Poissy and Auvers-sur-Oise, respectively) while continuing to create works aimed primarily at the American market. So strongly did Knight's French peasant genre appeal to current taste that his huge opus *Hailing the Ferry* (Illus. 105) won a medal at the World's Columbian Exposition in Chicago in 1893. With this honor, Knight's work held its own against the extensive collection of genuine French peasant paintings at the Exposition in the section entitled "Foreign Masterpieces Owned by Americans."[15]

As the market developed for works of art portraying peasants of all European nationalities, Americans, both as students and professionals, followed in Hunt's footsteps. Many sought out art colonies in the most picturesque villages of rural France, where they could paint pastoral landscape and peasant life. Succeeding Hunt at Barbizon were J. Appleton Brown, Wyatt Eaton, and Will Hicok Low. During the 1860s and later a group of young American painters sojourned at Pont-Aven in wild, archaic Brittany, including Earl Shinn,

Robert Wylie, Frederick Bridgman, J. Alden Weir, Willard Metcalf, and Thomas Hovenden. For some, peasant painting was only an episode in careers that later took different directions. The fact that so many passed through the peasant phase, however, is a revealing index of its popularity in the last third of the century.[16]

Knight's *Hailing the Ferry* epitomizes the Franco-American peasant image (though it is not meant to represent what was a fairly broad range of treatments). This painting portrays a world far distant from that of the American farm scene. Its heroic scale alone—seldom matched by earlier American efforts—marks it as the product of European tradition. Knight's vision is of an archaic world veiled in nuanced grays, which evoke both the silvery palette of Corot and the tonalities of the photograph. This monochromatic scheme serves to unify a design that incorporates Bastien-Lepage's technique of loosely brushed peripheral areas combined with a tight, naturalistic rendering of the figures. The girls themselves are the perfection of French artistic peasanthood—full-figured, healthy, clear-skinned, and picturesquely uniformed in tight bodices, much-mended skirts, and ungainly clogs. With their rough baskets at their sides, they call and gesture lustily to the ferryman across the shining river. The work expresses that spirit of peasant health and gladness upon which Knight chose to focus, to the satisfaction of his critics.[17]

A primitive idyll created with empty virtuosity by a sophisticated cosmopolitan, *Hailing the Ferry* stands diametrically opposed to the images produced by Mount and his contemporaries a mere half century earlier, or less. There is nothing Yankee about it, not even the subject. Contrived, artificial, and riddled with crossed signals as American farm genre paintings may have been, they had the fundamental virtue of maintaining a vital and meaningful connection with the culture out of and for which they were made. What, on the other hand, did French peasants have to do with America?

For one thing, peasant paintings represented highly desirable acquisitions for rich collectors. Indeed, no one else could

afford the high prices, which continued to escalate in the last two decades of the century. At a time when Winslow Homer's oil paintings fetched sums of $300 or $400, works by Breton and Troyon could command $10,000, sometimes much more. By 1889, prices for certain canonical works rose to dizzy heights. At the auction of the Secrétan collection of paintings in Paris, July 1889, the American Art Association bought Millet's *Angelus* (c. 1858–59; Louvre, Paris) for $110,000.[18]

These facts suggest that in an age notorious for its cultural imperialism, possession of fabulously expensive French paintings both conferred and announced status. Images of grubby toilers though they were, they cast about them a bright aura of glamour and privilege, which many could vicariously enjoy by owning prints after *The Angelus* or Breton's *Song of the Lark* (1884; Art Institute of Chicago). Predictably, floods of warm and reverential praise accompanied the progress of French peasant paintings in America; at the same time, they remained valuable counters in a game of conspicuous consumption.

One of the major factors in American emulation of the French, then, was economic. Younger Americans abandoned their farmer compatriots because farm subjects, no longer on the cutting edge of fashion, were less likely to survive in competition with French works. To lure their potential patrons, they had to use proven bait. The degree to which they subscribed to this tactic is suggested by the illustrations in G. W. Sheldon's *Recent Ideals of American Art* (see note 17), which aligned itself squarely with the young cosmopolitans. Large populations of mostly female French peasants, by painters such as Knight and Pearce, far outweighed the mere handful of American farm scenes allowed between the covers of Sheldon's book.

Crass economic motives were well-concealed, operating at a subliminal level; most artists and critics were probably not even conscious of these drives. Rather, the new European orientation found justification in a revisionist view of Old World peasant culture which substantially reversed earlier opinions about the American farmer's glorious superiority to the wretched agricultural underdogs across the Atlantic. Hardly by coincidence, the exaltation of the French peasant paralleled rising American tendencies to debunk old agrarian ideals and to discount the nobility of the yeoman.

The American response to Millet and other peasant painters graphed the peasant's soaring stock. Although a handful of critics saw in Millet's imagery an indictment of the oppression relentlessly visited upon the agricultural laborer everywhere, the majority did nothing but praise the poetry and spirituality of his vision. Writing in *Harper's Monthly*, M. D. Conway described *The Gleaners* (1857; Louvre, Paris) as a pictorial hymn to the "peacefulness of peasant life and its harmony with nature." This was a realm that the jaded city dweller must envy: "the simple life which gladly lets the deluded world go by while it still dwells in the dear old days when Adam delved and Eve span." This rhetoric is entirely familiar; many an agrarian fantasist of American country life had voiced the same thoughts. Millet's imagery, however, offered the opportunity to enjoy a depth of feeling seldom evoked by the American farmer. His peasants were at once noble and pathetic, his paintings filled with a sad lyricism. As another writer said, "Your sympathy is won for the toiler whose labor is so unremitting, whose life is so lonely," the subject in this case being a solitary shepherd at twilight, with his sheep and his dog.[19]

In the illustrated magazines, reproductions of peasant genre paintings were sometimes accompanied by wholehearted paeans to peasant goodness. A painting by Frère, for example, which portrayed simple peasant children in the roughest of mud-walled, crudely furnished huts, inspired the commentator to praise French peasants as the backbone of the French economy and of the state itself. Simple and good, they worked so hard that they would astound American fieldhands (who were, by implication, a lazy lot). Unlike the Americans, so profligate with land, they harvested abundant crops on tiny bits of soil. They preserved a sense of independence and equality because they owned their land, and this

in turn gave them "an air of frank and self-respecting manliness." Even better, they were satisfied with their lot: "They do not behold a carriage or fine clothing enviously." Another article that had nothing but kind words for French peasants—models of industry to shame the rest of Europe (and probably America as well)—called Irish peasants "careless and slatternly," Germans "dull and apathetic." The French, however, loved the soil and tilled it industriously, "never whining about scanty returns, or fancying that they have any special grievance of which to complain."[20] The equation of such unparalleled goodness with peasanthood signaled the final phase in the demoralization of the American farmer in art. The lowliest classes of rural France had come to be regarded as better than he.

Even the peasant physique seemed to surpass that of the American rustic. John M. Welding, one of the most thoroughgoing debunkers of the agrarian ideal, scoffed at the concept of "the ideal country girl—her of the novels—with lissome form, rosy cheeks, clear complexion, artless ways and quiet costume, etc., etc." The actual (and severely disappointing) country girl belonged to "one of two distinct classes . . . namely, the short and squabby form with greasy complexion, and the lean and gaunt with insipid and freckled complexion." French peasant girls were unrefined yet most appealing, as an admirer of Breton observed of *The Potato Harvest* (1868; Pennsylvania Academy of the Fine Arts, Philadelphia): "These potato gatherers elevate the whole sex. They are not painted above their station but in their station; not with delicacy and gentle grace, but teeming with strength and vigor and robust health. The painter thus gives them their own idea of perfect beauty, and by this idealization of nature he excites admiration."[21]

According to artists themselves, another powerful attraction of Old World peasant culture was its archaism. Here once more the displacement process was at work, shifting value symbolism from one group to another. Innocence and distance from the mad pace of progress had once been admired in the life of the ideal American farm; now, the basic complaint was that the American farmer was no longer picturesque. Mass manufacturing, transportation, marketing, and communication had made him mentally and physically indistinguishable from any other ordinary, dull American.

Will H. Low had gone through a phase of peasant painting under the impact of Millet, whom he came to know at Barbizon in the early 1870s. Meretricious mass education, Low believed, had robbed the American farmer of that precious simplicity and integrity which the French peasant still owned:

The peasant lacks the superficial refinement and quasi-education with which our common schools have veneered our masses; in this land of plenty we have as yet no conditions that parallel those that confront the rural population of France; but in this environment the peasant has wrested comparative comfort, self-support, and cheerful contentment under conditions we must respect.

Willing to admit that the peasant's lot was hard, Low nonetheless asserted that it was morally and spiritually better (being closer to nature) than the American farmer's, not to mention more interesting to paint.[22]

Contemporaries condemned the American farmer for his unpictorial modernity. As painter and critic Samuel Isham wrote, the native agriculturist was "too independent, too sophisticated; his machinery, his reapers and threshers lacked the epic note; they were new like his clothes, his house, all of his surroundings." Echoing Isham, culture critic Lewis Mumford found nothing to connect American farming with romantic concepts of nature. That this had ever been believed, he said, was "one of the most sardonic jests in history." The American yeoman could hardly wait to put as much distance as possible between himself and the natural world, "to barter all his glorious heritage for gas light and paved streets and starched collars and skyscrapers." In fiction, the drab American agriculturist inspired the same distaste. William Dean Howells opened *The Coast of Bohemia* with the young artist Ludlow, fresh from Paris and Impressionism, morosely observing the scene at the Pymantoning County Fair:

Ludlow believed that if the right fellow came to the work, he could get as much pathos out of our farm folks as Millet got out of his Barbizon peasants. But the fact was that he was not the fellow; he wanted to paint beauty not pathos. . . . there was nothing in the fair-house, with those poor, dreary old people straggling through it, to gladden an artistic conception. Agricultural implements do not group effectively, or pose singly with much picturesqueness.[23]

In short, the American farmer was not "peasant" enough for art, even though since the earliest years of the century his image, always ambiguous, had incorporated elements traditionally identified with peasant status. Artists of the nineteenth century turned deaf ears to the new epic note sounded from the spacious plains of the West, tilled and harvested by mechanical armies. Winslow Homer's "peasant" New Englanders, strangers to the mechanized reaper, found limited appreciation, but with the exception of a handful, few American painters of native themes succeeded (or were interested) in duplicating a Barbizon sentiment in an American subject.[24] Only in the French or perhaps the Dutch peasant, it seemed, could be found the traditional costumes, the picturesque patches and tatters, the archaic methods, the primitive rituals, and the oneness with the earth that both bound and fed them. Listening still to the old music of pastoral convention and romanticism, ambitious younger Americans had to cross the ocean in search of a new rural ideal.

In broad cultural terms, the peasant vogue was only the recurrence, in new guise, of that old bourgeois craving for green pastures well removed from the roads trampled by industrial development, technological innovation, urban sprawl, and social upheaval, all of which had accelerated dramatically in America during the final decades of the century. Perhaps at that time such imagery—of harmonious workers, uncomplaining and content with their lot—represented an ideal that industrialists might well dream of in an age of increasing tension between labor and capital. This was an international phenomenon as well: similar anxieties and impulses had motivated those very French painters the Americans so deeply admired. How deep or sincere this nostalgia ran is an open question; it is sometimes difficult to distinguish between lip service and true sentiment.

In retrospect, the American taste for French peasants seems contrived, an old pattern of nostalgia reworked into an exotic but superficial design. Comfortable in their townhouses or urban mansions, patrons who bought Barbizon or American Barbizon paintings could indulge in the luxury of a sigh for the simplicity of rural life, but in general that was probably little more than a pose. With perfect sincerity, writers may have preached the peasant as *exemplum virtutis,* but American life became inexorably more complex nonetheless. The peasant craze was, finally, a cult of hollow nostalgia, formed at the point where cosmopolitan fashion and the art market coalesced.[25]

It may only have been fortuitous, but the intensification of belittlement observable in both painting and graphic arts depicting the American farmer after the Civil War coincided with the rise of agrarian agitation and radicalism—first the Grange movement and later the Farmers' Alliances. Though their achievements fell far short of their original goals, these organizations gained widespread visibility and notoriety during their periods of activity, which also coincided with social unrest in urban and industrial sectors. It would be rash to imagine that portrayals of the farmer as enfeebled geezer or peasant clod were deliberate attempts to undermine the farmer's political threat by reducing him to the level of fool or dimwit; nevertheless, such imagery, rooted perhaps in subterranean currents of anxiety, could generate destructive side effects. At the very least, these depictions left little doubt of the farmer's peripheral status and political irrelevance in modern urban society.

98.   Winslow Homer, *Girl with a Pitchfork,* 1867. Oil on canvas, 24″ × 10½″. (The Phillips Collection, Washington, D.C.)

99. Jean-François Millet, *Going to Work,* c. 1850–55. Oil on canvas, 22″ × 18″. (Cincinnati, Ohio, Art Museum; bequest of Mary M. Emery)

100.   Winslow Homer, *The Last Load*. Wood engraving. *Appleton's Journal* 1 (August 7, 1869). (Bowdoin College Museum of Art, Brunswick, Maine)

101.   Winslow Homer, *Answering the Horn,*
1876. Oil on canvas, 38⅛″ × 24⅜″. (Courtesy of
The Muskegon Museum of Art, Muskegon,
Michigan, Hackley Picture Fund)

102. John Whetten Ehninger, *Bringing in the Hay,* 1868. Oil on canvas, $35\frac{1}{2}'' \times 59''$. (Private collection; photograph courtesy of Kenneth Lux, New York)

103. Winslow Homer, *Gloucester Farm,* 1874. Oil on canvas,
20½″ × 30½″. (Philadelphia Museum of Art, John H. McFadden Jr.
Fund)

104. George Fuller, *Turkey Pasture in Kentucky* (also known as *The Turkey Pasture*), 1878. Oil on canvas, $27\frac{3}{8} \times 40\frac{3}{4}''$. (Chrysler Museum, Norfolk, Virginia; gift of Walter P. Chrysler, Jr.)

105.   Daniel Ridgway Knight, *Hailing the Ferry,* 1888. Oil on
canvas, 64½″ × 83⅛″. (Courtesy of The Pennsylvania Academy of
the Fine Arts, Philadelphia; gift of John H. Converse)

THE ANXIETIES OF NOSTALGIA

11 ▪ *Rural Heavens and Urban Hells*

HE growth of cities played a major role in shaping and giving meaning to images of rural life. In the early decades of the nineteenth century the reckless economic life of the metropolis and its extravagance of consumption and display served as counterpoint to depictions of country life and country people as uncorrupted elements in the moral and political structure of an agrarian republic. Paradoxically, such polarization was only the obverse of a symbiotic relation, mutually antagonistic yet to a greater and greater degree binding the country to the city.

The rhetoric and iconography of rural-urban dualism crystalized in the middle decades of the century. At that time urban growth suddenly seemed to mushroom, creating a sharpened awareness of a society in flux and disorder. Evidence of concern abounded in literature, in popular prints, and in the periodicals of the day, where urban nightmares and rural felicities routinely appeared, often side by side for maximum didactic force. The same concern found expression in books and images that conjured up visions of a middle-class rural Arcadia providing refuge for the culture now menaced by the strange new metropolis. It is uncertain whether Americans unquestioningly embraced such black-and-white notions, or whether many were tormented by the paranoia that painted the city as a phantasmagoria, in hues of fire and brimstone. With few exceptions, neither urban horrors nor bourgeois Edens found a substantial place in midcentury academic painting. In the popular media, though, pictures and prose alike reinforced this ancient yet newly urgent dichotomy and in so doing helped to perpetuate simplistic, preconceived ways of viewing and judging the two realms.[1]

In what came to be a fixed stereotype, the city was a place of anything but moderation. Within its boundaries were vast fortunes and extreme poverty, straitlaced decorum and abandoned degeneracy, pious benefactors and criminals of unimaginable viciousness. More often than not, the perverse glamour of the netherworld—sinister alley mazes, saloons, and brothels—possessed a fascination that no scenes of rectitude could match. Therefore, the creators of sensationalist city exposés and the even more extravagant visionaries of the city as embodiment of Gothic terrors mined those vast caverns of wickedness for the most lurid and shocking details.

The image of the city as an earthly hell of chaos, death, and decay occurred repeatedly. Even a sophisticated New Yorker like diarist George Templeton Strong could write: "Cities are bad enough at the best, but a rich commercial city (like this) I regard as a *hell*—a sink of vice and corruption and misery—lightened on the surface by the false glare of unhealthy exhalations." Novelist George Lippard portrayed a Gothic New York, exuding an overheated miasma of rottenness, in *The Empire City* (1850), its pages awash with horrible murders, beautiful bare-bosomed female corpses, madhouses, graveyards, the power and greed of the rich, the hopeless debasement of the poor. Lippard envisioned the Empire City as a morbid Whore of Babylon,

clad in purple and rags, splendid with countless wealth, festering with countless crimes! . . . a voluptuous queen sitting in her gorgeous palace . . . that palace built on the hideous dungeons of poverty and crime—and as the cup is to her lips, and the music in her ears, you see the shroud beneath her robes of purple.

George C. Foster, author of several midcentury collections of urban sketches, used the same terms, especially to describe such notorious areas of depravity as the New York slum neighborhood called Five Points, "the skeleton of City Civilization." When stripped of the "cloud of appearances" that veiled it, Foster's "magnificent city" was "but a vast abyss of crime and suffering, with here and there a crystal shooting out over the horrid recess of filth."[2]

As the growing urban world seemed more and more to menace not only hapless individuals but the whole of society, the prose detailing its depravity could only seek to paint in ghastlier terms what earlier sketches and tales had mapped. In *Sunshine and Shadow in New York* (1868), Matthew Hale Smith honored the established convention of high contrast in descriptions of urban life. Smith's New York was full of parvenu rich, shifty stockbrokers, and models of righteousness. He delighted in tales of greatness and pride brought low: belles of one season become starving paupers the next.

Five Points, that region of "wickedness, filth, and woe," was only a stone's throw from Broadway, where costly plate-glass windows displayed the richest consumer goods. Despite the presence in *Sunshine and Shadow* of worthies like General Grant and Henry Ward Beecher, it was degeneracy that called forth Smith's purplest prose and stood in the spotlight at the end: "The motto over bad New York," Smith wrote, "is the startling words, 'Whoso entereth here leaves hope behind.' . . . A worse population . . . does not inhabit the globe. The base men of every nation, and the crimes, customs, and idolatries of every quarter of the world, are here. . . . A portion of New York is Paradise: a large part is Pandemonium."[3] New York thus reincarnated the capital of Hell in Milton's *Paradise Lost* and borrowed its motto from Dante's *Inferno,* where that dreadful warning emblazoned the entrance to the nether regions.

Reporters for the periodical press were equally inclined to exploit the sensational even while assuming the stance of reformer or social critic. The 1863 draft riots in New York served as an awful reminder of how explosively pandemonium could erupt from the lower depths, tearing away the city's facade of order. As columnist Eugene Lawrence put it,

Those who saw that troubled period, so full of doubt and terror, will remember the strange sensations with which they passed streets deserted by all save bands of plunderers; by houses, banks, and shops barred and guarded; beside the blazing ruins of fine buildings and the wrecks of stately manufactories; in the midst of fierce mobs who chased unfortunate colored men . . . and hanged them ruthlessly to the nearest lamp post.

Lawrence went on to describe the terrible sight of vast multitudes, maddened by rapine and bloodshed, sweeping down the avenues in a "resistless tide," setting fire to great blocks of buildings and dancing wildly around the corpses of their victims. Even the Gothic novelists could hardly surpass the horrors of such a reality.[4]

The trope of the metropolis as a virulent, spreading sickness was repeatedly called into service as well. Tenement houses, bad enough in actuality, were given lurid colors as "cesspools of disease." The Reverend Josiah Strong, secretary of the American Home Missionary Society, wrote forebodingly of modern cities as a "serious menace to our civilization" and "tainted spots in the body-politic," where "the dangerous elements are each multiplied and all concentered." Echoing Strong's words, a writer in the *North American Review* called great cities the "plague-spots of the nation." The basic rhetoric was not new: Jefferson had equated urban mobs with sores leaching strength from the body. The tone, however, had risen to a higher pitch in response to increasingly ominous signs.[5]

Illustrations of city life, scattered throughout the popular weeklies of the middle decades, followed the path laid down by writers of fiction and fact (however embellished). Pictorial exposés of urban crime and squalor did not by any means claim a disproportionate share of space; the illustrated weeklies peddled variety, and their offerings typically included an assortment of topical subjects, views of famous or exotic places, and portraits of the eminent and the notorious, along with various real and ideal scenes of country life. Depictions of the evil city, however, did appear regularly.

Several composites of Boston and New York street characters appeared in the 1850s, all of them emphasizing the picturesque while glossing over the sufferings of poverty. *City Sketches* (Illus. 106) shows dock loafers, pauper children, a charcoal peddler, immigrants on the dock, and a trash collector as a collection of interesting urban oddments. It is a very limited range of urban species; there is no reference to middle- or upper-class life. Only the tiny vignette of the night watchman at the bottom suggests the mechanics of social order in the city, while "Life in Town" at the top conveys little more than the seething flux of a commercial street. *City Sketches* is a portrait of the metropolis as the abode chiefly of the low, the shiftless, and the vagrant.

By the 1860s, images of the urban dispossessed concentrated more explicitly on squalor and depravity in a dark, dangerous underworld populated by drunks, criminals, and scavengers. Stanley Fox's *Evading the Excise Law—Laying in Rum for Sunday* (Illus. 107) depicts a grog shop where one could behold "more squalor, degradation, and misery" than at any other time, or in any other place. Here are the urban poor on parade: black and white, men and women, and even children, queueing for their Sabbath ration of the devil's brew, all of them ill clad, and all of them drawn with coarse features, the very opposite of the clear-cut Anglo-Saxon faces admired as the mark of the superior type and the standard of beauty. The same is true of Paul Frenzeny's *Rag-Pickers Disposing of Their Gatherings* (Illus. 108). Every face among these scavengers is grotesque by virtue of some gross exaggeration. They wear the nightmarish masks of the underdogs, constructing the visage of the mob that threatened to destroy the cultured classes. These underdogs lurked in the nether regions: the fetid tenements, the rum dives, or the comfortless shelters where the homeless might temporarily find a berth. The subterranean gloom and ghastly highlights of A. Gault's *Shelter for the Homeless: Night Scene in a New York Station-House* (Illus. 109) evoke a dungeon out of Edgar Allan Poe. No mere dormitory, it is a sinister cavern where evil spirits of the netherworld lie beneath the fitful glare of gaslights.[6]

Any man might tumble to damnation if he failed to see the shroud beneath the purple robes. At first glance, the wood engraving *The Wickedest Man in New York* (Illus. 110), showing the interior of John Allen's Dance House, appears to be a scene of vigorous festivity, a social hall where couples twirl and flirt so exuberantly that one man flings his partner like a prima ballerina above his head. It is not so unlike Winslow Homer's rowdy cornhusking frolics (see Illus. 15). This is no spectacle of innocent relaxation, however. The women who sip whiskey over a plunging décolletage are loose and vicious; the men are coarse and boisterously intoxicated. One has slumped to the floor in a stupor. This was not just a dance hall but a Five Points brothel, the kind of place from which, as Matthew Hale Smith wrote, men began the long fall into irredeemable depravity:

From the stews of New York, heated and often maddened by poisoned liquor, men come for a dance. . . . The room is full of thieves, pick-pockets, fighters, bullies. . . . Bank clerks, and young men in confidential positions, go to laugh and have a jolly time of an evening. They are ensnared before they know it. In the lap of Delilah their locks are shorn, and their strength departs.

Smith told the tale of an upright young man, representing a New England business house, who went to the dance hall and to ruin with drink and fancy women. Having squandered a million dollars on these fatal pleasures, he spent his shameful days "reeling about the street, lounging around barrooms." In this light, John Allen's Dance House might symbolize the very gate of Hell itself.[7]

The most powerful visual metaphor of the metropolis as the gateway to Inferno was Thomas Nast's *A Warning Light* (Illus. 111), a macabre parody of Frédéric Bartholdi's Statue of Liberty, soon to stand in the harbor of New York. Like a guardian at the mouth of Hell, the statue stands with a death's head under its radiant crown, one skeleton arm holding aloft the inverted torch, ancient symbol of life extinguished, and the other clutching a tome titled *Roll of Death*. On the pedestal is carved another variation of Dante's words: "New York—Leave All HOPE Ye That Enter." The cartoon reflected current citizen ire against the spoils system of political patronage, blamed for the filthy streets that had been responsible (it was thought) for a winter of rampant epidemics and an alarmingly high death rate. Despite its topicality, Nast's image, simple and forceful in conception and design, transcends its referent to become a baleful symbol of the evil city incarnate, place of darkness, mystery, and death.

As gloom over the city deepened and its infernal forces rumbled in menacing crescendo, the ideal of the country by contrast could only appear more paradisiacal; its inhabitants, if not angels, at least untainted. Such meanings were implicit in the pastoral landscapes and poetic rustic labor scenes so ubiquitous at midcentury. They came into play overtly and didactically, however, in popular literature and illustrations that deliberately juxtaposed the rural and the urban in order to leave no doubt which was good and which bad. The fact that such imagery coincided precisely with the emergence of the lampoonable bumpkin is a sticky paradox, but it effectively demonstrates the way in which details may be selected and bent to serve the promulgation of cultural ideas, however contradictory they may seem.

In Anna Ogden Mowatt's highly successful play *Fashion* (1845) the countryside functioned as antidote to urban ailments. The plot, as in so many Yankee plays, hinges on the confrontation of city and country, but here country life offers the means of redemption to a city businessman (once a country boy), Mr. Tiffany, whose slavery to wealth and status has driven him into bankruptcy. Tiffany and his extravagant, fashion-besotted wife are rescued by old friend Adam Trueblood, who has remained and prospered on the farm. The honest Trueblood consents to help his stricken and humbled friends on one condition: "You must sell your house and all these gew gaws, and bundle your wife and daughter off to the country. There let them learn economy, true independence, and home virtues, instead of foreign follies."[8]

At midcentury, story after story in such magazines as *Godey's* and *Gleason's* played variations on that theme, contrasting the shallow hypocrisy of elegant town girls with the pure sincerity of simple country maidens, or telling the tale of jaded urban lives restored by country air. "The Hypochondriac" offers a hero who, having exhausted himself seeking stimulation in New York, sinks into a melancholy funk. His canny physician tricks him into going to the countryside to take a cure under the supervision of a country doctor. Once the cure has succeeded, even the news that he may have lost all his money through a bank failure does not ruffle his tranquillity: "The crowded city has been the scene of all my miseries, and this quiet village has been the scene of all my happiness."[9]

The moral also operated in reverse, when after a visit to town taught a country dweller to appreciate the true luxury of rural life. In one tale the village wife of an up-and-coming builder longs to go to New York to become as genteel and fashionable as her city cousins. She appreciates the comforts of her life, but she "had no piano, and wore chintzes instead of mousselines and silks, while, do all she could to prevent it—even in the face and eyes of Mr. Spears [the city cousin], Mr. Clarke [her husband] *would* dine in his shirtsleeves, and shave only every other day!" Predictably, the scales fall from her eyes when she eventually visits New York: "There were brick walls, heaps of garbage, the odor of stables and drains, in place of the cheerful yard and tidy vegetable garden, the shady street and elms that surrounded Mr. Clarke's good two-story frame house at Toddesville." Crowning her disillusion is the discovery that the cousins live squalidly at home so that they can afford to shine in public.[10]

Didactic-contrast illustrations pointed the same moral. Visually, these contrast pictures may seem little different from those by Edmonds or Oertel (see Illus. 76, 80), in which the rustic is the butt of the joke. The context, however, determines meaning: the country dwellers are meant to appear sincere and natural, while the city types—as shown by their devotion to appearances—are seen as shallow and artificial. One of the most painstakingly elaborated is *Town and Country* (Illus. 112), which compares three types: doctors, belles, and storekeepers. The pictures speak very well for themselves. The country doctor is paunchy, wears a swallowtail coat and a soft, low hat; the city doctor is a trim dandy in a close-fitting frock coat and shiny top hat. The country belle is in calico and sunbonnet, with no hoops; the city belle is a fashion plate with vastly distended crinoline skirts and the latest in headgear. The country storekeeper is a brawny fellow in agrarian uniform, while his city counterpart in sleek black has wavy, oiled locks and a fussy little mustache. The text enlarges on what the eye can see, filling out a picture of hypocrisy, materialism, and superficiality as opposed to honesty and simplicity. The city belle is high-style but has no ideas, whereas the country belle is natural and has sensible things to say. The handsome city store-keeper measuring out ribbon has "sweet hands" and a low voice, but the rough-looking country storekeeper is the honest man who works hard for a living. The same meanings are implicit in Jules Tavernier's *Town and Country* (Illus. 113), which needed no caption to illuminate the contrast between the city maiden choosing her spring wardrobe in her hothouse, rococo boudoir and the country girls out in the fields decking each other with wildflowers, the only ornaments they need.[11]

Such stories and pictures might not mean a great deal were it not for the circumstances that generated them. Against the backdrop of a society in transition, a culture still rehearsing one set of ideals (rural, agrarian, individualistic) while acting more and more on another (urban, capitalistic, corporate), each bit of the cultural ephemera that reinforced traditional preconceptions staunchly proclaimed their validity in an uncertain present. The verbal and graphic message was both reassuring and conservative, in the sense that it upheld an ideological status quo.

A related form of conservatism, upholding a social status quo, lay at the bottom of the middle-class retreat to Arcadian rusticity. This movement began as early as the 1840s with the publication of Andrew Jackson Downing's *Cottage Residences* (1842) and his influential *Architecture of Country Houses* (1850), which inspired further treatises on the subject by disciples such as Calvert Vaux, who published *Villas and Cottages* in 1857. To those of privilege and means, these works offered the practical basis and the philosophical justification for escaping the infernal city and taking full advantage of the therapeutic and morally healthful paradise of rural America.

Downing democratically embraced the full range of American society, proposing honest homes for the honest yeoman and modest ones for mechanics and other workingmen. His heart, however, lay with the genteel, middle-class villa modeled on the ideal of the English country house but carefully divested of the outward trappings, at least, of aristocracy.

This house, with its Gothic or Italianate trimmings and picturesque landscaping, would stand as material emblem of bourgeois, Anglo-Saxon values: "the love of order, the obedience to law, the security and repose of society, the love of home." The rural villa represented the perfected type of the American family home. Far more elegant and beautiful than the simple cottage and plain farmhouse, it stood for higher civilization:

The villa, or the country house proper, then, is the most refined home of America—the home of its most leisurely and educated class of citizens. Nature and art both lend it their happiest influence. Amid the serenity and peace of sylvan scenes, surrounded by the perennial freshness of nature, enriched without and within by objects of universal beauty and interest—objects that touch the heart and awaken the understanding—it is in such houses that we should look for the happiest social and moral development of our people.

By its very existence, the rural villa would exert a happy persuasion: "There is a moral influence in a country home," Downing wrote, "—when, among an educated, truthful, and refined people, it is an echo of their character—which is more powerful than any mere teachings of virtue and morality." The villa of the cultured and the prosperous was a hedge against the creeping disease of urban growth and change. It would be a bulwark protecting the social order and civilized values from the inchoate dangers of the American city at midcentury. While Downing insisted on the need to maintain republican simplicity in style, taste, and manner, it is clear nonetheless that his country gentlemen were just that. As one farmer-critic perceived, Downing's designs were intended for the gentleman farmer who worked, "if at all, in gloves"; something was still needed to suit the "industrious working-man." Downing's idealized rural homeowner was as clearly superior to the farmer and the mechanic as he was safely removed from (though no doubt financially indebted to) the realm of urban squalor and turmoil.[12]

This vision of a middle-class Arcadia had an immediate and powerful appeal, fostered not only by the Downing treatises and their successors but by journalists and essayists who turned out articles and books on the new ideal of country life. Nathaniel Parker Willis, who had commissioned Calvert Vaux to design a Gothic villa on his new Hudson River estate, Idlewild, (acquired in 1850) published a series of "Idlewild Papers" in his magazine the *Home Journal*. These papers generated so much interest (including tourism to the region) that in 1858 writer and illustrator T. Addison Richards visited Idlewild to report on what seemed to be Downing's ideal, ravishingly realized as a "sweet idyl of Art-embellished and Fancy-vailed landscape":

Here our poet, while secluded to his heart's content amidst the primitive wildness and wealth of Nature, has yet within his reach, when it pleases him to extend his hand, all the resources and delights of the most cultivated and generous society. On all sides villages, villas, and farms, teeming with happy, intelligent, and elegant life, encompass him about. . . . high as he seems to be above the great flood of life, he has only to don the "wishing cap" of steam and stand in the heart of the metropolis.

Here it had been Willis's task not to wrest his sustenance from the land but to create a bower of refinement and a landscape of picturesque delights. To achieve this, he employed a number of men "in the stables and on the grounds," but these fellows were never allowed to mar Willis's perfect landscape pictures. Idlewild, quintessence of the country-gentleman ideal in America, was a monument to what money could buy and taste dictate. Safely sequestered from the rabble, it sheltered within its walls an existence of privilege, order, and refinement. Willis himself was fully aware that such a life amounted to a heaven for the elite. Showered with readers' requests for more information on the area (near Cornwall, on the west bank of the Hudson), Willis scouted out a dozen or so sites that he called "Paradises" and envisioned as future homes of "the wealthier class, in search of a villa-site rather than a farm."[13]

Willis's popular work *Outdoors at Idlewild* was one among a substantial number of country books published in the 1850s and 1860s, all of them concerned with the moral and spiritual influence of country life, its curative properties for the city-stressed, and its unending material pleasures. Perhaps the most paradisiacal of all was Henry Carmer Wetmore's *Hermit's Dell* (1854), reprinted in 1856 as *Rural Life in America*. The title might lead us to expect an essay on the sturdy yeoman and the simple republican goodness of his life; it is instead a paean to a bourgeois life of bucolic ease: an existence of cultivated pleasure, wholesome communication with nature, and manual work of only the lightest and most aesthetically pleasing sort.

Teddy, the hired man, performed the real labor of gardening, while the family took charge of embellishments:

So Teddy dug all day, and I raked off a bed for our first sowing of letuce [*sic*] and peas. . . . My fair cousin Blanche is out on the lawn near by, equipped with scissors and cord, clipping off the dead shoots from the rose-bushes and tying up their refractory branches: another one still [the narrator's wife Minnie] is sitting in the sunshine not far distant, weaving airy ladders for wild creepers to climb and mantle the dead maple that stands by the garden gate.

As in all such country sanctuaries, a division of beauty from utility was the norm. In the garden, "a wide border of lilacs and syringas mingled with lesser shrubs and plants, divides it from the lawn and serves as a screen to veil from the house our prospective cabbage and potato patches, which are not very ornamental appendages." This hierarchy of plants affords a paradigm of the social hierarchy that structured the country gentleman's perception of his rural universe. In this scheme of things the plain farmer was a worthy neighbor but seldom to be included in the gatherings of society. Rather, the cultivated banded together to enjoy the higher forms of amusement appropriate to their status. Taking his ladies for an afternoon drive, the narrator draws the reader's attention to the seats of these desirable associates:

Here and there, where the high ground commands a fine river or mountain view, or both combined, the forest has been long since cleared away, and tasteful dwellings with velvety lawns and well-kept enclosures, mark the hand of wealth and taste. They are the abodes of those upon whose intercourse and society we are dependent for much of our present and prospective pleasure.

Aside from ornamental gardening, diversions and pastimes were many. A typical postprandial hour would be one during which

Blanche practises the last new Polka, which she does not fancy much because it is not difficult enough. . . . Minnie is almost lost in my great reading chair . . . and deeply absorbed with the glowing pages of Hans Anderson's "Improvisatore." . . . The couch before the fire looks inviting, and, taking up "Cosmos," which I have nearly finished, I read till the book drops out of my hand.

There were also shooting, fishing, and riding—sports of the leisured. On occasion, an unfortunate Pole or a vagabond family of Irish immigrants would excite sympathy and allow Arcadians to enact the roles of Ladies and Gentlemen Bountiful. The presence of such outcasts served to introduce a decorative but very temporary cloud of sadness and rumination over the sunny landscape of rural pleasure.[14]

Such heavenly realms were celebrated in a number of contemporary prints from Frances Palmer and Currier & Ives. The periodicals also pictured and praised rural and suburban felicities, mirroring the assumptions of the country books and of Downing and his disciples. Some portrayed actual estates, homes of culturati or, later, of well-to-do capitalists who reaped wealth in the city but commuted to their rural-suburban estates to renew spiritual health. The Currier & Ives prints, however, depicted the most highly idealized fantasy world, the very incarnation of the middle-class heaven.

Palmer's 1855 quartet *American Country Life* explicitly set forth the idea of social hierarchy in rural America. Palmer was probably acquainted with the popular and familiar country books, and her own English background no doubt furnished her the conventions of a traditional country-house iconography, forged to assert the rightness of an existing hierarchy and system of property ownership.[15] *May Morning* (Illus. 114) might be a scene out of Wetmore's *Rural Life in America.* The house is a high-style, towered, bracketed Italianate villa, framed by tastefully grouped trees and fronted by a sloping and surely velvety lawn. Near the gate two fashionably dressed ladies perform some decorative horticultural tasks; on the lawn a small girl communes with a lamb. Riding by on sleek mounts are the top-hatted master of the house and his son, who wears a natty cap. It is perfectly obvious that these people are the aristocrats of the scene. Beyond their *hortus conclusus,* on both sides, the viewer is allowed glimpses of a lower social plane. On the left, and railed off from the landscape of beauty, is a stable, in front of which a groom curries a horse and chickens peck at the dirt. On the other side a man drives a plow, pulled by a team of workhorses, and behind him is the plain gable of a farmhouse, some humble yeoman's abode.

Summers Evening (Illus. 115) is substantially the same, although there is more agrarian activity for the country gentlefolk to observe. In the foreground a well-dressed young couple with two frolicking children occupy a picturesque knoll under venerable trees. The man's gesture invites us to observe the spectacle on the right, where harvesters rake hay into heaps and fork it onto a wagon, and a queue of cows ambles toward the barn for milking time. In the background, carefully set off from the utilitarian farmscape, is a high-style house with a wide piazza and Gothic touches: craggy roof line and lacy barge boards. Other prints, such as *Summer in the Highlands* (Illus. 116), focus exclusively on the middle-class paradise, where gardeners and laborers are invisible and only the privileged occupants are left to admire the view from the velvety lawn to the tranquil Hudson, from which in turn the occupants of leisurely sailboats might spy the elaborately ornamented Gothic "cottage" crowning the hill.

This was not a countryside of action and endeavor but of revery and recreation. New York writer and onetime landscape gardener Charles Wyllis Elliott summed up something of this mood in his article "About Piazzas" and its small but eloquent illustration (Illus. 117). Elliott's essay is a city-dweller's rumination on the restorative delights of country life as seen from the porch of a friend's country house in the Berkshires. The narrator tells the tale of two men who vowed to add to their incomes one thousand dollars for every year of their lives. One had a stroke, and the other died at the age of forty-two. He then proceeded to muse about his own rustic activity, or its lack:

What do I do there? What do I do? I cannot say I *do* anything, but I *enjoy* much. . . . After breakfast . . . I am careful not to plunge my head into a cellar or garret filled with vapors exhaled from foul gutters and filthy sewers; I try to keep tobacco smoke out of my lungs, by filling them with good mountain air; my ears are not deafened with the distracted din of omnibus wheels, nor my eyes blinded with the dust and grime of dray horses; my wits are not strained to get some other man's money away from him, and I entertain no schemes for lobbying a horse railroad along the banks of the Housatonic. . . .

No, my friend, I step out on your piazza and lift up mine eyes unto the hills; and there I praise God for the beautiful world he has spread at my feet, and am filled with his goodness.

Later, after dinner, he looks out and muses on a pastoral landscape:

The white June clouds float lazily in the serene azure, and the beautiful hills lie so peacefully in the soft sunlight, that my too impatient soul is stilled. . . .

I hear the soft moo-moo of the cows ready to give down their milk, and it is so still, I hear distant voices from far-off farm houses, and the whippoorwill sings her melancholy note. . . . The candles burn across the valley through open doors, and I can fancy good farmers are there eating their peaceful suppers. . . . They can sleep in peace, and so can we; for we have had a good, dull, wholesome day; have drank no whiskey; smoked no tobacco; cheated nobody, nor fretted our souls to grow rich or great.[16]

The illustration communicates the essence of the bourgeois rustic idyll. The man casually seated on the piazza is doing nothing in particular, though the means of diversion—a folded newspaper on his knee and a fishing creel at his feet—are present. Vines frame the view upon which he gazes, resting cheek on hand. Somewhere farmers are working, but it is for him simply to take his ease and absorb the balmy atmosphere. The most cursory glance at other pictorial categories of rural life—such as the defiant yeomen of the Granger posters; Winslow Homer's rugged, reticent harvesters—suffices to permit measurement of the chasm between yeoman and gentry.

The gulf between visions of rural bourgeois felicity and the imagery of the virtuous pastoral farmscape was wide indeed, yet the glaring incompatibility of the two did not preclude their coexistence. The yeoman could be now noble, now risible; now a republican *exemplum virtutis*, now a low-comedy figure. An urban audience could profess to admire the artless simplicity and sincerity of country manners or laugh at their boorishness, meanwhile securing in rural life what they chose of middle-class culture, comfort, and, especially, status. Would-be country gentlefolk co-opted the country for their own purposes and fashioned an idea of it to match: one that consisted mainly of refined pleasure, having little to do with homespun or huskings. It was heaven to the hell of the city, therapy to mend frazzled urban nerves, and sanctuary for middle-class values. The farmer's place there was only to produce; that of the privileged solely to consume.

106. *City Sketches.* Wood engraving. *Ballou's Pictorial* 8 (March 31, 1855).

107. Stanley Fox, *Evading the Excise Law—Laying in Rum for Sunday.* Wood engraving. *Harper's Weekly Magazine* 11 (February 6, 1868).

SKETCHES OF CITY LIFE—THE RAG-PICKERS DISPOSING OF THEIR GATHERINGS.—Sketched by Paul Frenzeny.—[See Page 727.]

108.   Paul Frenzeny, *The Rag-Pickers Disposing of Their Gatherings.* Wood engraving. *Harper's Weekly Magazine* 11 (November 14, 1868). (Prints and Photographs Division, Library of Congress)

109.   A. Gault, *Shelter for the Homeless: Night Scene in a New York Station-House*. Wood engraving. *Harper's Weekly Magazine* 17 (December 13, 1873).

"THE WICKEDEST MAN IN NEW YORK"—SCENE AT JOHN ALLEN'S DANCE HOUSE, 304 WATER STREET, NEW YORK CITY.—See Page 331.

110. *"The Wickedest Man in New York"— Scene at John Allen's
Dance House, 304 Water Street, New York City.* Wood engraving.
Frank Leslie's Illustrated Newspaper, August 8, 1868. (Prints and
Photographs Division, Library of Congress)

A WARNING LIGHT.

WILL IT BE NECESSARY TO ERECT AN ADMONITION OF PESTILENCE AND DEATH IN OUR HARBOR? A QUESTION WHICH OUR CITIZENS MUST DECIDE.

111.   Thomas Nast, *A Warning Light*. Wood engraving. *Harper's Weekly Magazine* 25 (April 2, 1881).

112. *Town and Country*. Wood engraving. *Harper's Weekly Magazine* 2 (February 6, 1858).

113. Jules Tavernier, *Town and Country*. Wood engraving. *Harper's Weekly Magazine* 17 (August 16, 1873).

AMERICAN COUNTRY LIFE.

May Morning

114. Frances Palmer, *American Country Life: May Morning,*
1855. Lithograph, $16\frac{7}{8}'' \times 23\frac{15}{16}''$. Published by Currier & Ives, New
York. (Prints and Photographs Division, Library of Congress)

AMERICAN COUNTRY LIFE.

Summers evening

115. Frances Palmer, *American Country Life: Summers Evening*, 1855. Lithograph, $16\frac{11}{16}'' \times 23\frac{7}{8}''$. Published by Currier & Ives, New York. (Prints and Photographs Division, Library of Congress)

'SUMMER IN THE HIGHLANDS.

116.   *Summer in the Highlands,* 1867. Lithograph, $14\frac{15}{16}'' \times 20\frac{7}{16}''$.
Published by Currier & Ives, New York. (Prints and Photographs
Division, Library of Congress)

117. E. B. Bensell [?], title vignette, "About Piazzas." Wood engraving. *The Galaxy* 1 (1866).

12 ■ *The Homestead*

HE emotion of nostalgia has come to be inseparable from visions of idealized country life. Any social change trails behind it the shadows of reminiscence and longing for days gone before. For centuries, men and women had sighed for lost youth and the scenes (almost always poetically rural) of their early and most innocent associations, their sighs of regret becoming ever gustier as the nascent forces of technology and capitalism coalesced into the dynamo of expansion that underlay the metamorphosis of Western society and culture in the nineteenth century.

In antebellum America a romantic, Wordsworthian nostalgia found expression in outpourings on the long-ago, faraway, humble cottage home. This theme was a staple of popular music and verse. The song "Home Sweet Home," written by John Howard Payne for the opera *Clari* (1823), became an enduring popular favorite, as did Samuel Woodworth's poem "The Old Oaken Bucket" (1826), a rueful tribute to simple days of boyhood on the farm. The ideas of youth and rural happiness were often so closely intertwined that one could scarcely appear without the other:

The places which we were accustomed to frequent in childhood and early youth are seldom, if ever, forgotten. . . .

The smoothly-shorn meadows upon which we played—the newly-mown hay, to us so sweet and healthful—the shady woods through which we roved during the summer noontides in search of wild flowers and berries—all come within our mental vision as though they had never faded or changed with the lapse of years. . . .

I have looked on many a glorious view from lake, river, and high mountain-top, but never have I forgotten those quiet spots, so dear with youthful and tender associations.

This pleasant regret could bear a bitter edge. However vivid such images of the past, they were without substance and indeed without physical trace:

Look back again to the scenes of your boyhood. Where are the landmarks that you loved, the pleasant things around which cluster the memories of youth? Where the tall forest tree that was spared when the old woods were swept away? Where the clustered plum-trees, the wild hazels, the willows along the brook, the maples that shaded the spring that came out from among their roots? Gone! all gone! The old school-house and the play-grounds—the path across

the fields that led to them—where are they? Gone again, all gone!
. . . Do you remember how in the long winter nights you sat around
the fire-place wherein logs were blazing, and how the pitcher of
cider and the platter of doughnuts were placed upon the old cherry
table that sat out in the middle of the kitchen . . . and how happy
each one was as he sat with his pewter mug of cider in one hand
and a doughnut in the other before that old-fashioned kitchen fireplace? Those were pleasant times. But they are memories now.[1]

These passages, taken from two popular country books of
the 1850s, are typical of contemporary nostalgic sentiment,
which ranged from cozy reminiscence to wails of despair in
the face of the relentless progress that was destroying precious rural things and places.

In painting as in literature, rural things signified what
could never be recaptured. Asher B. Durand created an allegory of nostalgia in landscape form in *An Old Man's Reminiscences* (1845; Albany, New York, Institute of History and
Art), a panoramic inventory of motifs that construct an iconography of recollection. Durand explained its meaning in a
discourse on the power of landscape painting to trigger recollection. He imagined a weary city dweller whose country
days were infinitely long behind him:

Suppose such an one, on his return home, after the completion of
his daily task of drudgery—his dinner partaken, and himself disposed of in his favorite arm-chair, with one or more faithful landscapes before him . . . in proportion as it is true and faithful,
many a fair vision of forgotten days will animate the canvas, and
lead him through the scene: pleasant reminiscence and grateful
emotions will spring up at every step, and care and anxiety will
retire far behind him. . . . He shifts the scene, and stretching
fields and green meadows meet his eye—in such he followed the
plow and tossed the new-mown hay; by the road-side stands the
school-house, and merry children scatter from its door—such was
the place where he first imbibed the knowledge that the world was
large and round, while ambition whispered that the village grounds
were too narrow for him,—and with the last rays of the setting
sun, the picture fades away.[2]

All the delightful rural activities described here were fig-
ments of memory, emblems laden with associations of days
gone by. Resurrected on canvas, they had no tangible, worldly
counterparts. They were gone as surely as the willows, the
schoolhouse, the kitchen hearth, the cider and doughnuts
mourned by the author of the "country book."

The rural nostalgia that found widespread expression in
the last third of the nineteenth century formed a line of
continuity with the conventions established earlier. There
was, however, a shift toward greater intensity and idealization. After the Civil War, reminiscent reveries of country
life took on new tints of rosy sentiment, even while the
agrarian dream itself faded as the debunkers exposed it to
the unfiltered light of truth. The impact of the war, combined with a sharpened awareness of social and economic
changes previously set in motion but now impossible to ignore, made the country of the imagination all the more a
ravishing dream world, an earthly paradise lost, which acted
as a powerfully evocative symbol among the insecurities of
the postbellum decades. This is not to say that the America
of the 1870s and after was dominated by escapist fantasy; on
the contrary, nostalgia was a wistful subcurrent in an era of
brassy optimism and greedy aggrandizement. But like the
subconscious mind of Freudian theory, cultural subcurrents
reveal what the brassy, public facade refuses to acknowledge, and they offer clues thereby to deep-seated cultural
malaise.

Many looked back on the era before the war as a time of
blissful provincial ignorance, now demolished. As Henry James
wrote in 1879, "the immense, uninterrupted material development of the young Republic" in the "broad morning sunshine" of its life had

implanted a kind of superstitious faith in the grandeur of the country, its duration, its immunity from the usual troubles of earthly
empires. This faith was a simple and uncritical one, enlivened with
an element of genial optimism, in the light of which it appeared

that the great American state was not as other human institutions are, that a special Providence watched over it, that it would go on joyously for ever, and that a country whose vast and blooming bosom offered a refuge to the strugglers and seekers of all the rest of the world, must come off easily, in the battle of the ages.

The war had "rudely dispelled" the illusions cherished by that "earlier and simpler generation," forced to behold "the best of all possible republics given over to fratricidal carnage." The new mood was darker, less certain. The Civil War had "introduced into the national consciousness a certain sense of proportion and relation, of the world being a more complicated place than it had hitherto seemed, the future more treacherous, success more difficult."[3]

The technological and industrial progress that had done so much to transform the older society (and bring about the war) ushered in a legion of doubts even while it swelled America's power and wealth in the 1870s. As a onetime Unitarian minister wrote, progress had wrought profound, permanent change: "Our former rural civilization, with its simple manners, moderate desires, and autonomous life, has as good as disappeared; the country is now just the suburb of the city." Because the present "ruling order" was inadequate to new conditions, the entire system was in danger of collapse:

Disorders increase, oppressions multiply; the nation is plundered in pocket, imperilled in morals; angry discontent is the mood of millions, distrust of all; agitation, insecurity, unhealthy excitement, hope to win and fear to lose . . . unsettle conserving customs, break up the traditions of honesty and honor, reduce intellect to skipping, snatching processes, and prey even upon physical health.[4]

No longer was rural virtue the moral and political backbone of American society. Agrarian simplicity was no match for the complicated, treacherous world envisioned by James and other contemporaries too skeptical to endorse wholeheartedly the advance of American civilization.

Beneath the general malaise lay anxieties about personal security in a world no longer composed of familiar faces. A doctor concerned about the hazards of child rearing in the modern world lamented:

In the times that are past and never to return, "everybody knew everybody"; the exact value, mental, bodily, and pecuniarily, of every person in the town, village, or little city was known. . . .

Times are different now. Those halcyon days of innocence and purity, will never return again. . . . Locks, and bars, and bolts are needed for our dwellings, our families also require watching, and our young sons and delicate daughters must be guarded against the company they keep.[5]

The doctor's words seem overwrought, but his fears were real enough. In the changing times of the Gilded Age many shared his vision of an embattled remnant of the old society threatened by new, dangerous forces. His complaint also reveals a powerful craving to be enfolded by a familiar, predictable, stable world, now lost yet never so sorely needed. Such elemental, pervasive desires fed the burgeoning production of nostalgic prose, poetry, and pictures from the 1860s on. Only a flight back into youth and innocence could hold the present, and the more terrifying future, at bay.

In the 1860s, stories of old New England achieved best-seller status. Henry Ward Beecher's *Norwood; or, Village Life in New England*, first serialized in the *New York Ledger*, was a great popular success when it appeared in book form in 1868. His sister Harriet Beecher Stowe published several novels and collections of stories based, like her brother's fiction, on memories of their childhood in the archetypal New England village of Litchfield, Connecticut. *The Minister's Wooing* (1859), her first in this vein, was followed by *The Pearl of Orr's Island* (1862), *Oldtown Folks* (1869), *Sam Lawson's Oldtown Fireside Stories* (1872), and *Poganuc People* (1878). Although none of these equaled the phenomenal success of *Uncle Tom's Cabin*, they won solid critical approval and sold briskly.

The novels of both writers portrayed the New England village as the source of American moral, political, and (especially) spiritual strength. Although Beecher subjected Norwood to the ordeal of the Civil War, all of Stowe's little towns existed in the "ante-railroad times" of old New England, not long after the Revolutionary War. Lovely pastoral oases with white houses embowered in graceful elms, these towns throve on Calvinist individualism, an unflagging work ethic, and democratic institutions. In the foreground of these pastoral communities, both Beecher and Stowe staged spiritual dramas bearing on the reconciliation of old Calvinism with the new liberalism and free-agency of democratic America. For all such pondering of theological issues, it is likely that many of the reading public enjoyed *Norwood, Oldtown Folks,* and the rest primarily as rich tapestries worked upon the New England social fabric at a time when, as Stowe put it, "our worst form of roaring dissipation consisted in being too fond of huckleberry parties, or in the immoderate pursuit of chestnuts and walnuts." Reviewers' reactions to *Norwood* suggest that this may have been the case. Its serious philosophical intent escaped many of them entirely; they perceived it, rather, as a quaint, local-color Yankee narrative.[6]

If the popular success of *Norwood* may be taken as evidence of post–Civil War nostalgic cravings, the rapturous reception of John Greenleaf Whittier's *Snow-Bound* testifies to their intensity. Whittier published his "winter idyll" in 1866, when the war had scarcely begun to subside into history. By consensus Whittier's masterpiece, its sentiment contained within a coherent and beautiful form, *Snow-Bound* was balm to the spirits of readers, who snatched up 18,000 copies of the poem within the first six months of its publication and 10,000 more before the year was out. In a letter to Whittier, publisher James T. Fields made mock complaint about the ravenous demand: "We can't keep the plaguey thing quiet. It goes and goes, and now, today, we are bankrupt again, not a one being in the crib. I fear it will be impossible to get along without printing another batch! Pity us!"[7]

An imaginative recreation and synthesis of boyhood experience, *Snow-Bound* tells the simple story of the Whittier family—the archetypal agrarian social unit—isolated for several days after a mighty New England blizzard. The introductory stanzas describe the ferocity of the storm, which cuts off the farm from the world, heaps its chill whiteness in fantastic shapes upon the homely structures of the barnyard, and makes ordinary chores exhilarating adventures for the little boys who must tunnel through the drifts in order to reach the barn where hungry animals await their care. The middle, and longest, section portrays family and friends grouped close around the welcoming hearth for a long evening of companionship and tale-spinning, warmly sequestered from the pallid wilderness outside. In the final stanzas, the farmstead slowly reestablishes contact with the world, and the idyll must come to a close.

Elegiac and gentle, *Snow-Bound* evokes the very texture of happy, simple country life in those long-gone days of old New England. The homestead itself—the ancestral Whittier house in Haverhill, Massachusetts, where the poet had grown up—is not so much described in concrete terms as it is felt, as a protective entity. The reader learns nothing of its external appearance; it is the interior that matters here. At its center, and at the center of Whittier's extended revery upon the past, is the image of the ample kitchen hearth, focus of happy family gathering and communion:

> hovering near,
> We watched the first red blaze appear,
> Heard the sharp crackle, caught the gleam
> On whitewashed wall and sagging beam,
> Until the old, rude-furnished room
> Burst, flower-like, into rosy bloom.

Outside, a full moon sheds cold light on the silvery drifts; but inside, parents, children, and friends, defying the frigid elements beyond the walls, bask in "tropic heat." To this picture, Whittier added a cluster of cozy details. The house dog and cat luxuriate before the flames, and

Between the andirons' straddling feet,
The mug of cider simmered slow,
The apples sputtered in a row,
And, close at hand, the basket stood
With nuts from brown October's wood.

A poignant note interrupts when the poet reflects that "the voices of that hearth are still" and the ruddy light shines no more on the "dear home faces" of that long-ago winter's circle. He proceeds, however, to a long narrative of the evening's games and tales, with sharply drawn sketches of each personality in the group. Late in the evening the great fire burns low, and the children go off to the "summer-land of dreams." The next morning they awaken to the sound of the teamsters—the world returning—breaking open the highway. In the end, the poet moralizes that present duty calls us from our dreams of the past to heed the "larger hopes and graver fears" of the present. Yet there remains a place for these precious memories, for heartening visits back to the place of origins and early joys:

Sit with me by the homestead hearth,
And stretch the hands of memory forth
To warm them at the wood-fire's blaze![8]

An intensely realized dream of the past, the poem created the sense of the home as refuge, an intimate oasis of rosy light and warmth, resurrected in a series of vignettes so minutely particularized that they rise in the mind's eye only a shade less vivid than present reality itself. The homestead and the fireside of *Snow-Bound* offered themselves as symbols of every individual's primeval world of sheltered dependence and happy ignorance of the trials that lay beyond protecting walls. Focusing on the hearth as an emblem of memory, a symbol of the peace and safety of the past, and the metaphorical heart of family community, Whittier threw open to his readers a temporary sanctuary from the stress and turmoil of their maturity in postwar America. Dead and gone, the homestead yet provided spritual nurture and strength to those who cherished it in their memories.

Snow-Bound, which remained popular long after its remarkable debut in 1866, is the quintessential expression of the postwar American homestead dream. Less and less was the rural homestead invoked as nursery and stronghold of the agrarian ideal. It stood now for a complex of emotional associations centering on lost youth and family ties, talismans of security in a disordered present. It symbolized what had been good and what was now lost. Its image became that of a reliquary, preserving beneath its sheltering roof the irretrievable joys and extinguished visions of a younger America.

Paintings and popular prints of the old homestead after the Civil War clearly signaled these new dimensions of nostalgic emotionalism. Hudson River School painter Worthington Whittredge's *Home by the Sea* (Illus. 118) and Jasper Cropsey's *The Old Home* (also called *The Old Homestead;* Illus. 119) are nostalgic, even elegiac; significantly, both depict homes rather than emotionally neutral houses. In Whittredge's painting of the countryside near Newport, Rhode Island, long late-afternoon shadows creep toward the ancient house on the left, where a woman stands by the door feeding a flock of geese. Behind the house is an orchard, which gives way to a salt marsh where harvesters work. Farther off are headlands and a calm sea. The mood emanates partly from the expansive horizontality of the design, partly from the mellow light of a day just beginning to wane, and partly from the character of the house itself, which speaks its great age in every line and surface, from the wavering edges of its roof ridge to its weathered skin of shingles. Symbol of another time, the image of this venerable homestead is meant to evoke nostalgic revery in the beholder.[9] Cropsey's painting follows the old Claudian formula used in many a Hudson River School design. The message is less muted than Whittredge's: the brown Dutch Colonial farmhouse is empty, and all around it are signs of decay, of culture crumbling into wilderness: rotting boards, missing shingles, collapsing fences, weeds. *The Old Home* mourns the past that is slowly vanishing before our very eyes.[10]

Old-home pictures by artists like Whittredge and Cropsey reflect the vision of the older generation of the Hudson River School, once the dominant native movement but after the Civil War (like the homestead) a dying anachronism. Something of that feeling of having outlived a golden age might be read into these paintings. It is not simply a case of old age, however: younger artists, such as impressionist Childe Hassam, would later paint and paint again the ancient homesteads of rural Connecticut and other enclaves of old New England.

If the number of homestead subjects published by popular printmakers is any indication, the demand for them was strong.[11] Currier & Ives homestead scenes of the late 1860s display the familiar, conventional pastoral iconography of the American farm. In some instances it is mainly by inference that we may assign them a slot in the nostalgia category. That is the case with the set of four *American Homestead* prints published in 1868 and 1869. Depicting the homestead in spring, summer, autumn, and winter (Illus. 120), these compositions conform to the pastoral formula Frances Palmer used in her American farm scenes of the 1850s (see Illus. 3), and the configuration of *Winter* was to be repeated almost exactly in the related 1871 print *Peace and Plenty* (see Illus. 42). There is nothing new about the imagery. In *Winter* there is simply the repetition of standardized artifacts: the plain, unfashionable farmhouse with its kitchen ell projecting to the rear; the simple, functional barn, piled with hay and grain to feed the inhabitants of the barnyard; the fine stands of trees and the winding lane. With its inventory of agrarian symbols, the print reads as visual manifesto of traditional American ideals.

Such meanings, despite the erosion of their links with factuality, continued to resonate in postbellum farmscapes. It is the context, however, that alters the reading. Currier & Ives issued this set of lithographs within the same short span of years that witnessed the publication and rousing success of *Norwood, Oldtown Folks,* and *Snow-Bound.* What may appear to be well-worn agrarian imagery was surely more than that to print consumers in 1868 and 1869. Like its counterparts in literature, the pictorial homestead had come to serve as icon of remembrance, reminder of peace and stability in a tattered world, and repository of abandoned youthful dreams. The *American Homestead* set enjoyed notable success as well. In the opinion of one cataloguer, in fact, it was "undoubtedly the most popular set of small folios ever published by Currier & Ives."[12]

Other prints are more explicitly nostalgic. These include *My Boyhood's Home* and *Home, Sweet Home* (Illus. 121, 122). In the first, the title directs the viewer to understand the scene as the rural terrain of memory, with its simple farm cottage, hayrick, ancient trees, and distant vista of lake and hills. The composition itself is pedestrian; it is the signal given by the title that makes the print significant in specific cultural terms. *Home, Sweet Home* is more elaborate in its imagery and more rewarding as an emblem of nostalgia. The design is conventional but carefully rendered and precise in detail. Here once more is a variation on the standardized pastoral theme: winding, tree-shaded lane, snug cottage with trellised vines, a neat barn behind. Father is just arriving home from work, or perhaps from travels more extensive and prolonged. The family dog leaps a welcome; his two small children rush out to greet him; his wife waits more decorously at the door. The scene recapitulates every element of the nostalgic journey to the old homestead: the voyager weary from strife and struggle in the world returns to the blissful, tranquil haven where "dear home faces," in Whittier's words, await him.

The verses from John Howard Payne's "Home Sweet Home" printed below the title illuminate the sentiment embodied in the design itself. A wanderer's lament, Payne's poem expresses weariness with the false dazzlement of foreign splendors and dolefully voices the single desire to be once more under the roof of the "lowly, thatched cottage" of earlier, and happier, days.[13] While the song itself was nearly half a century old by 1870, never was its bittersweet sentimentality more eloquently pertinent than during the aftermath of the Civil War. In the postwar decade its affecting refrain might almost have been a domestic national anthem, voicing what many may have wished: to retreat (metaphorically at least) from an ominous present into the safe refuge of the unblemished past, for which the archetypal homestead stood as symbol.

At the same time, actual old homes and old places gained new status as precious physical remnants of earlier years. Again and again, writers on domestic architecture or America's few remaining pockets of rural archaism found the present a feeble substitute for the past. In the late 1870s, journalist Ernest Ingersoll rambled among the isolated villages along the south shore of Long Island, relishing every ancient house he discovered there. On a country road beyond the village of Greenport, he noted with approval that

the houses are almost all old, and of generous proportions. . . . These big, low-browed houses, stone-gray with the long weathering and utter absence of paint, shaded by their huge cherry groves, and surrounded by fields ploughed a century ago, are real homesteads, and the occasional innovation of a spruce new cottage or pretentious "villa" seems almost a sacrilege.

It was not simply their venerability that made them shrines to the past; it was the thought of how many generations must have occupied them, forming a chain of continuity that contrasted painfully with a present day blemished by upstart architecture and afflicted with rootlessness. These old houses, each one built around an enormous chimney, had attics where children played on rainy days, "where their grandfathers and grandmothers did, and grew up to see their own sons and grandchildren amuse themselves in that same brown old garret, with its massive rafters and one little window." The ancient Johnes house in Southampton (Illus. 123) was a true reliquary, "still inhabited by a Johnes, who preserves many

a piece of antiquated furniture and quaint relic of his forefathers." Although even in remotest Long Island the old was crumbling before the onslaught of the new, and one could see the landscape disfigured by "modern improvements," "clever agricultural machines," and even fashionable "spring bonnets," it was still possible there to commune with "the Long Ago." [14]

The antiquated villages of Long Island and similar places served as symbols of memories both personal and cultural. The same was true of individual homesteads, which allowed even the city-raised reader or tourist to experience vicariously, at several removes, the pleasure of remembering the way things used to be. The Colonial Revival style in architecture, which began to develop in the 1870s, represented yet another response to new cravings for identification with national history in its pure and noble dawn. The identical impulses underlay the contemporary vogue for collecting antiques, those portable relics of the ancestral past. [15]

Among all these romantic artifacts the ancestral homes of American authors excited particular sentimental interest. Predictably, John Howard Payne's original family home in rural Long Island was the subject of fervent praise. The house and its kitchen hearth were illustrated by Harry Fenn in William Cullen Bryant's monumental, patriotic armchair travel book *Picturesque America* (Illus. 124, 125). Fittingly, the house was the rambling, unadorned homestead of the agrarian ideal, a swaybacked, rough-skinned saltbox with a crumbling chimney and a venerable guardian tree. As O. B. Bunce's text pointed out, this was truly a homely home, but what mattered was that the family around the once-blazing hearth had been happy in its simple joys. Warming to that idea, Bunce declared (wishfully thinking) that an abundance of such "simple, happy homes" existed yet in America. Payne's, however, was especially to be cherished and preserved. "Let no sacrilegious hand touch the old timbers of this precious relic!" he warned. "In a land where memorials of the past are so few . . . it is specially fit that we should preserve the roof which sheltered one who has expressed the memories that cling around the hearthstone in words that thrill the hearts of millions."[16]

In several instances the authors themselves figured in rituals of revisiting and even repossessing their birthplaces, thus acting out a major cultural fantasy. When *Appleton's Journal* published a series in the 1870s on "old Houses of historical or family interest," one week's feature was "The Bryant Homestead," a "venerable house" where "our veteran poet, Wiliam Cullen Bryant, was born." The illustration (Illus. 126) showed a structure in full conformity with the seasoned stereotype of the virtuous yeoman's home: the ample, unornamented box, its steep gable punctuated by dormer windows and tall chimneys; the surrounding trees bestowing grace and shade. Not long before, the poet had purchased his "youthful home," buying along with the house itself the precious ownership of its memories and associations. The same was true of popular poet James Whitcomb Riley, whose dialect poems celebrating the culture of the old rustic Midwest became tremendously popular late in the century. Hamlin Garland interviewed Riley in 1893 and reported that their conversation took place on the porch of the "old homestead" where Riley had passed his childhood and which he had bought "because of old-time associations."[17]

When Whittier's biographer Samuel T. Pickard published a travel guide to the poet's old haunts in rural Massachusetts, he devoted a long chapter to the "birthplace" in Haverhill. Built in 1688 by pioneer and patriarch Thomas Whittier, this place was a genuine ancestral homestead, though it had passed out of the family in 1836 when the Whittiers moved to nearby Amesbury. Pickard took the reader on a tour, reverently pausing at the hearth in the room "consecrated" by *Snow-Bound* and now "a shrine toward which the pilgrims of many future generations" would find their way. Indeed, the house had already achieved the status of genuine historical monument, having been bought, restored, and opened to visitors (numbering thousands yearly, as of 1904)

by a group of Haverhill citizens. "Here on these very bricks," wrote Pickard, "simmered the mug of cider. . . . The table now standing between these windows is the same that then stood there, and many of the dishes on the shelves . . . are the family heirlooms occupying their old places." Illustrating the text were photographs of the shrine (Illus. 127, 128), a perfect realization of the ideal agrarian farmscape given vivid presence by the immediacy of the photographic gaze: the square, gabled farmhouse, flanked by the barn and mature trees, set upon a slight rise of ground with smoothly rolling, appropriately snow-shrouded pastureland surrounding it. Inside, the great hearth fitted out in andirons, cauldrons, chains, and pothooks dominated the "consecrated" kitchen, sparsely furnished with Windsor chairs, a lean Queen Anne table, a desk, and a spinning wheel.

Whittier had entertained the idea of buying the Haverhill house to make it once more a Whittier family homestead, but his intentions did not bear fruit. He did pay a last ritual visit to his birthplace in the autumn of 1882, thus enacting a kind of ceremonial homecoming duly recorded by Pickard, who accompanied him. Whittier had been born in his mother's room off the famous kitchen. Making his pilgrim's way into this chamber, "he expressed a wish to see again a fire upon its hearth, not for warmth, for it was a warm day, but for the sentiment of it." Whittier's impulse underscores the sacral nature of hearth and homestead which he himself (one of the so-called "fireside poets," indeed) had fostered through his well-loved poetry. His association of the hearth not with function but with feeling reveals the symbolic resonance that this artifact had acquired in the later decades of the nineteenth century.[18]

In contemporary fiction of reminiscence the hearth played that same role. The compound of ancestors, homestead, happy recollections, family warmth, and the blazing fireplace figured prominently in Harriet Beecher Stowe's *Oldtown Folks* in a chapter the very title of which—"Fire-Light Talks in My Grandmother's Kitchen"—suggests the narrator's nostalgic, memory-misted perspective. This remembered kitchen was strikingly similar to its Haverhill counterpart. It was wide and roomy, "resplendent with the sheen of a set of scoured pewter plates and platters which stood arranged on a dresser," and dominated by the huge fireplace that took up all of one wall. The remembered autumn day was the Sabbath. The family had come home from the usual New England rigors of the second Sunday service and had eaten a meal of earthy simplicity—brown bread and baked beans. It was time for the central domestic ceremony of the evening:

There was an uneasy, chill moaning and groaning out of doors showing the coming up of an autumn storm,—just enough chill and wind to make the brightness of a social hearth desirable,—and my grandfather had built one of his most methodical and splendid fires.

The wide, ample depth of the chimney was aglow in all its cavernous length with the warm leaping light that burst out in lively jets and spurts from every rift and chasm. The great black crane that swung over it, with its multiplicity of pot-hooks and trammels, seemed to have a sort of dusky illumination.

Later, other details fleshed out a scene of homely tranquility:

Now the kitchen was my grandmother's own room. In one corner of it stood a round table with her favorite books, her great work-basket, and by it a rickety rocking-chair. . . . My grandfather had also a large splint-bottomed arm-chair, with rockers to it, in which he swung luxuriously in the corner of the great fireplace. By the side of its ample blaze we sat down to our family meals, and afterwards, while grandmother and Aunt Lois washed up the tea-things, we all sat and chatted by the firelight. . . . In the kitchen each member of the family had established unto him or her self some little pet private snuggery, some chair or stool, some individual nook—forbidden to gentility, but dear to the ungenteel natural heart.

In this warm haven the talk ranged from the highminded to the frivolous: "religion, theology, politics, the gossip of the day, and the legends of the supernatural all conspired to weave a fabric of thought, quaint and various." [19]

Not everything was perfect in this best of all possible American worlds, but those quiet times by the fireside symbolized the very spirit of family life in the rural New England of yesteryear, before industrialization, mechanized transport, urbanization, immigrants, and the Civil War—to name the chief culprits—had begun their fatal inroads on a once homogeneous (as it then seemed) society. Because of its wholesome associations, one writer on family life recommended a wood fire as a prescription for happiness: "It burns up many a quarrel and morbid speculation, rights many a wrong, and promotes peace. No picture is so utterly cheerful as that of the family gathering around it as evening falls." [20]

Laden with meaning, the hearth with its evocative language of memory became a totem, the most precious relic encased within the reliquary that was the homestead. As re-created artifact it even became quite concretely a totem to the cult of nostalgia. During the Civil War the "Sanitary Fairs," which were staged to raise funds to provide home comforts and health care to the Union Army, introduced historical reconstructions among their attractions. A fair in Poughkeepsie in 1864 presented a popular "Dutchess County Room One Hundred Years Ago," featuring young women in period costume and a "huge fireplace with old Dutch tiles." Later that year the biggest of the Sanitary Fairs, on Union Square in New York City, offered an elaborately equipped "Knickerbocker Kitchen" furnished with a motley collection of heirlooms. The most famous of the colonial kitchens was the one in the much-visited New England Log House at the 1876 Centennial Exposition in Philadelphia. Ears of corn and garlands of dried apples hung from a low ceiling; a turkey turned on the spit within the immense fireplace; costumed women served old-time Yankee fare and explained the workings of the antiquated cooking paraphernalia to the "victim of modern improvements" mystified by their simplicity. [21]

Physical embodiments of the old days, these kitchens with

their welcoming firesides gave utterance to a whole complex of emotions about the warmth and simplicity of home feeling in the past, and the negative implications of progress. Like the "consecrated" Whittier kitchen at Haverhill, they were shrines, only temporary but nonetheless promising to shed some moral or spiritual grace upon the hectic present. This antiquarian symbolism carried over into the theater: in Denman Thompson's enduringly popular play *The Old Homestead* (1886), one of the dominant features in archaic Yankee farmer Whitcomb's living room was a large fireplace, not simply a piece of picturesque rustic decor but the very emblem of the old days. Heaped with crackling hickory logs and festooned like the New England log house kitchen with bundles of corn and strings of dried apples, it was meant to evoke those cultural memories of cold evenings spent in the radiant haven of the homestead fireside.[22]

This was the cultural climate in which painters and illustrators after the Civil War created images of the old-fashioned rustic hearths, which like their literary counterparts signaled a very specific set of ideas and emotions. Like the archetypal hearth in *Snow-Bound*, they beckoned the viewer to "stretch the hands of memory forth / To warm them at the wood-fire's blaze."

For Eastman Johnson and others the hearth functioned symbolically in just such a way, inviting thoughts of the past rather than referring to it directly. As early as 1863 Johnson's oil study *New England Kitchen* (private collection) bore witness to a dawning interest in observing and recording primitive Yankee artifacts: this is the archetypal kitchen at its roughest, the walk-in fireplace gaping like a cave beneath a crudely hewn oak mantletree, and the clutter of elemental implements—iron pots, earthenware jars, a long-handled dipper—gently illuminated by outside light filtering in (Dutch fashion) from a high, small window. This may be a room full of memories, but Johnson's intention was primarily to document its characteristics.

The *Nantucket Interior* (Illus. 129), however, is a New England fireplace with a reflective and intimate mood. In this dim room, little beyond the hearth is visible. What can be seen exemplifies the rudest country simplicity: the plain brick fireplace and bare plank floor, the old ginger jar, cannister, and candlestick on the mantel, their mellow surfaces sending back flickers of light, and the short ladderback chair upon which a bearded man hunches forward, nursing his clay pipe as he contemplates the low-burning fire. Although the title (conferred later, apparently) is misleading—Johnson visited Nantucket for the first time five years after he painted this picture—the rustic, homey New England atmosphere already embodies those qualities later to be identified more particularly with a nostalgic vision of Nantucket, the artist's own regionalist pictorial territory. To him and his admirers, Nantucket culture represented a precious, archaic remnant of old New England, a place in "ante-railroad times," as Stowe had described Oldtown. As one of Johnson's critics pointed out: "The man and the place have a natural sympathy for each other. He is a chronicler of a phase of our national life which is fast passing away."[23] Johnson's "Nantucket" interior is surely more than an essay in preservation. The man with the pipe is lost in revery, so naturally stimulated by the glowing remnants of the fire. The old hearth, the pensive figure, and the muted atmosphere invite the beholder also to engage in sentimental thoughts on things long since passed away.

Philadelphia genre painter George Cochran Lambdin's *Winter Quarters in Virginia—Army of the Potomac, 1864* (Illus. 130) used the hearthside theme to evoke the idea of home reveries in the more specific context of the Civil War soldier, exiled to the perils of a battlefield far away. Lambdin's composition depicts the interior of a rough log-walled shelter where, amid a great clutter of gear, a young officer broods, warming his boots before the fire. A clue to his abstraction lies in the torn-open envelope resting on the floor beneath his camp chair—a letter from home, perhaps—but it is hardly needed. As he stares into the flames upon the hearth—symbol of home, family, and the happy past—what else could be the subject of the handsome soldier's thoughts?[24]

What this painting expressed by inference, popular illustration represented with extreme literalness. Alfred Fredericks's *And Ashes Lie upon the Hearth* (Illus. 131) was one of the illustrations to accompany the title piece in Wallace Bruce's *Old Homestead Poems*, published in 1888. "The Old Homestead" is a weak and uninspired echo of *Snow-Bound*, but the illustration is a diagram of memory-in-process, catalyzed by the hypnotic flicker of fire on the hearth. In the bottom half of the composition the middle-aged man before the fire slumps forward in a doze, while the flames and smoke stream upward to metamorphose into a vision of the family fireplace at Christmas time long ago. The memory-vision, festive and vivid, shows a united family basking in the warmth of a brilliant blaze. Parents look on fondly as a young man (the narrator's erstwhile self, probably) teases a girl under the mistletoe; children play; all participate happily in a celebration of home and family love. In contrast, the chamber occupied by the older, sadder self is dark and solitary.[25] This picture fills in the blanks, stating in clear and visible terms the content (unseen though sensed) of Lambdin's fireside revery and of works on the same theme by Eastman Johnson and other artists after the Civil War. Johnson's later paintings of ancient Nantucket sea captains sitting by the fireside—in particular, the melancholy *Embers* (c. 1880; private collection) in which an old man stares into the coals soon to be ashes—become more intelligible, in contemporary sentimental terms, when viewed in this established context of symbolism and meaning.

The same context lent significance to another genre of hearthside picture in which old-fashioned people and their rooms full of quaint country comforts recapture more completely the tone and texture of the simple life in America's rural past. Evocative of ancestors or grandparents, such figures dovetail and sometimes merge with the stereotype of the antiquated bumpkin, in his sentimental rather than laughable mode. Thomas Hovenden's *Old Version* (see Illus. 88), for example, would also fit neatly into this category, but this interior lacks the hearth which, with its rich layers of association, gives poignant meaning to figures elderly or quaint.

Representative of these hearthside pictures is Thomas Hicks's *No Place like Home* (Illus. 132). Hicks, a successful portrait and genre painter at midcentury, summered at Trenton Falls in far upstate New York and rather late in his career became interested (like his contemporary, Johnson) in portraying the archaic kitchen interiors and rustic fireplaces still to be discovered among the old homesteads of the area. Hicks's painting is a mood-saturated portrait of a room and its inhabitants rather than an unemotional catalogue of facts. While it is not entirely clear whether the old couple warming themselves near the hearth are meant to be seen as figures in a past era or merely as surviving human relics from a better time, there is little doubt that the imagery is intended to recall the fireside worlds so fondly enshrined in the works of such writers as Whittier and Stowe. Here are the spotlessly swept floor, and the humble but devotedly polished objects of use, ranged along the mantel. The old man is busy at the fire with a pair of tongs; within the fireplace itself a black kettle boils water for the couple's tea. Behind the old woman, who sits in a rocking chair, the table is prettily laid for the meal; under it, two house cats lap companionably from a common dish. The imagery expresses a deeply nostalgic indulgence, looking in, or back, upon an ideal of rural contentment not to be found in the busy life of the Gilded Age.[26]

More self-consciously antiquarian were works by colonial nostalgia specialist Edward Lamson Henry and by others such as Enoch Wood Perry, who occasionally ventured into historical genre. Henry was a passionate collector of America's heirloom artifacts and a zealous campaigner for the preservation of historic buildings. His *Figures in an Interior* (Illus. 133) exemplifies the precious quaintness of his interior scenes, which shrank the past down to the scale of historic dollhouses. Although the couple posed formally on either side of the well-wrought Federal fireplace lack the cozy ease of

Hicks's pair, the sense of the old American home and its virtues is the same. The hearth is a household altar. The fire burns behind highly polished andirons. The mantelpiece enshrines ancestral memorabilia: portrait miniatures of a man and woman, a framed sampler, bits of porcelain and brass. The chairs seating the quaintly garbed couple are also heirlooms: a Chippendale-style side chair for him, a tall ladder-back for her. Although an air of ceremonial stiffness governs the design, the cat rubbing itself against the woman's skirt introduces an accent of intimate domesticity.

Enoch Wood Perry's *Woman Sewing by Firelight* (Illus. 134) reflects the late nineteenth-century vogue for the costume genre painting, the recreation of colonial or early republican home life in meticulously researched interiors. Like his friend Eastman Johnson, Perry was the product of schooling in Düsseldorf and Paris in the 1850s. He enjoyed a successful career as a genre painter, specializing in homespun rustic subjects and domestic themes set in the American past. Unlike Henry's class-portrait formality, Perry's work offers what purports to be a candid glimpse of quiet feminine industry long ago in the kitchen of a colonial homestead. The iconography of the good country past conforms closely to the established type for the rustic kitchen. Here are the gaping hearth, the polished fire tools, the black cauldron suspended above the flames, the sleek roundness of an earthenware pitcher on the mantel. There is even a butter churn to the left of the fireplace, and the woman's infant sleeps in an antique cradle. Detachment from any hint of the present is carefully maintained (except for the arrangement of the model's hair, in the current fashion of chignon and bangs) in a hushed tranquility appropriate to what is clearly meant to be a consecrated place, like the kitchen of the Whittier homestead in Haverhill.

Perry's painting might be regarded as a devotional image of sorts, created for a cult of the past variously compounded of escapism and veneration and having at its core the idea and image of the ancestral hearth. Reviewers were quick to respond to Perry's sentiment; they praised the "simplicity and homelike character" of his subjects and succumbed to their nostalgic charm. Writing during the centennial year, when the celebration of the American past reached its first peak, one critic made specific connections between Perry's work and the world of literary legend and regionalism: "Quilting-scenes, such as we in middle life recollect as events in our childhood, and old kitchens, with their big fireplaces, are here; and it is Irving and Sleepy Hollow . . . and Mrs. Stowe's 'Old Town' that they recall."[27]

The cult of the past, which found expression in colonial revival architecture and costume genre painting, in historic preservation and antique collecting, also fostered a heightened sentimental regard for traditional American festivities—Thanksgiving perhaps most prominent among them. The essence of this holiday was the ceremonial return to hearth and home of even the most far-flung family members, and the ritual reenactment of family gatherings—once (so insisted the belief) the daily norm in old New England, as pictured, for example, in the 1855 illustration *A New England Fireside* (Illus. 135). Crude though it may be, this image epitomizes the ideal that contemporary Thanksgivings tried to recapture: the large extended family from grandparents to infant, all sheltering under the ancestral roof; the atmosphere of contented family communion and useful occupation, warmed by the blaze of a cavernous fireplace. After the violent years of the war the theme of the Thanksgiving return acquired new interest and pertinence. Thousands of soldiers had in fact returned to their homes and families, and the institutionalized visit to the old home associated with the Thanksgiving holiday accordingly took on heightened significance as symbol of those reunions. Beneath that topical meaning, however, lay the enduring vision of home as haven, a return to which meant both glad regression and the opportunity for spiritual replenishment. Significantly, Thanksgiving was also a specifically Yankee occasion:

We have called it an American holiday, but, strictly speaking, it belongs to New England, and is nowhere else celebrated with the same gusto. When the last of November comes, New England people, wherever scattered throughout the world, turn with yearning hearts to the land of their birth; and thousands upon thousands who have made their home in the far West and the South return to eat the Thanksgiving turkey in the old homestead of their fathers.[28]

The Currier & Ives lithograph after George Durrie's *Home to Thanksgiving* (Illus. 136) expresses the essence of postwar Thanksgiving imagery and symbolism. The design is thoroughly familiar: it is the standard New England agrarian scene in winter white, with the unpretentious homestead and big, plain barn, a few majestic though skeletal trees, and hazy mountains in the distance. The homecoming scene takes place almost inconspicuously on the porch off to the right, where the old farm parents stand to welcome the young married pair, just arrived in a smart cutter. Their small child is already in Grandmother's arms. The young couple's dress, more stylish than the parents', suggests that they have come from the city. They are true exiles celebrating a happy—though poignantly brief—return to the old homestead. In its simple and direct way, Durrie's design emblematically glosses over the scars of postwar culture by playing on the theme of union and reunion: parents and children, old and young, country and city, antebellum and postbellum. Portraying three generations together, the imagery exalts the idea of family continuity and proclaims the strength of American (Yankee, northern) traditions, at the same time giving a very literal and basic form to the nostalgic yearnings of the period. This was the meaning also of other popular images of holiday family reunions, such as F. A. Chapman's illustration *Thanksgiving at a New England Farmhouse* (Illus. 137). Here, the old country grandparents sit squarely before the primitive, capacious hearth, like votive figures framed by ceremonial architecture. Ranged round the amply spread table are the Yankee clan, children and children's children, some plain

and some apparently urban and fashionable but all temporarily united to celebrate the rite of family communion.[29]

Images like the Durrie lithograph and the magazine illustration were occasional, yet they cannot be dismissed as insignificant. That they meant something to magazine readers and print consumers of the time is clear. Casually encountered, so familiar as to sink into the consciousness without a ripple, they enacted a ritualistic joining of the present with the past. They endorsed the conception of the New England family as close-knit, clean-living, morally rugged, and spiritually strong. They acknowledged and assuaged nostalgia, and they proclaimed the sanctity and healing graces of traditions. They perpetuated the idea of the ancestral homestead as shrine, the hearth within it as domestic altar.

The old New England family, its hearth and homestead, also represented another vanishing ideal: that of racial homogeneity. It recalled a distant era when (in the minds of popular mythologizers) the Anglo-Saxon blood of America had been unadulterated by foreign strains. As one culture critic noted, American forefathers had been of the sternest moral fiber, and this fiber ran through a social fabric that was strong because it was woven of one homogeneous people. By the late nineteenth century, however, the righteous Puritan lifeblood of society had been diluted by "that foreign admixture which is now so remarkable and in some respects so disturbing an element in our national condition."[30] This concern for the purity of American bloodlines was one among a number of anxieties that nourished nativism in the last three decades of the century.

The full force of developed nativist feeling was not to be exerted until the 1890s, but well before that time the presence of immigrant aliens had occasioned unease, resentment, and hostility. The 1850s had seen a strong wave of anti-immigrant, anti-Catholic feeling in the Know-Nothing organizations, which attracted membership in the tens of thousands, published propaganda journals, and succeeded in lodging candidates in several state legislatures before the larger crisis and impending conflict of North versus South engulfed all lesser issues. For several decades before the war, and for some time after it, the major thrust of nativist prejudice was against the Irish—that most Roman Catholic of races—who constituted a very large percentage of foreign immigrants in the 1840s and 1850s. Arriving in the millions after the disastrous potato famines of the 1840s, Irish immigrants collected in northeastern urban slums in such numbers that by 1860 "slum" and "Irish neighborhood" meant virtually the same thing.[31]

Although the reputation of the Irish was on the upswing in the last decades of the century, in the 1860s and 1870s they were still regarded by established (Anglo-Saxon) Americans as an inferior breed, drunken, slatternly, and shiftless. From the established residents' viewpoint their influx was most severe in New England. Concerning the migration of New Englanders to lands of western opportunity, one journalist observed:

We are forever felicitating ourselves that the West is being peopled in great measure by the hardy citizens of Maine, but we are continually forgetting what sort of an effect this is likely to have upon Maine. As the poor but ambitious farmers of the East leave their domicile, a new stream must flow in to take their place, and that stream is Irish. The moment this movement begins, it accelerates the other; the two races are in the field of labor to one another as specie and paper are in the field of finance; the poorer driving the better out.

According to William Dean Howells, the arrival of an Irish family in a settled American neighborhood was something like the introduction of a plague germ:

When the calamitous race . . . appears, a mortal pang strikes to the bottom of every pocket. Values tremble. . . . None but the Irish will build near the Irish . . . fear spreads to the elder Yankee homes about, and the owners prepare to abandon them. . . . Where the Celt sets his foot, there the Yankee . . . rarely, if ever . . . returns.

The presence of this "calamitous race" not only tainted the present, it was thought, but made mockery of the great historical past. When poet and culture critic Thomas Bailey Aldrich wrote about his birthplace, the once solidly Yankee town of Portsmouth, New Hampshire, he sketched a telling and depressing (to him and his readers) vignette in the description of a venerable colonial home now fallen upon hard times. On its doorstep, "Mr. O'Shaughnessy now stretches himself . . . revolving the sad vicissitude of things (made very much sadder by drink)—that same doorstep has been pressed by the feet of generals and marquises and grave dignitaries." The very traditions sacred to Yankeedom faced the insult of attrition by degraded foreign influence.[32]

The threat of the Irish, however, paled before the potential menace of other nationalities. Between 1860 and 1900, fourteen million immigrants arrived to swell the American population. Directly following the Civil War, prospering industries welcomed foreigners to the labor pool and even encouraged them to cross the Atlantic to become the basis for a new industrial working class. The immigrant tide ebbed somewhat in the mid-1870s, when the American economy was foundering in a depression, but still it came on in the hundreds of thousands, rising again in the 1880s. In the 1870s most immigrants continued to arrive from the countries of northern Europe: the British Isles, Germany, Scandinavia; only a small proportion were southern or eastern Europeans. During the next decade this began to change, as more and more Italians and Slavs left their native lands; by the 1890s these groups made up the majority of immigrants to the United States. Clinging together in noisome metropolitan slums, these people—so unlike the generally more acceptable groups from northern Europe—loomed increasingly large as menaces to the American social order: its language, its culture, its very gene pool. In the worried eyes of contemporary social commentators, whatever the problems that beset America—unchecked urban growth; an epidemic of slums, poverty, and crime—were all exacerbated by the presence and continuing invasion of strange and unwelcome foreigners. Many considered their fears justified by the labor upheavals of the middle 1880s, most horrible among them the 1886 Haymarket riots in Chicago, in which bomb-throwing foreign anarchists were supposed to have played a leading part.[33]

In the 1870s, nativist currents ran deep but did not often rise vehemently to the surface. They were disturbingly present, however, and though the troubles of that decade were only a pale foreshadowing of later developments and lay half-hidden beneath the surface optimism and lavish bravado of the era, they were serious enough. By 1876 industrial wages, atrophied by the depression, had been cut by 50 percent. The second half of the decade—coinciding, ironically, with the centennial celebrations—saw the stirrings of labor organization and outbreaks of industrial violence. Most notorious was the episode of the Molly Maguires, an alleged secret organization of Irish miners working for the Reading Coal and Iron Company, suspected and finally accused of murdering their supervisors; in 1877 twenty of those miners were executed for the crimes. Even worse was the widespread railroad strike of July 1877, violently carried out by the workers and violently suppressed by state and federal troops. Many believed that these bloody disturbances could only be the work of immigrant radicals. One critic wrote indignantly that the railroad strike was "nothing less than communism in its worst form . . . not only unlawful and revolutionary, but anti-American." Helen Campbell, a reformer who wrote extensively about the problems besetting the poor in urban America, imagined a conversation among public-spirited friends about slum housing, in the course of which the narrator pinpointed middle-class fears: respectable Americans paying more than $13 million in taxes a year to support legions of the poor and the vicious in urban slums, only to "sit and shiver" as they read of "Pittsburgh riots, or the spread of German socialism."[34]

American urban slums inspired fear as the foul breeding grounds of the baleful, un-American forces that menaced social stability. Books and articles on the subject repeatedly drew the reader's attention to the pressing dilemma of the slums, where poverty, unbearably overcrowded tenement housing, or—possibly worse—homeless vagrancy spawned vice and crime barely imaginable to the decent minds of the American bourgeois. Time and again, writers pointed to the foreign element and the absence of true homes as the chief poisons in this compound of degradation.

Reformer Charles Loring Brace, who established the Children's Aid Society in New York, summarized these interconnected associations in his book *The Dangerous Classes of New York,* the fruit of his two decades' work in attempting to improve the lot of children growing up in the slums. Bereft of salubrious and civilizing home influences, he warned, the population of urban poor was a living time bomb. If the law withheld its hand or the civilizing influences of American life failed to reach these masses, "we should see an explosion from this class which might leave this city in ashes and blood." Only a small number among this fearful mob were true Americans in any sense: "An immense proportion of our ignorant and criminal class are foreign-born; and of the dangerous classes here, a very large part, though native born, are of foreign parentage." Such people had no sense of what was right, moral, and good in the traditional American scheme of things. Home and family values, and the sanctity of the marriage bond, were of little weight in their lives. It was extraordinary, wrote Brace, "in how large a number of cases a second marriage, or the breaking of marriage, is the immediate cause of crime or vagrancy among children." One had only to behold the noxious interior of a slum tenement to understand why a sweet moral atmosphere could never prevail there. Brace described one dark, smoke-filled cellar room where fourteen ill-asssorted people—mothers, small children, adolescent girls and boys, and grown men—lived and slept together. In this environment no one could remain innocent. The indiscrimate packing of humans in those foul places had only the most predictable and deplorable results: it sowed pestilence and bred "every species of criminal habits."[35]

Another reformer, W. H. Tolman, reported on work performed by the New York Association for Improving the Condition of the Poor. Repeatedly emphasizing the connections among immigrants, bad housing, bad morals, vice, and crime, Tolman described immigrants in their un-Americanized state as ignorant, degraded, half-civilized, and wholly demoralized by the filth in which they wallowed. "The result of tenement house life," he said, "was the existence of a proletarian class who had no interest in the permanent well-being of the community, with no sense of home, but lived without any deep root in the soil, the mere tools of demagogues and designing men." It was as if Jefferson's nightmare—of seething urban masses, raw energy to be tapped by ill-intentioned schemers—were taking dreadful physical form at last. The foreign anarchists and ne'er-do-wells who lurked in those lower depths were less than human, less even than animal. In 1892, after the bloody suppression of a strike and plant takeover at the Carnegie Steel factory in Homestead, Pennsylvania, one editor fulminated: "The iron region of Pennsylvania, like New York, is infested with a class of foreigners who are scarcely above beasts in intelligence, and are far below them in savage bloodthirstiness; and these people seize upon occasions of temporary anarchy to indulge their brutal instincts."[36]

These pictures of the urban underclass impressed middle-class Americans as glimpses into an ominous jungle of savage impulses, unrestrained by the traditional and honorable domestic instruments of social order and control. It was a nightmare vision common to many in a time when the American social structure seemed about to tip over and crumble under the weight of those unwelcome hordes. The words of one worried physician reflect what was undoubtedly widespread feeling:

This country is the refuge of the poor and oppressed, the bold and the daring, the speculative and hopeful of every land. The suffering poor, and the criminal refugee, flock to these shores. . . .

The past freedom of intercourse is not to be seen at present, nor expected in the future. The foreigners, who flood our country, have brought with them, from their effete homes, the vices of a rotten world. Virtue is but a name with them, and honor too often but an imagination. The pure and simple manners of our past days, are to them but the evidence of deprivation, and liberty is supposed by them to mean license.

But be the cause as it may be, the days of security are past.[37]

Such apprehensions constructed the subtext of nostalgia symbolism after the Civil War. The more obvious meanings—the yearning for a vanished past, the craving to escape an uncertain present—are readily to be seen, just beneath the surface of hearth and homestead imagery. Under the heavy layers of sentiment that sweetened and gilded those reminders of the past there lurked a thin but resilient thread of xenophobic nationalism centering on the belief in Anglo-Saxon hegemony in America as an idea natural, traditional, necessary, and divinely ordained.

As John Higham observed, the concept of Anglo-Saxon hegemony was not a new one. It had gained currency in the 1840s as a "romantic cult," emphasizing the Anglo-Saxon's gift for political freedom, special capacity for self-government, and self-appointed mission to spread those blessings throughout the less fortunate world. After a period of dormancy the Anglo-Saxon doctrine enjoyed a resurgence in the 1870s and 1880s, when the more cultivated of the middle and upper classes—and especially the Brahmins of New England—espoused this elitist notion wholeheartedly and probably a little desperately.[38] And though not all established Americans may have ranked themselves among the Anglo-Saxon aristocracy, the strong upswing of nativism late in the century suggests that many considered themselves apart from, superior to, and besieged by the ever more alien refugees crowding onto American shores.

The Last Yankee (Illus. 138), a cartoon about unrestricted immigration and its results, diagrams the racial dilemma from the Anglo-Saxon viewpoint. The figure in the center is a Jonathan type, with his spare height, craggy features, goat whiskers, and round-brimmed hat. Like a specimen on exhibit, he stands surrounded by an ogling mob of foreigners. The stereotypes portrayed include a Dutch boy, a Chinese, a Scot, a Frenchman, an Arab, and an Irishman. All these immigrant Americans are much shorter than the Last Yankee; indeed, some seem deformed, stunted. In comparison with the Yankee's features, those of many among the onlookers are grotesque, accurately reflecting the prevailing prejudice that cast aliens in debased, subhuman roles. The cartoonist, with heavy-handed irony, sketched in some shop signs behind the crowd: "Boomelheimer American Grocery," "Jean Bouçois Americaine Bakery," and "Yan-Kee American Laundry." As paradigm of Anglo-Saxon embattlement, nothing could be more transparent than this racist image.

This was the covert content of the nostalgic pictures, poetry, and fiction of the later decades of the nineteenth century. Threatened and besieged by forces profoundly un-American, "Yankees" made a metaphorical last stand in the archetypal homestead, ranged before the archetypal hearth. In addition to its generalized meaning as emblem of the good, simple past, the New England style of homestead—and what it contained—was identified specifically with fundamental Anglo-Saxon qualities. As one writer asserted near the beginning of the Civil War, were it not for the New England home, culture would scarcely exist: "I am confident that whatever of good in morals, laws, religions, in enterprise, in literature and art, may be justly attributable to the New England influence, may be as justly traced to the New England home." By the same token, what made the New Englander a "man of special qualities" was intimately bound up with his ancestral home, so much so that "his Anglo-Saxon blood would have availed him little, but for his Anglo-Saxon home." Harriet Beecher Stowe, whose regionalist fiction provided such a clear mirror of contemporary yearnings, wrote that the very concept of "home" was an Anglo-Saxon one: "Let any try to render the song, '[Home] Sweet Home,' into French, and one finds how Anglo-Saxon is the very genius of the word."[39]

In an era when it was customary to equate bad homes and immigrants with crime that threatened the very roots of the social order, the image of the homestead—sacred wellspring of Anglo-Saxon virtue—read not simply as wishful thinking or escapist fantasy, nor even as paean to the moral fiber of the past, but as refutation of all that was alien and, by implication, debased in contemporary America. Fortress against the dangerous classes, the homestead represented security not just from a disordered present but from a foreign present. It was a monument to xenophobia and a shrine to a racial ideal, to a still-attainable vision of social and cultural hegemony that should be held, rightfully, by those of Anglo-Saxon blood: the original, the true Americans.

Nor were the "last Yankees" ready to retire behind homestead walls and forget the jungle outside. On the contrary, the rhetoric of Manifest Destiny ran strong during this period. Writer John Fiske, Congregationalist home missionary spokesman Josiah Strong, and lawyer Dexter Arnoll Hawkins vigorously prophesied that the liberty-loving, Protestant God–fearing Anglo-Saxon American race was intended to control and shape the world. As Strong put it:

Does it not look as if God were not only preparing in our Anglo-Saxon civilization the die with which to stamp the peoples of the earth, but as if he were also massing behind that die the mighty power with which to press it? . . . I look forward to what the world has never yet seen united in the same race; viz., the greatest numbers *and* the highest civilization.[40]

Like *The Last Yankee,* which so baldly announced the head-and-shoulders superiority of the Anglo-Saxon American, the images of hearth and homestead asserted Yankee precedence and preeminence in the American nation. Purporting to be images of the real America, they canceled out other versions of it. In an age when the common immigrant was subjected to vitriolic verbal and pictorial abuse (the distortions in the cartoon are, relatively speaking, quite benign for the time), the New England hearth and homestead claimed status as the norm and by implication dismissed and downgraded whatever was not so authentically American. In a milder light the homestead and its hearth might also be seen as symbols of the norm that must be imposed on the alien masses in order to defuse their social time bomb and press them into a home-loving, law-abiding mold.

As the beholder can see, there is nothing of bluff or bombast about the old-homestead images. It would be absurd to claim that they were overtly xenophobic or racist. On the surface and for quite a way below it, they were sentimental, wistful, and elegiac. Nor were these necessarily hollow professions of feeling; on the contrary, they expressed the nostalgia and emotion that many sincerely felt. The other, more negative ideas appear elusively, like vague shadows glimpsed from the corner of the eye. If it were not for the context that generated them, the old-homestead images would be at worst only innocuous. The emerging nativist ambience that surrounded their production, however, edged their nostalgia with the finest line of acid.

118. Worthington Whittredge, *Home by the Sea,* 1872. Oil on
canvas, 35½″ × 53½″. (Addison Gallery of American Art, Phillips
Academy, Andover, Massachusetts)

119. Jasper Cropsey, *The Old Home*, 1884. Oil on canvas, 60″ × 48″. (Courtesy of Richard York Gallery, New York)

PUBLISHED BY CURRIER & IVES.   ENTERED ACCORDING TO ACT OF CONGRESS IN THE YEAR 1868 BY CURRIER & IVES IN THE CLERKS OFFICE OF THE DISTRICT COURT OF THE U.S. FOR THE SOUTHERN DISTRICT OF NEW YORK.   152 NASSAU ST NEW YORK.

AMERICAN HOMESTEAD WINTER.

120.   *American Homestead: Winter,* 1868. Lithograph, 8″ × 12½″.
Published by Currier & Ives, New York. (Prints and Photographs
Division, Library of Congress)

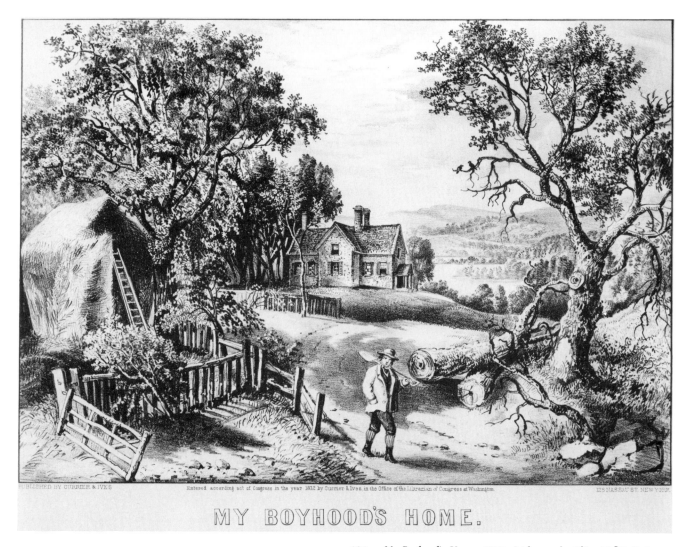

MY BOYHOOD'S HOME.

121. *My Boyhood's Home,* 1872. Lithograph, $8\frac{1}{2}'' \times 12\frac{7}{16}''$. Published by Currier & Ives, New York. (Prints and Photographs Division, Library of Congress)

HOME, SWEET HOME.

122. *Home, Sweet Home*, 1869. Lithograph, 24″ × 29⅝″. Published by Currier & Ives, New York. (Prints and Photographs Division, Library of Congress)

280 ■ *The Anxieties of Nostalgia*

123. *Johnes House* (and other old homesteads, Southampton, Long Island). Wood
engraving. *Harper's New Monthly Magazine* 57
(October 1878).

124.   Harry Fenn, *Home of John Howard Payne*. Wood engraving.
Published in William Cullen Bryant, ed., *Picturesque America; or,*
The Land We Live In, vol. 1 (New York: Appleton, 1872).

282 ■ *The Anxieties of Nostalgia*

125.   Harry Fenn, *Interior of Payne's "Home, Sweet Home."* Wood engraving. Published in William Cullen Bryant, ed., *Picturesque America; or, The Land We Live In*, vol. 1 (New York: Appleton, 1872).

126.   *The Bryant Homestead.* Wood engraving. *Appleton's Journal* 9
(February 8, 1873).

127. Alfred A. Ordway, *Birthplace in Winter*. Photograph of the Whittier homestead in Haverhill, Massachusetts. Published in Samuel T. Pickard, *Whittier-Land* (Boston: Houghton Mifflin, 1904).

128.   Alfred A. Ordway, *Snow-Bound Kitchen, Eastern End*. Photograph of the Whittier homestead in Haverhill, Massachusetts. Published in Samuel T. Pickard, *Whittier-Land* (Boston: Houghton Mifflin, 1904).

129. Eastman Johnson, *Nantucket Interior—Man with a Pipe*, 1865. Oil on board, 11″×9″. (Whereabouts unknown; photograph courtesy of Kennedy Galleries, New York)

130.   George Cochran Lambdin, *Winter Quarters in Virginia—
Army of the Potomac, 1864, 1866.* Oil on canvas, 16″×20″. (Pri-
vate collection; photograph courtesy Berry-Hill Galleries, New
York)

131. Alfred Fredericks, *And Ashes Lie upon the Hearth*. Wood engraving. Published in Wallace Bruce, *Old Homestead Poems* (New York: Harper, 1888).

132. Thomas Hicks, *No Place like Home,* 1877. Oil on canvas,
21½″ × 28½″. (M. R. Schweitzer of Schweitzer Gallery, Inc., New
York)

133. Edward Lamson Henry, *Figures in an Interior,* 1878. Oil on canvas, $9\frac{1}{2}'' \times 11\frac{7}{8}''$. (Collection of Dr. and Mrs. Marvin A. Perer; photograph courtesy of Hirschl & Adler Galleries, New York)

134. Enoch Wood Perry, *Woman Sewing by Firelight*, 1892. Oil
on canvas, 20″ × 24″. (Private collection; photograph Copyright
Sotheby's, Inc., 1989)

A NEW ENGLAND FIRESIDE.

135.   A. Coolidge Warren, *A New England Fireside*. Wood engraving. *Ballou's Pictorial* 8 (March 10, 1855).

HOME TO THANKSGIVING.

136.   Jno. Schutler after George Henry Durrie, *Home to Thanksgiving*, 1867. Lithograph, $14\frac{3}{4}'' \times 25\frac{1}{16}''$. Published by Currier & Ives, New York. (The Harry T. Peters Collection, Museum of the City of New York)

294 ■ *The Anxieties of Nostalgia*

137. Frederick A. Chapman, *Thanksgiving at a New England Farmhouse*. Wood engraving. *Harper's Weekly Magazine* 15 (December 9, 1871).

138. Matthew Morgan, *Unrestricted Immigration and Its Results—A Possible Curiosity of the Twentieth Century: The Last Yankee*. Wood engraving, *Frank Leslie's Illustrated Newspaper*, September 8, 1888. (Prints and Photographs Division, Library of Congress)

UNRESTRICTED IMMIGRATION AND ITS RESULTS.—A POSSIBLE CURIOSITY OF THE TWENTIETH CENTURY.
THE LAST YANKEE.
SEE PAGE 32.

13 ▪ *Barefoot Boys and Other Country Children*

N THE post–Civil War era the ubiquitous and popular image of the country child, epitome of happy youth, counterbalanced the nostalgic image of the homestead, symbol of old times. Like the homestead imagery, that of the country child stemmed from the same general set of social and cultural factors that lent such romantic appeal to what was simple, rural, and untroubled by the problems of modern urban life. The mature urban patrons and readers to whom such themes were meant to appeal were invited to enjoy vicariously the carefree, unthinking existence of rural boyhood or girlhood, to project themselves back into their own early days, to refresh their jaded souls at an American fountain of youth.

These versions of rural childhood were stringently selective and idealized. However innocuous on the surface, such images offer clues to anxieties buried or ignored. It is just as important here to consider what was left out of childhood imagery as to examine what was represented. The gap between real and ideal was in this instance an uncommonly deep and wide one. To descend into it is to discover the logistics of the process which, in creating a myth of unsul-

lied rural childhood, left so far behind the facts that contradicted it.

Later nineteenth-century attitudes toward children were rooted in earlier decades when, under the impact of romantic ideas derived from Jean-Jacques Rousseau and William Wordsworth, previously held doctrines of infant depravity began to dissolve into sentimental exaltations of the child's innocence, and closeness both to nature and to God. By the 1830s significant changes had begun: child-rearing authorities were recommending that children should be allowed freedom to act out their impulses rather than subjected to restraint. No longer a mere proving ground for adulthood, the youthful years came more and more to be regarded as a precious time of joy that would never again be so pure, so close to divinity. In the 1830s and 1840s a vast amount was written about childhood in this Wordsworthian vein. One essay objected to the practice of sending children to school too early and cramming their heads with facts:

O leave him to play, and grow, and be happy; and in the luster of his joyous innocence, remind men of the kingdom of heaven! Let him play out childhood's sweet little prelude to the busy drama of life entirely *ad libitum*. . . . Let him spend the livelong day, if he pleases, *sub Dio;* let him bring home every night a face embrowned by Phoebus, or reddened by Aquilo . . . let him rival the Fawns in archness, and the Satyrs in merriment . . . the stronger his preference for the outside of a house over the inside . . . the more hopeful you may think him. And boon Nature, be sure—whose impulses he is obeying—whose laws he is living by—whose child he is—will impel his little mind to all the action that will benefit it . . . teaching him, by other inspiration than the birch's terrors.[1]

Along with the relaxation of discipline came the foundations of a new literature of childhood that sought to entertain rather than terrify the little reader. At the same time, poetry for and about children began to incorporate realistic details of play, romps, and games.[2]

It is debatable to what extent (and how quickly) these romantic ideas penetrated American society. Most country children, at least, found themselves treated less as messengers of heavenly joy than as a pair of hands, the sooner put to work (usually about the age of seven) the better. The atmosphere of many rural households was, as one scholar put it, that of a "moral pressure cooker" in which early contact with death and the early introduction of piety and religious anxiety marked the childhood years with sobering preoccupations that frequently climaxed in a religious crisis during adolescence.[3] Even without the inculcation of spiritual fear, there was little room for idleness. Play itself had useful functions, as the diary entry of a fourteen-year-old farm boy reveals: "April 3 [1803]. Went down in the orchard and broke up three bumble-bee's nests. I got stung on my hand. Went over back of the school house and dug out a woodchuck. Went a gunning. Went to the corn barn and killed some rats."[4]

Exhortations sprinkled throughout many editions of the *Farmer's Almanac* also emphasized the necessity of work and discipline for farm children and showed a pronounced tendency to regard them as nuisances unless properly trained. Barns were serious, utilitarian places. In one of editor Rob-

ert Thomas's agricultural anecdotes (standard features in the *Almanac*), one character grumbled, "I want none of your dirty, wasteful slovens, nor romping boys and girls, in my barn." In another, Thomas sounded a summons to tackle a number of seasonal tasks: "Come, where are the boys? Here is business enough for an army of us! Now is the time, you know, to clear out the ditches and to carry the mud into the barnyard. We must also be about ploughing." Another piece offered a terse statement on how boys must be controlled:

It is now a capital time to keep the boys at work, and use them to the yolk. Boys are like calves, they need management and much practice to make them handy; and can there be a better time to do this than when spring work comes on? Show them the benefit of every operation; let them understand that he who would reap must sow and he that would enjoy life must use rational means for it.[5]

Again and again, the *Almanac* fumed about farmers' boys who were spoiled and coddled, or put into stores to become great dandies instead of remaining on the farm to do honest work. The country childhood, then, while it was surely not without happiness (as many autobiographical accounts confirm), was no Wordsworthian romance of ecstatic communion with nature, either.

Both moralistic and sentimental strains were present in William Sidney Mount's paintings of country boys. *The Truant Gamblers* (see Illus. 60), *The Disagreeable Surprise* (1843; private collection), and *Boys Caught Napping in a Field* (1848; Brooklyn Museum, New York) are moralistic, if humorous, essays. Such themes were derived from English and Dutch predecessors in whose work children's activities served as emblems of adult folly. All three paintings, featuring gambling and cardplaying, also reflect what was probably the prevailing climate of middle-class religious opinion regarding those games as forms of deep-dyed evil. Charles Dudley Warner, in his account of a typical early nineteenth-century farm boy reflecting on the sins of his neighbors, wryly suggested the horror such activities could inspire:

John knew a couple of desperately bad boys who were reported to play "seven-up" in a barn on the hay-mow, and the enormity of this practice made him shudder. He had once seen a pack of greasy "playing-cards," and it seemed to him to contain the quintessence of sin. If he had desired to defy all Divine law and outrage all human society, he felt that he could do it by shuffling them. And he was quite right. The two bad boys enjoyed in stealth their scandalous pastime, because they knew it was the most wicked thing they could do. . . . John sometimes drove past a brown, tumble-down farmhouse, whose shiftless inhabitants, it was said, were card playing people; and it is impossible to describe how wicked that house appeared to John. . . . In old New England, one could not in any other way so express his contempt of all holy and orderly life as by playing cards for amusement.

The Truant Gamblers and its kin, then, are moral comedies, more than simple scenes of naughty children yet less than thundering sermons. These little anecdotes, which deliver the wages of sin with a chuckle, echo the exhortations in the *Farmer's Almanac* to control and manage boys for their future good.[6]

Other paintings by Mount depict ordinary childhood adventures. In *Turning the Leaf* (1848; The Museums at Stony Brook, New York) a country girl and boy discover a cache of eggs; in *The Trap Sprung* (1844; Terra Museum of American Art, Chicago) two boys out by themselves in the snowy forest are happily snaring rabbits. Such scenes neatly straddle the space betwen factuality and sentiment. The activities they portray—half play, half work—were common to the lives of all farm children in the early nineteenth century. But the depiction of joyous young folk on their own, without adult supervision or intervention, may allude (rather obliquely, perhaps) to those new concepts exalting the child as a free being, at one with nature.

To what extent (if at all) Mount projected personal nostalgia into his images of country children is difficult to determine. What is more certain is that they could (or were presumed to) stimulate nostalgic reflexes in his audience.[7] When *The Trap Sprung* (engraved by Joseph Ives Pease) ap-

peared in *The Gift* for 1845, the custom-written caption was a lament for the lost happiness of boyhood: "Oh, how those days will rush to our hearts again at times; days when we looked lovingly yet reverently on the rabbit, and the white mouse, and the unfledged bird. . . . Many pleasures we may have hereafter, but this one never returns. It is brushed away with the morning dew." Whether or not the trapping of rabbits was consistent with boyish love and reverence for them was an issue the writer failed to resolve. The point, however, is that images of country youth almost invariably called forth such responses. H. Hinshelwood's engraving after John Gadsby Chapman's painting of a rustic fisherboy was embellished with verses expressing the same conventionalized rue for the past: "Back to my days of boyhood!—Fresh and fair / Again they spring before my age-dimmed eyes."[8]

The litany of nostalgia pervaded other forms of literature as well. Charles Lanman's fantasy in the essay "The Dying Year" will stand for all. He dreamed of being carried

right back to the dear little village where I was born. I am a bright-eyed, rosy-cheeked laughing boy again. It is Saturday afternoon. The sun is shining brightly but not very warm. A large party of us children are going on a 'chestnut gathering excursion' over the fields and in the woods. We are a dozen thoughtless, innocent, happy boys and girls. . . . O Time! Thou ruthless tyrant! Why dost thou take from us the joys of childhood, so soon after we have clasped them in a fond embrace?[9]

Post–Civil War nostalgia for youth was compounded of much the same romantic and sentimental elements. On the basis of general similarities one could easily make the case that this later sensibility was only by coincidence a direct response to cultural conditions. It is true that no absolute dividing line may be inscribed between the nostalgias of the two periods on either side of the great watershed. After all, Whittier's popular poem "The Barefoot Boy," which had such meaning for the Gilded Age, was first published in 1856 and reflected sentimental attitudes then prevalent. After the war, however, the context of historical circumstance and social reality endowed nostalgia for childhood with intensified meanings, specific to the time.

The status childhood assumed as a precious, magical state—so happily insulated from the evils of the adult (real) world—can be measured in part by the pronounced increase in the production of a specialized literature both for and about children in the 1870s—including poetry, stories, and magazines—along with a rise in the incidence of paintings, prints, and illustrations commemorating and exalting the beauties of childhood, rural childhood in particular. It was not the increase alone that was important but rather that it occurred together with a change in tone. Wordsworth aside, the dominant note before the Civil War had remained rather humorlessly moralistic and religious. Now, the literature exhibited a liberal, indulgent, sentimental tolerance for all the little joys and even peccadilloes of childhood. Such tendencies had begun to bud in earlier decades, but they came decisively to fruition during the Gilded Age.

Once more, the success of Whittier's *Snow-Bound* serves as an index of postwar sensibility, because this poem was not only a fond backward glance at the vanishing homestead ideal but also an evocation of the innocent happiness of rural boyhood. The boys in the poem—in life, Whittier and his brother—are shadowy figures, but it is through their eyes that the narrative unfolds, through their imaginations that the drifts outside assume bizarre shapes, and through their enthusiasm that digging out a path to the barn becomes a delightful adventure. Their presence and their perceptions are central to the poem, and implicit in the point of view expressed is the idea of the country childhood as a good childhood.

The same equation announced itself in the *Four Seasons of Life* series published by Currier & Ives in 1868 (the year that saw the debut of the firm's popular *American Homestead* series as well). Childhood is "the season of joy," (Illus. 139). The setting is a spring landscape, with trees coming into leaf and flowers into bloom, and new life beginning for the little spring lambs with their mothers on a plump knoll in the middle distance. This is the ideal pastoral landscape once more, now serving as terrain for childish games and pleasures. One foursome poses prettily in the foreground with a lamb and a harvest of blossoms; another romps on the lawn behind.

The association of early youth with spring is an ancient one. There is nothing new about the Currier & Ives imagery nor, strictly speaking, anything particularly American about it. The same sort of imagery was appearing in contemporary English art, for roughly the same reasons: war (in the Crimea) and its aftermath; the sense of loss occasioned by the swift advances of industrialization, urbanization, and expansion. In the 1850s and 1860s, members of the rural Cranbrook Colony devoted themselves to the production of rustic genre scenes in the Wilkie tradition, often dwelling with sentiment on the sport of children. The painting *Spring* (1855; location unknown), for example, by Cranbrook Colony figurehead and mentor Thomas Webster, employed precisely the same bucolic childhood iconography as displayed in the *Four Seasons* print: pastoral terrain, children of various ages, posy gathering, and sheep in the background. Only two years before the appearance of *Childhood, "The Season of Joy,"* an engraving after Webster's painting was published and widely distributed in the *Art Journal,* a major midcentury British magazine. Webster's *Spring* could easily have served as model or inspiration for *The Season of Joy.* The similarities between such images offer a paradigm of American culture in its right relation with the older nations of the Western world, most particularly Britain. An outgrowth of its parent culture across the sea, American culture was subjected to the same range of extreme pressures and, like its British counterpart, attempted to discover solace in the iconography of rustic youth, innocence, and happiness.[10]

Despite its conventionality, childhood imagery in postwar America bore meanings and developed a style reflecting American cultural conditions and needs. *The Season of Joy,* banal though it may be, rehearses the familiar visual language of the idealized American countryside, and its vision of children privileged to dwell in this earthly paradise was meant to nurture the same nostalgic hungers as those that fed upon the idea of the old homestead and the ancestral hearth.[11] Its moral blandness and sentimentality afford additional insight into the revised role of childhood iconography in the later decades of the nineteenth century. This becomes apparent if we compare it with one of the great allegories of antebellum landscape painting, Thomas Cole's four-part *Voyage of Life* (1839–40; Munson-Williams-Proctor Institute, Utica, New York; a second version, painted 1841–42, is in the National Gallery of Art in Washington), which as a set of engravings had reached a wide audience through distribution by the American Art-Union in 1848. Cole's *Childhood* (Illus. 140) symbolizes pristine, happy innocence, at one with nature, in the figure of the baby emerging from a cavern in Mother Earth to sail (with his guardian angel at the helm) through a lush, dawn-radiant landscape.

In Cole's series the baby floats on down the river of life to become an optimistic youth and then a storm-tossed man, finally to reach the end of mortal existence in a calm, twilight sea above which the heavens open to receive his soul. Life unfolds on a continuum. It is a passage through time, using the connecting motif of a river along which the dewy bliss of childhood inevitably gives way to the lashing tempest of maturity. The theme of swiftly passing time and the finite nature of earthly life is one component in the moral. The other consists in a serious pictorial admonition to look to Heaven for salvation, as the frantically praying man does while riding the perilous rapids of adulthood. To Cole, childhood was a lovely but evanescent stage in the course of human life, as it also was in the poetry of William Wordsworth.

The Currier & Ives *Four Seasons* is by contrast secularized and domesticated. In *Youth* a courting couple dawdles down a country lane bordering a summer wheatfield. In *Middle Age* the scene is a middle-class homecoming, mother and children rushing to greet father, returned from the busy world. *Old Age,* finally, depicts a cosy and prosperous interior where grandfather and grandmother sit by the fire, safe from the snowy scene visible through their fashionably draped parlor window. The Currier & Ives series views life as a set of compartmentalized episodes rather than an inexorable continuum. There is no dynamic connection between the romping spring children of the first print and the doting summer couple of the second, and there is little moral weight to the outcome, a vision of life's finale as a heaven of domestic comfort. Instead of flowing into the later stages of growth and development, childhood remains sealed off, suspended and arrested.

This shift in emphasis occurred chiefly in the childhood imagery of the Gilded Age, contrasting broadly with modes and meanings of representation in earlier decades. Childhood became an enchanted realm, a no-man's-land, longingly viewed from afar by those prevented by age, experience, and the trials of history from recrossing its borders. Children's author William Allen White described this division in the introduction to his collection of tales called *The Court of Boyville.* Once the gates of Boyville shut behind a grown youth, wrote White, "he is banished forever. From afar he may peer over the walls at the games inside, but he may not be of them. . . . In vain does he haunt the swimming hole; the water elves will have none of him." The concept of childhood as an exclusive, fortified kingdom complemented the growing tendency Anne Trensky has observed in period literature for or about children to regard childhood as a "static substitute for adulthood" and children as unchanging inhabitants of some idyllic Golden Age.[12]

These perspectives on child life found expression in a new genre: novels and tales of realistically drawn boy heroes: that is, boys not paragons of virtue but natural children, little scapegraces all the more likable for their flaws. From 1869, when Thomas Bailey Aldrich's autobiographical *Story of a Bad Boy* was published (first as a serial in the magazine *Our Young Folks*), such works continued to enjoy great popularity well past the turn of the century. Generated by a wave of reaction against excessive sentiment and piety in earlier children's literature, the Bad Boy tales—almost invariably played out in a rural setting—aimed to glorify the state of boyhood and stimulate nostalgia in the adult readership. The manifest intention of Mark Twain's *Tom Sawyer* (1876) is typical. Twain declared that it had been part of his plan "to try to pleasantly remind adults of what they once were themselves, and of how they felt and thought and talked." And in a glowing (albeit calculated) review of the book, William Dean Howells praised the manner in which the author had brought to life that realm exclusive to the young: "The story is a wonderful study of the boy-mind, which inhabits a world quite distinct from that in which he is bodily present with his elders, and in this lies its great charm and its universality, for boy-nature, however human nature varies, is the same everywhere." Another reviewer later admitted a preference for *Tom Sawyer* over *Huckleberry Finn* because the first so brilliantly illuminated a boy's very heart.[13]

Even more fondly evocative of an ideal past and a never-ending paradise of boyhood was the loosely autobiographical narrative *Being a Boy* (1877) by Charles Dudley Warner (Twain's collaborator on the 1873 novel *The Gilded Age*). In the preface to a later edition Warner explained that he had been writing of a New England golden day:

The rural life described is that of New England between 1830 and 1850, in a period of darkness, before the use of lucifer matches; but when, although religion had a touch of gloom and all pleasure was heightened by a timorous apprehension that it was sin, the sun shone, the woods were full of pungent scents, nature was strong in its invitations to cheerfulness, and girls were as sweet and winsome as they are in the old ballads.

In creating this memoir of idyllic youth, Warner had determined to keep "the man out of the boy's life" by carefully avoiding the adult's point of view:

The object of the papers composing the volume . . . was to recall scenes of the boy-life of New England, or the impressions that a boy had of that life. There was no attempt at the biography of any particular boy; the experiences given were common to the boyhood of the time and place. . . . as soon as I became conscious that I was dealing with a young life of the past, I tried to be faithful to it, strictly so, and to import into it nothing of later experience, either in feeling or performance.[14]

As in the case of *Tom Sawyer* and many contemporary tales of childhood, *Being a Boy* represented the insular child's Arcadia, that state of blessedness which by the 1870s had assumed the status of a potent emblem of what had been lost, both from the individual life and from the life of the nation.

Adulation of country boyhood centered on a romantic craving for innocent closeness to nature in an age when civilization and its ills were suffocating the earth under a toxic crust of artifice. According to George M. Beard, a pioneering researcher in nervous disorders, American civilization had exacted a high toll from the "indoor-living and brain-working classes"—who probably made up the major audience for the works of Warner and Twain. The pace and stresses of life had been increased to near-intolerable levels, thanks to "the invention of printing, the extension of steam power into manufacturing interests and into means of conveyance, the telegraph, the periodical press," along with the enormous increase in business and business transactions, all acting as forces against nature and her rhythms. The victim of civilization must obey mechanical clocks and watches instead of moving and acting according to the biological, seasonal pace of life. Everything in the civilized world, including its sounds, cruelly assaulted the senses:

The noises that nature is constantly producing—the moans and roar of the wind, the rustling and trembling of the leaves and swaying of the branches, the roar . . . of waterfalls, the singing of birds . . . are . . . often pleasing, sometimes delightful and inspiring.

Many of the appliances and accompaniments of civilization, on the other hand, are the causes of noises that are unrhythmical, unmelodious, and therefore annoying, if not injurious; manufactures, locomotion, travel, housekeeping even, are noise-producing factors, and when all these elements are concentred, as in great cities, they maintain . . . an unintermittent vibration in the air that is more or less disagreeable to all, and . . . may be unbearable and harmful.[15]

Against such a background of modern dissonance (in every sense), the idea of the natural country boy held out a powerful appeal.

John Greenleaf Whittier's tender poem of reminiscence, "The Barefoot Boy," established a prototype for literary country boys of the Gilded Age. Whittier's ideal boy is brown, healthy, and cheerful:

> Blessings on thee, little man,
> Barefoot boy, with cheek of tan!
> And thy turned-up pantaloons,
> And thy merry whistled tunes;
> With thy red lip, redder still
> Kissed by strawberries on the hill;
> With the sunshine on thy face,
> Through thy torn brim's jaunty grace.

Whittier's barefoot boy is the creation of a Nature who is both mother and teacher. All year in Nature's world, he absorbs "knowledge never learned of schools":

> How the robin feeds her young,
> How the oriole's nest is hung;
> Where the whitest lilies blow,
> Where the freshest berries grow,
> . . . .
> For, eschewing books and tasks,
> Nature answers all he asks;
> Hand in hand with her he walks,
> Face to face with her he talks,
> Part and parcel of her joy,—
> Blessings on the barefoot boy!

Unlike the later Bad Boy narratives, Whittier's poem ends with a rueful allusion to the carefree boy's inevitable growth and transformation. Those changes are symbolized by the act of confining his bare feet, emblems of the state of nature:

> All too soon those feet must hide
> In the prison cells of pride,
> Lose the freedom of the sod,
> Like a colt's for work be shod.

Charles Dudley Warner saw the same significance in the country boy's shoeless happiness: "The country boy," he wrote, "goes barefoot just as naturally as the trees burst their buds." The equation never varied: unshod youth plus nature equaled perfect happiness.[16]

Some writers, among them William Allen White, sustained Whittier's unabashed romanticism late in the century. White's boys were mystically attuned with nature:

Among the trees they scampered; into the haystacks they wormed; over barrels and boxes they wriggled; they huddled under the sunflowers and horse-weeds. . . . But when the moon's silver had marked itself upon the grass, the boys were lying prone on a haycock. . . . They chatted idly. . . . But the chatter was only a seeming. For in truth the boys were absorbing the glory of the moonlight. And the undertones of their being were sounding in unison with the gentler music of the hour. Their souls—fresher from God than are the souls of men—were a-quiver with joy, and their lips babbled to hide their ecstacies.[17]

At the opposite extreme was a quasi-Darwinian evolutionary model. Warner—who was certainly romantic enough in other parts of *Being a Boy*—asserted:

Every boy who is good for anything is a natural savage. The scientists who want to study the primitive man, and have so much difficulty finding one in this sophisticated age, couldn't do better than to devote their attention to the common country boy. He has the primal, vigorous instincts and impulses of the African savage, without any of the vices inherited from a civilization long ago decayed, or developed in an unrestrained barbaric society. You want to catch your boy young, and study him before he has either virtues or vices, in order to study the primitive man.

Contemporary science, indeed, pursued the same line of thought. Influential educator and psychologist G. Stanley Hall sought to apply the theory of biological recapitulation (that is, the apparent repetition of earlier evolutionary stages during embryonic development) to psychology. Each individual, Hall argued, passes through stages that recapitulate racial history. Before the age of twelve, the child—mirroring some prehistoric time "when in a warm climate the young of our species once shifted for themselves"—revels in all the savage's "tribal, predatory, hunting, fishing, fighting, roving, idle, playing" instincts. In themselves, such feral instincts are healthy; they should be "fed and formed." But these wild impulses were just what modern culture suppressed, and what made their currency so high. As Dr. George Beard observed, "Laughter and tears are safety-valves; the savage and the child laugh or cry when they feel like it . . . in a high civilization like the present, it is not polite either to laugh or to cry in public."[18]

Such theorizing amounted to a marriage of the romantic Noble Savage with a later primitivism based on the scientific thinking of the post-Darwin universe. While there remained some disagreement concerning the moral status of this unconditioned, primitive purity, there was virtual consensus that it represented a state of grace in an overcivilized and disillusioned world. The more civilization encrusted the earth, the more did primitive youth seem an enviable and ideal condition. It was the sheer perfection of this immaturity that made even the children in contemporary fiction wish not to grow up. In Louisa May Alcott's *Little Women*—in some respects a kind of feminine counterpart to the Bad Boy stories—tomboy Jo retorts passionately when sister Meg asks whether she will ever cease her "romping ways": "Never till

I'm stiff and old, and have to use a crutch. Don't try to make me grow up before my time, Meg; it's hard enough to have you change all of a sudden; let me be a little girl as long as I can."[19]

Art gave pictorial flesh to the current idea of the country boy. Paintings such as Eastman Johnson, *The Barefoot Boy*, issued as a chromolithograph by Louis Prang in 1867; John George Brown, *The Berry Boy*; Enoch Wood Perry, *Country Boy*; and Winslow Homer, *Boys in a Pasture* (see Illus. 141–144) show complete agreement with the popular literary conception. These painters were all major producers of country-childhood imagery in the 1860s and 1870s. The English-born Brown (who moved to America in 1853 and came to enjoy huge popular and financial success), Johnson, and Homer shared an interest in naturalistic outdoor effects, and their paintings often hint of reciprocal influence. In the 1860s Homer and Johnson both had studios in the University Building in New York; in 1872 Homer moved to the Tenth Street Studio, where Brown had established himself twelve years earlier. Homer and Perry were also good friends. Homer was closely connected with the emergent literature of childhood and rural childhood themes through his affiliation as illustrator with *Our Young Folks*, a major youth periodical of the time.[20]

By its very title, Johnson's *Barefoot Boy* (Illus. 141) proclaims its connection with Whittier's famous poem, and Brown's *Berry Boy* (Illus. 142) is a variation on the theme. Both evoke the innocent joy and health of Whittier's country boy, gloriously at one with nature. They also find a parallel in Charles Dudley Warner's description of his generic country boy "John":

If you had seen John at this time, you might have thought he was only a shabbily dressed country lad, and you never would have guessed what beautiful thoughts he sometimes had as he went stubbing his toes along the dusty road, nor what a chivalrous little fellow he was. You would have seen a short boy, barefooted, with trousers at once too big and too short, held up, perhaps, by one suspender only; a checked cotton shirt; and a hat of braided palm leaf, frayed at the edges and bulged up in the crown. It is impossible to keep a hat neat if you use it to catch bumble-bees and whisk 'em; to bail the water from a leaky boat; to catch minnows in; . . . to transport pebbles, strawberries, and hens' eggs.[21]

This is what Johnson and Brown wanted to express in their paintings of the archetypal country boy. Johnson's poses winningly, hands in the pockets of his baggy, suspendered, rolled-up trousers and round straw hat jauntily tipped back. He stands on a rock above a stream (perpetual source of wonders to the rustic lad), and around him all is nature: forest, hills, sky. This is the country boy in his element, meant to be seen as child and part of an uncorrupted world. Brown's is even more winning, gazing with a smile directly out at the beholder and standing under a bright sun that strikes glaring highlights upon his hat and shirtsleeves. He stands with both hands braced, about to skip over the stone wall that blocks off the foreground. We cannot see his feet, but we know he must be barefoot. And even though the stone wall functions as a reminder of human artifice, this boy—hardly less than Johnson's—dwells in a kingdom of ecstatic youth in company with nature.

That the literary and the pictorial correspond so closely demonstrates less that one copied the other than that both drew from a pool of common ideas. Picture after picture, the country boy remains constant. In Perry's *Country Boy* (Illus. 143) he has the same rolled-up trousers and battered hat. Lingering by a weathered barn door, with a loaded basket of apples at his bare feet, he whittles a stick with energy and concentration, an activity signaling his identity as an old-fashioned Yankee youngster. The fact that he has abandoned an errand to dawdle by the wayside recalls the wholesome naughtiness of the rustic Bad Boys, just then entering into fame.

Homer's boys too are old-time Yankee lads, even though they were based on studies of their contemporary counterparts. Homer had already essayed several versions of the subject in the mid-1860s. Some, like *Haymaking* (1864; Columbus, Ohio, Museum of Art), showed boys doing the work of the men who had gone to war; others, such as *Boys on a Bough* (1864; Museum of Fine Arts, Springfield, Massachusetts) were evocations of carefree rustic pleasure. Subsequently, Homer left the subject of serious youthful toil behind. Never-failing sunshine beams down upon his untroubled terrain of pastoral childhood, seen with a fonder eye than that which scrutinized the American "peasant."

It may seem inconsistent that Homer could treat aspects of the same rural scene so differently, but the subject of rustic youth was intrinsically a more emotional one, especially in the nostalgic context of the period. Homer had more personal stake in these images as well. In 1878 he told art writer G. W. Sheldon some of the facts and circumstances of his own early years, tracing his taste for rural life back to boyhood experience. Sheldon wrote, "He has a great liking for country life—a liking which he thinks had its origin in the meadows, ponds, fishing and beautiful surroundings of that suburban place [Cambridge]. To this day there is no recreation that Mr. Homer prefers to an excursion into the country." This element of personal nostalgia may have played its part in investing Homer's childhood imagery with a certain sweetness and rue. [22]

Like the other country lads, the two figures in Homer's *Boys in a Pasture* (Illus. 144) wear oversized trousers and rustic hats. The sun beats down upon them, making one boy's shirt a patch of starchy white and the other's straw hat a golden helmet. They let their bare feet luxuriate in the juicy coolness of the meadow grass where they rest, all alone. There is no anecdote here, only a mood of happy calm. Further, there is no moralizing. Whereas Mount's *Boys Caught Napping in a Field* was a humorous warning against indolence, Homer's painting depicts simple rustic joy and celebrates that vital oneness of boys with nature which preoccupied writers and scientists alike during the period. One of Clifton Johnson's photographs illustrating the 1897 edition of *Being a Boy* is strikingly similar in mood, even if so different in medium and obviously contrived in making. Straw hat tipped over his eyes, the subject in *The New England Boy* (Illus. 145) luxuriates so intently in the grass that grass and boy almost literally merge into oneness. All these boys—Homer's, Brown's, Perry's, Eastman Johnson's, and Clifton Johnson's—are the most privileged of beings, blessed in the state of nature. Far from betraying bumpkin unrefinement, their unshod feet betoken their enviable primitivism and unity with Mother Earth.[23]

Nowhere was that primitivism more exuberantly displayed than in Homer's *Snap the Whip* (Illus. 146). In this painting the expression of ecstatic freedom is heightened by contrast: beyond the line of barefoot boys—a model of disciplined spontaneity in design—stands their red clapboarded school-house, emblem of confinement, foursquare and stolid. In relation to the building the sinuous, passionately energetic human chain becomes the pictorial equivalent of the idea of sudden and joyous liberation. Two boys in the middle are in midflight; their feet fly through the air above the ground. The painting is about animal joy, recalling Warner's description of boys bursting out of school for recess:

Was ever any enjoyment so keen as that with which a boy rushes out of the school house for the ten minutes of recess? He is like to burst with animal spirits; he runs like a deer; he can nearly fly; and he throws himself into play with entire self-forgetfulness, and an energy that would overturn the world if his strength were proportioned to it. For ten minutes the world is absolutely his; the weights are taken off, restraints are loosed, and he is his own master for that brief time,—as he never again will be if he lives to be as old as the king of Thule, and nobody knows how old he was.

One reviewer used precisely the same terms in an appreciation of *Snap the Whip*. Homer, he wrote, liked "boys and young animals" and delighted in "a strong sense of animal life": "Head over heels the children go topsy-turvy, but it is with a sense of good spirits that makes them delight to use their legs and pull hard with their strong young arms." Happy in their elemental vitality, these youthful rural savages were immune to the ills of civilization.[24]

The consensus among literary and pictorial images of barefoot boys holds generally in other themes of rustic childhood during the period, and the same agreement extended from painting to popular illustration. All media contributed to a standardized iconography of nostalgia for country childhood. Homer's illustrations *Chestnutting* (Illus. 147) and *Gathering Berries* (Illus. 148), based on a Gloucester watercolor done the previous year, and W. L. Sheppard's *The Last Apple* (Illus. 149) reflect the charm invested in the spectacle of young country people playing at work in their summer and fall gathering expeditions. According to Charles Dudley Warner, nutting of any kind was an especially delightful pursuit:

One of the best things in farming is gathering the chestnuts, hickory-nuts, butternuts, and even beech-nuts, in the late fall, after the frosts have cracked the husks and the high winds shaken them, and the colored leaves have strewed the ground. On a bright October day, when the air is full of golden sunshine, there is nothing quite so exhilarating as going nutting. Nor is the pleasure of it altogether destroyed for the boy by the consideration that he is making himself useful in obtaining supplies for the winter household. The getting-in of potatoes and corn is a different thing; that is the prose, but nutting is the poetry, of farm life.[25]

This is the sentiment expressed in Homer's illustration, a scene of youthful enjoyment in which two boys and two girls—one with quaint rustic pigtails—hold up the corners of the great sheet into which the chestnuts tumble, propelled by the boy who sits aloft, shaking them down. Sheppard's picture is close to Homer's in both feeling and design, though the subject is apples rather than nuts. Here three little girls, one with apron spread, wait beneath the boughs of a majestic old apple tree as the boy on the branch above prepares to toss the last apple down. The comment written for Sheppard's illustration responded appropriately to the nostalgic poetry of the scene: "Our illustration tells its own story—a pretty autumn idyll which almost everyone remembers from youth."[26] *Gathering Berries*, one of Homer's strongest graphic designs, sustains the spirit of *Chestnutting*. Boys and girls cull berries in a scrubby, rocky pasture near the Atlantic shore. The stiff wind sending the clouds scudding and hat ribbons flying amplifies the buoyant mood of carefree rustic pleasure in the open air.

The same sensibility tinted the childhood verse produced by writers such as Lucy Larcom, who had been assistant editor of *Our Young Folks*. Her collection *Childhood Songs* (1874) included many poems previously published in the magazine. The verses were written, she said, "as one may write who in mature life retains a warm sympathy with childhood, through a vivid memory of her own." Most dwelt upon childhood wonder at nature or children's innocent games. The "Berrying Song" is a chant to the beauty and healthfulness of spending the day amidst the charms of the rural landscape.

> Red lilies blaze out of the thicket;
>   Wild roses blush here and there:
> There's sweetness in all the breezes,
>   There's health in each breath of air.
> Hark to the wind in the pine-trees!
>   Hark to the tinkling rill!
> O, pleasant it is a-berrying
>   In the pastures on the hill![27]

Homer's *Gathering Berries* shares the spirit of Larcom's verse in its evocation of the bright, exhilarating breeziness and creature happiness of a child's summer day. That this should be so is not exactly coincidence. While *Gathering Berrries*

was not an illustration to any specific text, four of Homer's pictures in *Our Young Folks* in 1867 and 1868 accompanied verses by Larcom and by John Townsend Trowbridge, another prominent poet of childhood. Homer also executed two illustrations for Whittier's poem of reminiscence "My Playmate," published both in *Our Young Folks* in 1869 and in Whittier's *Ballads of New England* in 1870. Homer's early professional affiliation with the emergent literature of childhood in the years immediately following the Civil War probably helped to mold his subsequent approach to country childhood themes and to color his sensibility with the romantic childhood nostalgia that permeated so much of that literature.[28]

The theme of children in barns was also loaded with sentiment. The mere thought of the old-fashioned barn was enough to catalyze one writer's nostalgic meditations:

Now, nothing is more essential than good impressions in childhood, and nothing secures them like a good old barn. I speak well of my mother, who was formed in a large mold, but I insist on my grandfather's barn, and I am sure that I had more pleasure in it than I have had in the new opera house, and I would not exchange the recollections of the one for the other. . . . Every Saturday afternoon, my sister and I, with two other boys, played there; and on Sunday morning we went (she and I) to look for the eggs. . . . There was no floor but the "thrashing" floor (as in a barn built for children there should not be), but on either side of it the deep bays extended, and high up the dusky light filled the roof, through which a pencil of sunshine showed the dancing motes. In that dim space the swallows wheeled.

The writer recalled the joys of jumping in the hay and other delectable amusements, and concluded by advising mothers to supply their boys with "country air and a good barn" rather than "fringed pantaloons, a small cane, kid gloves, and long curls."[29] Play in the barn was also a subject fondly treated by Lucy Larcom. In "The Barn Window" a woman recalls happy times long ago:

Have you forgotten, John,
    That Wednesday afternoon
When the great doors were open wide,
    And all the scents of June
Came in to greet us, side by side,
    In the high-seated swing,

．　．　．　．　．　．　．　．　．　．

Up to the barn eaves, John,
    We swung, two happy things,
At home and careless in the air
    As if we both had wings. [30]

The old-fashioned barn interior coalesced perfectly with rural childhood nostalgia in a series of sketches and finished paintings done in 1877 and 1878 by Eastman Johnson. These include *In the Hayloft* (Illus. 150), *The Quiet Hour* (c. 1877–78; private collection), *Barn Swallows* (1878; Philadelphia Museum of Art), and *The Confab* (1878; Wadsworth Atheneum, Hartford, Connecticut). Although both the barn and the children existed in the present, the images evoked the innocent, wholesome past lamented by Larcom and other writers. The barn, inhabited by groups of children romping, chatting, or quietly resting, is not at all a functional structure but a playhouse. *In the Hayloft,* with its children balancing on the massive crossbeam and frolicking in the hay below, reveals a private world of childhood, a kingdom of freedom and bliss. Similarly, in Aldrich's *Story of a Bad Boy,* the barn is a clubhouse for the schoolboys' secret society. The illustration *A Visit to Grandfather's Home* (Illus. 151) is an entire visual catalogue of nostalgic rustic joys, including a romp in the cavernous barn and play in the garret of the old homestead. More succinctly than any other image, perhaps, this cluster of motifs objectifies the idea of the American farmscape as a never-never land, where kindly old people exist mainly to keep traditions alive for the young, whose realm it is. It is worth noting how radically such barn scenes differ from William Sidney Mount's. In *The Truant Gamblers* (see Illus. 60) the boys play a dangerous game and are soon to be punished by the grim farmer sneaking up on their

jolly group. In the later pictures indulgent sentiment is all: the children's play is blessed. [31]

Images like Homer's, Brown's, and Johnson's represented ideals based on certain facts but given a golden aura of sentiment that meshed smoothly with postbellum nostalgia and the new adulation of the childhood state. In contemporary culture the vision of happy, rustic youth, like those of hearth and homestead, had the overt and primary function of catering to that nostalgia, softening the sour present with gentle reminders of former sweetness, and counterposing the state of natural, primitve grace against the overcivilized world of modern adulthood.

It was also a glaringly false and misleading facade that concealed, or simply failed to take account of, the social realities surrounding the largely urban and suburban audiences toward whom nostalgic visual and literary products were directed. The false front of childhood felicity functioned as immunization against the anxiety-generating social ills of impoverished urban youth, already a major problem at mid-century. The degree to which artists and writers detached themselves from those issues was virtually complete. With the exception of a handful of mill and city scenes, Winslow Homer looked only at the terrain of play and sport in the world out-of-doors. Larcom's case affords an interesting parallel. She passed much of her life in the factory town of Lowell, Massachusetts, and as a young girl had worked in the mills herself, yet she published only two poems on the theme of child labor and poverty. [32] The imagery of Larcom, Homer, and their colleagues supported an ideology of childhood that few were fortunate enough to share. At the same time, however, it sustained a powerful myth that significantly shaped the philosophy and actions of reformers in the late nineteenth century.

The circumstances of other sorts of childhood—particularly in the cities—throw the passive mendaciousness of country childhood scenes into high relief. Children of the slums and children of immigrants (often one and the same) lived in a world that could not have been further from that of the generic Barefoot Boy, or even the Bad Boy. As the pace of industrialization quickened, so rose the demand for child labor, which could be had at bargain prices. In the 1870s, reform had barely begun to improve the lot of the child worker. Massachusetts passed a law in 1876 prohibiting the employment of children under ten in any capacity, but as previous attempts had shown, enforcement was erratic at best and at worst dwindled to nothing. Even after 1900 few states had made any attempt to regulate such laws as did exist, and the very young had little protection against consignment to mills and mines. (Children on farms, of course, were routinely put to work at a tender age, but few people regarded this as oppressive.) In the factories of New York alone in 1873 as many as 100,000 children were employed for the meagerest wages. Many were sent to work by immigrant parents, driven by necessity or ambition to scrape a living with every possible hand. Others worked in the streets as newsboys, bootblacks, and messengers, occupations that struck H. G. Wells as "social abominations" and revelations of "the weakest spot in America's fine front of national well being." Many children were homeless, or so neglected by their families that they were all but feral, bedding down in flophouses and roaming the streets in gangs. In the 1870s, New York had some 10,000 of these urban vagabonds.[33]

Slum children, puny and pathetic though they might be, represented one of the greatest menaces to the status quo (white, Anglo-Saxon, and bourgeois). In their frail, tattered persons rested the seeds of that great, barbaric danger that might visit apocalyptic destruction upon the social order, rending the fabric of civilization. One journalist commented balefully: "Never in the history of our city has infant wretchedness stalked forth in such multiplied and such humiliating forms. . . . even pagan Rome . . . never witnessed a more rapid and frightful declension in morals, nor witnessed among the young a more utter disregard of honor, of truth, and piety, and even the commonest decencies of life." Such children reminded reformer Charles Loring Brace of a species of "street-rats," who "gnawed away at the foundations of society and scampered away when light was brought near them."[34]

Brace, founder of the Children's Aid Society and author of *The Dangerous Classes of New York,* believed that the offspring of the immigrant poor represented the most ominous threat to the social order, a poison that would ferment into greater deadliness as these children became adults:

All the neglect and bad education and evil example of a poor class tend to form others, who, as they mature, swell the ranks of ruffians and criminals. So, at length, a great multitude of ignorant, untrained, passionate, irreligious boys and young men are formed, who become the "dangerous classes" of our city. They form the "Nineteenth-Street Gangs," the young burglars and murderers, the garroters and rioters, the thieves and flash-men, the "repeaters" and ruffians, so well known to all who know this metropolis.

Reminding his readers of recent riots in New York—the draft riots of 1863; the Orange riot of 1871, when Catholic and Protestant Irish immigrants clashed—Brace pointed out that the separate members of these "riotous and ruffianly masses" were "simply neglected and street-wandering children . . . come to early manhood."

Brace attributed the deviate development of slum children to the environment itself rather than to inherent weakness. In this he was among the pioneers of a new social thought which—repudiating Social Darwinism and laissez-faire philosophies—would become fundamental to reform by the last decade of the century. Looking back in 1880 over the quarter-century of his efforts to rescue children from the "dens of misery" that corrupted them, Brace portrayed the nightmare world of evil that had confronted him in the early years:

There were the thieves' Lodging-houses in the lower wards, where the street-boys were trained by older pickpockets and burglars for their nefarious callings; the low immigrant boarding-houses and vile cellars of the First Ward, educating a youthful population for courses of guilt; the notorious rogues' den in Laurens Street . . . and, farther above, the community of young garroters and burglars around

"Hamersley Street and Cottage Place." And, still more north, the dreadful population of youthful ruffians and degraded men and women in "Poverty Lane."[35]

A *Harper's Weekly* report on conditions in a Mulberry Street tenement house illuminated all the loathsomeness of slum nurture. The atmosphere was "rank poison." "Sickening odors and gases" rose from the "choked sewers." The drunken tenants were "steeped in ignorance and degradation." In such places lived unblessed boys who were barefoot because of poverty and neglect, primitive in ways far more ominous than the country boy's innocent savagery.[36]

In the world of academic painting, although images of country children far outnumbered those of their urban counterparts, several painters (including J. G. Brown) made a specialty of city urchins—newsboys, bootblacks, and the like. In periodicals, pictures of homeless young wretches appeared more frequently, yet curiously they seldom attained anything near the high pitch of apocalyptic rhetoric so often encountered in contemporary prose on the same subject. Depictions of adult slum dwellers were more acerbic, but many pictures of slum children, portraying them as pathetic victims or engaging scamps, failed to come to terms with either their presumed depravity or the depths of their despair. That this was so underscores the role of much American art— high and popular—throughout the nineteenth century. Carefully sidestepping the uncomfortable issues of the day, it offered reassuring versions of American life—cleaned up, optimistic, comic, or sentimentalized.

Harper's Weekly staff artist Sol Eytinge's illustration *The Hearth-Stone of the Poor* (Illus. 152) exemplifies that strategy of defusing the time bomb represented by abandoned urban youth. The illustration depicts a group of homeless children, one a bootblack, huddled over the steam vent of a printing plant. On the sidewalk behind them stroll warmly and fashionably dressed pedestrians: a tall, stout man and a young mother, whose two children stare and point as they pass by the raggedy clutch of urchins. While the latter are not a merry band, neither are they grotesque; indeed, save for their rags, they could be siblings of the well-to-do children. At worst, they look forlorn, not vicious. The accompanying text confirms the suggestions of the illustration: "The poor street children, girls and boys together, take comfort at these free hearth-stones—rather cold comfort, think the warmly dressed children who look at them in passing: but the waifs evidently enjoy themselves, and are not disturbed by envious feelings."[37] If the "waifs" were so innocently enjoying themselves, then presumably no one need lie awake at night, dreading their day of wrath.

John George Brown, who portrayed cute city urchins even more often than winning country lads, and owed to the former a hefty measure of his popularity, never permitted the slightest hint of misery (except the occasional dash of pathos) to dim the cheerful aura surrounding his cheeky, roguish newsboys, bootblacks, and street sweepers. Like the plucky Horatio Alger heroes whom they so much resembled, Brown's urchins were healthy, street-wise, and appealing. Like Alger's first hero, Ragged Dick (of the novel by the same name, published in 1867), they were upward bound, never destined to descend into metropolitan sinks of sin and despair. Thus did art pull the claws of the "dangerous classes," offering instead images of optimism. In this respect, at least, the cheery bootblacks become cousins to the rustic barefoot boys whose images, seen everywhere, contradicted what every gallery-goer might have passed en route to an exhibition.

Pictorial journalism on occasion presented less reassuring images. One contemporary illustration, *Story of a Waif* (Illus. 153), mirrors Brace's assumptions in showing a deterministic model of slum development. Unlike Ragged Dick, this boy progresses from ragged urchin, nurtured on the filth of the streets, to gin-swilling ruffian picking his teeth with the same knife he doubtless uses to commit crimes, and finally to grizzled bum behind bars. When police photographer and social reformer Jacob Riis embarked on his sensational exposés of slum life and child exploitation in the 1890s, he too followed Brace in attributing to the squalid environment of the slums the infection of vice and crime in the young. It was only with the appearance of Riis's photographs, which portrayed slum children with unprecedented objectivity, that sentimental and picturesque stereotypes like Brown's stood exposed in their falsehood.[38]

The Barefoot Boys served as models of what reformers and educators hoped city children, with proper guidance, might become. In order to ameliorate destructive external conditions, Brace and his colleagues worked ardently to establish workshops, nightschools, and lodginghouses for young vagrants and tenement dwellers; more important was the idea of (even temporary) country childhood as the best cure for the environmental and social ills of urban youth. Once a city child absorbed the beneficent influence of nature, it was believed, he or she would become a better person; even if forced back to the city, the child would have been "vaccinated" and better able to ward off the invasion of moral disease.

A form of benevolent deportation, then, became the cornerstone of the course of action formulated by Brace's Children's Aid Society:

The Founders . . . early saw that the best of all Asylums for the outcast child, is the *farmer's home.*

The United States have the enormous advantage over all other countries, in the treatment of difficult questions of pauperism and reform, that they possess a practically unlimited area of arable land. The demand for labor on this land is beyond any present supply. Moreover, the cultivators of the soil are in America the most solid and intelligent class. From the nature of their circumstances, their laborers, or "help," must be members of their families, and share in their social tone. It is, accordingly, of utmost importance to them to train up children who shall aid in their work, and be associates of their own children.

In Brace's vision, the old agrarian ideal, notions of democracy, and the long-favored theory of the frontier as a safety valve combined to justify what was in part at least (ideology aside) a method simply of getting undesirables out of the way. To demonstrate the success of the program, Brace recounted a number of successful case histories and embellished them with before and after illustrations (Illus. 154, 155), eloquent testimonial to the transformation (in only one year) of a homeless, undernourished tatterdemalion into a clean, happy farm boy. In the country he has achieved a state of nature and grace, although—as a symbol of his new, respectable status, perhaps—he is now well shod.[39]

If a child could not be sent away from the slum or factory permanently, even the briefest exposure to country air and country ways (reformers hoped) might implant the seeds of virtue in the impressionable young soul. In July 1873 the *New York Times* underwrote a scheme providing slum children with one-day excursions into the country. Inspired by the benevolent *Times*, reformers followed suit, augmenting the original plan with such variations as "Country Weeks" with farm families. "Fresh Air Funds," which by 1897 had been established in seventeen cities, began in 1877 when the Reverend Willard Parsons of Sherman, Pennsylvania, brought sixty children out of New York to enjoy a respite from the suffocating heat of the metropolis. The *New York Tribune* took over the program in 1882 and sent some 5,500 urchins to the countryside to become temporary barefoot boys and girls. By 1889, beneficiaries of Fresh Air charities in New York alone numbered over 10,000. Faith in the purifying influence of country air was considerable. Bostonian William Cole maintained that "the importance to the child of becoming acquainted with country sights and sounds cannot be overestimated. Without such acquaintance . . . its mental growth cannot but be dwarfed and distorted." Cole went so far as to assert that without the "essential spiritual nurture" provided by nature alone, the child "must inevitably grow up with twisted and vicious views of life." Even nodding acquaintance with the country, therefore, must be infinitely better than none.[40]

Such measures, undertaken with genuine charitable spirit for the most part (though with an eye on public image, as in the newspapers' conspicuous sponsorship), no doubt saved many an itchy conscience and enabled the privileged to bask in the glow of their own self-satisfaction. Whether a Country Week exerted any enduring influence upon those who had to pass the remaining fifty-one weeks in a slum environment is dubious. What the enthusiasm for the Country Week so clearly shows is the power of the Barefoot Boy ideal and the immense amount of sentiment invested in it.

William Allen Rogers's illustration *The Tribune Fresh Air Fund—Children's Excursion to Lake Champlain* (Illus. 156) views this urchins' pilgrimage through the sentimental haze that so often and so unobtrusively erected a barrier between the observer and the bedrock of alien experience. At the top of the page are four dispirited little city girls (one with a crutch) and a small boy, en route to the Eden that awaits them. The three principal scenes show some young city visitors agape at a bee-swarming, paddling barefoot and straw-hatted in the lake, and going to church with their rustic sponsors. At the bottom, a boy carries the "trophies of his visit" in a carpetbag: a litter of kittens, destined to become alley cats should they travel to the great city. The realities and severities of the children's native environment form no part of Rogers's design. They seem to come from and return to nowhere. Only the felicities of the country visit itself are admitted: we see how simple the stereotyped country folks are and how good (their church being so dominant), and how serene the lake where the children enjoy their brief rustic status. There is a sweetness and a sprightliness, too, in Rogers's style, almost a cartoonish playfulness, in keeping with the simplistic emotionalism of the presentation.

The same kind of self-serving sentimentality is present in Will Carleton's poem "Let the Cloth Be White," which was dedicated to the poor children's excursions. Carleton, a popular writer of pastoral poetry, put the words into the mouth of old Farmer Harrington, a rustic philosopher who, having seen the metropolis and its evils, resolves to treat several underprivileged city children to a month on his farm. These children, as he describes them—with their features "pinched an' spare"—are the very opposite of the Barefoot Boy:

They come from out the dungeons where they with want were chained;
From places dark an' dismal, by tears of sorrow stained;
From where a thousand shadows are murdering all the light:
Set well the table, Mary dear, an' let the cloth be white!

They ha' not seen the daisies made for the heart's behoof;
They never heard the rain-drops upon a cottage roof;
They do not know the kisses of zephyr an' of breeze;
They never rambled wild an' free beneath the forest trees.

The farmer goes on to praise the men and women "of noble brain an' heart, / Who go down in the folk-swamps an' take the children's part."[41]

William Allen Rogers, who illustrated the poem (Illus. 157), depicted the archetypal geriatric yeoman and his wife—both stout and benevolent—surrounded by symbols of country goodness and nurture: a butter churn; a great bustle of cooking on a woodstove, with substantial kettles and cauldrons; a cat with kittens on the porch; a barnyard full of chickens and cows. Here, the picture says, is the pastoral paradise that will cure those sick young souls, transform them into wholesome country boys and girls, and fortify them against their inevitable descent back into the urban underworld. Like the Fresh Air Fund illustration, this one focuses optimistically on a fleeting interval in lives otherwise antithetical.

So stubbornly did the ideal cling of the country child, taught by nature, that many urban educators late in the century strove to introduce programs of nature study into school curriculums in the hope that this knowledge and experience would foster something approaching the normal (that is, rural) childhood experience and help mold good character as well. Urging that such courses in nature study be initiated, G. Stanley Hall asserted: "As our methods of teaching grow more natural, we realize that city life is unnatural, and that those who grow up without knowing the country are defrauded of that without which childhood can never be complete or normal." Surrounded by urban artifacts, the city child knew next to nothing about nature. Hall discovered to his dismay that 180 of some 200 Boston children he tested did not know what an elm tree was, or a field of wheat.[42]

Galvanized by such appalling facts, schools in the late nineteenth century attempted to mold children into "miniature Jeffersonian yeomen," as William Bullough put it. [43] They introduced not only academic courses in natural history but also school gardens, vacation schools (emphasizing nature study and microcosmic agriculture), and manual training (inspired by the idea of the village workshop). Such programs had little if any effect on urban children, however, and were generally regarded as failures. The fundamental problem lay in the irreconcilability of rural values and the new urban environment. Seeing this, educational psychologist Charles DeGarmo criticized the persistence of faith in rural values that did not fit contemporary circumstances:

A city represents a system of reciprocal activities, duties, concessions, and benefits. Social co-operation in the city . . . is a necessity . . . . Yet even in these vast centers of population the ideals of a primitive community still prevail; for the dominant ideal . . . in this country is that of essentially non-social individualism.[44]

Viewed in this context, images of happy country children in prose, poetry, painting, and the graphic arts communicate a complicated set of signals. On the one hand, they symbolize all those longings, overt or submerged, to escape from the pressures of the present, to burrow back into an ideal past, to be a child again, to shed the burden of adult responsibility for a retreat into a sheltered, pastoral never-never land. Turning their backs on what was real life for hundreds of thousands of real children in the period, the Barefoot Boy images were the ultimate in willful avoidance and ignorance. On the other hand, they functioned as emblems of an ideal to which those multitudes of alien, impoverished, nature-starved wretches of metropolitan tenements must be made to conform, less in order to save their souls (though such was the rhetoric) than to blunt and ultimately vanquish the threat that their very existence posed to middle-class society and its values. Just as Frederick Law Olmsted's Central Park—nature brought to the city—was in theory an instrument of social control that would teach nature, decorum, and democracy while undermining the immigrant (alien, dangerous) culture flourishing in slum streets and tenements, in the same way the model of the country child, the blessed Barefoot Boy, represented an Anglo-Saxon, middle-class norm to be impressed upon the youth of the slums. Only thus would they be Americanized; only thus would they acquire values that would render them harmless. Although the country boy pictures and tales themselves were not at all moralistic in the old sense, they embodied a very specific set of values, a template for American youth.[45]

The image of the country child, then, implied a strategy for social control, based on venerated traditions and beliefs, which might help redeem civilization (as that concept was understood by the culturemakers) from an awful fate. Such meanings, like those submerged beneath the image of the old homestead, did not thrust themselves into prominence. Rather, they were undercurrents, insinuations, shadows of cultural hegemony, paranoia, and xenophobia lingering beyond the bright rays of the sunshine that illuminated the mythic terrain of American rural childhood.

THE FOUR SEASONS OF LIFE: CHILDHOOD.
"The Season of Joy"

139.   James Merritt Ives after Frances Palmer and J. Cameron,
The Four Seasons of Life: Childhood, "The Season of Joy," 1868.
Lithograph, $15\frac{13}{16}'' \times 23\frac{7}{8}''$. Published by Currier & Ives, New York.
(Prints and Photographs Division, Library of Congress)

140.   Thomas Cole, *Childhood,* from *The Voyage of Life,* 1839.
Oil on canvas, 52″ × 78″. (Munson-Williams-Proctor Institute,
Utica, New York)

141. Eastman Johnson, *The Barefoot Boy,* 1860. Oil on board, $12\frac{3}{4}'' \times 9\frac{1}{2}''$. (From the collections of Katherine Smith Miller and Lance Smith Miller; photograph courtesy of Sotheby's, New York)

142. John George Brown, *The Berry Boy,* c. 1875. Oil on canvas, 23″ × 14¼″. (George Walter Vincent Smith Art Museum, Springfield, Massachusetts)

143. Enoch Wood Perry, *Country Boy,* 1872. Oil on canvas, $20'' \times 15\frac{1}{4}''$. (Private collection; photograph courtesy of R. H. Love Galleries, Inc., Chicago)

144.   Winslow Homer, *Boys in a Pasture,* 1874. Oil on canvas, 15¼″×22½″. (Courtesy, Museum of Fine Arts, Boston, Charles Henry Hayden Fund)

145. Clifton Johnson, *The New England Boy*. Photograph. Published in Charles Dudley Warner, *Being a Boy* (Boston: Houghton Mifflin, 1897).

146. Winslow Homer, *Snap the Whip*, 1872. Oil on canvas,
22″ × 36″. (Butler Institute of American Art, Youngstown, Ohio)

147. Winslow Homer, *Chestnut-ting*. Wood engraving. *Every Satur-day*, October 29, 1870. (Bowdoin College Art Museum, Brunswick, Maine)

322 ▪

148.   Winslow Homer, *Gathering Berries*. Wood engraving. *Harper's Weekly Magazine* 18 (July 11, 1874). (Bowdoin College Art Museum, Brunswick, Maine)

149. W. L. Sheppard, *The Last Apple*.
Wood engraving. *Harper's Weekly Magazine* 18
(November 28, 1874).

150.   Eastman Johnson, *In the Hayloft,* c. 1877–78. Oil on canvas, 27″ × 33″. (San Diego Museum of Art, San Diego, California)

151. Granville Perkins after Eva Muller, *A Visit to Grandfather's Home*. Wood engraving. *Harper's Weekly Magazine* 20 (August 19, 1876).

152. Sol Eytinge, *The Hearth-Stone of the Poor*. Wood engraving. *Harper's Weekly Magazine* 20 (February 12, 1876).

THE STORY OF A WAIF.—Drawn by W. L. Sheppard, from a Sketch by M. Woolf.—[See Page 234.]

153. W. L. Sheppard after M. Woolf, *The Story of a Waif.*
Wood engraving. *Harper's Weekly Magazine* 16 (March 23, 1872).

154. *Please, Sir, May I Have a Bed?* Wood engraving. Published in Charles Loring Brace, *The Dangerous Classes of New York, and Twenty Years' Work among Them,* 3d ed. (New York: Wynkoop & Hallenbeck, 1880).

155. *The Street Boy on a Farm (A Year Later)*. Wood engraving.
Published in Charles Loring Brace, *The Dangerous Classes of New
York, and Twenty Years' Work among Them*, 3d ed. (New York:
Wynkoop & Hallenbeck, 1880).

Little Pilgrims On The Way

At a Bee-Swarming

Sunday Morning in the Country

In the Waters of Lake Champlain.

Trophies of his visit

156.   William Allen Rogers, *The Tribune Fresh Air Fund—Children's Excursion to Lake Champlain*. Wood engraving. *Harper's Weekly Magazine* 26 (July 29, 1882).

"THE HUNGRY CITY CHILDREN ARE COMING HERE TO-NIGHT."

157.   William Allen Rogers, *Let the Cloth Be White*. Wood engraving. Published in Will Carleton, *City Ballads* (New York:
Harper, 1885).

CONCLUSION

HE connections between nineteenth- and twentieth-century images of rural life are direct. We owe our vision of what American agriculture should be to the old ideals and stereotypes, shaped and perpetuated by art and literature. Visions of country life in the nineteenth century expressed concepts that had nothing to do with the miseries of life in prairie sod houses or the brutalizing monotony of rural labor everywhere. Instead, the ideal farmscape of a Currier & Ives print and the lively rustic shrewdness of William Sidney Mount's farmers communicated a complex of cultural ideas, while realities were the province of journalists and artist-reporters. Such a fractured mode of looking and perceiving is just as common today. No more than nineteenth-century viewers and readers can we reconcile facts with fictions or find the line between them.

Periodically in twentieth-century life and art there have been swells of enthusiasm for getting back to the land where, theoretically, one can become whole and good and natural. In the 1930s, the agrarian ideal attained renewed, meaningful life in the art of Grant Wood and other regionalists. In the 1960s, getting back to the land became a form of protest against the Establishment as well as a path to happiness and self-realization.

The farm crises of the 1980s have revealed how deeply the old veneration of the homestead still colors our perceptions of agriculture in America. Periodically, news anchors lament the passing of the family farm; dispossessed and displaced farmers are seen as both pathetically helpless and nobly heroic in their fruitless efforts to keep their forefathers' acres out of the bank's cold fingers. We fear for the future of America should the well-known family farm—this cherished icon—vanish from the landscape; without it the country would be a different place, perhaps a worse one.

The condescension and denigration embedded in nineteenth-century images of the bumpkin have also survived, although the geographic focus has shifted west and south of Yankeeland. On television country people are seen as amiable fools (*The Beverly Hillbillies*); movies caricature backwoodsmen as a grotesque, subhuman species: inbred, moronic, vicious, and perverse (*Deliverance*). The ambiguous political status of today's farmer is partially reflected in such simplistic or degrading stereotypes.

In the mid-1980s several well-received feature films focused on American farm life, past and present. Of these, *Witness* (1985) forcefully and poetically expresses modern urban longing for the simplicities of a virtuous life close to the soil. In this picture the farmers of the peaceful Amish community live on their land and labors. They have no modern appliances at all. The whole community gathers to help a neighbor raise his barn; while the men hammer and saw, the women prepare a huge, festive dinner. Although Amish life is more or less like this, it represents a tiny minority of American rural communities; nevertheless, it is the one (aside from its sectarianism) most evocative of our ideal nineteenth-century American farm. The film makes a point of showing the nearly disastrous confrontation between these archaic, noble yeomen and the modern city world of technology, drugs, and violent crime. There is no common ground; harmony returns to the community only with the departure of the tough, urban detective who, as fugitive, has taken shelter in an Amish household, bringing after him all the forces of city corruption that the gentle country people most fear. Such opposing concepts of country and city are most directly the legacy of the nineteenth century, when art and literature gave form and definition to the persisting dichotomy of urban hell, rural heaven; urban knowledge, rural innocence.

A corollary to twentieth-century anxieties about dying agricultural traditions is the nostalgia business, descended from the more sentimental categories of nineteenth-century rural life imagery. Such artists as Norman Rockwell and Grandma Moses are perennially in favor because their paintings evoke the ideal farm and village of the old days. Currier & Ives homestead scenes appear on countless collectors' plates and calendars, and the original prints are hotly collected. Only the scale and refinement of nostalgia merchandising is new today. In a flyer promoting the magazine *Early American Life,* publisher Robert G. Miner calls it "a new kind of magazine—about *old* things like New England saltboxes and Pennsylvania stone farmhouses, hand-pegged beams and hand-split cedar shakes." It promises to take the subscriber back

to "a time of house warmings and barn-raisings, festive bowls and groaning boards, quilting bees and bundling, rugged individualism, old-fashioned neighborliness and honest furnishings made by people not machines." For those with the money to purchase their nostalgia ready-made, there are emporia such as Jenifer House in the Berkshires, where an old farm has been restored to provide an appropriate atmosphere for selling synthetic country artifacts. A mail-order catalogue enumerates the delights of the interior: "In the huge main barn, with its massive stone fireplace, the old horse stalls now display unusual and exciting imports. . . . In the hayloft—looking perfectly at home—are colorful hooked and braided rugs. . . . and especially for the ladies our exclusive designs [are] . . . housed in our Gambrel Roofed Colonial Shop for Fashion and Fine Furniture."

More egregious is the country commercialism of the advertising business. Images of wholesome farm and village life continue to help manufacturers sell their wares, especially food products. A television advertisement for bottled salad dressing depicts a county fair and uses the nineteenth-century iconography of capacious barns, abundant harvests, and sturdy farm people to suggest how good and natural the product is. An oatmeal commercial shows a group of ancient geezers in overalls, grouped around the potbellied stove in some village general store; except for the prominent display of brand names, this could be Eastman Johnson's *Nantucket School of Philosophy.* In every case, what is being advertised has been produced by agribusiness and processed in factories, yet the creators of such scenes, so flagrantly hollow, are confident that the powerful sentimental and ideological associations of rural imagery will ensure our complicity in the commercial fiction of wholesomeness and naturalness.

We seek country charm while the real country is increasingly charmless. We deplore the sorry state of farm life as the news presents it, with crazed farmers slaughtering bankers about to seize their land, and auctions of foreclosed farms attended by ranks of depressed country people who look like ordinary Americans. At the same time, we manage to nurse a soft spot for the virtue and simplicity of country life in some American never-never land, and we cherish those artifacts that symbolize the good rural existence: the rugged, primitive furniture and laboriously handmade quilts, the butter churn, the sleigh, the porch rocker, the ancestral farmhouse, the red barn.

These easily acceptable symbols serve purposes in a general way similar to those they served in the nineteenth century. They mask truths and proffer illusions. They pretend (by ignoring them) to resolve tensions that remain unresolved. They continue to reveal how images may be put to work for a range of ideological, sentimental, or commercial purposes. They keep alive a vision of an America that almost never was, is not, and never will be.

NOTES AND INDEX

Notes

INTRODUCTION

1. Classical and European pastoral ideas have been the subject of much study. See, e.g., two articles by Paul H. Johnstone: "In Praise of Husbandry," *Agricultural History* 11 (April 1937): 80–95; and "Turnips and Romanticism," *Agricultural History* 12 (July 1938): 224–55, which deal with agrarian and pastoral ideas in eighteenth-century England and still offer a concise yet thorough survey. See also Renato Poggioli, *The Oaten Flute: Essays on Pastoral Poetry and the Pastoral Ideal* (Cambridge, Mass.: Harvard University Press, 1975), on the broader European tradition, and for a useful overview of the poetry, John Heath-Stubbs, *The Pastoral* (London: Oxford University Press, 1969). A revisionist investigation is Raymond Williams, *The Country and the City* (New York: Oxford University Press, 1975). This provocative and stimulating Marxist critique of pastoral literature and ideology also manages to offer an intensely detailed history and reading of texts from classical antiquity to modern times.

2. J. Hector St. Jean de Crèvecoeur, *Letters from an American Farmer and Sketches of Eighteenth-Century America,* ed. Albert E. Stone (1782; rpt. New York: Viking Penguin, 1981), 67, 80. On Crèvecoeur, see Gay Wilson Allen and Roger Asselineau, *St. Jean de Crèvecoeur: The Life of an American Farmer* (New York: Viking Penguin, 1987).

3. Thomas Jefferson, *Notes on the State of Virginia,* 2d American ed. (Philadelphia: Matthew Carey, 1794), 240–41.

4. Scholars have begun to examine the aesthetics and significance of the "settled landscape," theme of Roger B. Stein, *Susquehanna: Images of the Settled Landscape,* exhibition catalogue (Binghamton, N.Y.: Roberson Center for the Arts and Sciences, 1981). Stein pointed out (129 n.1) that the prevailing view of American landscape painting has focused on "the attachment to wilderness and the uniqueness of that vision." Examples are James Thomas Flexner, *That Wilder Image: The Painting of America's Native School from Thomas Cole to Winslow Homer* (Boston: Little, Brown, 1962); and Barbara Novak, *Nature and Culture: American Landscape and Painting, 1825–1875* (New York: Oxford University Press, 1980). *Susquehanna* is intended to be a revisionist work challenging the older canons. Another study with a similar thesis and regional focus is, *Arcadian Vales: Views of the Connecticut River Valley,* exhibition catalogue (Springfield, Mass.: George Walter Vincent Smith Art Museum, 1981).

5. "Middle landscape" is the term used by Leo Marx to define the "moral position perfectly represented by the image of a rural order, neither wild nor urban, as the setting of man's best hope"; see *The Machine in the Garden: Technology and the Pastoral Ideal in America* (1964; rpt. New York: Oxford University Press, 1967), 101. The issue of rural equilibrium is central to John R. Stilgoe,

Common Landscape of America, 1580 to 1845 (New Haven, Conn.: Yale University Press, 1982). Stilgoe describes "equilibrium" as a state of hard-won agricultural balance: "land cleared of wilderness and defended against the evils of weeds and blights and the return of wilderness," supporting a fertile, well-kept, traditional farm (202–6). Edward Halsey Foster, *The Civilized Wilderness: Backgrounds to American Romantic Literature, 1817–60* (New York: Free Press, 1975), viewing the same issue from a different angle, surveys a wide range of cultural ideas surrounding the middle-class vision of ideal rural life—combining urban refinement with bucolic tranquillity—promulgated by authors, tastemakers, and architects during the period. Also see Roderick Nash, *Wilderness and the American Mind* (New Haven, Conn.: Yale University Press, 1975), for a discussion of ambivalence in American attitudes toward primeval nature, seen for many decades as a "moral and physical wasteland fit only for conquest and fructification in the name of progress, civilization, and Christianity" (xv) and only gradually, in the nineteenth century, assuming value as a precious, sanctified resource. As Nash points out, even such devotees of wilderness as James Fenimore Cooper and Thomas Cole experienced clouds of doubt and felt at times the "antipodal attraction to civilization" (74–83)

6. Patricia Hills, "Images of Rural America in the Works of Eastman Johnson, Winslow Homer, and Their Contemporaries: A Survey and Critique," in Hollister Sturges, ed., *The Rural Vision: France and America in the Late Nineteenth Century* (Omaha, Neb.: Joslyn Art Museum, 1987), 78. This essay is a development and revision of certain ideas originally proposed in Hills, *The Painters' America: Rural and Urban Life, 1810–1910*, exhibition catalogue (New York: Praeger in association with Whitney Museum of American Art, 1974). This groundbreaking work conclusively argues that "scenes of everyday life in America were synthetic constructions, reflecting the cultural ideals and social myths of the picture producers and picture consumers . . . rather than the actual social circumstances of the majority of the people" (1). Once Hills's catalogue appeared, it became impossible to think of genre painting any longer as a simple record of daily life. I am much indebted to her innovative scholarship, which mapped certain major directions and suggestions for my own work. For an example of the older, more naive perception of nineteenth-century rural life in art, see Frank Weitenkampf, "Country Life in American Prints," *Print Connoisseur* 11 (1931): 296–315, and 12 (1932): 51–57.

7. "Irving Park, Tarrytown," *Harper's Weekly Magazine* 4 (January 28, 1860), 52. Information on circulation, editorial stance, and other aspects of the magazine's publishing history are given in Frank Luther Mott, *A History of American Magazines* (Cambridge, Mass.: Belknap Press of Harvard University Press, 1957), 2:472–482. Mott's encyclopedic study is the standard authority.

8. Bernard F. Reilly, Jr., introduction to *Currier & Ives: A Catalogue Raisonné* (Detroit, Mich.: Gale Research Company, 1984), 1:xxi, xxx.

9. See Marx, *The Machine in the Garden*; Leo Marx, "The Railroad-in-the-Landscape: An Iconographical Reading of a Theme in American Art," *Prospects* 10 (1985): 77–117; *The Railroad in the American Landscape, 1850–1950*, exhibition catalogue (Wellesley, Mass.: Wellesley College Museum, 1981).

CHAPTER 1
THE ICONOGRAPHY OF THE
AGRARIAN WORLD, c. 1825–1875

1. Palmer came to the United States from England around 1844 and worked as an artist for Currier & Ives after unsuccessfully attempting to establish her own lithography business. See Charlotte Streifer Rubinstein, "The Early Career of Frances Flora Bond Palmer (1812–1876)," *American Art Journal* 17 (Autumn 1985): 71–88.

2. Richard Hofstadter, *The Age of Reform* (New York: Knopf, 1955), 28. That the "agrarian myth" was in fact a "mass creed" has not gone undisputed; see Chapter 4, note 1 below.

3. Extract from a speech by Edward Everett, cited in *Gleason's Pictorial Magazine and Drawing-Room Companion* (hereafter *Gleason's Pictorial*) 4 (January 29, 1853): 75.

4. Leo Marx, "The Garden," chap. 3 in *The Machine in the Garden: Technology and the Pastoral Ideal in America* (1964; rpt. New York: Oxford University Press, 1967), 73–144, offers a detailed examination of the pastoral design in early writings about the American landscape. Examples of this conventionalized rhetoric, full of gentle zephyrs and flowery groves, may be found in Gilbert Imlay, *A Topographical Description of the Western Territory of North America* (London: J. Debrett, 1797), 28; and Philip Freneau, "The Rising Glory of America," in *The Poems of Philip Freneau*, ed. Frederick Lewis Pattee (Princeton, N.J.: Princeton University Library, 1902–7), 1:67–68.

5. Timothy Dwight, *Greenfield Hill: A Poem in Seven Parts* (New York: Childs & Swaine, 1794), 377, 380, 381. Perry D. Westbrook, *The New England Town in Fact and Fiction* (East Brunswick, N.J.: Associated University Presses, 1982), 40, notes that both in *Greenfield Hill* and in his prose writings Dwight followed a course of "systematic idealization, amounting to mythologizing, of the New England town." Also see Ima Honaker Herron, *The Small Town in American Drama* (Dallas, Tex.: Southern Methodist University Press, 1969), on similar tendencies in nineteenth-century theater to present the American village under a glaze of idealized rusticity.

6. William Cullen Bryant, "The Tempest," in *Poetical Works* (New York: Appleton, 1883), 1:108.

7. Nathaniel Parker Willis, *Letters from under a Bridge* (1840), in *Rural Letters and Other Records of Thoughts at Leisure* (1849; rpt. Auburn, N.Y.: Alden & Beardsley, 1856), 206; Willis, *Hurry-Graphs; or, Sketches of Scenery, Celebrities, and Society, Taken From Life,* 2d ed. (Auburn, N.Y.: Alden & Beardsley, 1856), 74. Willis first wrote about the Susquehanna and Owego landscapes in a series of letters describing his life at Glenmary, his rural retreat during the 1830s; they were published in the *New-York Mirror, Graham's Magazine,* and *Godey's Ladies' Book* beginning in 1838 and first collected in *A l'abri; or, The Tent Pitch'd* (New York: Colman, 1839) and *Letters from under a Bridge* (London: Virtue, 1840). With occasional revisions and supplements, Willis's best-selling letters were reissued in various collections and at least seven editions or reprintings up to 1856.

8. Gilbert Le Feure, "My Rival," *Gleason's Pictorial* 6 (May 20, 1854): 311; Mary A. Lowell, "Kitty and I," *Ballou's Pictorial* 12 (June 27, 1857): 406–7 (the Boston-based *Gleason's Pictorial* became *Ballou's Pictorial Drawing Room Companion* in 1855 when Maturin M. Ballou purchased the magazine from its founder, Frederick Gleason).

9. Henry William Herbert, "Two Scenes in the Life of a Young American," *Gleason's Pictorial* 6 (March 18, 1854): 166.

10. Richard A. Bartlett, *The New Country: A Social History of the American Frontier, 1776–1890* (New York: Oxford University Press, 1974), 123. Henry Nash Smith's landmark study *Virgin Land: The American West as Symbol and Myth* (1950; rpt. Cambridge, Mass.: Harvard University Press, 1981) investigated in great depth the idea of the West as primitive frontier and agrarian utopia, the "garden of the world." Although I focus largely upon eastern versions of the agrarian pastoral, I have found Smith's work a stimulating source of suggestions and ideas. The "garden of the world" is Whitman's epithet: *Leaves of Grass,* ed. Harold W. Blodgett and Sculley Bradley (1855; rev. ed. 1860; rpt. New York: Norton, 1968), 90.

11. Henry Theodore Tuckerman, *Book of the Artists: American Artist Life* (New York: Putnam, 1867), 193. Aspects of parallels and relations between nineteenth-century American art (emphasizing the Hudson River School) and literature are explored in James T. Callow, *Kindred Spirits: Knickerbocker Writers and American Artists, 1807–55* (Chapel Hill: University of North Carolina Press, 1967). Also see *William Cullen Bryant and the Hudson River School of Landscape Painting,* exhibition catalogue (Roslyn, N.Y.: Nassau County Museum of Fine Art, 1981).

12. The English-born Cole had come to America at the age of seventeen. Though he was trained as an engraver of wood blocks for printing calico, he soon turned to landscape painting, gradually picking up technical skill. He took his first sketching trip up the Hudson River in 1825; the dramatic wilderness paintings based on that trip won him immediate fame among New York artists and patrons, and he rose to become a key figure in the establishment of an American landscape school. Although he produced many a regional scene to satisfy his patrons, he reserved his most passionate efforts for large-scale imaginary landscapes embodying lofty, philosophical themes. See Louis L. Noble, *The Course of Empire, Voyage of Life, and Other Pictures of Thomas Cole, N. A . . .* (New York: Cornish, Lamport, 1853); Howard S. Merritt, *Thomas Cole,* exhibition catalogue (Rochester, N.Y.: Memorial Art Gallery of the University of Rochester, 1969); Matthew Baigell, *Thomas Cole* (New York: Watson-Guptil, 1981).

13. A valuable study and critique of the Hudson River School is *American Paradise: The World of the Hudson River School,* exhibition catalogue (New York: Metropolitan Museum of Art, 1987).

14. The most comprehensive studies of Durand are David B. Lawall, *Asher Brown Durand: His Art and Art Theory in Relation to His Times* (New York: Garland, 1977), and Lawall, *Asher B. Durand: A Documentary Catalogue of the Narrative and Landscape Paintings* (New York: Garland, 1978).

15. Charles Lanman, "A Pair of Landscapes. By Durand," *Literary World* 1 (February 6, 1847): 16. Durand, in a letter to the editor, dated August 20, *Crayon* 2 (August 29, 1855): 133, declared himself "unqualified to penetrate the 'untrodden ways' " of

the sublime. For him, the "beautiful aspect" of scenery (i.e., the pastoral) had the greater appeal. Among Durand's bucolic, Claudian compositions are the very early *Landscape with Children or View Near Rutland, Vermont* (1837; private collection); *Sunday Morning* (1839; New-York Historical Society); *Farmyard on the Hudson* (1843; Mr. and Mrs. George J. Arden); *The Solitary Oak* (1844; New-York Historical Society); and *Landscape Composition, Forenoon* (1847; New Orleans Museum).

16. Sources on Cropsey include Peter Bermingham, *Jasper F. Cropsey, 1823–1900: A Retrospective View of America's Painter of Autumn*, exhibition catalogue (Silver Spring: University of Maryland Art Gallery, 1968); William S. Talbot, *Jasper F. Cropsey, 1823–1900*, exhibition catalogue (Washington, D.C.: Smithsonian Institution Press for the National Collection of Fine Arts, 1970); and Talbot, *Jasper F. Cropsey, 1823–1900* (New York: Garland, 1977); and *Jasper F. Cropsey (1823–1900), Artist and Architect: Paintings, Drawings, and Photographs from the Collections of the Newington-Cropsey Foundation and the New-York Historical Society*, exhibition catalogue (New York: New-York Historical Society, 1987).

17. Similar combinations of "bold scenery and habitable plain" appeared repeatedly in views by Cropsey, Alvan Fisher, John Frederick Kensett, Aaron Shattuck, James McDougal Hart, Charles H. Moore, Alfred Bricher, Worthington Whittredge, George Inness, and a host of other painters over the early to middle decades of the century.

18. Roger B. Stein, *Susquehanna: Images of the Settled Landscape*, exhibition catalogue (Binghamton, N.Y.: Roberson Center for the Arts and Sciences, 1981), 59–64, studies Cropsey's interpretations of that region.

19. See Martha Young Hudson, *George Henry Durrie. American Winter Landscapist Renowned through Currier & Ives*, exhibition catalogue (Santa Barbara, Calif.: Santa Barbara Museum of Art, 1977).

20. Rubinstein, "Frances Palmer," 87. See Chapters 5–8 for a detailed investigation of Mount's rural imagery.

21. For regional barn forms, see Thomas C. Hubka, *Big House, Little House, Back House, Barn: The Connected Farm Buildings of New England* (Hanover, N.H.: University Press of New England, 1984); Allen G. Noble, *Barns and Farm Structures*, vol. 2 of *Wood, Brick, and Stone: The North American Settlement Landscape* (Amherst: University of Massachusetts Press, 1984); John R. Stilgoe, *Common Landscape of America, 1580 to 1845* (New Haven, Conn.: Yale University Press, 1982); Joseph W. Glass, *The Pennsylvania*

Culture Region: A View from the Barn (Ann Arbor: University of Michigan Research Press, 1975); Henry Glassie, "The Variation of Concepts within Tradition: Barn Building in Otsego County, New York," *Geoscience and Man*, 5 (June 10, 1974): 177–235.

22. Hubka, *Big House, Little House*, 80. See also Howard S. Russell, *A Long, Deep Furrow: Three Centuries of Farming in New England* (Hanover, N.H.: University Press of New England, 1976), chap. 28, "Horses, Cheese, and Sheep," 280–291; and chap. 34, "Sheep and Other Livestock," 351–65.

23. H. Shaw, "Influence of Different Pursuits on Character," *Prairie Farmer* 8 (April 1848): 124. In any region, of course, there was bound to be a range from careful order to slovenly chaos, depending on the abilities and energies of the individual farmer. Timothy Pickering, in the *New England Farmer*, 4 (October 14, 1825): 89, commented that lack of care in housing livestock was generally typical of New England farms.

24. Lowell, "Kitty and I"; Samuel Goodrich, *Recollections of a Lifetime* (New York: Miller, Orton, & Mulligan, 1856), 78–81.

CHAPTER 2
THE POETRY OF LABOR

1. Review of the agricultural periodical *Farmer's Register* in "The Book Table," *New-York Mirror* 11 (March 8, 1834): 282. Roxana Barry offered a short survey of American harvest scenes in *Land of Plenty: Nineteenth Century American Picnic and Harvest Scenes*, exhibition catalogue (Katonah, N.Y.: The Katonah Gallery, 1982).

2. John Burroughs, "Phases of Farm Life" (1886), in *The Works of John Burroughs* (Boston: Houghton Mifflin, 1904), 252.

3. Henry Ward Beecher, "Haying," in *Eyes and Ears* (Boston: Ticknor & Fields, 1862), 63.

4. On Thompson, see Lee M. Edwards, "The Life and Career of Jerome Thompson," *American Art Journal* 14 (Autumn 1982): 5–30.

5. "Fine Arts: National Academy of Design," *Home Journal*, June 4, 1859, p. 2.

6. Among many contemporary examples, academic and popular, that share the iconography and mood of Thompson's painting are John B. Hudson, *Haying at Lapham's Farm, Auburn, Maine* (1859; Karolik Collection, Museum of Fine Arts, Boston); John Whetten

Ehninger, *Bringing in the Hay* (see Illus. 102); George T. Devereux, *July,* wood engraving in *Gleason's Pictorial* 5 (July 2, 1833): 1.

7. Fisher, a Massachusetts native, was one of the earliest nineeteenth-century painters to make a successful career of landscapes and genre subjects. See Fred Barry Adelson, "Alvan Fisher (1792–1863): Pioneer in American Landscape Painting" (Ph.D. diss., Columbia University, 1982).

8. Joel Barlow, "The Hasty-Pudding" (1793), in *The Works of Joel Barlow* (Gainesville, Fla.: Scholars' Facsimiles and Reprints, 1970), 2:95–96.

9. Homer is discussed in greater detail in Chapters 10 and 14. The most comprehensive catalogue of his magazine illustrations is Philip C. Beam, *Winslow Homer's Magazine Engravings* (New York: Harper & Row, 1979).

10. The major sources on Johnson are John I. H. Baur, *Eastman Johnson, 1824–1906: An American Genre Painter* (Brooklyn. N.Y.: Institute of Arts and Sciences, 1940); Patricia Hills, *Eastman Johnson,* exhibition catalogue (New York: Clarkson N. Potter in association with Whitney Museum of American Art, 1972), and Hills, "The Genre Painting of Eastman Johnson: The Sources and Development of His Style and Themes" (Ph.D. diss., New York University, 1973).

11. Lewis Leary, *John Greenleaf Whittier* (New York: Twayne, 1961), 148. Whether Whittier's verse was what his many listeners ought to have heard and where it stands aesthetically are issues peripheral to this discussion, which focuses on the nature and appeal of idealized and popularized versions of reality.

12. Cited in Leary, *Whittier,* 63.

13. John Greenleaf Whittier, "The Huskers," in *The Poetical Works of John Greenleaf Whittier* (Boston: Houghton Mifflin, 1892), 91.

14. John Woods, *Two Years' Residence in the Settlement on the English Prairie, in the Illinois Country, United States* (London: Hurst, Rees, Orme, & Brown, 1822), 213–14; Rowland E. Robinson, "Glimpses of New England Farm Life," *Scribner's Monthly Magazine* 16 (1878): 527. Jack Larkin, "The View from New England: Notes on Everyday Life in Rural America to 1850," *American Quarterly* 39 (1982): 254, suggests that future research should attempt to answer such questions as "How much work was actually done communally in the American countryside? . . . What was the real frequency of occurrence and social 'grammar' of husking frolics and quiltings, barn and house raisings?"

15. See Warder H. Cadbury, *Arthur Fitzwilliam Tait: Artist in the Adirondacks, An Account of His Career* (Newark: University of Delaware Press, 1986). Hills, *Eastman Johnson,* 49–68, discusses and illustrates examples of the maple sugar camp series.

16. "Making Maple Sugar," *Gleason's Pictorial* 2 (June 5, 1852): 368.

17. Charles Dudley Warner, *Being a Boy* (1877; rpt. Boston: Houghton Mifflin, 1897), 120–21.

18. New England crops and their transformation in response to competition and changing markets are thoroughly discussed in Howard S. Russell, *A Long, Deep Furrow: Three Centuries of Farming in New England* (Hanover, N.H.: University Press of New England, 1976).

19. Farmers did appear occasionally as consumers in genre paintings of peddlers showing their goods to country people; these include Asher B. Durand, *The Peddler Displaying His Wares* (1836; New-York Historical Society, New York), and Thomas Waterman Wood, *The Yankee Peddler* (1872; lost). The emphasis in such pictures, however, is on display and negotiation, rather than actual cash transaction. The shrewd Yankee peddler was a stereotype derived from regional folklore and characters featured in the popular Yankee plays of 1820–1860; see Chapter 7.

20. In a lecture given November 1981 at a Northwestern University symposium, Wayne Craven discussed the absence of agricultural machinery in Asher B. Durand's pastoral landscapes, suggesting that his businessmen patrons preferred nostalgic views recalling their own rural origins in a simpler day. The symposium was held in conjunction with the exhibition *Life in Nineteenth-Century American Art,* curated by David M. Sokol, at the Terra Museum of American Art in Evanston, Illinois.

21. Rodney Welch, "The Farmer's Changed Condition," *Forum,* 10 (February 1891), 691–92.

22. The self-destructing tensions within and without the pastoral ideal are central to the thesis of Leo Marx, *The Machine in the Garden: Technology and the Pastoral Ideal in America* (1964; rpt. New York: Oxford University Press, 1967), which explores the conflict (as expressed, for the most part, in eighteenth- and especially nineteenth-century American literature) between the traditional image of the pastoral state as fantasized emblem of ultimate earthly perfection and the impossibility of its reconciliation with the real, aggressive, expanding realm of technology and industry. More recent studies have taken on an ancient issue from fresh

perspectives; e.g., Annette Kolodny, *The Lay of the Land: Metaphor as Experience and History in American Life and Letters* (1975; rpt. Chapel Hill: University of North Carolina Press, 1984), uses the tools of linguistics and psychohistory to argue that in order to understand the shape and course of the pastoral impulse as it developed in America, one must examine the use of language itself. It is Kolodny's contention (7, 9) that the American pastoral was unique in hiding at its core the promise of fantasy as daily reality; that with the discovery of America the dead conventions of the European pastoral tradition suddenly became "the vocabulary of everyday reality," centering on metaphors of the land as female (mother, womb, virgin, and the like). The pattern of the pastoral in America, she writes, furnished a paradigm of its ultimate failure: "the dream about to be fulfilled, the momentary grasping of its reality, and its inevitable disruption and destruction," which happened in both a literal and a metaphorical sense.

CHAPTER 3
"UNLOVABLE THINGS":
FARMSCAPES REAL

1. On the American village as symbol of ideal society, see Perry D. Westbrook, *The New England Town in Fact and Fiction* (East Brunswick, N.J.: Associated University Presses, 1982).

2. For major ideas and directions in the history of American agriculture, I am especially indebted to Paul Gates, *The Farmer's Age: Agriculture, 1815–1860*, vol. 3 in Ray A. Billington, ed., *Economic History of the United States* (New York: Holt, Rinehart & Winston, 1960); John T. Schlebecker, *Whereby We Thrive: A History of American Farming, 1607–1972* (Ames: Iowa State University Press, 1975); Howard S. Russell, *A Long, Deep Furrow: Three Centuries of Farming in New England* (Hanover, N.H.: University Press of New England, 1976); Walter Ebeling, *The Fruited Plain: The Story of American Agriculture* (Berkeley: University of California Press, 1979); Willard W. Cochrane, *The Development of American Agriculture: A Historical Analysis* (Minneapolis: University of Minnesota Press, 1980); John R. Stilgoe, *Common Landscape of America, 1580 to 1845* (New Haven, Conn.: Yale University Press, 1982); William N. Parker, "The American Farmer," in Jerome Blum, ed., *Our Forgotten Past: Seven Centuries of Life on the Land* (London:

Thames & Hudson, 1982), 181–96; and Thomas C. Hubka, *Big House, Little House, Back House, Barn: The Connected Farm Buildings of New England* (Hanover, N.H.: University Press of New England, 1984)

3. Alexis de Tocqueville, *Democracy in America*, Part 2: *The Social Influence of Democracy*, trans. Henry Reeve (1840; 5th ed. Boston: John Allyn, 1873), 191–92.

4. James F. W. Johnston, *Notes on North America: Agricultural, Economical, and Social* (Edinburgh: William Blackwood, 1851), 1:162; Henry David Thoreau, *Walden; or, Life in the Woods* (1852; rpt. New York: Harper & Row, 1965), 147.

5. John Johnston, cited in *Country Gentleman* 13 (February 10, 1859): 90.

6. Orasmus Turner, *Pioneer History of the Holland Purchase of Western New York* (Buffalo, N.Y.: Jewett, Thomas, 1849). For a survey of publication and sales practices associated with county histories and atlases, see Gerald Carson, "Get the Prospect Seated . . . and Keep Talking," *American Heritage* 9 (August, 1958): 38–41, 77–80.

7. "Speculation and Production," *New England Farmer* 16 (July 12, 1837): 5.

8. Alfred Bunn, *Old England and New England, in a Series of Views Taken on the Spot* (London: R. Bentley, 1853), 243.

9. *Homestead* 2 (August, 1857): 745–46, and 3 (October 1857): 80; *Cultivator*, n.s., 4 (May 1847): 155, all summarized in Gates, *The Farmer's Age*, 254, 412. Russell, *Long, Deep Furrow*, 412–13, points out that research still needs to be done on the interplay of economics with farming, observing that the effects of the panics on farms were "so interwoven with other influences of the time as often in retrospect to be difficult to measure."

10. The history of the Anti-Rent struggle is treated in Henry Christman, *Tin Horns and Calico: A Decisive Episode in the Emergence of Democracy* (New York: Henry Holt, 1945).

11. Useful sources for the history of agricultural mechanization include Paul C. Johnson, *Farm Inventions in the Making of America* (Des Moines, Iowa: Wallace-Homestead, 1976); Michael Partridge, *Early Agricultural Machinery, and Farm Tools through the Ages* (Greenwich, Conn.: New York Graphic Society, 1973); Stewart Holbrook, *Machines of Plenty* (New York: Macmillan, 1955); and Gates, *The Farmer's Age*.

12. The canonical work is Leo Marx, *The Machine in the Garden: Technology and the Pastoral Ideal in America* (1964; rpt. New

York: Oxford University Press, 1967), although his methods and assumptions—such as the concentration on "high" cultural products as the most accurate and most meaningful reflections of deep cultural preoccupations—have been attacked by later scholars; see Bruce Kuklick, "Myth and Symbol in American Studies," *American Quarterly* 24 (1972): 435–50. In art history, Barbara Novak, *Nature and Culture: American Landscape and Painting, 1825–1875* (New York: Oxford University Press, 1980), addresses a number of paradigmatic issues implied by the dichotomy of the title: the collisions of science and belief, tradition and progress, wilderness and civilization; chap. 8, "Man's Traces: Axe, Train, Figure" (157–65), deals specifically with those nineteenth-century emblems of progress which ultimately despoiled and transformed wilderness. That is also the theme of Nicolai Cikovsky, Jr., " 'The Ravages of the Axe': The Meaning of the Tree Stump in Nineteenth-Century American Art," *Art Bulletin* 61 (December 1979): 611–26.

13. Robert Thomas, "Fifty Years Ago," *Farmer's Almanac* (Boston, 1842); untitled report, *Prairie Farmer* 6 (August 1846): 262.

14. Henry Ward Beecher, "Mowing-Machines and Steam Ploughs," in *Eyes and Ears* (Boston: Ticknor & Fields, 1862), 70.

15. "Reaping at Syracuse," *Harper's Weekly Magazine* 1 (August 1, 1857): 484.

16. "Walks and Talks on the Farm," *American Agriculturist* 27 (February 1869): 50.

17. "Farming in the Great West," *Harper's Weekly Magazine* 15 (September 23, 1871): 899.

18. "Harvesting on a Bonanza Farm," *Harper's Weekly Magazine* 35 (August 29, 1891): 663. Rogers was a *Harper's Weekly* illustrator and writer whose work embraced both documentary and humorous subjects. It was only with the turn of the twentieth century that fiction, at least, discovered the epic note of vast spaces and agricultural capitalism when literary naturalist Frank Norris published *The Octopus* (1901) and *The Pit* (1903), the two completed works of his projected trilogy *The Epic of the Wheat*.

19. Coffin's diary is published in part in Robert H. George, "Life on a New Hampshire Farm, 1825–36," *Historical New Hampshire* 22 (Winter 1967): 3–16.

20. John Muir, *The Story of My Boyhood and Youth* (1913; rpt. Boston: Houghton Mifflin, 1923), 220–24.

21. Isaac Phillips Roberts, *Autobiography of a Farm Boy* (1916), cited in Ben Maddow, *A Sunday between Wars: The Course of American Life from 1865 to 1917* (New York: Norton, 1979), 152.

22. As noted by Frank Weitenkampf, "Country Life in American Prints," *Print Connoisseur* 11 (October 1931): 314, luminist landscape painter Fitz Hugh Lane produced two lithographs on farm troubles: *Mortgaging the Farm* and *Lifting the Mortgage,* "which two form a bit of temperance sermon." Edwin Austin Abbey, creator of the *Hard Times* illustration, was employed by *Harper's* in the 1870s but is best known for his later illustrations of themes from Elizabethan and Georgian English literature.

23. *Harper's Weekly Magazine,* 17 (June 21, 1873): 526.

24. Any attempt at generalization is bound to produce some distortion. New England farm life can best be described as diversified, embracing a range of circumstance from comfort or even luxury to hardscrabble poverty. The best assessment is probably Russell, *Long, Deep Furrow,* esp. chap. 38, "The Typical Farmer," 403–14.

25. George, "Life on a New Hampshire Farm," 10; editorial, *The Homestead,* 4 (February 3, 1859): 320.

26. Hubka, *Big House, Little House,* 193–95; Richard Wines, "The Nineteenth-Century Agricultural Transition in an Eastern Long Island Community," *Agricultural History* 55 (1981): 50–63.

27. Isaac Weld, *Travels through the States of North America* (London: John Stockdale, 1799), 23–24. For a thorough analysis, see Cikovsky, "The Ravages of the Axe." Hubka, *Big House, Little House,* 74, points out that while the Cobblestone Farm photograph was taken c. 1900, its rough appearance was "probably similar to most common farms in the early nineteenth century."

28. Donald Grant Mitchell, "An Old-Style Farm," *Hours at Home* 3 (June 1866): 101–5.

29. "Farming Life in New England," *Atlantic Monthly* 2 (August 1858): 334–41.

30. George Lyman Kittredge, *The Old Farmer and His Almanac,* 4th ed. (1904; rpt. Cambridge, Mass.: Harvard University Press, 1924), 172.

CHAPTER 4
BENEATH THE IDYLL

1. Richard H. Abbott, "The Agricultural Press Views the Yeoman," *Agricultural History* 42 (January 1968): 35–48, challenges the assumption that the "agrarian myth" was universally accepted during this period. In particular, he queries whether farmers themselves believed in their special status. By surveying a number

of agricultural magazines and their contradictory evidence, Abbott concluded that "not only did farmers fail to believe the agrarian myth; they were not even sure what the agrarian myth was" (48). See also Richard Hofstadter, "The Myth of the Happy Yeoman," *American Heritage* 7 (April 1956): 43–53.

2. American Art-Union sale catalogue (c. 1840s), cited by John William Ward, *Red, White, and Blue: Men, Books, and Ideas in American Culture* (New York: Oxford University Press, 1969), 278. The American Art-Union in New York (1844–52) supported the establishment of a native school by purchasing the works of living American artists and distributing them in the form of engravings to thousands of subscribers, who also had a chance to win an original painting through an annual Art-Union lottery.

3. Asher B. Durand, "Letters on Landscape Painting," no. 4, *Crayon* 1 (February 14, 1855): 98.

4. The relatively modern, strongly Marxist critique of the English pastoral tradition (both poetry and painting) as celebration and justification of the class hierarchy and of agrarian capitalism has been taken up and vividly argued in several works: see Raymond Williams, *The Country and the City* (New York: Oxford University Press, 1975); John Barrell, *The Dark Side of the Landscape: The Rural Poor in English Painting, 1730–1840* (Cambridge: Cambridge University Press, 1980); David H. Solkin, *Richard Wilson: The Landscape of Reaction*, exhibition catalogue (London: Tate Gallery, 1982); and Ann Bermingham, *Landscape and Ideology: The English Rustic Tradition, 1740–1860* (Berkeley: University of California Press, 1986). Two of the foremost producers of escapist or class-validating rural imagery were Francis Wheatley and George Morland; their work is discussed in Chapter 6.

5. James A. Henretta, *The Evolution of American Society, 1700–1815: An Interdisciplinary Analysis* (Lexington, Mass.: Heath, 1973), 211.

6. Studies on the morality of simplicity and sincerity in nineteenth-century America include David E. Shi, *The Simple Life: Plain Living and High Thinking in American Culture* (New York: Oxford University Press, 1985), and Karen Halttunen, *Confidence Men and Painted Women: A Study of Middle-Class Culture in America, 1830–1870* (New Haven, Conn.: Yale University Press, 1982). See also Neil Harris, *The Artist in American Society: The Formative Years, 1790–1860* (1966; rpt. New York: Simon & Schuster, 1970), esp. chap. 2, "The Perils of Vision: Art, Luxury, and Republicanism,"

28–53, and chap. 8, "Crusades for Beauty," 188–216, for a discussion of the role bestowed upon art in the nineteenth-century endeavor to elevate American culture from the slough of materialism.

7. "Fashion. By a Reformed Dandy of the Eighteenth Century," *New England Magazine* 4 (May 1833): 346; *New York Sun*, February 2, 1838; "The Progress of Luxury," *Gleason's Pictorial* 7 (September 2, 1854): 141.

8. G., "American Society," pt. 2, *Knickerbocker Magazine* 8 (August 1836): 210–11.

9. "Domestic Architecture," *New England Magazine* 3 (January 1832): 35.

10. Andrew Jackson Downing, *The Architecture of Country Houses* (1850), 2d ed. (New York: D. Appleton, 1852), 138.

11. Lewis F. Allen, *Rural Architecture* (New York: C. M. Saxton, 1852), 189.

12. Thomas Cole, letter to Luman Reed, September 18, 1833, in Louis Legrand Noble, *The Life and Works of Thomas Cole*, ed. Elliott S. Vessell (1853; rpt. under 1856 title, Cambridge, Mass.: Belknap Press of Harvard University Press, 1964), 129. As Vessell points out in his introduction (xxi), the popular press manifested a skewed perception of *The Course of Empire* as "signalizing the destruction of old-world tyrannies and the triumph of American democracy." But, he adds "many understood it, and everyone praised it." Alan Wallach advances an interesting interpretation in "Thomas Cole and the Aristocracy," *Arts Magazine* 56 (November 1981): 94–106; he argues that *Consummation* suggests the transition from democracy to mob rule in America, whereas *The Pastoral State* stands for the recent past of "the aristocracy": i.e., Cole's wealthy patron class, some of whom at least had ties with the old Federalist elites of the early republic.

13. "Judge Buel's Address, to the Agricultural Institute of New London and Windham Counties," *Western Farmer* 1 (March 1840): 188; "Agriculture and Rural Economy of Europe: Notes of a Traveler in England," no. 6, *Cultivator*, n.s. 4 (August 1847): 251–52.

14. M. Bradley, "Intelligence among Farmers," *Prairie Farmer* 8 (August 1848): 257.

15. John Greenleaf Whittier, *Justice and Expediency* (1833), in *The Works of Whittier* (Boston: Houghton Mifflin, 1892), 7:32–33.

16. Whittier, "The Panorama," in *The Panorama and Other Poems* (Boston: Ticknor & Fields, 1856), 10–11.

17. Republican critiques of the South are surveyed in Eric Foner, *Free Soil, Free Labor, Free Men: The Ideology of the Republican Party before the Civil War* (New York: Oxford University Press, 1970), 40–44.

18. Henry Ward Beecher, "The Nation's Duty to Slavery" (speech delivered October 30, 1859), in *Patriotic Addresses, 1850–85*, ed. John R. Howard (New York: Ford, Howard, & Hulbert, 1891), 219. A very useful source of information and ideas on images of the South is Howard R. Floan, *The South in Northern Eyes 1831 to 1861* (Austin: University of Texas Press, 1958).

19. The subject of northern self-superiority even in climate is discussed in Larzer Ziff, *Literary Democracy: The Declaration of Cultural Independence in America* (New York: Viking Press, 1981), 51–54. Ziff points out the contemporaneity of the New England "fireside poets" (Whittier, Henry Wadsworth Longfellow, Oliver Wendell Holmes, James Russell Lowell) with the popularity of George Durrie's snow scenes for Currier & Ives and a "widespread interest" in Arctic and Antarctic exploration in the 1850s as evidence that the complementary images of cold clime and warm hearth symbolized and reflected current belief in the moral ascendancy of the North over the South. After writing this chapter I heard an interesting paper, Angela Miller's "Region and Nation in the 1850s: Claiming the Part as the Whole," presented to the American Studies Association meeting in New York, November 1987. Focusing on Frederic E. Church's *New England Scenery* (1851; George Walter Vincent Smith Art Museum, Springfield, Massachusetts), Miller argued that the image of the New England landscape spoke a subtle language of propaganda for that region's right to cultural and political dominance over all of America. In certain points, her argument parallels mine.

20. Robert Thomas, "Farmer's Calender," in *Farmer's Almanac* (Boston, 1817).

21. Henry Christman, *Tin Horns and Calico: A Decisive Episode in the Emergence of Democracy* (New York: Henry Holt, 1945), 305, 70; *Congressional Globe*, 31st Cong., 2d sess., app., 136 (January 29, 1851), cited in Henry Nash Smith, *Virgin Land: The American West as Symbol and Myth* (1950; rpt. Cambridge, Mass.: Harvard University Press, 1981), 173; Walt Whitman, "American Workingmen, versus Slavery," *Brooklyn Daily Eagle*, September 1, 1847, reprinted in Emory Holloway, ed., *The Uncollected Poetry and Prose of Walt Whitman* (New York: Peter Smith, 1932), 171–74.

22. Connections between millennialism and the rural New England village are explored in Perry D. Westbrook, *The New England Town in Fact and Fiction* (East Brunswick, N.J.: Associated University Presses, 1982). Peter Bermingham discusses Cropsey's *Millennial Age* in *Jasper F. Cropsey, 1823–1900: A Retrospective View of America's Painter of Autumn*, exhibition catalogue (Silver Spring: University of Maryland Art Gallery, 1968), 14–15. James Moore, "The Storm and the Harvest: The Image of Nature in Mid-Nineteenth Century American Landscape Painting" (Ph.D. diss., Indiana University, 1974), 232, proposes a millennial interpretation of midcentury pastoral landscapes, arguing that in paintings such as Cropsey's *American Harvesting* the millennial impulse, in a typologically and historically real sense, found covert expression in a secularized image of progress in which agriculture was a central focus.

23. William N. Parker, "The American Farmer," in Jerome Blum, ed., *Our Forgotten Past: Seven Centuries of Life on the Land* (London: Thames & Hudson, 1982), 185, gives a succinct and useful summary of the economic motives underlying the war between North and South.

24. Christopher Kent Wilson, "Winslow Homer's *The Veteran in a New Field*: A Study of the Harvest Metaphor and Popular Culture," *American Art Journal* 17 (Autumn 1985): 2–27, makes a detailed survey of the use of battle-harvest imagery in the illustrated journals and popular literature of the Civil War period, and its meanings in the context of contemporary history and culture.

25. Horace Bushnell, "Our Obligations to the Dead," commemorative oration at Yale University, July 1865, in Bushnell, *Building Eras in Religion* (New York: Scribner, 1881), 328; Henry Ward Beecher, *Norwood; or, Village Life in New England* (New York: Ford, Howard, & Hulbert, 1867), 494.

26. N. G. Shepherd, "Harvest on Historic Fields," *Harper's Weekly Magazine* 11 (July 20, 1867): 455. Sheppard, a native of Richmond, Virginia, did a series of watercolors showing army life during the Civil War and illustrations for several popular magazines in the 1860s and after. Other *Harper's Weekly* harvest and farm scenes during the postwar era delivered similar messages, sometimes quite explicitly. In vol. 13 (August 21, 1869), e.g., Edwin Forbes's *Harvesting on the Battlefield of Bull Run* was intended to make two points: to demonstrate the rapid healing of the wounds of war, and to illustrate the improvements of agriculture "upon the arena where

then a feudal system of labor arranged its boastful champions" (532). On Inness, see Nicolai Cikovsky, Jr., *George Inness* (New York: Praeger, 1971), and Nicolai Cikovsky, Jr., and Michael Quick, *George Inness*, exhibition catalogue (Los Angeles: Los Angeles County Museum of Art, 1985).

CHAPTER 5
THE NOBLE YEOMAN

1. James Silk Buckingham, *America: Historical, Statistic, and Descriptive* (New York: Harper, 1841), 2:121–22; Catherine Maria Sedgwick, *Means and Ends; or, Self-Training* (1839), 4th ed. (Boston: Marsh, Capen, Lyon, & Webb, 1840), 137; G., "American Society," pt. 2, *Knickerbocker Magazine* 8 (August 1836): 210.

2. Donald Grant Mitchell, *Dream-Life: A Fable of the Seasons* (1851; rpt. New York: Scribner, 1893), 66–72. *Dream-Life* went through at least twenty-two editions or reprintings, a good index of its strong and enduring popularity. It also appeared in British and German editions.

3. William Sidney Mount, Diary/Journal (1848–57), November 14, 1852, MS, Museums at Stony Brook, Long Island, cited in Alfred Frankenstein, *William Sidney Mount* (New York: Abrams, 1975), 249. After writing this section I read Elizabeth Johns, "The Farmer in the Work of William Sidney Mount," *Journal of Interdisciplinary History* 17 (Summer 1986): 258–281, which proposes interpretations parallel in some respects to those I have advanced.

4. "The Mower in Ohio," *Harper's Weekly Magazine* 8 (Aug. 6, 1864): 497. Related in spirit to this illustration and its iconographic predecessors is Winslow Homer's painting *Veteran in a New Field* (1865; Metropolitan Museum of Art), which also appeared two years later as a wood-engraved illustration in *Frank Leslie's Illustrated Newspaper*. The design comprises the basic agrarian-ideal components of yeoman, scythe, and harvest field, but to the conventional meanings are fused historically precise metaphorical associations with the war (harvest of death; grim reaper) and its aftermath (peace and prosperity). This interpretation is the subject of detailed examination in Christopher Kent Wilson, "Winslow Homer's *The Veteran in a New Field*: A Study of the Harvest Metaphor and Popular Culture," *American Art Journal* 17 (Autumn 1985), 2–27.

5. Buckingham, *America* 2:91–92; "Tour in England," *American Agriculturist* 1 (May 1842): 41.

6. Francis and Theresa Pulszky, *White, Red, Black: Sketches of Society in the United States during the Visit of Their Guest* (New York: Redfield, 1853), 1:65.

7. See Richard R. and Caroline B. Brettell, *Painters and Peasants in the Nineteenth Century* (New York: Rizzoli, 1983). According to travelers, in the North only German farmers in Pennsylvania continued the Old World tradition of field work for women. In the South, by contrast, slave women routinely labored in the fields.

8. Donald Grant Mitchell, "English and American Wayside," *Hours at Home* 3 (July 1866): 204.

9. Noah Webster, cited in Walter Blair and Hamlin Hill, *America's Humor: From Poor Richard to Doonesbury* (New York: Oxford University Press, 1978), 31; Alexander Mackay, *The Western World; or, Travels in the United States in 1846–47*, 4th ed. (London: Richard Bentley, 1850), 3:11. A surprising number of travelers remarked on Americans' reading habits, perhaps because they presented a particularly striking difference from those of ordinary Europeans. Frances Trollope, *Domestic Manners of the Americans*, ed. Herbert van Thal (1832; rpt. London: Folio Society, 1974), 83, noted that Americans were all too busy to read anything except the newspaper. The Italian Jesuit Giovanni Grassi agreed with Mackay: there would be newspapers even in homes destitute of the Bible, and because of newspaper reading, politics was the most frequent subject of conversation: *Notizie varie sullo stato presente della republica degli Stati Uniti dell' America . . .* (Milan, 1819), cited in Oscar Handlin, ed., *This Was America* (Cambridge, Mass.: Harvard University Press, 1949), 144.

10. Relevant paintings from the Mexican War period include James Goodwyn Clonney, *Mexican News* (1847; Munson-Williams-Proctor Institute, Utica, New York); Richard Caton Woodville, *War News from Mexico* (1848; National Academy of Design, New York), and *Politics in an Oyster House* (1848; Walters Arts Gallery, Baltimore, Maryland). Tait's own *Arguing the Point—Settling the Presidency* (1854; R. W. Norton Art Gallery, Shreveport, Louisiana) is another treatment of the newspaper theme, this time in a frontier setting. Patricia Hills, "Images of Rural America in the Works of Eastman Johnson, Winslow Homer, and Their Contemporaries: A Survey and Critique," in Hollister Sturges, ed., *The Rural Vision: France and America in the Late Nineteenth Century* (Omaha, Neb.: Joslyn Art Museum, 1987), 65–67, discusses the newspaper motif in American genre painting as pictorial visualization of "the individualism nurtured by participatory democracy."

11. For the history of the Grange I am indebted especially to Fred A. Shannon, *The Farmer's Last Frontier: Agriculture, 1860–1897*, vol. 5 in *The Economic History of the United States* (New York: Rinehart, 1945); and the useful popular history by Robert West Howard, *The Vanishing Land*, 2d ed. (New York: Ballantine Books, 1986).

12. The only recent study of Wood is *Thomas Waterman Wood, PNA (1823–1903)*, exhibition catalogue (Montpelier, Vt.: Wood Art Gallery, 1972). Other paintings by Wood on the political life of the ordinary American include *American Citizens (To the Polls)* (1867), and *The Day before the Election* (1875), both in the collection of the Wood Art Gallery.

13. See Glyndon G. Van Deusen, *Horace Greeley, Nineteenth-Century Crusader*, 2d ed. (New York: Hill & Wang, 1964); and Erik S. Lunde, *Horace Greeley* (New York: Twayne, 1981).

14. For the discussion of the minuteman and George Washington agrarian symbolism, I have relied on the valuable scholarship of Mark Edward Thistlethwaite, *The Image of George Washington: Studies in Mid-Nineteenth-Century American History Painting* (New York: Garland, 1979), 116–51.

15. Mason Locke Weems, *The Life of Washington* (c. 1800), ed. Marcus Cunliffe (rpt. of 9th ed. [1809], Cambridge, Mass.: Harvard University Press, 1962), 128.

16. Some similar suggestions about the Ritner lithograph are made in Roger Butterfield, "The Folklore of Politics," *Pennsylvania Magazine of History and Biography* 79 (April 1950): 165–70, a useful introduction to the the subject of the politician as country boy. For a related topic, see James D. Hart, "They Were All Born in Log Cabins," *American Heritage* 7 (Aug. 1956): 32–33, 102–5. On the 1840 election itself, see Robert Gray Gunderson, *The Log-Cabin Campaign* (Lexington: University Press of Kentucky, 1957).

17. Van Deusen, *Greeley*, 412.

CHAPTER 6
HICKS

1. Both the moralizing and idealizing aspects of Dutch peasant painting are considered in Peter C. Sutton, *Masters of Seventeenth-Century Dutch Painting*, exhibition catalogue (Philadelphia: University of Pennsylvania Press for Philadelphia Museum of Art, 1984), esp. xxxiv-xxxvi, lxi.

2. The most interesting recent consideration of Morland, which includes the observation that engravers edited his imagery, is John Barrell, *The Dark Side of the Landscape: The Rural Poor in English Painting, 1730–1840* (Cambridge: Cambridge University Press, 1980), 89–130. On Wheatley, see Mary Webster, *Francis Wheatley* (London: Routledge & Kegan Paul, 1970).

3. Interpretations of *Farmers Nooning* have tended to focus on the depiction of the black man; there is some controversy about Mount's attitude toward this figure. Karen Adams, "The Black Image in the Paintings of William Sidney Mount," *American Art Journal* 7 (Nov. 1975): 47, argues that Mount's sympathies lie with the black man, used here as chief weapon in "a subversive attack on the Puritan maxim to make hay while the sun shines." Carol Troyen refutes this view in the catalogue entry for *Farmers Nooning* in Theodore E. Stebbins, Jr., Carol Troyen, and Trevor J. Fairbrother, *A New World: Masterpieces of American Painting, 1760–1910*, exhibition catalogue (Boston: Museum of Fine Arts, 1983), 257. The black man's pose, she suggests, is similar to that of the Barberini Faun, a second-century B.C. Hellenistic statue well known in Mount's time and then considered "undignified, indecent, and even immoral." This putative association with the Faun suggests that the picture "may not be nearly as sympathetic a portrayal of the black man as has been previously supposed."

4. The influence of British and Dutch art on nineteenth-century American painters is discussed in Donald Keyes, "The Sources for William Sidney Mount's Earliest Genre Paintings," *Art Quarterly* 32 (1969): 258–68; Catherine Hoover, "The Influence of David Wilkie's Prints on the Genre Paintings of William Sidney Mount," *American Art Journal* 13 (Summer 1981): 4–33; H. Nichols B. Clark, "A Taste for the Netherlands: The Impact of Seventeenth-Century Dutch and Flemish Genre Painting on American Art, 1800–1850," *American Art Journal* 14 (Spring 1982): 23–38, and Clark, "A Fresh Look at the Art of Francis W. Edmonds: Dutch Sources and American Meanings," *American Art Journal* 14 (Summer 1982), 73–94.

5. James Kirke Paulding, *Koningsmarke, the Long Finne: A Story of the New World* (1823), rev. ed. titled *Koningsmarke; or, Old Times in the New World* (New York: Harper, 1835), 2:14.

6. Cornelius Mathews, *The Politicians*, (1840) in *The Various Writings of Cornelius Mathews* (New York: Harper, 1863), 126.

7. Donald Grant Mitchell, *My Farm of Edgewood* (1863), 16th ed. (New York: Scribner, 1894), 83.

8. Mitchell, *The Lorgnette; or, Studies of the Town by an Opera Goer* (1850); 9th ed. (New York: Scribner, 1853), 201.

9. Uncle Toby, "Mr. and Mrs. Cowpen: A Humorous Sketch," *Gleason's Pictorial* 1 (September 13, 1851): 171.

10. Standard works on Mount are Mary Bartlett Cowdrey and Hermann Warner Williams, Jr., *William Sidney Mount, 1807–1868: An American Painter* (New York: Columbia University Press, 1944); Alfred Frankenstein, *Painter of Rural America: William Sidney Mount, 1807–1868*, exhibition catalogue (Stony Brook, N.Y.: Suffolk Museum, 1968); and Frankenstein, *William Sidney Mount* (New York: Abrams, 1975). For a fine introductory essay and detailed entries on many major works, see Janice Gray Armstrong, ed., *William Sidney Mount: Works in the Collection of the Museums at Stony Brook* (Stony Brook, N.Y.: The Museums at Stony Brook, 1983). Joseph Hudson, "Banks, Politics, Hard Cider, and Paint: The Political Origins of William Sidney Mount's *Cider Making*," *Metropolitan Museum of Art Journal* 10 (1975): 107–18, offers a clever argument to support a connection between Mount's painting and the Log Cabin Campaign.

11. Donald Keyes, "William Sidney Mount Reconsidered," *American Art Review* 4 (August 1977): 116–28, argues convincingly that like his British and Dutch predecessors, Mount extolled the "righteous life" by injecting an "emblematic level" of meaning into many of his paintings; his pictorial sermons against drink and gambling coincided with the rise of the temperance movement in the Northeast during the antebellum decades.

12. For a useful list of prints made after Mount's paintings, see Cowdrey and Williams, *Mount, American Painter*, 38–41.

13. Mount to Lanman, March 7 and December 3, 1847, and Diary/Journal (1848–57), December 7, 1848, MS, The Museums at Stony Brook; cited in Frankenstein, *Mount*, 117, 122, 197.

14. National Academy of Design exhibition reviews, *Knickerbocker Magazine* 5 (June 1835): 554; *New-York Mirror* 12 (June 13, 1835): 395; Edgar Allan Poe, "Review of New Books," *Graham's Magazine* 19 (November 1841): 249–50; John Hassell, *Memoirs of the Life of the Late George Morland* (London: J. Cundee, 1806), 154.

15. Charles Lanman, *Haphazard Personalities, Chiefly of Noted Americans* (1866; rpt. New York: C. T. Dillingham, 1886), 170; Henry Theodore Tuckerman, *Book of the Artists, American Artist Life* (New York: Putnam, 1867), 421.

16. National Academy of Design exhibition reviews, *New-York Mirror* 9 (June 9, 1832): 391 and 13 (June 18 and 25, 1836): 406,

414; W. Alfred Jones, "A Sketch of the Life and Character of William S. Mount," *American Whig Review*, n.s. 8 (August 1851): 125.

17. Barrell, *The Dark Side*, 114–15.

18. Mount's musical activities and associations are carefully explored in Janice Gray Armstrong, ed., *Catching the Tune: Music and William Sidney Mount* (Stony Brook, N.Y.: The Museums at Stony Brook, 1984). For information on Mount's musical life, I am indebted to Martha V. Pike's title essay (8–21), and M. Hunt Hessler, " 'Rusticity and Refinement': Music and Dance on Long Island, 1800–1870" (40–55).

19. The connections with Krimmel are discussed in Hoover, "The Influence of David Wilkie's Prints"; and Keyes, "The Sources for Mount's Earliest Genre Paintings." Their findings are summed up in David Cassedy, "William Sidney Mount (1807–1868)," in Armstrong, *Mount: Works*, 16–18. The German-born Krimmel, who lived and exhibited in Philadelphia, was one of the earliest painters to specialize in American genre themes; see Milo M. Naeve, *John Lewis Krimmel: An Artist in Federal America* (Newark: University of Delaware Press, 1987).

20. Background for the discussion of New England dialect verse comes from Jennette Tandy's invaluable *Crackerbox Philosophers in American Humor and Satire* (1925; rpt. Port Washington, N.Y.: Kennikat Press, 1964), 1–23.

21. Royall Tyler, "Ode Composed for the Fourth of July," *Farmer's Weekly Museum* 4 (July 19, 1796): 4.

22. Thomas Greene Fessenden, "The Country Junket, or Rustic Revel," *Farmer's Weekly Museum* 4 (September 6, 1796): 4; Fessenden, "Horace Surpassed; or, A Beautiful Description of a New-England Country-Dance," in *Original Poems* (London: J. Cundee for T. Hurst, 1806), 56–59. On the history of the Sambo type, see Joseph Boskin, *Sambo: The Rise and Demise of an American Jester* (New York: Oxford University Press, 1986).

23. "A Sleigh Ride," *Yankee and Boston Literary Gazette* 2 (March 19, 1829): 96. As "Johnny's Sleigh Ride" and with minor changes, the tale was published serially in Robert Thomas's *Farmer's Almanac* (Boston, 1830, 1831, 1833). A virtually identical story, *John Beadle's Sleigh Ride, Courtship, and Marriage* (New York: C. Wells, 1841) appeared under the authorship of a Captain M'Clintock of the U.S. Army. Undoubtedly, other versions were published as well; indeed, the basic elements of the story correspond precisely to regional folklore: e.g., Asa Greene, *The Life and Adventures of Dr. Dodimus Duckworth, A. N. Q.* (New York: Peter Hill, 1833), 2:159–

60, in which the same ritual is described, minus the Beadle narrative. John Neal himself, in *Wandering Recollections of a Somewhat Busy Life* (Boston: Roberts Brothers, 1869), 342, claimed ignorance of the true author's identity but admitted that he had made alterations and additions to the manuscript before publishing it in his gazette.

24. The Long Island dance schools are discussed in Hessler, "Rusticity and Refinement," 45–48.

25. Edward P. Buffet, "William Sidney Mount and His Environment," *New-York Historical Society Quarterly Bulletin* 7 (1923): 83.

26. The list was sent by Mount to his brother from Stony Brook, January 26, 1837 (cited in Frankenstein, *Mount,* 52). Details of Italian peasant types from Robert's works were widely circulated through lithographic reproduction beginning about 1843; there is a chance, therefore, that the similarities between Robert's dancers and Mount's are more than fortuitous. On Robert, see Gabriel P. Weisberg, "Breton, Robert, and the Poetic Vision of Rural Life," in Hollister Sturges, ed., *The Rural Vision: France and America in the Late Nineteenth Century* (Omaha, Neb.: Joslyn Art Museum, 1987), 43–52.

27. Mount's 1847 painting *The Power of Music* (Century Association, New York) departs from the content of the other barn-dance scenes even while retaining the basic format; it seems to embody dimensions more personal to the artist himself. The theme—the quiet pleasure of listening to the music of a rustic violin—directly reflects his own deep interest in that instrument. Even though the black man here, barred from white society, enjoys the tunes from outside the barn, there is barely a trace of fun or caricature in this work.

CHAPTER 7
JONATHANS

1. Joshua C. Taylor, "The American Cousin," in *America as Art* (Washington, D.C.: Smithsonian Institution Press, 1976), 37–94, discusses general parallels between stage Yankees and types in American painting.

2. George Handel Hill, *Scenes from the Life of an Actor* (1853; rpt. New York: Benjamin Blom, 1969), 121; Mount is quoted in

Charles Lanman, *Haphazard Personalities, Chiefly of Noted Americans* (1866; rpt. New York: C. T. Dillingham, 1886), 170.

3. For examples of the Yankee in political cartoons, see Allan Nevins and Frank Weitenkampf, *A Century of Political Cartoons: Caricature in the United States from 1800 to 1900* (New York: Scribner, 1944).

4. "The Drama," *Knickerbocker Magazine* 7 (June 1836): 646.

5. The indispensable source for the history of the stage Yankee is Francis Hodge, *Yankee Theatre: The Image of America on the Stage, 1825–1850* (Austin: University of Texas Press, 1964). Also useful are Daniel F. Havens, *The Columbian Muse of Comedy: The Development of a Native Tradition in Early American Social Comedy, 1787–1845* (Carbondale: Southern Illinois University Press, 1973); and Ima Honacker Herron, *The Small Town in American Drama* (Dallas, Tex.: Southern Methodist University Press, 1969).

6. Samuel Woodworth, *The Forest Rose; or, American Farmers* (1825; rpt. Boston: W. Spencer, 1855).

7. Seba Smith, *The Life and Writings of Major Jack Downing of Downingville, Away Down East in the State of Maine, Written by Himself* (1833); 3d ed. (Boston: Lily, Wait, Colman, & Holden, 1834), 38–39. The first edition contained six wood-engraved illustrations by comic artist David Claypoole Johnston. His image of Major Jack did not feature any outstandingly Yankee characteristics. On Johnston's images, see David Tatham, "Jack Downing: A Jacksonian Hero Personalized," *Imprint* 6 (Autumn 1981).

8. Charles Augustus Davis, *Letters of J. Downing, Major, Downingville Militia, Second Brigade, to His Old Friend Mr. Dwight of the N.Y. Daily Advertiser* (New York: Harper, 1834).

9. Mary Alice Wyman, *Two American Pioneers: Seba Smith and Elizabeth Oakes Smith* (New York: Columbia University Press, 1927), a valuable earlier account of Smith's career, suggests the possible influence of Smollett (32) and attempts to sort through the complexities of the real and false Downing letters and of the statistics regarding the newspapers that printed them (233–35). In Wyman's view, Seba Smith through his mouthpiece Jack Downing attacked principles, not men, and while he "had his fun" with the "Gineral," he did not destroy his readers' faith in the president's sincerity (79). Both Jennette Tandy, *Crackerbox Philosophers in American Humor and Satire* (1925; rpt. Port Washington, N.Y.: Kennikat Press, 1964), 25, and the later study by Milton and Patricia Rickels, *Seba Smith* (Boston: Twayne, 1977), argue that the Downing letters represented a conservative and even negative view of Jack-

sonian democracy. The epistolary form had been used earlier in the Joe Strickland letters, written by George Arnold as a "puff" for his lottery parlor in New York and published in the *National Advocate* in 1825.

10. James Hackett's master notebook, ca. 1827, Enthoven Collection, Victoria and Albert Museum, London, cited in Hodge, *Yankee Theatre*, 91–92.

11. James Kirke Paulding, *The Diverting History of John Bull and Brother Jonathan* (1812) 2d ed. (New York: Harper, 1835), 81; Alexander MacKay, *The Western World; or, Travels in the United States in 1846–47*, 4th ed. (London: Richard Bentley, 1850), 2:62.

12. Nathaniel Parker Willis, *Letters from under a Bridge* (1840), in *Rural Letters and Other Records of Thoughts at Leisure* (1849; rpt. Auburn, N.Y.: Alden & Beardsley, 1856), 79, 157.

13. Thomas Low Nichols, *Forty Years of American Life* (London: J. Maxwell, 1864), 2:193; Bill Severn, *The Long and the Short of It: Five Thousand Years of Fun and Fury over Hair* (New York: David McKay, 1971), 105.

14. Peter G. Buckley, " 'The Place To Make an Artist Work': Micah Hawkins and William Sidney Mount in New York City," in Janice Gray Armstrong, ed., *Catching the Tune: Music and William Sidney Mount* (Stony Brook, N.Y.: Museums at Stony Brook, 1984), 22–39, is to date the most concentrated examination of Mount's connections with the New York stage in the 1820s and 1830s. Six of his theater sketches (The Museums at Stony Brook) are illustrated and discussed in Buckley's essay (29–35).

15. "The National Academy of Design," *New-York Mirror* 14 (June 17, 1837): 407; Edgar Allan Poe, "Review of New Books," *Graham's Magazine* 19 (November 1841): 250; unidentified comment cited in *Life in America*, exhibition catalogue (New York: Metropolitan Museum of Art, 1939), 119; *International Magazine* 3 (June, 1851): 328. *Who'll Turn the Grindstone?* was an illustration for a moralizing tale in Robert Miner, *Essays from the Desk of Poor Robert the Scribe* (1815).

16. Mount, Diary/Journal (1848–57), MS, Museums at Stony Brook, cited in Janet Gray Armstrong, ed., *William Sidney Mount: Works in the Collection of the Museums at Stony Brook* (Stony Brook, N.Y.: The Museums at Stony Brook, 1983), 51.

17. *The Wintergreen: A Perennial Gift for 1844*, ed. John Keese (New York: C. Wells, [c. 1843]), 47.

18. Edward J. Nygren's entry for *The Long Story* in *Of Time and Place: American Figurative Art from the Corcoran Gallery*, exhibition catalogue (Washington, D.C.: Smithsonian Institution and Corcoran Gallery of Art, 1981), 31, notes that "in 1837 the railroad was in its infancy, extending only to Hicksville." The pinned-up notice thus emphasizes the "currentness of the image." Nygren also suggests that it "may reflect Mount's mixed feelings about life in the country. It is possible that the artist saw in the coming of the Long Island line the promise of easy access to the city he enjoyed visiting and the means of escape from the provincial world he loved to paint."

19. Mount, letter to Robert Gilmor, Jr., December 5, 1837, Archives of American Art, quoted in Alfred Frankenstein, *William Sidney Mount* (New York: Abrams, 1975), 75.

20. Seba Smith, "The Tough Yarn," in *'Way Down East; or, Portraitures of Yankee Life* (New York: J. O. Derby, 1856), 53–75.

21. Paulding, *John Bull and Brother Jonathan*, 82.

22. Donald Grant Mitchell, *Dream-Life: A Fable of the Seasons* (1851; rpt. New York: Scribner, 1893), 83.

23. Frederick Marryat, *A Diary in America*, ed. Jules Zanger (1839; rpt. Bloomington: Indiana University Press, 1960), 147, 148.

24. Reed to Mount, October 29, 1835; Mount to Reed, November 12, 1835, both quoted in Frankenstein, *Mount*, 70. The Downing story, published in the *New York Gazette and Daily Advertiser*, October 28, 1835, is cited in the *Catalogue of the Gallery of the New-York Historical Society* (New York, 1915), 10.

25. Mount was probably familiar with some examples of the seventeenth-century Dutch theme of a man, often a soldier, visiting a comely young woman; Gabriel Metsu's *Soldier Visiting a Young Woman* (c. 1665; Louvre) was available to him in an eighteenth-century engraving by P. Audouin and as an illustration in John Burnet, *A Treatise on Painting in Three Parts* (London, 1827), a book Mount knew. Other examples of the English rustic courtship include Sir David Wilkie, *The Refusal* (1814; Victoria and Albert Museum, London), which was engraved by Francis Engleheart under the title *Duncan Gray* and published by Wilkie in 1828; Francis Wheatley, *The Smitten Clown* (mezzotint engraved by S. W. Reynolds, published by I. Read, 1795), and William Mulready, *The Village Buffoon* (1815–16; Royal Academy, London). For a more detailed look at these sources see my "Yankee Romance: The Comic Courtship Scene in Nineteenth-Century American Art," *American Art Journal* 18, no. 4 (1986): 52–75.

26. Thomas Greene Fessenden, "The Country Lovers," in Evert Augustus and George L. Duyckinck, *Cyclopedia of American Literature* (New York: Scribner, 1866), 1:597–99.

27. Kadanda [pseud.], "Yankee Phrases," *Port Folio*, 3 (March 12, 1803): 87; Jemimah [pseud.], "Jonathan to Jemima," *Port Folio* 2 (May 15, 1802): 152.

28. "William Sidney Mount," *New-York Mirror* 14 (December 24, 1838): 206; "The National Academy of Design," *New-York Mirror* 14 (June 17, 1837): 407. Despite what the first review claims, there is no knife visible on the floor, only the whittled stick. Perhaps in recollecting the painting for the review, this writer misremembered, thinking that since there was a stick, there must have been a knife as well.

29. John Russell Bartlett, *A Glossary of Words and Phrases Usually Regarded as Peculiar to the United States* (1848), 3d ed. (Boston: Little, Brown, 1860), 514.

CHAPTER 8
BUMPKINS BY CONTRAST

1. Samuel Woodworth, *The Forest Rose; or, American Farmers* (1825; rpt. Boston: W. Spencer, 1855), 1.1. Social incongruities, contrasts, and collisions were important devices of antebellum American humor in print and on stage; see Walter Blair and Hamlin Hill, *America's Humor: From Poor Richard to Doonesbury* (New York: Oxford University Press, 1978), 158–60.

2. J. S. Jones, *The Green Mountain Boy* (1833; rpt. New York: S. French, 1860), 1.2.

3. Cornelius Logan, *The Wag of Maine* (1833); rewritten as *Yankee Land* (1842; rpt. Boston: W. Spencer, [1856?]). Francis Hodge, *Yankee Theatre: The Image of America on the Stage, 1825–1850* (Austin: University of Texas Press, 1964), 144–45, 235–36, 282, clarifies the history of this play, which was performed at the Bowery Theatre under its new title; the plot remained the same, but Logan gave the characters different names.

4. Hodge, *Yankee Theatre*, 96, 130.

5. Although the long-tailed coat was quite early identified with the stage Yankee, this cut was also actually in style during the 1820s and 1830s. It was the tasteless, idiosyncratic combination of garments, rather than the tailcoat alone, that identified the Yankee in these early years.

6. Hodge, *Yankee Theatre*, 70.

7. Cornelius Mathews, "The Great Charter Contest in Gotham," in *The Motley Book* (1839), reprinted in *The Various Writings of Cornelius Mathews* (New York: Harper, 1863), 42. Opinions differ on the issue of dress and status in nineteenth-century America before the Civil War. There seems to have been a leveling tendency, produced in part by the industrialization of clothing manufacture and the mass distribution of standardized fashions, but this leveling did not become obvious until the 1850s or later, and not until the 1840s did the wearing of black begin to signify a democracy of costume. Henry Tuckerman, "Costume," *Godey's Ladies' Book* 30 (January–June 1845): 139, remarked that men's dress was blighted by a dreary conformity: "The limited privileges of mankind on the score of raiment are but typical of the monotony which society in this age seems to have entailed on life. It is in good taste that black is the accredited color, for doubtless it is the best fitted to subdue all inequalities of form, and is associated with the idea of simplicity and dignity." A decade later the writer of "American Servants," *Gleason's Pictorial* 7 (June 3, 1854): 333, satirically commented on the dress of rich men's servants, so spruce in their elegant black suits that they could be mistaken for aristocrats.

8. Frances Trollope, *Domestic Manners of the Americans*, ed. Herbert van Thal (1832; rpt. London: Folio Society, 1974), 106–7; James Fenimore Cooper, *The American Democrat* (Cooperstown, N.Y.: H. & E. Phinney, 1838), 156.

9. Nathaniel Parker Willis, "Editorial Confab III," in *Rag-Bag: A Collection of Ephemera* (New York: Scribner, 1855), 297–98.

10. Robert Thomas, *Farmer's Almanac* (Boston, 1796). Another shade of interpretation is suggested by the title. In antebellum America, "sportsman" sometimes denoted not a hunter but a professional gambler. In this light, the sermon of *The Sportsman's Last Visit* might preach against the pitfalls of trusting to luck (rather than honest work) to succeed in life. Since Mount's figure is literally a hunter, however, the gambling allusion—if intended at all—is only an oblique or secondary reference.

11. Mrs. H. Seeley Totten, "Fashion in a Village," *Godey's Ladies' Book* 30 (January–June 1845): 208.

12. On Edmonds, see Maybelle Mann, *Francis W. Edmonds:*

Mammon and Art (New York: Garland, 1977), and H. Nichols B. Clark, *Francis W. Edmonds: American Master in the Dutch Tradition,* exhibition catalogue (Washington, D.C.: Smithsonian Institution Press for the Amon Carter Museum, Fort Worth, Texas, 1988). In 1842 comic genre painter James Goodwyn Clonney also produced a scene of comic contrast: *Jonathan's Introduction to Good Society* depicted a Yankee bumpkin sorely incongruous among elegant surroundings and fashionable people. A study for the painting is illustrated in Lucretia H. Giese, "James Goodwyn Clonney (1812–1867): American Genre Painter," *American Art Journal* 11 (October 1979): 19, which notes that the *Knickerbocker Magazine* reviewer found it affected and ridiculous, as well as technically inept.

13. R. Turner Wilcox, *The Mode in Hats and Headresses,* rev. ed. (New York: Scribner, 1959), 212; Penelope Byrde, *The Male Image: Male Fashion in Britain, 1300–1970* (London: Batsford, 1979), 134. British and European styles set the standard for American dress, male as well as female, during the nineteenth century. What was fashionable in England would soon be fashionable in America, as was the case with these greatcoats, which were said to have their origin in traditional eastern European costume.

14. Nathaniel Parker Willis, *Letters from under a Bridge* (1840), reprinted in *Rural Letters and Other Records of Thought at Leisure* (1849; rpt. Auburn, N.Y.: Alden & Beardsley, 1856), 157. Patricia Hills, *The Painters' America: Rural and Urban Life, 1810–1910,* exhibition catalogue (New York: Praeger in association with the Whitney Museum of American Art, 1974), 26, first pointed out the social cues conveyed by costume in *Raffling for the Goose.*

15. National Academy of Design exhibition review, *Literary World* 12 (April 30, 1853): 358. For political readings of *The Herald in the Country,* see Alfred Frankenstein, *William Sidney Mount* (New York: Abrams, 1975), 203; Barbara Groseclose, "Politics and American Genre Painting of the Nineteenth Century," *Antiques* 120 (1981): 1214; catalogue entry, Janice Gray Armstrong, ed., *William Sidney Mount: Works in the Collection of the Museums at Stony Brook* (Stony Brook, N.Y.: Museums at Stony Brook, 1983), 63. Details vary in these interpretations, but there is agreement that Mount's painting, originally exhibited as *Politics of 1852, or Who Let Down the Bars?,* alluded to the presidential election of 1852, when the right-wing Democrats allied themselves with the right-wing Whigs in order to elect Democrat Franklin Pierce, a supporter of the Compromise of 1850.

16. Mount, Diary/Journal (1848–57) February 1854, MS, The Museums at Stony Brook, cited in Frankenstein, *Mount,* 65. Hills, *The Painters' America,* 12, notes that sometimes only the first part of Mount's remark is quoted (and thereby rendered out of context) to lend support to the idea of his democratic intentions; Hills also concludes, on the evidence of the entire passage, that Mount thought of the "public" in the narrow sense of the coterie of buyers and critics who would acquire his paintings and support his efforts.

17. National Academy of Design exhibition review, *Knickerbocker Magazine* 45 (May 1855): 531. Oertel was trained as a painter and engraver at the Polytechnic Institute in Nuremburg. In the 1850s he lived in New Jersey, painting portraits and executing engravings for banknotes. Later he became an Episcopal priest and concentrated on religious paintings for churches.

18. National Academy of Design exhibition review, *Town and Country,* no. 14 (April 1, 1854): 2.

19. "Cheated of a Whole Year," by One Who Knows, *Ballou's Pictorial* 10 (June 28, 1856): 411.

20. Hoppin, a successful midcentury illustrator of humorous and satirical subjects, illustrated George William Curtis, *The Potiphar Papers* (New York: Putnam, 1853), and Mark Twain and Charles Dudley Warner, *The Gilded Age* (Hartford, Conn.: American, 1873), among others.

CHAPTER 9
GRANDFATHERS AND GEEZERS

1. For thought-provoking studies of transformations in late nineteenth-century America, see Robert H. Wiebe, *The Search for Order, 1877–1920* (New York: Hill & Wang, 1967); and Alan Trachtenberg, *The Incorporation of America: Culture and Society in the Gilded Age* (New York: Hill & Wang, 1982).

2. Frederic C. Howe, *The City, the Hope of Democracy* (New York: Scribner, 1905), 9, 23.

3. R. K. Munkittrick, "Farming," *Harper's Weekly Magazine* 35 (January 17, 1891): 52.

4. Rodney Welch, "The Farmer's Changed Condition," *Forum* 10 (February 1891): 689–700.

5. John M. Welding, "The Country Boy versus the Town Boy," *Social Economist* 3 (1892): 11–22, 98–107, 179–184. Richard R. Wohl treats late nineteenth-century debunkers of country life in "The 'Country Boy' Myth and Its Place in American Urban Cul-

ture: The Nineteenth-Century Contribution," *Perspectives in American History* 3 (1969): 140–155.

6. Rebecca Harding Davis, "In the Gray Cabins of New England," *Century Magazine* 49 (1895): 620–22.

7. Helen Maria Fiske Hunt Jackson, *Bits of Travel at Home* (Boston: Roberts Brothers, 1882), 182.

8. Whittier, "Among the Hills," in *The Poetical Works of John Greenleaf Whittier* (Boston: Houghton Mifflin, 1892), 235.

9. Rose Terry Cooke, "Some Account of Thomas Tucker," in *The Sphinx's Children and Other People's* (Boston: Ticknor, 1886), 167–69. See "A Taste of Honey" and "A Mistaken Charity" as representative examples of Mary E. Wilkins Freeman's tales in *A Humble Romance and Other Stories* (New York: Harper, 1887). Excellent general discussions of regionalism are Jay Martin, *Harvests of Change: American Literature, 1865–1914* (Englewood Cliffs, N.J.: Prentice-Hall, 1967), 133–52; and Robert Spiller, Willard Thorpe, Thomas H. Johnson, Henry Seidel Canby, Richard M. Ludwig, and William M. Gibson, eds., *Literary History of the United States*, 4th rev. ed. (New York: Macmillan, 1974), 1:843–48.

10. Harold Frederic, *Seth's Brother's Wife: A Study of Life in Greater New York* (1887; rpt. New York: Greenwood Press, 1969), 2, 7, 13.

11. Edgar Watson Howe, *The Story of a Country Town,* ed. Claude M. Simpson (1883; rpt. Cambridge, Mass.: Belknap Press of Harvard University Press, 1961).

12. Hamlin Garland, "Up the Coulee," in *Main-Traveled Roads* (1891; rpt. New York: New American Library, 1962), 60, 95, 97. Roy W. Meyer, *The Middle Western Farm Novel in the Twentieth Century* (Lincoln: University of Nebraska Press, 1965), 13–34, provides a useful survey of the nineteenth-century backgrounds touched upon here.

13. For the facts on Shaw, I have relied on the discussion in Jennette Tandy, *Crackerbox Philosophers in American Humor and Satire* (1925; rpt. Port Washington, N.Y.: Kennikat Press, 1964), 146–57.

14. Henry Wheeler Shaw, *Josh Billings' Farmer's Allminak* (New York: G. W. Carlton, 1872).

15. Ima Honaker Herron, *The Small Town in American Drama* (Dallas, Tex.: Southern Methodist University Press, 1969), 78.

16. Denman Thompson and George W. Ryer, *The Old Homestead* (New York, 1887), act 2. For more information on Thompson, see Herron, *Small Town.* Other popular rural plays cited in Herron include *A Midnight Bell* (1888), *Shore Acres* (1892), and *David Harum* (1900).

17. Merit Osborn, *Farmer Larkin's Boarders* (Clyde, Ohio: Ames, [c. 1897]).

18. See Sarah Orne Jewett, *Deephaven* (Boston: J. Osgood, 1877). The paintings by Johnson are illustrated and briefly discussed in Patricia Hills, *Eastman Johnson,* exhibition catalogue (New York: Clarkson N. Potter in association with Whitney Museum of American Art, 1972), 101–11.

19. Lee M. Edwards, "Noble Domesticity: The Paintings of Thomas Hovenden," *American Art Journal* 19, no. 1 (1987): 23–24, interprets *The Old Version* as a celebration of the " 'old version' of marriage" in an era of concern over the erosion of the family.

20. Marguerite Tracy, "In the Paths of the Poets," *Quarterly Illustrator* 3 (1895): 231. Howland, a native of New Hampshire, started out as an engraver, then studied painting for several years in New York, Düsseldorf, and Paris. He specialized in landscape and genre painting.

21. Henry studied at the Pennsylvania Academy of Fine Arts and briefly in Paris. A successful genre painter of the Gilded Age, he kept a studio in the famous Tenth Street Studio Building in New York. He settled in Cragsmoor in 1887; Peter Brown, the town drunk, was one of his favorite models. See Elizabeth McCausland, *The Life and Work of Edward Lamson Henry N. A., 1841–1919, New York State Museum Bulletin,* no. 339 (September 1945); *E. L. Henry's Country Life: An Exhibition* (Cragsmoor, N.Y.: Cragsmoor Free Library and New York State Museum, 1981); and Barbara Ball Buff, "Mr. Henry of Cragsmoor," *Archives of American Art Journal* 21 (1981): 2–7.

22. Howard S. Russell, *A Long, Deep Furrow: Three Centuries of Farming in New England* (Hanover, N.H.: University Press of New England, 1976), 466–67, notes that in the later nineteenth century the summer visitor became an important source of supplemental income for farmers in New England.

23. A useful examination of Populism in relation to the agricultural problems of the time is Fred A. Shannon, *The Farmer's Last Frontier: Agriculture, 1860–1897,* vol. 5 in *The Economic History of the United States* (New York: Rinehart, 1945), chap. 13, "The Agrarian Uprising," 291–328.

24. Wallace Irwin, "The Sick Cow," in *A Book of Drawings by A. B. Frost,* introd. Joel Chandler Harris (New York: P. F. Collier, 1904).

CHAPTER 10
PEASANTS

1. Rodney Welch, "The Farmer's Changed Condition," *Forum* 10 (February 1891): 700. Cf. Robert Redfield, *Peasant Society and Culture: An Anthropological Approach to Civilization* (Chicago: University of Chicago Press, 1956). Redfield argues that the peasant is a generic type, to be found the same everywhere and holding a set of universal values, including suspicion of town life and the world of the market; reverence for ancestral ways; conservatism toward social change; disinclination to adventure or speculate; productive industry as a prime virtue.

2. Lloyd Goodrich, *Winslow Homer* (New York: Macmillan for Whitney Museum of American Art, 1944), 50. Other standard works are John Wilmerding, *Winslow Homer* (New York: Praeger, 1972); and Gordon Hendricks, *The Life and Work of Winslow Homer* (New York: Abrams, 1979).

3. Richard R. and Caroline B. Brettell, *Painters and Peasants in the Nineteenth Century* (New York: Rizzoli, 1983), 145, suggests that for Homer the American farmer was quite literally a peasant, because his paintings "focused on the hard labor of the fields, a subject which became increasingly out of date as the relentless mechanization of the American farm continued, and only in these few canvases . . . [and a handful by Eastman Johnson] does the American farm worker attain the emblematic stature of the European peasant." The Brettells make this observation in passing, however, without examining its implications.

4. Painter John LaFarge thought that Homer was little affected by what he had seen in France: "I do not know what more he got beyond what he had already." LaFarge also asserted, however, that as a student of lithographs after Barbizon painters, Homer—like himself—had been "largely made by them": LaFarge to *New York Herald*, December 4, 1910, cited in Goodrich, *Homer*, 39–40; Royal Cortissoz, *John La Farge: A Memoir and Study* (Boston: Houghton Mifflin, 1911), 70. Goodrich, *Homer*, 37, conceded some influence but only in a "quite general" sense, as "part of the whole spirit of the time." Representing prevailing contemporary directions of argument, Helen A. Cooper, *Winslow Homer Watercolors*, exhibition catalogue (New Haven, Conn.: Yale University Press for the National Gallery of Art, Washington, D.C., 1986), 52–54, sees Homer's development as virtually inseparable from the wave of Barbizon-inspired peasant painting by Americans beginning in the 1860s and gathering force through the 1870s; similarly, Brettell and Brettell, *Painters and Peasants*, 147, describes Homer's *Girl with a Pitchfork* as a work "almost quoted from Millet or Breton."

5. Kathleen A. Pyne, catalogue entry for *Answering the Horn*, in *The Quest for Unity: American Art between World's Fairs, 1876–1893*, exhibition catalogue (Detroit, Mich.: Detroit Institute of Arts, 1983), 56, suggests that the direct inspiration for Homer may have been Jules Breton's *Recall of the Gleaners* (1859; Musée des Beaux-Arts, Arras), one of the sensations at the 1867 Exposition Universelle. The simple massiveness of Homer's figures, however, is closer to the style of Millet. Wilmerding, *Homer*, 50, has also pointed out Homer's obvious debt to Millet.

6. Hendricks, *Winslow Homer*, 113–14, believes that the title *Gloucester Farm* is wrong. Since there are "virtually no" farms in Gloucester, he writes, it is more likely that this painting came from sketches made in the Hurley, New York, area, which furnished material for several other contemporary rustic scenes. Hendricks proposes that the correct title should be *A Temperance Meeting*, which was the title of a painting Homer exhibited at the Palette Club in 1874, described by a reviewer as a milkmaid giving a "shepherd lad" a draught of milk.

7. Goodrich, *Homer*, 51–52; "The National Academy of Design," *Art Journal*, n.s. 2 (June 1876): 189; "Art," *Atlantic Monthly* 37 (June 1876): 760; "The Academy Exhibition," *Art Journal*, n.s. 3 (May 1877), 159.

8. Henry James, "On Some Pictures Lately Exhibited," *Galaxy* 20 (July 1875): 90, 93–94.

9. Ibid., 93.

10. Shepherdess themes formed the basis of the bucolic designs Homer executed as a project in the Tile Club later that year; see Goodrich, *Homer*, 60–62. Cooper, *Homer Watercolors*, 60–64, discusses the shepherdesses of 1878 and sees their reception as a turning point in the artist's career. Houghton Farm, in Mountainville, New York, was owned by Homer's patron Lawson Valentine. There were, of course, some exceptions to the general rule of reticence in Homer's art. An occasional work such as *Song of the Lark* (1876; Chrysler Museum, Norfolk, Virginia), which depicts a young farmer enchanted by birdsong in a meadow, is (relatively speaking) full of romantic, quasi-Barbizon sentiment. Homer's illustrations and paintings of country children (see chapteer 13) cannot be divorced from the contemporary climate of nostalgia that encouraged the production of such images, and they have an understated yet per-

ceptible emotional resonance. For a different view of Homer's farmers, see Patricia Hills, "Images of Rural America in the Works of Eastman Johnson, Winslow Homer, and Their Contemporaries: A Survey and Critique," in Hollister Sturges, ed., *The Rural Vision: France and America in the Late Nineteenth Century* (Omaha, Neb.: Joslyn Art Museum, 1987), 73–75, which argues that the farmer in *Song of the Lark* is "no peasant, but a heroic individual who works for himself."

11. Henry Theodore Tuckerman, *Book of the Artists: American Artist Life* (New York: Putnam, 1867), 462, 464. There seems to have been a rather high incidence after the Civil War of paintings and illustrations depicting cooperative groups working happily in the fields. Eastman Johnson stands out as an important formulator of such imagery, in paintings such as his 1876 *Husking Bee* (see Illus. 17), the 1860s maple-sugar camp series, and a series of studies and finished paintings (1875–80) of the cranberry harvest on Nantucket. Similar treatment was given to harvest scenes in popular magazines: e.g., Julian Scott, *Picking Raspberries* (*Harper's Weekly Magazine* 17 [July 26, 1873]), and Granville Perkins, *A Cranberry Bog* (*Harper's Weekly Magazine* 21 [September 15, 1877]).

12. Tuckerman, *Book of the Artists*, 467; S. G. W. Benjamin, *Some Modern Artists and Their Work* (New York: Cassell, 1883), 158. For a revealing contemporary evaluation of Frère, see M. D. Conway, "Edouard Frère and Sympathetic Art in France," *Harper's New Monthly Magazine* 43 (November 1871): 801–14.

13. Edward Wheelwright, "Three Boston Painters," *Atlantic Monthly*, 40 (December 1877): 711–12. Recent studies of Hunt include Marchal E. Landgren and Sharman Wallace McGurn, *The Late Landscapes of William Morris Hunt*, exhibition catalogue (College Park: University of Maryland Art Gallery, 1976); and Martha J. Hoppin and Henry Adams, *William Morris Hunt: A Memorial Exhibition* (Boston: Museum of Fine Arts, 1979). A valuable survey of the Barbizon presence in America is Peter Bermingham, *American Art in the Barbizon Mood*, exhibition catalogue (Washington, D.C.: National Collection of Fine Arts, 1975); also see Laura L. Meixner, *An International Episode: Millet, Monet, and Their American Counterparts*, exhibition catalogue (Memphis, Tenn.: Dixon Gallery and Gardens, 1982). I have not yet identified the painting discussed by Wheelwright.

14. Mariana Van Rensselaer, catalogue essay in *Memorial Exhibition of the Works of George Fuller* (Boston: Museum of Fine Arts, 1884), 21. On Fuller, see my article "A Study of the Life and Poetic Vision of George Fuller (1822–1884)," *American Art Journal* 13 (Autumn 1981): 11–37.

15. For an itemization of the paintings shown at the Chicago fair, see Daniel H. Burnham, et al., *The Art of the World, Illustrated in the Painting, Statuary, and Architecture of the World's Columbian Exposition*, 2 vols. (New York: Appleton, 1893).

16. Michael Jacobs, *The Good and Simple Life: Art Colonies in Europe and America* (Oxford: Phaidon Press, 1985), is an informative account of the history of these colonies and their inhabitants. See also David Sellin, *Americans in Brittany and Normany, 1860–1910*, exhibition catalogue (Phoenix, Ariz.: Phoenix Art Museum, 1982); and Michael Quick, *American Expatriate Painters of the Late Nineteenth Century*, exhibition catalogue (Dayton, Ohio: Dayton Art Institute, 1976).

17. See, e.g., George William Sheldon, *Recent Ideals of American Art* (1888; rpt. New York: Garland, 1977), 18–19, 23–24.

18. Ibid., 22–24. On American patronage of French peasant paintings, see Madeleine Fidell-Beaufort, "Jules Breton in America: Collecting in the Nineteenth Century," in Hollister Sturges, *Jules Breton and the French Rural Tradition*, exhibition catalogue (Omaha, Neb.: Joslyn Art Museum, 1982), 51–61.

19. Conway, "Frère and Sympathetic Art," 806; Charles Henry Hart, "The Collection of Mr. Henry C. Gibson, Philadelphia," in Walter Montgomery, ed., *American Art and American Art Collections: Essays on Artistic Subjects* (Boston: S. Walker, 1889), 1:115–16. American opinion on Millet is analyzed in Laura L. Meixner, "Popular Criticism of Jean-François Millet in Nineteenth-Century America," *Art Bulletin* 65 (March 1983): 92–105. Meixner argues that the major direction in Millet criticism was sentimental and served to engender a smugly superior national self-image because American farmers, relative to French peasants, were so much better off. Only to a more sensitive and concerned few did Millet's images mirror the misery of rural poverty in America itself after the Civil War, especially in the South, but their attempts at social criticism via Millet failed, overwhelmed by the persistent strength of the religio-sentimental view. The Meixner argument is effective but does not take into account the prevalence of agrarian debunking during the period, or of countertendencies purporting to regard the peasant as the moral and spiritual superior of the materialistic American farmer. See also Meixner, "The 'Millet Myth' and the American Public," in *An International Episode*, 68–91.

20. Editorial commentary on Edouard Frère's *Breakfast, Harper's Weekly Magazine* 21 (May 5, 1877): 357; "French Peasants," *Harper's Weekly Magazine* 24 (April 24, 1880): 269–70.

21. John M. Welding, "The Country Boy versus the Town Boy," *Social Economist* 3 (1892): 103; Hart, "The Collection of Mr. Henry C. Gibson," 115.

22. Will H. Low, *A Chronicle of Friendships 1873–1900* (New York: Scribner, 1908), 130. Low was a figure painter who specialized in monumental allegorical murals in the late nineteenth and early twentieth centuries.

23. Samuel Isham, *History of American Painting* (1905), rev. ed. with Royal Cortissoz (New York: Macmillan, 1927), 495; Lewis Mumford, *The Golden Day* (New York: Boni & Liveright, 1926), 80; William Dean Howells, *The Coast of Bohemia* (1893; rpt. New York: Harper, 1899), 6.

24. In addition to William Morris Hunt and George Fuller, Elliott Dangerfield devoted himself to painting Millet-like subjects in America. So completely did he model himself on Barbizon examples that critics christened him the "American Millet." This title was also conferred on Canadian-born Horatio Walker, who painted the peasants of French Canada. Like Fuller and Homer, several painters depicted southern blacks as New World peasants: Thomas Anschutz, Gilbert Gaul, William Aiken Walker.

25. The association between Barbizon painting and nostalgia for a preindustrial past is of long standing; it is probably the first and most obvious idea to arise in the consideration of the pastoral landscape and peasant genre. See, e.g., Robert L. Herbert, "City vs. Country: The Rural Image in French Painting from Millet to Gauguin," *Artforum* 8 (February 1970): 50; Bonnie L. Grad and Timothy A. Riggs, *Visions of City and Country: Prints and Photographs of Nineteenth-Century France,* exhibition catalogue (Worcester, Mass.: Worcester Art Museum and American Federation of Arts, 1982), 135.

CHAPTER 11
RURAL HEAVENS AND URBAN HELLS

1. The theme of rural-urban polarity is so pervasive in American culture and its interpretation that the literature is extensive. Certain works, however, have proved especially valuable for my own study. John R. Stilgoe, *Common Landscape of America, 1580 to 1845* (New Haven, Conn.: Yale University Press, 1982), using the artifacts of American material culture, examines the duality of the primitive-agrarian and the civilized-artificial realms. Neil Harris, *The Artist in American Society: The Formative Years, 1790–1860* (1966; rpt. New York: Simon & Schuster, 1970); Jan Cohn, *The Palace or the Poorhouse: The American House as Cultural Symbol* (East Lansing: Michigan State University Press, 1979); and Edward Halsey Foster, *The Civilized Wilderness: Backgrounds to American Romantic Literature, 1817–60* (New York: Free Press, 1975), all discuss aversion to or ambivalence about the city, and the middle-class Arcadias envisioned by designers such as Andrew Jackson Downing. Karen Halttunen, *Confidence Men and Painted Women: A Study of Middle-Class Culture in America, 1830–1870* (New Haven, Conn.: Yale University Press, 1982), considers middle-class responses to the treacherous, fluid urban world of midcentury. Paul Boyer, *Urban Masses and Moral Order in America, 1820–1920* (Cambridge, Mass.: Harvard University Press, 1978), 67–84, discusses middle-class fears of the city in the mid-nineteenth century. Literary treatments are most usefully surveyed and criticized in Janis P. Stout, *Sodoms in Eden: The City in American Fiction before 1860* (Westport, Conn.: Greenwood Press, 1976); and (more superficially) in Eugene Arden, "The Evil City in American Fiction," *New York History* 35 (July 1954): 259–79.

The history of the anti-urban idea in America is explored in Morton and Lucia White, *The Intellectual versus the City* (Cambridge, Mass.: Harvard University Press and M.I.T. Press, 1962). The evil city–virtuous country polarity is anything but unique to America; it extends as far back as the Virgil of the *Eclogues* and was the basis for English pastoral poetry (and some fiction, such as Henry Fielding's *Joseph Andrews*) in the eighteenth century. In the nineteenth, Charles Dickens's horrific portraits of cities established an important precedent for American writers. In antebellum painting the significant exception to the rule of avoiding urban problems was David Gilmore Blythe, whose images of working-class Pittsburgh—with its sometimes sinister denizens, and urchins already hardened and corrupt—strike a blunt and sour note. Bruce Chambers, *The World of David Gilmore Blythe*, exhibition catalogue (Washington, D.C.: National Museum of American Art, 1982), 40–55, considers Blythe in relation to contemporary urban problems.

2. George Templeton Strong, *Diary*, ed. Allan Nevins and Milton Halsey Thomas (New York: Macmillan, 1952), 1:104, entry for

May 5, 1839; George Lippard, *The Empire City; or, New York by Night and Day* (1850; rpt. New York: Books for Libraries Press, 1969), 42; George C. Foster, *New York in Slices, by an Experienced Carver* (New York: William H. Graham, 1849), 4, 5.

3. Matthew Hale Smith, *Sunshine and Shadow in New York* (Hartford, Conn.: J. B. Burr, 1868), 205, 707–9.

4. Eugene Lawrence, "Mr. Tilden's Friends as Rioters," *Harper's Weekly* 20 (September 2, 1876): 715.

5. "Tenement-House Abuses," *Harper's Weekly* 11 (April 24, 1867): 537; Josiah Strong, *Our Country: Its Possible Future and Present Crisis*, ed. Jurgen Herbst (1885); rev. ed. (1890; rpt. Cambridge, Mass.: Harvard University Press, 1963), 172, 177; George Nelson, "National Plague-Spots," *North American Review* 145 (December 1887): 687.

6. Paul Frenzeny, a Frenchman who came to America in the late 1860s, did his first illustration for *Harper's Weekly* in 1868; his work, including a series of western sketches, appeared there through the 1870s and 1880s. The identities of Stanley Fox and A. Gault have proved difficult to trace. Fox did several illustrations of lower-class city life for *Harper's* in the late 1860s. Gault's career with the magazine was also brief; the luridly illuminated, boldly contrasted treatment in this illustration, however, suggests that he nourished vivid memories of Gustav Doré's *London*, with its gloomy, dramatic illustrations, which *Harper's Weekly* had published in serial form in 1872. The caption cited here to Fox's illustration is in *Harper's Weekly Magazine* 11 (February 6, 1867): 96. It should also be noted that the text for Frenzeny' *Ragpickers*, in *Harper's Weekly Magazine* 12 (November 14, 1868): 727, made a halfhearted attempt to mitigate the scavengers' fearsome appearance by calling these people honest, decent workers, however low their trade—but the words do little to neutralize the visual message.

7. Smith, *Sunshine and Shadow*, 442–45.

8. Anna Cora (Ogden) Mowatt Ritchie, *Fashion* (1845), in Allan Gates Halline, ed., *American Plays* (New York: American Book Company, 1935), 231–72.

9. Sylvanus Cobb, Jr., "The Hypochondriac," *Gleason's Pictorial* 4 (February 26, 1853): 134–35.

10. Alice B. Neal, "Two Sides to the Picture," *Gleason's Pictorial* 7 (July 22, 1854): 42.

11. *Harper's Weekly* 2 (February 6, 1858): 85–86. Jules Tavernier was born in Paris, studied art with F. Barries, exhibited at the Paris Salon 1865–70, and came to New York in 1871. He drew illustrations for *Harper's Weekly Magazine* and the *New York Graphic*, and worked occasionally with Paul Frenzeny.

12. Andrew Jackson Downing, *Rural Essays* (1853; rpt. New York: George A. Leavitt, 1869), 15; Downing, *The Architecture of Country Houses* (1850), 2d ed. (New York: Appleton, 1852), 257–58, v–vi; H. of Oneida Country, "Rural Architecture," *Cultivator*, n.s. 4 (March 1847): 73. Harris, *The Artist in American Society*, 208–16, briefly discusses Downing's thought in relation to midcentury "Crusades for Beauty"; with appropriate supporting evidence, Harris argues that despite the democratic veneer, Downing's essential vision was that of a stratified rural social order in which not every man was a democrat but "every democrat an aristocrat—so far as was possible" (213). The inegalitarian bias of such a philosophy, of course, could easily be wished away with the rationalization that given the unlimited opportunities of America, no man could be prevented from rising to attain his own higher estate and his own villa. See Stilgoe, *Common Landscape*, 162–70, for a more detailed look at practical farmers' reactions to the Downing aesthetic.

13. T. Addison Richards, "Idlewild: The Home of N. P. Willis," *Harper's New Monthly Magazine* 16 (January 1858): 147, 154; Nathaniel Parker Willis, *Out-Doors at Idlewild; or, The Shaping of a Home on the Banks of the Hudson* (New York: Scribner, 1855), 194. See Ann Bermingham, *Landscape and Ideology: The English Rustic Tradition 1740–1860* (Berkeley: University of California Press, 1986), chap. 4, "Middle Grounds and Middle Ways: The Victorian Suburban Experience of Landscape," 157–93, for a close examination of analogous phenomena occurring in England. According to Bermingham, the Victorian suburb was in its purest form "an abstraction of the rustic tradition, a utopian ideological construction that provided a refuge from the disappointing realities of both urban and rural life"; it was "a flight from both the old suffocating hierarchies of the country village and the new bureaucratic impersonality of the city"; and it reflected "the increasing tendency for Englishmen to separate their social lives into work and leisure and their social geography into workplace and home" (168). On suburbanization in America, see Kenneth T. Jackson, *Crabgrass Frontier: The Suburbanization of the United States* (New York: Oxford University Press, 1985); on the influence of Downing, see John Archer, "Country and City in the American Romantic Suburb," *Journal of the Society of Architectural Historians* 42 (May 1983): 142–65.

14. Harry Penciller [Henry Carmer Wetmore], *Rural Life in America; or, Summer and Winter in the Country*, 2d ed. (New York:

J. C. Derby, 1856), 13, 34, 102–3. Other country books included Susan Fenimore Cooper, *Rural Hours* (1850); Frederick William Shelton, *Up the River* (1853); Lewis Mansfield, *Up-Country Letters* (1852), and, with Samuel Hammond, *Country Margins and Rambles of a Journalist* (1855); Henry Ward Beecher, *Star Papers; or, Experiences of Art and Nature* (1855), and *Eyes and Ears* (1862); Donald Grant Mitchell, *My Farm of Edgewood: A Country Book* (1863). Foster discusses the country book phenomenon in *The Civilized Wilderness,* 99–118.

15. See Raymond Williams, *The Country and the City* (New York: Oxford University Press, 1975); Bermingham, *Landscape and Ideology;* and David H. Solkin, *Richard Wilson: The Landscape of Reaction,* exhibition catalogue (London: Tate Gallery, 1982), for discussions of the function of pastoral landscape and country-house iconography in English poetry and painting.

16. Charles Wyllis Elliott, "About Piazzas," *Galaxy* 1 (1866): 547–48, 550–51. The illustrator of the title vignette, signed only with the initial "B," may have been E. B. Bensell, who worked for various New York publishers in the 1860s and 1870s, sometimes specializing in initial letters and tailpieces, and occasionally signing only his last initial.

CHAPTER 12
THE HOMESTEAD

1. Harry Penciller [Henry Carmer Wetmore], *Rural Life in America; or, Summer and Winter in the Country,* 2d. ed. (New York: J. C. Derby, 1856), 213, 218; Samuel H. Hammond and Lewis W. Mansfield, *Country Margins and Rambles of a Journalist* (New York: J. C. Derby, 1855), 79, 162.

2. Asher B. Durand, "Letters on Landscape Painting," no. 4, *Crayon* 1 (February 14, 1855): 98.

3. Henry James, *Hawthorne* (London: Macmillan, 1879), 142, 144.

4. D. A. Wasson, "The Modern Type of Oppression," *North American Review* 119 (July–December 1874): 262, 284.

5. Augustus K. Gardner, *Our Children: Their Physical and Mental Development* (Hartford, Conn.: Belknap & Bliss, 1872), 203.

6. William G. McLoughlin, *The Meaning of Henry Ward Beecher: An Essay on the Shifting Values of Mid-Victorian America 1840–1870* (New York: Knopf, 1970), 63. Perry D. Westbrook, *The New En-*

gland Town in Fact and Fiction (East Brunswick, N.J.: Associated University Presses, 1982), 78–115, discusses the theological and political issues addressed by Beecher and Stowe in their novels; for the regionalist aspects of Stowe's work, see Jay Martin, *Harvests of Change: American Literature, 1865–1914* (Englewood Cliffs, N.J.: Prentice-Hall, 1967), 137–139. The references to "ante-railroad times" and "roaring dissipation" are from Harriet Beecher Stowe, *Oldtown Folks* (1869; rpt. Boston: Houghton Mifflin, 1884), 391.

7. James T. Fields to Whittier, April 2, 1866, cited in Thomas Franklin Currier, *A Bibliography of John Greenleaf Whittier* (Cambridge, Mass.: Harvard University Press, 1937), 98–99.

8. John Greenleaf Whittier, *Snow-Bound: A Winter Idyll,* in *The Poetical Works of John Greenleaf Whittier* (Boston: Houghton Mifflin, 1892), 209–14.

9. Whittredge was particularly attracted to the old colonial houses near Newport, Rhode Island. In the 1870s he made several studies of what was reputed to have been Bishop George Berkeley's house during the English philosopher's brief residence there (1729–31) and produced a painting, *A Home by the Sea-Side* (1872; Los Angeles County Museum of Art), similar in look and mood to the painting discussed here. For Whittredge's association with Newport, see Sadayoshi Omoto, "Berkeley and Whittredge at Newport," *Art Quarterly* 27 (1964): 43–56. On Whittredge, see Edward H. Dwight, *Worthington Whittredge (1820–1910): A Retrospective Exhibition of an American Artist,* exhibition catalogue (Utica, N.Y.: Munson-Williams-Proctor Institute, 1969), and Anthony F. Janson, "The Paintings of Worthington Whittredge" (Ph.D. diss., Harvard University, 1975).

10. William S. Talbot, *Jasper F. Cropsey, 1823–1900* (New York: Garland, 1977), 233, speculates that the melancholy content of *The Old Home* may have been related to financial reverses that had forced the sale of Cropsey's cherished country house "Aladdin," along with most of the contents of his studio.

11. A tally shows that Currier & Ives produced at least ten old-homestead or home-sweet-home prints from 1864 into the early 1870s: George Durrie, *The Old Homestead in Winter* (1864), and *Home for Thanksgiving* (1867); Frances Palmer, *The Old Oaken Bucket* (1864), *The Old Farm Gate* (1864), *Glimpse of the Homestead* (1865), and *My Cottage Home* (1866); plus *Pleasures of the Country—Sweet Home* (1869), *Home Sweet Home* (1869), *My Boyhood's Home* (1872), and *The Old Farm House* (1872). Other printmakers provided similar scenes: e.g., Stephen O. Duval and Thomas Hunter's chrom-

olithograph *Home Sweet Home* (1871; Library of Congress), a pastoral landscape with a venerable homestead; and the lithograph after Jerome Thompson's *The Old Oaken Bucket* (published in 1868 by A. D. Frye, Jr.; Library of Congress). On the theme of the *Old Oaken Bucket,* see Lee M. Edwards, "The Life and Career of Jerome Thompson," *American Art Journal* 14 (Autumn 1982): 19–25, which discusses in historical and social context Thompson's two painted versions (1860 and 1867) and the chromolithograph after the 1867 painting.

12. Frederic A. Conningham, *Currier & Ives Prints: An Illustrated Checklist* (New York: Crown, 1949), 12.

13. John Howard Payne, "Home Sweet Home," in Gabriel Harrison, *John Howard Payne: Dramatist, Poet, Actor . . . His Life and Writings,* rev. ed. (Philadelphia: Lippincott, 1885), 29.

14. Ernest Ingersoll, "Around the Peconics," *Harper's New Monthly Magazine* 57 (October 1878), 715–30. The 1870s saw an increase in books and magazine articles written about American homes and their individual or historical associations. In addition to William Cullen Bryant, ed., *Picturesque America; or, The Land We Live In* (New York: Appleton, 1872–74), Martha J. Lamb's *The Homes of America* (New York, 1879) reflected these new interests. The subject of the historic "house essay," which helped to foster the idea of house as shrine, is considered in Jan Cohn, *The Palace or the Poorhouse: The American House as Cultural Symbol* (East Lansing: Michigan State University Press, 1979), 193–212.

15. The most complete study of the Colonial Revival in American architecture is William B. Rhoads, *The Colonial Revival* (New York: Garland, 1977). On fashions in collecting, see Elizabeth Stillinger, *The Antiquers* (New York: Knopf, 1980). See also Celia Betsky, "Inside the Past: The Interior and the Colonial Revival in American Art and Literature, 1860–1914," in Alan Axelrod, ed., *The Colonial Revival in America* (New York: Norton for Henry Francis du Pont Winterthur Museum, Winterthur, Delaware, 1985), 241–77. David Lowenthal, *The Past Is a Foreign Country* (Cambridge: Cambridge University Press, 1985), is a fascinating and wide-ranging essay on the meanings of the past and our cult of preservation.

16. O. B. Bunce, "Scenes in Eastern Long Island," in Bryant, *Picturesque America,* 1:256. Harry Fenn, born in England, came to America at the age of eighteen; he became one of the leading American illustrators of the later nineteenth century, specializing in landscape scenes.

17. "The Bryant Homestead," *Appleton's Journal* 9 (February 8, 1873): 193–94; Hamlin Garland, "Real Conversations IV: A Dialogue between James Whitcomb Riley and Hamlin Garland," *McClure's Magazine* 2 (1893–94): 219.

18. Samuel T. Pickard, *Whittier-Land: A Handbook of North Essex* (Boston: Houghton Mifflin, 1904), esp. 14–39. The term "fireside poets" originated as a marketing gimmick devised by their publisher; see Larzer Ziff, *Literary Democracy: The Declaration of Cultural Independence in America* (New York: Viking Press, 1981), 51. The Whittier homestead had already been canonized visually as early as 1871, when Boston chromolithograph publisher Louis Prang issued *The Birthplace of Whittier,* after a design by the English-born landscape painter Thomas Hill.

19. Stowe, *Oldtown Folks,* 61–84.

20. M. E. W. Sherwood, *The Amenities of Home* (New York: Appleton, 1881), 120.

21. *Dutchess County and Poughkeepsie Sanitary Fair* (Poughkeepsie, N.Y., 1864), 21–22; J. S. Ingram, *The Centennial Exposition* (Philadelphia: Hubbard Brothers, 1876), 706. An excellent source of information on the colonial kitchen phenomenon in the 1860s and 1870s is Rodris Roth, "The New England, or 'Old Tyme' Kitchen Exhibit at Nineteenth-Century Fairs," in Axelrod, *The Colonial Revival in America,* 159–83.

22. Ima Honacker Herron, *The Small Town in American Drama* (Dallas, Tex.: Southern Methodist University Press, 1969), 78.

23. Lizzie W. Champney, "The Summer Haunts of American Artists," *Century Illustrated Magazine* 30 (September 1885): 854.

24. A year earlier Lambdin had painted *The Consecration, 1861* (1865; Indianapolis Museum of Art), in which a handsome officer—very much resembling the one in *Winter Quarters*—looks on as a lovely young woman (sweetheart? sister?) bestows a sacramental kiss upon the sword that he will soon carry into battle. Assuming that the two paintings are a loosely jointed pair, it is safe to surmise that the officer's home thoughts may include dreams of love. Lambdin exhibited at the Pennsylvania Academy of Fine Arts and the National Academy of Design. In addition to creating genre scenes, he was a successful portrait and still-life painter.

25. Wallace Bruce, *Old Homestead Poems* (New York: Harper, 1888). Alfred Fredericks was a New York painter and illustrator who did both comic sketches for magazines and more serious subjects for books. There were European precedents for his hearth symbolism, notably Célestin Nanteuil's *Souvenir* (1855; location

unknown), depicting a melancholy old man who stares into the fire of his cottage hearth while the billowing smoke forms visions of past love, hopes, and glory.

26. On Hicks, see David Tatham, "Thomas Hicks at Trenton Falls," *American Art Journal* 15 (Autumn 1983): 4–20, which surveys rustic hearth imagery in post–Civil War American painting (13–16). Tatham also notes a tradition among descendants of Edward Hicks (Thomas's second cousin) that "the fireplace implements and other furnishings" in *No Place like Home* are from a Hicks family kitchen in Newtown, Pennsylvania (20 n.30). Very similar to *No Place like Home* in content is Eastman Johnson's *Reading the Bible* (1879; Nelson-Atkins Museum, Kansas City, Missouri), which depicts a devout old couple sitting by the hearth in a simple Nantucket cottage. It would be possible to create an impressive roster of contemporary works bearing on this theme: e.g., the quaint rustic couple by the fireside in John George Brown's *Old Memories* (n.d., Sotheby's, Inc., N.Y., sale May 28, 1987); J. W. Ehninger's illustration for the 1870 edition of Whittier's *Ballads of New England,* depicting an old-fashioned couple before a huge, old hearth; E. W. Perry's *Old Cronies* (1876; National Academy of Design, New York), two old men chatting and smoking together in a rustic chimney corner. Eventually the subject entered the realm of photography, notably in the work of Wallace Nutting, Congregational minister turned preservationist, whose commercially successful costume-genre photographs include a number of ancestral hearth-side scenes; see Joyce P. Barendsen, "Wallace Nutting, an American Tastemaker: The Pictures and Beyond," *Winterthur Portfolio* 18 (Summer/Autumn 1983): 187–212.

27. "The National Academy of Design," *Art Journal,* n.s. 2 (1876): 158; "The Arts: The Academy Exhibition," *Appleton's Journal* 15 (April 22, 1876): 539. Other practitioners of historical genre were Edwin Austin Abbey, George Henry Boughton, and Francis David Millet, all cosmopolitans, all full- or part-time expatriates living chiefly in England. Their themes were often as much British as American, although Boughton's fame in his native land arose from his depictions of Puritan maidens. Abbey, an enormously successful and influential illustrator-painter, ranged in his selection of subject matter from the Middle Ages to eighteenth-century England, and Millet also essayed classical subjects in the partly decorative and partly naturalistic English neoclassical style of the later nineteenth century. Although they were important producers of period pieces, the variety of their themes took them upon many tangents of little relevance here. For examples of their work, see the respective entries in *The Quest for Unity: American Art between World's Fairs, 1876–1893,* exhibition catalogue (Detroit, Mich.: Detroit Institute of Arts, 1983).

28. "Thanksgiving Day," *Harper's Weekly Magazine* 17 (December 6, 1873): 1084. See Christopher Kent Wilson, "Winslow Homer's *Thangsgiving Day—Hanging up the Musket,*" *American Art Journal* 18 (1986): 77–83, for an analysis of the Thanksgiving subject as it pertained to the conclusion of peace and the soldiers' final return home.

29. Frederick A. Chapman, a painter of portraits, landscapes, and historical scenes, was also a stained-glass designer. He was known especially for a series of paintings depicting events of the Civil War.

30. Charles A. Deshler, "A Glimpse of Seventy-Six," *Harper's New Monthly Magazine* 49 (July 1874): 230.

31. Paul Boyer, *Urban Masses and Moral Order in America, 1820–1920* (Cambridge, Mass.: Harvard University Press, 1978), 67.

32. "The Decay of New England," *Nation* 8 (May 27, 1869): 411; William Dean Howells, *Suburban Sketches,* rev. ed. (1872; rpt. Boston: Houghton Mifflin, 1888), 62–70; Thomas Bailey Aldrich, "An Old Town by the Sea," *Harper's New Monthly Magazine* 49 (October 1874): 642–45.

33. The classic study of nativism is John Higham, *Strangers in the Land: Patterns of American Nativism, 1860–1925* (New Brunswick, N.J.: Rutgers University Press, 1955), indispensable for background and detail of late nineteenth-century attitudes. Other standard works on immigration are M. L. Hansen, *The Immigrant in American History,* ed. Arthur M. Schlesinger (1940; rpt. Cambridge, Mass.: Harvard University Press, 1948); and Oscar Handlin, *The Uprooted: The Epic Story of the Great Migrations That Made the American People* (Boston: Little, Brown, 1951). An important recent study is John Bodnar, *The Transplanted: A History of Immigrants in America* (Bloomington: Indiana University Press, 1985).

34. *National Republican,* July 28, 1877, cited in Lally Weymouth, *America in 1876: The Way We Were* (New York: Vintage Books, 1976), 206; Helen Campbell, "The Tenement-House Question," in *The Problem of the Poor: A Record of Quiet Work in Unquiet Places* (New York: Fords, Howard, & Hulbert, 1882), 113.

35. Charles Loring Brace, *The Dangerous Classes of New York and Twenty Years' Work among Them* (1872), 3d ed. (New York: Wynkop & Hallenbeck, 1880), esp. 29–56.

36. W. H. Tolman, "Half a Century of Improved Housing Effort, by the New York Association for Improving the Condition of the Poor," *Yale Review* 5 (1896–97): 301; editorial, *American Architect and Building News*, July 16, 1892, p. 33.

37. Gardner, *Our Children*, 203.

38. Higham, *Strangers in the Land*, 10, 32. The connections between Anglo-Saxon nationalism and period architecture are explored in Rhoads, *The Colonial Revival*, chap. 26. See also William B. Rhoads, "The Colonial Revival and the Americanization of Immigrants," in Axelrod, *The Colonial Revival in America*, 341–61. Certain aspects of the idea are also considered in Cohn, *The Palace or the Poorhouse*.

39. J. F. W. W[are], "The New England Home," *Monthly Religious Magazine* 26 (1861): 431, 356; Christopher Crowfield [Harriet Beecher Stowe], "House and Home Papers," *Atlantic Monthly* 13 (1864): 356. The significance of religious ideology and its symbolism in the nineteenth-century home and hearth (both Protestant and Catholic) is the subject of Colleen McDannell, *The Christian Home in Victorian America* (Bloomington: Indiana University Press, 1986).

40. Josiah Strong, *Our Country* (1886), ed. Jurgen Herbst, 2d ed. (1891; rpt. Cambridge, Mass.: Belknap Press of Harvard University Press, 1963), 205. Also see Dexter Arnoll Hawkins, *The Anglo-Saxon Race: Its History, Character, and Destiny* (New York: Nelson & Phillips, 1875); and John Fiske, "Manifest Destiny," *Harper's New Monthly Magazine* 70 (March 1885): 578–90.

C H A P T E R   1 3
B A R E F O O T   B O Y S   A N D   O T H E R
C O U N T R Y   C H I L D R E N

1. W. H. Simmons, "A Cry and a Prayer: Against the Imprisonment of Small Children," *Knickerbocker Magazine* 11 (January 1838): 50.

2. For the general background on American childhood, I am indebted to Bernard Wishy, *The Child and the Republic: The Dawn of Modern Child Nurture* (Philadelphia: University of Pennsylvania Press, 1968); Oscar and Mary F. Handlin, *Facing Life: Youth and the Family in American History* (Boston: Little, Brown, 1971); and Bert Roller, *Children in American Poetry, 1610–1900*, Contribution to Education, no. 72 (Nashville, Tenn.: George Peabody College for Teachers, 1930). Excellent essays on the material culture of American childhood and its meanings are collected in *A Century of Childhood, 1820–1920*, exhibition catalogue (Rochester, N.Y.: The Margaret Woodbury Strong Museum, 1984).

3. Joseph F. Kett, "Growing Up in Rural New England, 1800–50," in Tamara Hareven, ed., *Anonymous Americans: Explorations in Nineteenth-Century Social History* (Englewood Cliffs, N.J.: Prentice-Hall, 1971), esp. 2–10.

4. Cited in Elizabeth Speare, *Child Life in New England, 1790–1840* (Sturbridge, Mass.: Old Sturbridge Village, 1961), 16.

5. Robert Thomas, "Farmer's Calendar," *Farmer's Almanac* (Boston, 1818, 1819, 1835).

6. Charles Dudley Warner, *Being a Boy* (1877; rpt. Boston: Houghton Mifflin, 1897), 134–35. It seems clear that Mount was very much aware of English prototypes; in addition to evoking some of George Morland's works, his playing or misbehaving children recall those of William Mulready, a successful and popular genre painter who specialized in scenes of child life, often with a moral attached; e.g., *The Fight Interrupted* (1816; Victoria and Albert Museum, London), depicted scrapping schoolboys being forcibly separated, with an old man restraining one and several fingers pointing blame. Though the treatment was more sophisticated, Mulready's work shares strong points with Mount's early *Schoolboys Quarreling* (1830; The Museums at Stony Brook), in which a big boy champions a young one harassed by a bully. For a fine modern study of Mulready, see Kathryn Moore Heleniak, *William Mulready* (New Haven, Conn.: Yale University Press, 1980). The moralism and symbolism of children in Dutch genre painting is examined in Christopher Brown, *Images of a Golden Past: Dutch Genre Painting of the Seventeenth Century* (New York: Abbeville Press, 1984); and Mary Frances Durantini, *The Child in Seventeenth-Century Dutch Painting* (Ann Arbor, Mich.: UMI Research Press, 1983). Nonconformist David Gilmore Blythe, Mount's contemporary, produced bleakly unsentimental paintings of disturbing, vaguely sinister urban children; see Bruce Chambers, *The World of David Gilmore Blythe*, exhibition catalogue (Washington, D.C.: National Museum of American Art, 1982), 40–55. George H. Comegys painted several bad-boy subjects, such as *Boys Stealing Watermelons* (1839; private collection), in which somewhat repellent boys are viewed without Mount's humor.

7. The exception in Mount's *oeuvre* is *Eel Spearing at Setauket* (1845; New York State Historical Association, Cooperstown), which,

when exhibited at the National Academy in 1846, bore the title *Recollections of Early Days—"Fishing along Shore."* It was commissioned by George W. Strong and shows the Strong family estate in the background. The subject obviously had personal meaning for Mount's patron; perhaps it also embodied some of Mount's own memories. In a letter to Charles Lanman, November 17, 1847, he told of his first lessons in spearing flatfish along the shore, his mentor an old black man named Hector (cited in Alfred Frankenstein, *William Sidney Mount* [New York: Abrams, 1975], 120–22).

8. "Rabbit Catching," in *The Gift: A Christmas and New Year's Present* (Philadelphia: Carey & Hart, 1845), 85; "The Fisher-Boy," in Henry William Herbert, ed., *The Magnolia* (New York: Bancroft & Holley, 1837), 346. The title of the engraving after Chapman was *The Sunfish.* Chapman, a well-known and successful portrait and history painter, painted *The Baptism of Pocahontas* for the rotunda of the U.S. Capitol and was a founder of the Century Club in New York.

9. Charles Lanman, "The Dying Year," in *Essays for Summer Hours*, 2d ed. (Boston: Hilliard, Gray, 1842), 242. On the incidence of poems of nostalgia in the early decades of the century, see Roller, *Children in American Poetry*, esp. 51–52. Herbert Ross Brown, *The Sentimental Novel in America, 1789–1860* (Durham, N.C.: Duke University Press, 1940), makes numerous references to the subject of sentimental nostalgia for rural youth.

10. Webster painted so many childhood subjects that he was known as "Do-the-Boys" Webster. The Cranbrook Colony also included John Callcott Horsley, Frederick Daniel Hardy, Augustus Edwin Mulready, and George Bernard O'Neill. See Andrew Greg, *The Cranbrook Colony*, exhibition catalogue (Wolverhampton, Eng.: Central Art Gallery, 1977).

11. Currier & Ives published several such childhood scenes during the period; they include *Childhood's Happy Days* of 1863, and another *Season of Joy*, 1872.

12. William Allen White, *The Court of Boyville* (New York: Doubleday & McClure, 1899), xviii; Anne Trensky, "The Bad Boy in Nineteenth-Century American Fiction," *Georgia Review* 27 (Winter 1973): 516.

13. Mark Twain [Samuel Clemens], *The Adventures of Tom Sawyer*, vol. 4 of *The Works of Mark Twain*, ed. John C. Gerber, Paul Baender, and Terry Firkins (Berkeley: University of California Press for Iowa Center for Textual Studies, 1980), 33; William Dean Howells, unsigned review of *Tom Sawyer, Atlantic Monthly* 37 (May 1876): 621; T. S. Perry, review of *Huckleberry Finn, Century Magazine*, n.s. 8 (May 1885): 171–72. It should be noted that the Howells review, sincere though it undoubtedly was, had been planned as part of a strategy to generate interest in the forthcoming American edition of *Tom Sawyer*. For a discussion of contemporary criticism, see the editor's introduction to the Iowa *Tom Sawyer* cited above (27–29). For much essential information on this genre, I am indebted to Trensky's invaluable study "The Bad Boy," 503–17, which discusses fifteen representative examples published during the last thirty years (approximately) of the nineteenth century. Also useful is Alice M. Jordan's survey of late nineteenth-century children's literature, *From Rollo to Tom Sawyer* (Boston: Horn Books, 1948).

14. Warner, preface to the 1897 illustrated edition of *Being a Boy*, viii–x.

15. George Miller Beard, *American Nervousness: Its Causes and Consequences* (New York: Putnam, 1881), 98–116.

16. John Greenleaf Whittier, "The Barefoot Boy," in *The Poetical Works of John Greenleaf Whittier* (Boston: Houghton Mifflin, 1892), 143–44; Warner, *Being a Boy*, 115.

17. White, *The Court of Boyville*, 352–53.

18. Warner, *Being a Boy*, 150; Granville Stanley Hall, *Adolescence* (1905; rpt. New York: Arno Press, 1969), 1:vii–x; Beard, *American Nervousness*, 120. Child rearing and science in the nineteenth century are examined in Harvey Green, "Scientific Thought and the Nature of Children in America, 1820–1920," in *A Century of Childhood*, 121–37.

19. Louisa May Alcott, *Little Women; or, Meg, Jo, Beth, and Amy* (1868), centennial ed. (Boston: Little, Brown, 1968), 139. Wishy, *The Child and the Republic*, 92, discusses the theme of fear of adulthood, which emerged in the children's literature of the period.

20. For Homer's career as an illustrator, see Mavis P. Kelsey, *Winslow Homer Graphics*, exhibition catalogue (Houston, Tex.: Museum of Fine Arts, 1977); Philip C. Beam, *Winslow Homer's Magazine Engravings* (New York: Harper & Row, 1979); David Tatham, "Winslow Homer and the New England Poets," *Proceedings of the American Antiquarian Society* 89, pt. 2 (October 1979): 241–60. A relatively recent though brief assessment of Brown's life and work is Philip N. Grime, *John George Brown, 1831–1913: A Reappraisal*, exhibition catalogue (Burlington, Vt.: The Robert Hull Fleming Museum, 1975).

21. Warner, *Being a Boy*, 76. For the history of the chromolith-

ograph of Johnson's *Barefoot Boy,* see Peter C. Marzio, *The Demo-cratic Art: Pictures for a Nineteenth-Century America* (Boston: David R. Godine in association with the Amon Carter Museum of Western Art, Fort Worth, Texas, 1979).

22. George W. Sheldon, "American Painters—Winslow Homer and F. A. Bridgman," *Art Journal,* n.s. 4 (August 1878): 225.

23. Related works are Homer's unfinished oil *The Nooning* (c. 1872; Wadsworth Atheneum, Hartford, Connecticut), in the same spirit as *Boys in a Pasture* even though a farmhouse stands beyond the straw-hatted lad sprawled under the trees; and a variation on *The Nooning* in *Harper's Weekly Magazine* 17 (August 16, 1873), with two more boys, a dog, a line of washing, and another house added. Despite the complications introduced, the feeling holds of the boys' relaxation and simple closeness to natural things. Marzio, *The Democratic Art,* 124, notes that Johnson's *Barefoot Boy* proved so popular as a chromolithograph that other lithographers copied the genre. Clifton Johnson was a writer-photographer in Springfield, Massachusetts, whose chief subjects were the sights and people of rural New England. See William F. Robinson, *A Certain Slant of Light: The First Hundred Years of New England Photography* (Boston: New York Graphic Society, 1980), 129, 227.

24. Warner, *Being a Boy,* 49; "The Arts: The Academy Exhibition," *Appleton's Journal* 15 (April 22, 1876): 539. Other examples of contemporary interest in the theme of uninhibited childhood play are Eastman Johnson's *Old Stage Coach* (1871; Layton Art Collection, Milwaukee, Wisconsin, Art Museum), boys and girls playing and miming energetically around the shell of the abandoned coach; and J. G. Brown, *Boys Will Be Boys* (1873; Wood Art Gallery, Montpelier, Vermont), a group of merry young adventurers on a boat in the middle of a woodland pool.

25. Warner, *Being a Boy,* 56.

26. *Harper's Weekly Magazine* 18 (November 28, 1874): 972. Other children's gathering scenes in illustration include Homer's *Strawberry Bed* in *Our Young Folks* 4 (July 1868); Julian Scott's *Picking Raspberries,* in *Harper's Weekly* 17 (July 26, 1873); Edwin Austin Abbey's *Anticipation—Return from a Melon Scout,* and C. S. Reinhart's *Picking Huckleberries,* both in *Harper's Weekly* 21 (August 25 and September 1, 1877).

27. Lucy Larcom, "Note" and "Berrying Song," in *Childhood Songs* (1874), facsimile ed. (Great Neck, N.Y.: Granger, 1978), vii, 98.

28. The poems Homer illustrated in *Our Young Folks* were Lucy Larcom's "Swinging on a Birch Tree," in 3 (1867); and three by

Trowbridge in 4 (1868): "Watching the Crows," "Strawberries," and "Green Apples."

29. "About Barns," *Putnam's Magazine* 5 (1855), 630.

30. Larcom, *Childhood Songs,* 138–41.

31. Patricia Hills illustrates and discusses Johnson's barn scenes briefly in *Eastman Johnson,* exhibition catalogue (New York: Clarkson N. Potter in association with Whitney Museum of American Art, 1972), 86. Similar barn subjects include George Cochran Lambdin's *Feeding Time* (1876; private collection), a little boy and girl feeding a calf; and Thomas Waterman Wood's *Jump* (1883; Wood Art Gallery, Montpelier, Vermont), two children standing at the window of the haymow, ready to hop into the arms of the old farmer in the wagon below.

32. Roller, *Children in American Poetry,* 103.

33. H. G. Wells, *The Future in America: A Search after Realities* (New York: Harper, 1906), 109–15. The statistics on New York are from Handlin and Handlin, *Facing Life,* 168–69. Paul Boyer, *Urban Masses and Moral Order in America, 1820–1920* (Cambridge, Mass.: Harvard University Press, 1978), offers a valuable survey and discussion of urban problems and reform efforts in the period, including the issue of slum children.

34. "The Metropolitan Police," *Harper's Weekly Magazine* 9 (September 9, 1865): 570; Charles Loring Brace, *The Dangerous Classes of New York and Twenty Years' Work among Them* (1872), 3d ed. (New York: Wynkoop & Hallenbeck, 1880), 97.

35. Brace, *The Dangerous Classes,* 28, 30, 94.

36. "A City Tenement-House," *Harper's Weekly Magazine* 17 (September 13, 1873): 796.

37. "The Hearthstone of the Poor," *Harper's Weekly Magazine* 20 (February 12, 1876): 131. Eytinge was a prolific artist who illustrated works of Bret Harte and Charles Dickens, among many others.

38. Jacob Riis's works include *How the Other Half Lives: Studies among the Tenements of New York* (1890), *Children of the Poor* (1892), and *Children of the Tenements* (1903). Peter B. Hales, *Silver Cities: The Photography of American Urbanization, 1839–1915* (Philadelphia: Temple University Press, 1984), 161–276, discusses Riis, his ideals and techniques, and his impact on reform photography. Hales argues that while Riis's photographs, invoking the myth of the camera's verisimilitude, look artless and unmediated, their subjects were in fact selected and manipulated in order to endow the world of the slums with maximum horror and shock value. Others, how-

ever, would argue that Riis was, as he himself maintained, working as an intuitive, untutored amateur.

39. Brace, *The Dangerous Classes*, 225. Boyer, *Urban Masses and Moral Order*, 99, maintains that Brace himself, a more innovative thinker than many contemporaries, did not entertain romantic notions about rural virtue but sought through his migration program to give the freewheeling autonomy he admired in city children a "wider and more secure social arena in which to operate." All the same, it is difficult to conceive of Brace's program as completely independent of the still-powerful persuasions of agrarian idealism; certainly, in *The Dangerous Classes* (though possibly for propagandistic reasons) his rhetoric makes much of the American farmers' exceptional sense, honesty, goodness, and generosity. Henry Nash Smith, "The Garden as Safety Valve," in *Virgin Land: The American West as Symbol and Myth* (1950; rpt. Cambridge, Mass.: Harvard University Press, 1981), chap. 20, provides a useful summary of the myth of the frontier, its persistence, and its flaws.

40. William Cole, "Country Week," *New England Magazine* 14 (July 1896): 528. I have relied on Peter J. Schmitt, *Back to Nature: The Arcadian Myth in Urban America* (New York: Oxford University Press, 1969), 96–99, for facts on the Fresh Air charities of the late nineteenth century. The country weeks, Schmitt writes, played a significant role in the evolution of summer camps, a staple in American vacation culture ever since.

41. Will Carleton, "Let the Cloth be White," in *City Ballads* (New York: Harper, 1885), 172–75.

42. G. Stanley Hall, "The Contents of Children's Minds on Entering School," *Pedagogical Seminary* 1 (1891): 155, 146.

43. William A. Bullough, " 'It Is Better to Be a Country Boy': The Lure of the Country in Urban Education in the Gilded Age," *Historian* 35 (February 1973): 189. Bullough's is an excellent study; also useful is "Arcadia Comes to School," chap. 6 in Schmitt, *Back to Nature*, 77–85.

44. Charles DeGarmo, "Concentration of Studies as a Means of Developing Character," *National Education Association Journal of Addresses and Proceedings*, 1896, pp. 311–12, quoted in Bullough, "Better to Be a Country Boy," 193.

45. Alan Trachtenberg discusses the theory of Central Park as civilizer of the poor and the alien in *The Incorporation of America: Culture and Society in the Gilded Age* (New York: Hill & Wang, 1982), 107–12.

Index

The page numbers in italic type refer to illustrations.

Abolitionists, views on South of, 84
Agrarian ideal, negative opinions of, 191–93
Agrarianism: defined, 8; and land ownership, 5. *See also* Farmers; Farms; Land ownership; Rural life
Agricultural capitalism: and bonanza farms, 57; and Burr Oak Farm, 56
Agricultural commerce: absence of, in art, 37; spread of, 53
Agricultural depressions, and farmers, 52, 58–59
Agricultural machinery: absence of, in art, 37–39, 55; and agricultural capitalism, 54–57; development and introduction of, 53–54; enthusiasm for, 54–55; in the Midwest, 53, 55; in the Northeast, 59–60
Alcott, Louisa May, *Little Women,* 304
Aldrich, Thomas Bailey: on barns as clubhouses, 308; on Irish, 271; *Story of a Bad Boy,* 301, 308
Alger, Horatio, *Ragged Dick,* 310
Allen, Lewis, on farmhouse and republican values, 80, 99
American Art-Union, 77–78, 127, 348 n.2

Anglo-Saxon Doctrine, resurgence of, 273–74
Anti-Rent conflicts, 85; and radicalism, 52–53
Anti-urbanism, 237–41, 360 n.1; Jefferson's, 5
Apostle of Prosperity (lithograph), 109, *121*
Appleton's Journal, old houses series, 265
Arcadia, middle-class ideal of, 241–45
Art, Dutch, American painting and, 122–23
Art, English, American painting and, 123–24
Art colonies, American, in Europe, 222–23

Bad Boy stories, 301–2
Barbizon painting, 215, 221–22, 226
Barefoot state, symbolism of, 303, 306
Barlow, Joel, "The Hasty-Pudding," 34
Barns, in art, types of, 18; as playhouses, 307–8
Barrell, John, on Wilkie, 130
Bartlett, John Russell, *Glossary,* 160

Bastien-Lepage, Jules, 220; and D. R. Knight, 223
Beard, George M.: on children as savages, 304; on stresses of civilization, 302–3
Beard style, symbolism of, 199–202
Beecher, Henry Ward: on agricultural machines, 55; and Civil War harvest metaphor, 88; on haying, 33; *Norwood,* 88, 260–61, 263; on the South, 85
Benjamin, Samuel Green Wheeler, on E. Johnson, 220–21
Bensell, E. B. [?], "About Piazzas" vignette, 244–45, 257
Beverly Hillbillies (television series), 335
Blythe, David Gilmore, 365 n.6
Bonanza farms, 56–57
Brace, Charles Loring: *The Dangerous Classes of New York,* 272, 309; on slum children as social threat, 309; theory of environmental determinism and, 309–10
Breton, Jules, 220; class stratification in work of, 83; *works mentioned: The Gleaners,* 83, 92; *The Potato Harvest,* 224; *Song of the Lark,* 223

Breughel, Pieter, 122

British School, *Dixton Harvesters,* 83, *91*

Brouwer, Adriaen, 122

Brown, John George, 214; urban children, images of, 310; *works mentioned: The Berry Boy,* 304–5, *317; Boys Will Be Boys,* 367 n.24; *Old Memories,* 364 n.26

Bruce, Wallace, "The Old Homestead," 268

Bryan, William Jennings, presidential campaign of, 200–201

Bryant, William Cullen: homestead, purchase of, 265; and wilderness, 5; *works mentioned: Picturesque America,* 264; "The Tempest," 13

The Bryant Homestead (wood engraving), 265, *284*

Buchanan, James, 86

Buckingham, James Silk, on farmers, 99, 101

Bullough, William, 313

Bunn, Alfred, on farmers, 52

Burr Oak Farm, Illinois, 56

Burroughs, John, on haying, 32

Bushnell, Horace, 88

Campbell, Helen, on immigrants as social threat, 272

Carleton, Will, "Let the Cloth Be White," 312

Case, Jerome, 53

Chapman, Frederick A., *Thanksgiving at a New England Farmhouse,* 270, *295*

Chapman, John Gadsby, nostalgia in childhood scenes of, 299

Charles Mathews as "Jonathan W. Doubikins" (lithograph), 170, *178*

Child labor, statistics on, 309

Child rearing: romantic attitudes toward, 297–98; rural, 298–99

Childhood, postbellum, as Golden Age, 300–301, 302

Childhood, rural: ideology of, 308; as middle-class norm, 313; in popular illustrations,

306–7; and urban reform, 311–13. *See also* Country boys

Childhood literature, development of, 300

Childhood nostalgia, characterized, 299–300

Children: closeness to nature of, 302–3; in English and American art, 300, 365 n.6; as savages, 303–4

Children, slum: in art, 310; as social threat, 309–10

Children's Aid Society, 272, 309, 311

Children's play: in barns, 307–8; berry-gathering, 306–7

City: contrasted with country, 240–41; and disease metaphor, 239; and hell metaphor, 238

City Sketches (wood engraving), 239, *246*

Civil War: as economic conflict, 87; harvest metaphor in, 88; religious rhetoric of, 88

Civilization, stresses of, 302–3

Class, social, and culture, 7

Class stratification, rural: in America, 243, 245; in Europe, 83; in popular prints, 243–44. *See also* Villa, middle-class

Claude Lorraine, and pastoral landscape painting, 16–17

Claudian conventions. *See* Pastoral design

Clemens, Samuel [pseud. Mark Twain]: *Huckleberry Finn,* 302; *Tom Sawyer,* 302

Clonney, James Goodwyn: *Jonathan's Introduction to Good Society,* 356 n.12; *Mexican News,* 350 n.10

Cobblestone Farm (photograph), 60, *74*

Coffin, Thomas: on agricultural machinery, 59; on farm labor, 57

Cole, Thomas: and pastoral design, 15–16; warnings against materialism by, 81; and wilderness, 5; *works mentioned: Childhood,* 301, *315; The Course of Empire* cycle, 15–16, 81, 348 n.12; *The Pastoral State,* 15–16, *24; The Voyage of Life* cycle, 301

Colonial Revival, 264, 269

Conspicuous consumption, 79

Conway, M. D., on Millet, 224

Cooke, Rose Terry, 194; "Some Account of Thomas Tucker," 194

Coolidge, C. M., and Edwin Austin Abbey: "Hard Times"—Mortgaging the Old Homestead, 58–59, 73

Cooper, James Fenimore: *The American Democrat,* 171; on American manners, 171; conservatism of, 53; and wilderness, 5

Corn husking: in art and literature, 34–36; *Farmer's Almanac* on, 61

Corot, Camille, 222, 223

Cosmopolitanism, 190, 219, 222, 223

Costume: of archaic bumpkin, 197, 199, 200; as symbol of class, 169–71, 172–73, 174–75, 241, 355 n.7

Costume, Yankee. *See* Yankee costume

Country books, 243–44

Country boys, in art and literature, 304–6. *See also* Childhood, rural

Country gentleman, as middle-class ideal, 243

Country Sketches: Farmer Cronk and Farmer Bonk (wood engraving), 174–75, *185*

Country Weeks. See Fresh Air Funds

Couture, Thomas, 220, 221

Cowper, William, 4

Cranbrook Colony (England), 300

Crèvecoeur, Hector St. John de: and American art history, 6; on farmyards, 19; *Letters from an American Farmer,* 4; pastoral ideals of, 4, 105; pastoral ideals of, and reality, 50

Cropsey, Jasper Francis, 217; and pastoral design, 16–17; *works mentioned: American Harvesting,* 11, 15, 16, 17, 33, 20; *The Millennial Age,* 86; *The Old Home,* 262–63; *The Spirit of Peace,* 86

Currier, Nathaniel, *Washington at Mount Vernon, 1787,* 107

Currier & Ives, 217; history of, 7–8; home subjects, 362 n.11; home subjects, popularity of, 253; *works mentioned: American*

Homestead set, 263; *Childhood, "The Season of Joy,"* 300–301, *314*; *Childhood's Happy Days,* 366 n.11; *Farmer Garfield Cutting a Swath to the White House,* 108–9, 120; *The Four Seasons of Life* set, 300, 301; *Home Sweet Home,* 263–64, 280; *Maple Sugaring: Early Spring in the North Woods,* 36; *My Boyhood's Home,* 263, 279; *The Old Barn Floor,* 135; *Peace and Plenty,* 88, 263, 95; *Season of Joy,* 366 n.11; *Summer in the Highlands,* 244, 256; *Winter,* 263, 278. See also Durrie, George Henry; Maurer, Louis; Palmer, Frances; Tait, Arthur Fitzwilliam

Dakota Territory (wood engraving), 56–57, *71*
Dance, on Long Island, 131, 134
Dance, The (lithograph), 133, *144*
Dance-halls (New York), as brothels, 239–40
Darwin, Charles, 304
Davis, Charles Augustus, 161; Jack Downing letters of, 151, 154
Davis, Rebecca Harding, on New England rural decline, 193
Davis, Theodore: *The Centennial—State Exhibits in Agricultural Hall,* 200, 209; *Farming in the Great West—The "Burr Oak" Farm, Illinois,* 56, 70
Deere, John, 53
DeGarmo, Charles, on rural values, 313
Deliverance (motion picture), 335
Diaz, Narcisse, 215
Downing, Andrew Jackson: on farmhouse and republican values, 80, 99; on middle-class villa, 241–42, 361 n.12; *works mentioned: The Architecture of Country Houses,* 241; *Cottage Residences,* 241
Downing, Major Jack, 151–52, 196; as critic of Jacksonian democracy, 152, 353 n.9; in theater, 151
Draft riots (New York), 238, 309

Dress. See Costume
Durand, Asher B.: and pastoral design, 16, 17; pastoral scenes of, as sermons, 81; *works mentioned: The Beeches,* 15; *Dance of the Haymakers,* 135; *Farmyard on the Hudson,* 344 n.15; *Haying,* 80–81, 90; *The Hudson River Looking toward the Catskills,* 16, 25; *Landscape Composition, Forenoon,* 344 n.15; *Landscape with Children,* 344 n.15; *Letters on Landscape Painting,* 78; *An Old Man's Reminiscences,* 259; *The Solitary Oak,* 344 n.15; *Sunday Morning,* 344 n.15; *Thanatopsis,* 81
Durrie, George Henry: and study of farmhouses, 18; *works mentioned: Farmyard in Winter, Selling Corn,* 37; *Home to Thanksgiving,* 269–70, 294; *Winter in the Country: A Cold Morning,* 17, 27
Dwight, Timothy, *Greenfield Hill,* 13

Earlom, Richard. See Wheatley, Francis
Economic growth, and social change, 78–79
Edmonds, Francis William, 171–72, 241; *works mentioned: The City and the Country Beaux,* 171–72, 179; *The Speculator,* 58; *Taking the Census,* 174, *184*
Ehninger, John Whetten, 220; Tuckerman on, 220; *works mentioned: Bringing in the Hay,* 216–17, 344 n.6, *231*; *Gathering Pumpkins—An October Scene in New England,* 37, 220, 48; *October,* 37
Elliott, Charles Wyllis, "About Piazzas," 244–45
Enclosure (England), 78
Evans, George Henry, 106; and Anti-Renters, 53; and homestead measure, 85; and natural rights philosophy of land ownership, 85
Everett, Edward, on agrarian ideal, 12–13
Eytinge, Sol, *The Hearth-Stone of the Poor,* 310, 327

Farm women: in Europe and America, compared, 101–2, 224; in Homer, 217; in peasant paintings, 223
Farmer Larkin's Boarders (play), 197
Farmer Pays for All, The (lithograph), 104, *114*
Farmers: beard symbolism and, 199–200, 201–2; commercial ambitions of, 50–52, 53; literacy and political awareness of, 102–3; and peasants, compared, 101–2, 225; simplicity of, 99; and speculation, 52; status of, in decline, 192–93, 201–2, 226; in theater, postbellum, 197
Farmers' Alliances, 105, 200–201, 226
Farmer's Almanac, 171. See also Thomas, Robert
Farmer's Question, The—"Is Horace Greeley a Fool or a Knave?" (wood engraving), 106–7
Farmhouse: in art, 17–18; and republican values, 17–18, 80–81; as status symbol, 51
Farms: and Northern ideology, 83–87; as sermons against materialism, 80–82; unimproved, 60–61
Farmyards: in art and literature, 18; symbolism of, 19
Fenn, Harry: *Home of John Howard Payne,* 264, 282; *Interior of Payne's "Home Sweet Home,"* 264, 283
Fessenden, Thomas Green: *works mentioned:* "The Country Junket, or Rustic Revel," 132; "The Country Lovers," 150, 158–59; "Horace Surpassed; or, A Beautiful Description of a New-England Country-Dance," 132; *Original Poems,* 158; and Yankee poems, 131
Fireside poets, 265, 349 n.19
Fisher, Alvan, *Corn Husking Frolic,* 34, *41*
Fiske, John, and Anglo-Saxon doctrine, 274
Foster, George C., on city as hell, 238
Fox, Stanley, *Evading the Excise Law—Laying in Rum for Sunday,* 239, 247

Francis, John F., *Joseph Ritner, Governor of Pennsylvania*, 108, *119*

Frederic, Harold, *Seth's Brother's Wife*, 195

Fredericks, Alfred, *And Ashes Lie upon the Hearth*, 268, 289

Free Soil, as Free Labor slogan, 86

Freeman, Mary E. Wilkins, 194

Frenzeny, Paul, *The Rag-Pickers Disposing of Their Gatherings*, 239, 248

Frère, Edouard, 220; American praise of, 224

Fresh Air Funds, 311–12

Frost, Arthur Burdett: *A Book of Drawings*, 201–2; *The Game between the Squire and the Postmaster*, 201–2, 213; *The Sick Cow*, 201, 213

Fuller, George: and American Barbizon painting, 222; *works mentioned: The Afterglow*, 222; *Turkey Pasture in Kentucky*, 222, 233

Gainsborough, Thomas, 123

Garland, Hamlin: *Main-Traveled Roads*, 195; "Up the Coulee," 195–96

Gault, A., *Shelter for the Homeless—Night Scene in a New York Station-House*, 239, 249

George Handel Hill in Yankee Character (lithograph), 157, 170, *165*

Geremia, T. *See* Wheatley, Francis

Gift for the Grangers (lithograph), 104–5, *115*

Gillam, Alfred, *The Wily Farmer at His Old Tricks*, 200, *210*

Gi¹mor, Robert, Jr., 155

Gleason's Pictorial Magazine, city–country contrast stories in, 240–41

Godey's Ladies' Book: comic social contrast in, 172; city–country contrast stories in, 240

Goldsmith, Oliver, "The Deserted Village," 78

Goodrich, Lloyd, 217

Goodrich, Samuel, and ideal farm, 19

Goupil, Vibert, & Co., 127, 135

Grange (Patrons of Husbandry), 103–6, 201, 226, 245

Grant, Ulysses S., 106, 200

Greeley, Horace: beard style of, 200; caricatured, 108, 199–200; presidential campaign of, 106–7; as Yankee, 153

Hackett, James, 150; Yankee costume of, 169–70; on Yankees, 152

Hall, Grenville Stanley: on nature study, 312; recapitulation theory of, 304

Harper's Weekly Magazine: content of, 174; Republican bias of, 106–7

Harrison, William Henry, 87, 108

Harvests: of apples, 37; as metaphor in Civil War, 88; of pumpkins, 37; symbolism of, 87. *See also* Haying; Maple sugaring

Hawkins, Dexter Arnoll, and Anglo-Saxon doctrine, 274

Hawkins, Micah, *The Saw-Mill; or, A Yankee Trick*, 153, 157

Haying, in art and literature, 32–33

Haymarket Riot (Chicago), 272

Hearth: as altar, 269; in art, 267–70, 364 n.26; in Colonial costume genre, 268–69; symbolism of, 262, 266. *See also* Kitchens, rustic

Henry, Edward Lamson, 197; *works mentioned: Figures in an Interior*, 268–69, *291*; *Forty Winks*, 199, 207; *Uninvited Guests*, 199; *Watching for Crows*, 199

Herrick, Henry, *Life on the Farm*, 38, 56, *49*

Hicks, Thomas, *No Place Like Home*, 268, 290

Higham, John, on Anglo-Saxon hegemony, 273

Hill, George Handel, 149, 150; as Yankee whittler, 157

Hills, Patricia, 6, 342 n.6

Homer, Winslow, 214, 239, 245; and agrarian ideal, undercutting of, 217; and American farmer as peasant, in art of, 214–15, 217, 220, 225; and Barbizon painting, 358 nn.4, 5; and childhood literature, 307; criticism of, 218–20, 306; emotional distance of, 216; farm women in art of, 217; and Millet, 215–16; nostalgia of, 305; paintings, prices of, 223; and popular illustration, 214; selectivity of, 308; Yankee boys in art of, 305; *works mentioned: Answering the Horn*, 216, 230; *Boys in a Pasture*, 304, 305, *319*; *Boys on a Bough*, 305; *Chestnutting*, 306–7, *322*; *The Cotton Pickers*, 217; *The Course of True Love*, 218; *The Dance after the Husking*, 135, 148; *Gathering Berries*, 306–7, *323*; *Girl with a Pitchfork*, 215, 227; *Gloucester Farm*, 217, 232; *Haymaking*, 305; *The Husking Party Finding the Red Ears*, 34, 42; *Husking the Corn in New England*, 34; *The Last Load*, 215–16, 216–17, 229; *Milking Time*, 218; *The Nooning*, 367 n.23; *Prisoners from the Front*, 215; *Snap the Whip*, 306, 321; *The Straw Ride*, 61–62, 75

Homestead: ancestral, veneration of, 264–66; in art, 262–63; and nativism, 274; as shrine, 264; symbolism of, 262

Homestead Act: campaign for, 82; as deterrent to slavery, 85–86; and Republican Party, 86

Homestead (Pennsylvania) strike, 273

Hoppin, Augustus, "*You Want to See My Pa, I 'Spose?*", 175–76, *189*

Hovenden, Thomas, 197, 223; *The Old Version*, 198, 268, 204

How the New York Merchants Received Their Country Cousins Last Year; How They Received Them This Year (wood engraving), 175, *187*

How to Spend the Fourth (wood engraving), 175, 200, *188*

Howe, Edgar Watson, *The Story of a Country Town*, 195

Howe, Frederic C., *The City, the Hope of Democracy*, 191–92

Howells, William Dean: on Clemens' *Tom Sawyer*, 302; on Irish immigrants, 271; *The Coast of Bohemia*, 225

Howland, Alfred C., *Bargaining for a Calf*, 198–99, 206

Hudson, John B., *Haying at Lapham's Farm, Auburn, Maine*, 344 n.6

Hudson River School: as anachronism, 263; and pastoral landscape, 16

Hunt, William Morris, 222; criticism of, 221; and Millet, 221; *The Little Gleaner*, 221

Immigrants, as threat to social order, 271–73

Immigration, 270–71

Ingersoll, Ernest, on Long Island homesteads, 264

Inness, George, *Peace and Plenty*, 88, 93

Irwin, Wallace, "The Sick Cow," 201

Isham, Samuel, on unpicturesqueness of farmer, 225

Ives, James Merritt. *See* Palmer, Frances, with J. Cameron

Jackson, Andrew, 152

James, Henry: on antebellum innocence, 259–60; on Homer, 218–19; on E. Johnson, 219

Jefferson, Thomas: agrarian ideal of, vs. realities, 50; agrarian politics of, 3, 105; and agrarianism, 4–5; and American art history, 6; anti-urbanism of, 5; *Notes on the State of Virginia*, 5

Jewett, Sarah Orne, 194, 198

Johnes House, The (wood engraving), 264, *281*

Johns, Joseph, *Farmyard at Sunset*, 18, 29

Johnson, Clifton, *The New England Boy* (photograph), 305–6, 320

Johnson, Eastman, 214, 216; as chronicler of the past, 267; criticism of, 219, 220–21; and free labor, ideology of, 87; and literary regionalism, 197–98; *works mentioned: The Barefoot Boy*, 304–5, 316; *Barn Swallows*, 308; *The Confab*, 308; *Corn Husking*, 35, 60, 87, 101, *43*; *Embers*, 198–99, 199, 268; *The Evening Newspaper*, 102–3, *113*; *Husking Bee, Island of Nantucket*, 35, *44*; *In the Hayloft*, 308, 325; *Nantucket Interior—Man with a Pipe*, 267, 287; *The Nantucket School of Philosophy*, 198, 201, 336, *203*; *Nantucket Sea Captain*, 197; *New England Kitchen*, 267; *The Quiet Hour*, 308; *Reading the Bible*, 364 n.26; *Sugaring Off*, 36; *Woodcutter*, 104

Jones, Joseph, *The Green Mountain Boy*, 150, 169, 170

June (wood engraving), 100–101, *111*

Kitchens, rustic: in Sanitary Fairs, 266; as shrines, 267

Knight, C. *See* Wheatley, Francis

Knight, Daniel Ridgway, 222, 223; *Hailing the Ferry*, 222, 223, 234

Know-Nothing organizations, 270

Krimmel, John Lewis: *Country Frolic and Dance*, 131; *Dance in a Country Tavern* (lithograph), 131

LaFarge, John, 218, 219

Lambdin, George Cochran: *Feeding Time*, 367 n.31; *Winter Quarters in Virginia— Army of the Potomac, 1864*, 267, 268, 288

Land Ordinance of 1785, 55

Land ownership: in Jefferson's agrarianism, 5; and natural rights doctrine, 82; Northern and European systems of, compared, 82–83; Northern, and sectional pride, 81–84. *See also* Homestead Act

Land tenancy, New York State, 52

Lanman, Charles, 149; on Durand, 16; "The Dying Year," 299; on Mount, 129

Larcom, Lucy: selectivity of, 308; *works mentioned:* "The Barn Window," 307–8; "Berrying Song," 307; *Childhood Songs*, 307

Lincoln, Abraham, beard style of, 199

Lippard, George, *The Empire City*, 238

Livestock management, New England and Midwest, 19

Locke, John, and natural rights doctrine, 82

Log Cabin Campaign, 87, 108

Logan, Cornelius: comic social contrast, use of, 169; costume symbolism, use of, 169–70; *The Wag of Maine [Yankee Land]*, 150, 169–70, 172

Long Island (New York), dance in, 131, 134; homesteads on, 264

Low, Will Hicok, on French peasants, 225

Lowell, James Russell, "The Courtin'," 175–76

McCormick, Cyrus, 53

McCormick Reaper, 1847 (wood engraving), 54, 66

MacKay, Alexander: on literacy of American farmers, 102; on Yankees, 153

Magazines, audience for, 7

Manifest Destiny, 86, 151; resurgence of, in late 19th century, 274

Manners, American: nationalism and, 171; negative views of, 171

Maple sugar, and antislavery sentiment, 85–86

Maple sugaring, in art and literature, 36–37

Marryat, Captain Frederick, 157

Mathews, Charles, 208; Yankee costume of, 170

Mathews, Cornelius: costume symbolism, use of, 170; *The Politicians*, 125–26

Matteson, Tomkins, *Sugaring Off*, 36, *45*

Maurer, Louis, *Preparing for Market*, 37, *137*

Mechanization, agricultural. *See* Agricultural machines

Mexican War, paintings about, 350 n.10

Meyer, Ferdinand, *The Farm of Volney Lester, Esq.*, 51, *64*

Millennialism: and northern hegemony, 87; and northern landscape, 86

Millet, Jean-François, 220, 221; American criticism of, 224, 359 n.19; and American painting, influences on, 215–16, 221, 222; peasant types of, 215; romanticism of, 216; *works mentioned: Autumn Landscape with a Flock of Turkeys*, 222; *The Gleaners*, 224, *Going to Work*, 215, 216, 228; *The Sower*, 215

Mitchell, Donald Grant [pseud. Ik Marvell], 7; American farmers, criticism of, 126; English farmers, criticism of, 102; on farms of New England, 60; ideal farmer of, 100, 194; on Yankee whittling, 157; *works mentioned: Dream-Life: A Fable of the Seasons*, 100, 126; *The Lorgnette; or, Studies of the Town by an Opera-Goer*, 126

Molly Maguires, 272

Morgan, Matthew, *Unrestricted Immigration and Its Results: The Last Yankee*, 273–74, 296

Morland, George, 123, 128; *Alehouse Politicians*, 129; *Boys Robbing an Orchard*, 124, *140*

Mount, William Sidney, 127, 223; attitude toward public of, 173; city and country contrasted by, 128; costume symbolism, use of, 170, 172; courtship theme in, 158–61, 168; criticism of, 128–30, 154, 160; ideal American farmer of, 100; and Jack Downing lore, 154, 154–55, 157–58; on Long Island farmers, 128; moralism in paintings of, 127, 172, 298–99, 352 n.11; and Morland, 124; nostalgic sentiment in, 127, 299; patrons of, 161; Seba Smith inspired by, 155–56; and sleighing lore, 132–33; social contrast, use of, 170–73; and Wheatley, 124, 158; and Yankee poems, 131–32, 133, 158–59; and Yankee theater, 134, 153–54, 160–61, 169–70; Yankee types in works of, 154; on Yankees, 149; whittling in works of, 156, 160; *works mentioned: Bargaining for a Horse*, 130, 154, 156, 157–58, 198, 217, *164*; *Boys Caught Napping in a Field*, 298; *Cider Making*, 127; *Coming to a Point*, 154; *Dance of the Haymakers*, 130, 134–35, *146*; *Dancing on the Barn Floor*, 129, 130, 133–34, *145*; *The Disagreeable Surprise*, 298; *Eel Spearing at Setauket*, 127, 365 n.7; *Farmer Whetting His Scythe*, 100, 105, 127, 154, *110*; *Farmers Nooning*, 124, 125, 127, 130, 154, 351 n.3, *139*; *The Herald in the Country*, 170, 173, *182*; *Long Island Farmer Husking Corn*, 154–55, *162*; *Long Island Farmhouse*, 18, 28; *The Long Story*, 129, 154, 155, 155–56, 172, 354 n.18, *163*; *Loss and Gain*, 127, 135; *Music is Contagious* (lithograph after Mount), 135; *The Painter's Study* (engraving after Mount), 173; *The Painter's Triumph*, 170, 172–73, *181*; *Raffling for the Goose*, 154, 172, *180*; *Rustic Dance after a Sleigh-Ride*, 130–33, 135, *143*; *Schoolboys Quarreling*, 365 n.6; *The Sportsman's Last Visit*, 168–71, 172, *177*; *The Tough Story* (engraving after Mount), 129; *The Trap Sprung*, 299; *The Truant Gamblers*, 124, 127, 130, 298–99, 308, *141*; *Turning the Leaf*, 299; *Uncle Joshua* (engraving after Mount), 154–55;

Walking the Line, 128–29, 149, *142*; *Who'll Turn the Grindstone?*, 154; *Winding Up*, 154, 158–61, 168, 217, *166*

Mowatt, Anna Ogden, *Fashion*, 240

Mower in Ohio, The (wood engraving), 101, *112*

"Mr. and Mrs. Cowpen," 126

Muir, John, on agricultural labor, 57–58

Mulready, William: *The Fight Interrupted*, 365 n.6; *The Village Buffoon*, 354 n.25

Munkittrick, R. K., "Farming," 192

Nanteuil, Célestin, *Souvenir*, 363 n.25

Nast, Thomas: anti-Greeley cartoons, 106–7, 200; *works mentioned: Cincinnatus: H.G. the Farmer Receiving the Nomination from H.G. the Editor*, 200, 208; *The Transportation Problem*, 105, *116*; *A Warning Light*, 240, *251*

National Reform Association, 106; and Anti-Renters, 53

Nature study, in urban schools, 312–13

Neal, John (attrib.), "A Sleigh Ride," 132–33

New England: decline of, perceived, 193–94; and ideal pastoral landscape, 14–15, 37; village, in nostalgia literature, 260–61

Nichols, Thomas Low, on Greeley, 153

Norris, Frank: *The Octopus*, 347 n.18; *The Pit*, 347 n.18

Nostalgia: antebellum, 258–59; and nativism, 273–75; and social change, 259–60. *See also* Childhood nostalgia

Nostalgia business, 336

November (wood engraving), 17, 26

Oertel, Johannes, 175, 241; *The Country Connoisseurs*, 173–74, 175, *183*; criticism of, 174

Olmsted, Frederick Law, 84; and design of Central Park, 313

Ordway, Alfred A.: *Birthplace in Winter,* 265, 285 (photograph); *Snow-Bound Kitchen, Eastern End,* 265, 286 (photograph)

Ostade, Adriaen van, 122

O'Sullivan, Timothy, *The Harvest of Death* (photograph), 88

Our Young Folks, 301, 307; and Homer, 304

Palmer, Frances: and study of farmhouses, 18; types of farmhouses in, 17; *works mentioned: American Country Life: May Morning,* 244, 254; *American Country Life: Summers Evening,* 244, 255; *American Farm Scene: Spring,* 11, 12, 22; *New England Scenery,* 15, 23; with J. Cameron, *The Four Seasons of Life: Childhood, "The Season of Joy,"* 300–301, 314; *Haying-Time: The First Load,* 62, 76

Panic of 1837, 79, 81; impact on farmers of, 52

Panic of 1857, 175; impact on farmers of, 52

Panic of 1873, impact on farmers of, 58

Pastoral: defined, 8; European tradition of, 3–4

Pastoral design, 15–17

Pastoral ideal, tensions in, 345 n.22

Pastoral landscape: and agrarian ideal, 6, 13; in American literature, 13–14; in art and literature, parallels in, 15, 16–17; design conventions in, 12; in popular literature, 14

Paulding, James Kirke: *works mentioned: John Bull and Brother Jonathan,* 150, 152–53, 157; *Koningsmarke,* 125, 126; on Yankees, 152–53, 157

Payne, John Howard: "Home Sweet Home," 258, 263–64; homestead of, 264–65

Pearce, Charles Sprague, 222, 223

Peasants, characterized, 214

Peasants, French: American admiration of, 223–26; paintings of, by Americans, 222–25; paintings of, by French, 223. *See also* Bastien-Lepage, Jules; Breton, Jules; Frère, Edouard; Millet, Jean-François

Perkins, Granville: *An American Farm Yard—A Frosty Morning,* 18, 30; *A Cranberry Bog,* 359 n.11; *A Visit to Grandfather's Home* (after Eva Muller), 308, 326

Perry, Enoch Wood: criticism of, 269; *works mentioned: Country Boy,* 304, 305, 318; *Old Cronies,* 364 n.26; *Women Sewing by Firelight,* 269, 134

Pickard, Samuel T., on Whittier birthplace, 265

Pioneer Settler upon the Holland Purchase, and His Progress, The: Fourth Sketch of the Pioneer (wood engraving), 51, 63

Please, Sir, May I Have a Bed? (wood engraving), 311, 329

Poe, Edgar Allan, on Mount, 129, 154

Politicians, as farmers, 108–9

Popular art, and relation to academic art, 7

Populism, 105, 200

Populist Party, 200–201

Practical Experience of the Gift Book Enterprises (wood engraving), 175, 186

Progress, ambivalence toward, 260

Pughe, J. S., *"Blowing" Himself around the Country,* 200–201, 211

Pulszky, Francis, on absence of women in American fields, 101

Putnam, Israel, and image of farmer-patriot, 107

Railroad. *See* Transportation, mechanized

Railroad Strike (1877), 272

Realism, and literary regionalism, 195

Reaping in the Olden Time (wood engraving), 55, 68

Reaping in Our Time (wood engraving), 55, 69

Recapitulation theory, in psychology, 304

Reed, Luman, 157, 161

Regionalism: in literature, of Midwest, 195–96; in literature, of New England, 194; in painting, 197–99

Regnier, Claude, *Life of George Washington, the Farmer* (after Stearns), 107, 118

Richards, T. Addison, on Idlewild (Willis estate), 242

Riis, Jacob, 310–11

Riley, James Whitcomb, homestead of, 265

Robert, Léopold, *Return from the Pilgrimage to the Madonna dell'Arco,* 134, 147

Roberts, Isaac Phillips, on agricultural depressions, 58

Robinson, Henry R., *The Inhuman Anti-Rent Murder,* 52–53, 65

Rockwell, Norman, 336

Rogers, John, *Washington at Mount Vernon,* 107

Rogers, William Allen: *Harvesting on a Bonanza Farm,* 57, 72; *Let the Cloth Be White,* 312, 332; *The Tribune Fresh Air Fund—Children's Excursion to Lake Champlain,* 312, 331

Rousseau, Jean-Jacques: and child rearing, influence of, 297; pastoral sentiment of, 4

Rural hierarchy. *See* class stratification, rural

Rural life: and city life, contrasted, 240–41; escapism in images of, 77–78; as therapy, 244–45; and urban reform, 311–12. *See also* Agrarianism; all Agricultural entries; Arcadia; Child rearing, rural; Class stratification, rural; Country books; Country gentleman; Farmers; Villa, middle-class

Sambo, as black nickname, 132
Schutler, Jno. *See* Durrie, George Henry
Scott, E. *See* Morland, George
Scott, Julian, *Picking Raspberries,* 359 n.11, 364 n.26
Sedgwick, Catherine Maria, on American farmers, 99
Shaw, Henry Wheeler: and character of Josh Billings, 151, 196; *Josh Billings's Farmer's Allminak,* 196
Shearman, James, *Improved Buckeye Reaper with Table Rake,* 54, 67
Sheldon, George W., *Recent Ideals of American Art,* 223
Sheppard, William Ludlow: *Harvest on Historic Fields—A Scene at the South,* 88, 94; *The Last Apple,* 306, 324; *The Story of a Waif* (after M. Woolf), 310–11, 328
Slums, as threat to social order, 272–73
Smith, Matthew Hale: on dance-halls, 239–40; *Sunshine and Shadow in New York,* 238
Smith, Seba: *The Life and Writings of Major Jack Downing of Downingville,* 151, 154; *My Thirty Years out of the Senate,* 151; "The Tough Yarn," 155–56; *'Way Down East; or, Portraitures of Yankee Life,* 156. *See also* Downing, Major Jack
Social change, postbellum, 190
Social Darwinism, 309
South, contrasted with North, 84–85, 349 n.19
Spring in the Country (wood engraving), 11, 12, *21*
Stein, Roger, 5
Stowe, Harriet Beecher, 267; and concept of Anglo-Saxon home, 274; hearth symbolism, use of, 265–66, 268, 269; New England village themes in works of, 260; *works mentioned: The Minister's Wooing,* 260; *Oldtown Folks,* 260, 261, 263; *The Pearl of Orr's Island,* 260; *Poqanuc People,*

260; *Sam Lawson's Oldtown Fireside Stories,* 260; *Uncle Tom's Cabin,* 84–85, 260
Street Boy on the Farm—A Year Later, The, 311, 330
Strong, George Templeton, on city as a hell, 238
Strong, Josiah: and Anglo-Saxon doctrine, 274; on cities, 239

Tait, Arthur Fitzwilliam: *American Forest Scene: Maple Sugaring,* 36, 46; *Arguing the Point—Settling the Presidency,* 350 n.10; *The Latest News,* 103
Tavern scenes, vulgarity in, 128–29
Tavernier, Jules, *Town and Country,* 241, 253
Tenancy. *See* Land tenancy, New York State
Tenement housing, 310
Teniers, David, 122; compared with Mount, 128
Thanksgiving: in art, 270; as New England holiday, 269–70; postbellum symbolism, 269
Theater. *See* Yankee theater
Theocritus, 3
Thomas, Robert: on agricultural machines, 54; on farm children, discipline of, 298, 299; on husking bees, 61; on maple sugar, 85
Thompson, Denman: *The Old Homestead,* 197, 267
Thompson, Jerome, 216; idealism of, 60; idyllicism of, 33–34; and northern values, 87; *works mentioned: Apple Gathering,* 37, 87, *47; The Haymakers, Mount Mansfield, Vermont,* 33–34, 60, 61, 81, 87, 101, 102, *40*
Thomson, James, 4
Thoreau, Henry David, 7; on farmers, 51
Tocqueville, Alexis de, on farmers, 50–51

Tolman, W. H., on slums, 273
Town and Country (wood engraving), 241, 252
Transportation, mechanized, impact on agriculture of, 53
Trensky, Anne, 301
Trollope, Frances, on American manners, 171
Troyon, Constant, 215; *La Gardeuse de dindons,* 222
Tuckerman, Henry T.: on Durand, 15; on Ehninger, 220; on E. Johnson, 220; on Mount, 129, 135
Tumbledown Mansion—The House of Farmer Slack (wood engraving), 19, *31*
Turner, Orasmus, *Pioneer History of the Holland Purchase of Western New York,* 51
Twain, Mark. *See* Clemens, Samuel
Tyler, Royall: *works mentioned: The Contrast,* 150; "Ode Composed for the Fourth of July," 131–32; and Yankee poems, 131

Urban growth, 237
Urbanism, postbellum, 191

Van Buren, Martin, 87, 108
Van Rensselaer, Mariana, on Fuller, 222
Vaux, Calvert: design of Idlewild, 242; *Villas and Cottages,* 241
Villa, middle-class: in art, 243–44; as class symbol, 242
Virgil, 3–4

Warner, Charles Dudley: on barefoot boy, 303; *Being a Boy,* 302; on boys at recess, 306; on boys as savages, 303–4; on maple sugaring, 37; on nutting, 306; typical country boy of, 304–5

Warren, A. Coolidge, *New England Fireside,* 269, 293

Washington, George, agrarian iconography of, 107–8

Webster, Noah, on literacy of farmers, 102

Webster, Thomas, *Spring,* 300

Weems, Mason Locke, Washington myth of, 107

Welch, Rodney, agrarian ideal, debunking of, 192–93

Welding, John M., agrarian ideal, debunking of, 193

Wells, H. G., on child labor in America, 309

Wetmore, Henry Carmer, *Rural Life in America,* 243, 244

Wheatley, Francis: and rural life, images of, 123–24; *works mentioned: Preparing for Market* (engraving after), 123, *136; Rural Repose* (engraving after), 124, *138; The Rustic Lover* (engraving after), 158, *167; The Smitten Clown,* 354 n.25

Wheelwright, Edward, 221

White, William Allen: on children and nature, 303; *The Court of Boyville,* 301

Whitman, Walt, 84, 86

Whittier, John Greenleaf: birthplace of, as shrine, 265; as democratic poet, 34–35;

hearth symbolism of, 261–62, 265; homestead symbolism of, 262; nostalgia in work of, 300; popular success of, 261, 263; and the South, view of, 84; *works mentioned:* "Among the Hills," 194; *Ballads of New England,* 307; "The Barefoot Boy," 299, 303; "The Huskers," 35; *Justice and Expediency,* 84; "My Playmate," 307; *The Panorama,* 84; *Snow-Bound,* 261–62, 263, 265, 267, 300; *Songs of Labor,* 35

Whittredge, Worthington: *Home by the Sea,* 262, 276; *Home by the Sea-Side,* 362 n.9

"Wickedest Man in New York, The" (wood engraving), 239–40, *250*

Wilderness, attitudes toward, of painters and writers, 5–6

Wilkie, Sir David: and Mount, 128, 158; and rustic life, 123; *works mentioned: The Blind Fiddler,* 131; *The Refusal,* 354 n. 25; *Village Politicians,* 130

Willis, Nathaniel Parker, 242; on American manners, 171; Glenmary estate of, 142, 153; Idlewild estate of, 242, 243; and pastoral landscape, 14; on rustic costume, 172; on Yankees, 153; *works mentioned: American Scenery,* 17; "Idlewild Papers," 242; *Letters from Under a Bridge,* 172; *Outdoors at Idlewild,* 243

Witness (motion picture), 336

Wood, Grant, 335

Wood, Thomas Waterman, 197; *Cogitation,* 105–7; *Jump,* 367 n.31; *A Pinch of Snuff,* 198

Woodworth, Samuel: comic social contrast, use of, 169; costume symbolism, use of, 170; courtship theme in, 159–60, 161; *works mentioned: The Forest Rose; or, American Farmers,* 134, 150–51, 159–60, 169, 170, 172; "The Old Oaken Bucket," 258

Wordsworth, William, romantic view of childhood of, 297

Yankee: defined, 149–50; origin of term, 149

Yankee costume, 152–54, 169–70, 175, 176, 200

Yankee poetry, 131–33; courtship in, 158–59

Yankee theater, 134, 150; courtship in, 159–60, 169; later phases of, 197

Yankees: caricatures of, 174–76; characteristics of, 150–51, 152–53; as traders, 156–57; as whittlers, 157–58

AMERICAN CIVILIZATION
A series edited by Allen F. Davis

Gospel Hymns and Social Religion: The Rhetoric of Nine-teenth-Century Revivalism,
by Sandra S. Sizer
Social Darwinism: Science and Myth in Anglo-American Social Thought,
by Robert C. Bannister
Twentieth Century Limited: Industrial Design in America, 1925–1939,
by Jeffrey L. Meikle
Charlotte Perkins Gilman: The Making of a Radical Feminist, 1860–1896,
by Mary A. Hill
Inventing the American Way of Death, 1830–1920,
by James J. Farrell
Anarchist Women, 1870–1920,
by Margaret S. Marsh
Woman and Temperance: The Quest for Power and Liberty, 1873–1900,
by Ruth Bordin
Hearth and Home: Preserving a People's Culture,
by George W. McDaniel
The Education of Mrs. Henry Adams,
by Eugenia Kaledin
Class, Culture, and the Classroom: The Student Peace Movement in the 1930s,
by Eileen Eagan
Fathers and Sons: The Bingham Family and the American Mission,
by Char Miller
An American Odyssey: Elia Kazan and American Culture,
by Thomas H. Pauly
Silver Cities: The Photography of American Urbanization, 1839–1915,
by Peter B. Hales

Actors and American Culture, 1800–1920,
by Benjamin McArthur
Saving the Waifs: Reformers and Dependent Children, 1890–1917,
by LeRoy Ashby
A Woman's Ministry: Mary Collson's Search for Reform as a Unitarian Minister, a Hull House Social Worker, and a Christian Science Practitioner,
by Cynthia Grant Tucker
Depression Winters: New York Social Workers and the New Deal,
by William W. Bremer
Forever Wild: Environmental Aesthetics and the Adirondack Forest Reserve,
by Philip G. Terrie
Art and Labor: Ruskin, Morris, and the Craftsman Ideal in America,
by Eileen Boris
Paths into American Culture: Psychology, Medicine, and Morals,
by John C. Burnham
Pastoral Inventions: Rural Life in Nineteenth-Century American Art and Culture,
by Sarah Burns
Before It's Too Late: The Child Guidance Movement in the United States, 1918–1945,
by Margo Horn
Mary Heaton Vorse: The Life of an American Insurgent,
by Dee Garrison